Creativity and Academic Activism

Creativity and Academic Activism

Instituting Cultural Studies

Edited by
Meaghan Morris and Mette Hjort

Duke University Press
Durham and London, 2012

Hong Kong University Press
Hong Kong, 2012

Hong Kong University Press
14/F Hing Wai Centre
7 Tin Wan Praya Road
Aberdeen, Hong Kong
www.hkupress.org

ISBN 978-988-8139-39-2 (*Hardback*)
ISBN 978-988-8139-40-8 (*Paperback*)

Duke University Press
Box 90660
Durham, North Carolina
27708-0660
www.dukeupress.edu

ISBN 978-1-932643-20-6 (*Hardback*)
ISBN 978-1-932643-02-2 (*Paperback*)

This book is among a series of titles co-published by Duke University Press and Hong Kong University Press, a collaboration designed to make possible new circuits of circulation for scholarship. This title is available in Asia, Australia, and New Zealand from Hong Kong University Press; in the Americas and Europe from Duke University Press; and from either publisher in the rest of the world.

Library of Congress Cataloging-in-Publication Data
Creativity and academic activism : instituting cultural studies / edited by Meaghan Morris and Mette Hjort.
p. cm.
Includes bibliographical references and index.
ISBN 978-1-932643-20-6 (cloth : alk. paper) — ISBN 978-1-932643-02-2 (pbk. : alk. paper)
    1. Culture—Study and teaching (Higher)—Asia. I. Morris, Meaghan. II. Hjort, Mette.
HM623.C75 2012
    306—dc23
2012026869

10 9 8 7 6 5 4 3 2 1

Printed and bound by Liang Yu Printing Factory Limited, Hong Kong, China

For

Edward Chen Kwan-yiu

President of Lingnan University, 1995–2007

Scholar, Teacher, Visionary

Contents

Contributors

Tony BENNETT is Research Professor in Social and Cultural Theory at the Centre for Cultural Research at the University of Western Sydney. He was previously Professor of Sociology at the Open University in the United Kingdom, where he was also Director of the Economic and Social Science Research Centre on Socio-Cultural Change. He is Fellow of the Australian Academy of the Humanities. His publications include *Formalism and Marxism; Outside Literature; Bond and Beyond: The Political Career of a Popular Hero* (with Janet Woollacott); *The Birth of the Museum; Culture: A Reformer's Science; Accounting for Tastes: Australian Everyday Cultures* (with Michael Emmison and John Frow); *Pasts Beyond Memory: Evolution, Museums, Colonialism; New Keywords: A Revised Vocabulary of Culture and Society* (edited with Larry Grossberg and Meaghan Morris); *The Sage Handbook of Cultural Analysis* (edited with John Frow); and *Culture, Class, Distinction* (with Mike Savage, Elizabeth Silva, Alan Warde, Modesto Gayo-Cal, and David Wright).

Stephen Ching-Kiu CHAN is Professor in the Department of Cultural Studies and Academic Dean of the Faculty of Arts at Lingnan University. He has published in the areas of Hong Kong culture, film, literature, education and cultural studies, and coordinated projects on cultural pedagogy and policy, schooling as cultural process, urban creativity and cultural citizenship under the Kwan Fong Cultural Research and Development Program. He serves on the board of the international Association for Cultural Studies, representing the Asia constituency. He is a part-time member of the Central Policy Unit of the Hong Kong government, and a policy fellow of the think-tank Community Development Initiatives.

Kuan-Hsing CHEN is Professor in the Institute for Social Research and Cultural Studies at National Chiao Tung University, Hsinchu, Taiwan. The author of many books and articles in both English and Chinese, his most recent book is *Asia as Method: Toward Deimperialization*. He is a founder and co-executive editor of *Inter-Asia-Cultural Studies* and co-editor with Chua Beng Huat of *The Inter-Asia Cultural Studies Reader*.

Douglas CRIMP is the Fanny Knapp Allen Professor of Art History at the University of Rochester. He is the author of *Melancholia and Moralism: Essays on AIDS and Queer Politics*, *On the Museum's Ruins*, and a series of essays on Andy Warhol films.

DAI Jinhua has taught in the Department of Filmic Literature of Beijing Film Academy for ten years. Now Professor of the Institute of Comparative Literature and Comparative Culture and Director of the Cultural Studies Workshop of Peking University, she is also Adjunct Professor to the Department of East Asian Languages and Literatures, Ohio State University. She has published widely on film history, mass culture, and feminist literature. Her many books in Chinese include *Breaking Out of the City of Mirrors: Women, Film, Literature* (1995); *Invisible Writing: Cultural Studies in China in the 1990s* (1999); *The Views in the Mist: Chinese Film Culture 1978–1998* (1999); and *Writing Cultural Heroes: Cultural Studies at the Turn of the Century* (2000). Her most recent work, *Cinema and Desire: Feminist Marxism and Cultural Politics in Dai Jinhua's Works* (edited by Jing Wang and Tani Barlow, 2002) is a translated collection of her important articles.

John Nguyet ERNI is Head of Cultural Studies at Lingnan University and former Associate Head and Associate Professor of Media and Cultural Studies in the Department of English and Communication, City University of Hong Kong. He has published *Internationalizing Cultural Studies: An Anthology* (with Ackbar Abbas, 2005), and *Asian Media Studies: The Politics of Subjectivities* (with Siew Keng Chua, 2005). In 2005, he also completed a Master of Laws degree in Human Rights at the University of Hong Kong.

Mette HJORT is Chair Professor and Head of Visual Studies at Lingnan University, Affiliate Professor of Scandinavian Studies at the University of Washington, Seattle, and Honorary Professor at the Centre for Modern European Studies, University of Copenhagen. She has written, translated, and edited/co-edited a number of books. Recent titles include *Film and Risk* (2012); *The Danish Directors 2* (with Eva Jørholt and Eva Novrup Redvall, 2010); *Lone Scherfig's 'Italian for Beginners'* (2010); *The Cinema of Small Nations* (edited with Duncan Petrie, 2007); *Small Nation, Global Cinema* (2005); and *Stanley Kwan's Center Stage* (2006).

Josephine HO founded the Centre for the Study of Sexualities at National Central University in 1995. She has been writing both extensively and provocatively on many cutting-edge issues in the Taiwanese context, spearheading sex-positive views on female sexuality, gender/sexuality education, queer studies, sex work studies and activism, transgenderism, and most recently body modification. The author/editor of more than two dozen ground-breaking books, Josephine Ho has become a champion of sexual dissidence. Her academic website was forced out of the academic net space in 2001 because of its sex-positive stance on teenage sexuality. In 2003, a total of thirteen conservative NGOs banded together to bring a lawsuit against Josephine Ho for two hyperlinks on her massive sexuality studies databank that led to zoophilia websites. With the support of students, scholars, and activist groups, along with a widespread international petition drive, and her own articulate self-defence in court, Josephine Ho won the court case in both the District Court and the High Court in 2004. For her tireless efforts in resisting bigotry and prejudice, and her work on human rights and sex rights, she was selected as one of the thousand women from all over the world who were collectively nominated for the Nobel Peace Prize. Josephine Ho was one of the founding scholars for the Cross-Campus Program in Cultural Studies at the University System of Taiwan, and has been working on networking and scholarly exchange among Asian institutes since 2003. She was elected President of the Cultural Studies Association of Taiwan in 2005.

Koichi IWABUCHI is Professor in the Faculty of Arts of Monash University. He is Chair in Media and Cultural Studies and will also take on the role as Director of the Monash Asia Institute from 2013. He has researched on cultural globalization and transnationalism, media flows and cultural connections in East Asia, and multicultural politics in Japan. His recent publications include *Recentering Globalization: Popular Culture and Japanese Transnationalism* (2002); *Feeling Asian Modernities: Transnational Consumption of Japanese TV Dramas* (2004); and *Rogue Flows* (edited with Stephen Muecke and Mandy Thomas, 2004).

Meaghan MORRIS is Chair Professor of Cultural Studies and Coordinator of the Kwan Fong Cultural Research and Development Programme at Lingnan University, Hong Kong. She is also Professor of Gender and Cultural Studies at the University of Sydney. Her books include *Hong Kong Connections: Transnational Imagination in Action Cinema* (edited with Siu Leung Li and Stephen Chan Ching-kiu, 2005); *New Keywords: A Revised Vocabulary of Culture and Society* (edited with Tony Bennett and Lawrence Grossberg, 2005); *"Race" Panic and the Memory of Migration* (edited with Brett de Bary, 2001); *Too Soon, Too Late: History in Popular Culture* (1998); and *The Pirate's Fiancée: Feminism, Reading, Postmodernism* (1988). She is a former senior editor of *Traces: A Multilingual Journal of Cultural Theory and Translation*, and in 2004–08 was Chair of the international Association for Cultural Studies. Her most recent work is *Identity Anecdotes: Translation and Media Culture* (2006).

Tejaswini NIRANJANA is Director and Senior Fellow at the Centre for the Study of Culture and Society, Bangalore, which offers the first PhD in Cultural Studies in India. She is the author of *Siting Translation: History, Post-structuralism and the Colonial Context* (1992) and *Mobilizing India: Women, Migration and Music between India and Trinidad* (2006). She is the co-editor of *Interrogating Modernity: Culture and Colonialism in India* (1993).

WANG Xiaoming is Professor and Chair of the Department of Cultural Studies at Shanghai University, and Director of the Centre for Contemporary Culture Studies. He also holds the professorship in Chinese Literature at East China Normal University, where he serves as the Committee Chair of the Centre for Research on Modern Chinese Literature. Wang is the author of thirteen scholarly books, including *Between Literature and Thought* (2004), *The Myth of Half-Face* (2001), and *The Cold Face of Reality: A Biography of Lu Xun* (1993), and the editor of seven volumes, including the famous collection of essays that brought about the debate on "the humanistic spirit" (1996).

Audrey YUE is Senior Lecturer in Screen and Cultural Studies at the University of Melbourne in Australia. Her recent publications include *Ann Hui's Song of the Exile* (2010) and *Queer Singapore: Illiberal Citizenship and Mediated Cultures* (co-edited with Jun Zubillaga-Pow, 2012). She is currently Chief Investigator in two Australian Research Council-funded projects on transnational large screens and multicultural arts governance.

Acknowledgements

Creativity and Academic Activism: Instituting Cultural Studies was supported by two Direct Grants from Lingnan University (DA06A7, "University Culture: Markets, Globalization, Norms," 2006–07; and DA10A2, "Instituting Cultural Studies," 2010–11), which we are glad to acknowledge.

For their immense contribution to the project over the years, we would like to thank the present and former staff of the Department of Cultural Studies and the Kwan Fong Cultural Research and Development Programme at Lingnan University, in particular Ms Josephine Tsui Wai-shuen, Ms Selino Lo Tak-man, and Ms Flora Chung Choi-Nin.

Introduction

Instituting Cultural Studies

Meaghan Morris and Mette Hjort

[W]hat is essential to creation is not "discovery" but constituting the new: art does not discover, it constitutes; and the relation between what it constitutes and the "real", an exceedingly complex relation to be sure, is not a relation of verification. And on the social plane, which is our main interest here, the emergence of new institutions and of new ways of living is not a "discovery" either but an active constitution.

— Cornelius Castoriadis[1]

[One] way to create institutional reality often is to act as if it already existed.

— John R. Searle[2]

This is a book about the role played by creativity, collective invention and imaginative academic activism in "instituting" Cultural Studies as a new disciplinary practice over the past twenty years. More broadly, it is also a volume of stories in which internationally well-known scholars in the humanities and social sciences look back on what they now consider to be key moments of their trajectories as institution-builders, in the process reflecting in often personal terms on the art of the possible in academic life. Variously based in Australia, mainland China, Hong Kong, India, Japan, Taiwan, the United Kingdom and the United States, the contributors are all noted researchers whose scholarly work covers a wide range of fields, from film, popular music, literature, art and media to museum and urban cultural studies, political and intellectual history, and cultural policy studies. What brings them together here is that they are figures whose very notability rests also on their institutional inventiveness — be this as activists, researchers, teachers, editors, practitioners or all these things at once. Along with shared experience in developing new undergraduate degrees, these authors have built significant research centers (Tony Bennett, Josephine Ho, Tejaswini Niranjana, Wang Xiaoming) and postgraduate schools

(Dai Jinhua, Koichi Iwabuchi), edited field-shaping book series (Stephen Chan Ching-Kiu) and journals (Kuan-Hsing Chen, Douglas Crimp), established an international artist-in-residence program (Mette Hjort) and helped to found social activist networks (John Erni, Audrey Yue). The aim of the book, then, is to explore in some detail the many different ways in which the practices of cultural pedagogy and research can be a matter of forging — at times in contexts of considerable adversity — the types of institutional spaces where important questions can be asked, where networks and communities can be created and where, ultimately, progress on a number of socially significant issues can be made.

These emphases on practical detail and a plurality of ways to create "institutional reality" ground the book in an unusually constructive approach to the opportunities for action afforded by particular institutional locales. In part, this is a matter of disciplinary inclination: Cultural Studies attaches a great deal of importance to local contexts, both as objects of study and as the medium in which effective practices in cultural politics need to be conceived.[3] Accordingly, fifteen years ago Ted Striphas proposed that we set aside discussions of the pros and cons of "institutionalization" understood abstractly (and thus, by implication, those narratives of the formation of Cultural Studies written in terms of a history of ideas) in order to look closely at actually existing programs, documenting "the strategies by which they have gone about institutionalizing, and how they respond to the ongoing challenges that institutionalization brings."[4] While much has happened internationally in the intervening years, direct responses to this call have been fairly scarce, and upbeat or optimistic accounts of institutional experiment have been rare — especially ones fully bringing the rapid growth of new programs in non-Western and non-Anglophone contexts into the discussions of the discipline's future that are staged in the North American, British and Australasian heartlands of English-language scholarship.[5]

Certainly, these have been hard years generally for humanities and social sciences initiatives in public universities assailed by strategic budget cuts and escalating enrolments within a "New Public Management"-inspired reform aiming to remodel the university on "a corporate enterprise whose primary concern is with market share, serving the needs of commerce, maximizing economic return and investment, and gaining competitive advantage in the 'Global Knowledge Economy.'"[6] Since the 1985 Jarratt Report on "efficiency studies in universities" in the United Kingdom recommended introducing the corporate model and the language of new managerialism to higher education (a move rapidly exported around the world to widely differing national systems and cultures of education),[7] traditional disciplines and new "studies" areas alike have been forced in difficult circumstances to reinvent their rationales and rhetorics of value, as scholarly "reasons for being" became "reasons for getting resources." Yet as Simon Marginson and Mark Considine point out in their classic study of the "enterprise university," casual references to managerialism or corporatization in universities gesture at what are actually "titanic struggles for a new future" in which academic enterprise may better be understood as a "complex achievement of public purpose and economic energy."[8] Cultural Studies has an overt commitment to public purpose at the heart of its self-conception, and in places where it has been able to thrive the discipline should be contributing to at least some aspects of that "complex achievement." Many of the following chapters analyze situations in which that has indeed been the case, asking where, how and why. We see these questions as having more than disciplinary relevance. If Cultural Studies has taken shape as a distinct area of inquiry and practice in the midst of these titanic struggles, it has no monopoly on public engagement and no claim to a singular creativity in finding energetic ways to inhabit the new university landscape. Just as our contributors come to Cultural Studies from lives in other disciplines (including English, Chinese, Art History, Comparative Literature, Cinema Studies, Communication and Sociology) and other occupations (Douglas Crimp has been a curator and an editor; Koichi Iwabuchi worked in Japanese television for ten years; Audrey Yue was a full-time activist in Melbourne, supporting migrant women from Asia), so the value of their positive institutional stories and their analyses of achievement against the odds can travel to other contexts.

The project for this book began, however, not with the discovery of a "gap in the literature" but with a happy convergence of two empirical occasions for celebration and thought. One of these was a birthday. In 2006, the Department of Cultural Studies at Lingnan University, Hong Kong, completed six years of activity as the first such department in the Chinese-speaking world and one of the few stand-alone programs worldwide to deliver a full BA Honors in Cultural Studies. To mark the occasion and to stimulate thinking and future planning in Hong Kong's complex cultural and educational situation as a unique system of governance within the People's Republic of China (PRC),[9] Lingnan's Kwan Fong Cultural Research and Development Programme hosted an international symposium, "Cultural Studies and Institution," on the relations between

Cultural Studies and the process of "institution" itself. The invited participants were asked for critical reflections on institution-building across a range of cultural institutions, of which the university might be only one example; on the ways in which they saw social and historical contexts shaping the concrete possibilities and problems of institutionalization with which they dealt; and on the relationship between the potential of Cultural Studies as a discipline and the diverse institutions in which it dwells or could dwell in future. The essays published here have been developed from that symposium, and they respond to one or more of these three sets of questions.[10]

More diffuse in time, the second occasion for celebration and thinking was a friendship formed by institutional encounters. Having met at lively conferences in China and Hong Kong, the two editors found themselves working together from 2004 at Lingnan University, where Mette Hjort is now Chair Professor and Head of Visual Studies and Meaghan Morris has been Chair Professor of Cultural Studies since 2000. While sharing a base in cinema studies and the experience of postgraduate study in France, educationally we came to Hong Kong from different backgrounds. Schooled in Kenya, Holland and Switzerland, Mette had worked in Canada and Denmark while Meaghan arrived from Australia after itinerant teaching in the United States and more than a decade of involvement in the Inter-Asia Cultural Studies movement (discussed below by Kuan-Hsing Chen). Our disciplinary orientations also differ: Mette has worked with cognitive film theory and analytical as well as continental philosophy, while Meaghan (for some years a freelance writer) is an interpretive critic of rhetorical practices in popular culture. What led us to collaborate was none of these things but rather our sense of wonder in finding at Lingnan — a small, undergraduate-oriented liberal arts university — a milieu where teaching was valued, research encouraged without cut-throat competition, scholarly community promoted rather than scorned as an old-fashioned management model, and the handling of internal reforms and external threats alike approached through patient consensus-building.

As in most universities today, some of the structural changes that we witnessed or carried out were hard and controversial while some of the threats (amalgamation, possible crippling budget cuts and repeated exhausting "reviews," for example) were serious and time-consuming. However, having seen up close the miserably dysfunctional academic contexts inflicted on many of our colleagues in different types of institutions around the world by local modes of *implementing* "enterprise" university policies, we were astonished to find ourselves happy academics at Lingnan — at a time when the profession at large was becoming increasingly stressful for those over-employed within it and unattractive to junior staff who found a secure career path into it inaccessible. So for two years we conducted a small research project to try to work out what institutional conditions make for happy rather than wretched academics in today's university environments.[11] We were interested in the material aspects of university culture that seemed able to shape some places affectively as "livable institutions" for teaching, learning and research while other places facing similar or identical external constraints and policy imperatives became hell-holes of burn-out, exploitation, cynicism, precariousness and illness — both mental and physical.[12] After conducting interviews with senior academics responsible for the well-being of others in different countries and regions of the world,[13] asking in particular what values or practices they would *not* sacrifice in the interests of competitiveness, and what models or ideas they found inspiring in their work, we came to focus on "below the radar" features of discrete university cultures — not the top-down protocols, exportable models of good practice and the monotonous institutional bragging about "excellence" familiar from official university discourses, but rather the ways in which the local social bond is effectively imagined on a daily basis across the dense network of micro-practices that together in any institution articulate a story that people can "live by" (or not).[14]

For example, although Lingnan University's management at the time of our project was dominated by economists and business professors, and while we were busy like everyone else in Hong Kong's universities with performance indicators, role differentiation, quality assurance and the RAE (the government's policy settings being much the same for all), the primary *story* shaping the cultural practices of the institution was not about the corporation or a pseudo-business, but rather "the Lingnan family." Mary Douglas argues that institutions stabilize and legitimize themselves by analogies ultimately founded on "their fit with the nature of the universe."[15] In a Chinese society, the family is a powerful institution with its own naturalizing claims, and while this potentially patriarchal story was not for everyone (it did not encourage research celebrity-seeking at the expense of undergraduates, for example), it gave plenty of scope for skepticism, humor and conflict, and for those who could live by it "the Lingnan family" was an engaging rather than a debilitating or demoralizing story. Above all, the micro-practices of sociability, accessibility, and care that it authorized (discussed by Mette in her chapter) bound staff and students together in ways that gave meaning and collective purpose on a daily basis to our shared academic life. In turn, that sense of meaning and purpose was a source of energy for coping imaginatively with the tasks imposed by Hong Kong's version of new managerialism "with Chinese characteristics."[16]

After this research, we contend that creating the conditions for energy to be produced rather than depleted by academic life on an everyday basis is key to what Castoriadis calls the "active constitution" of "new ways of living" in universities today. There are many critiques of the adverse impact of marketization and managerialism on the academy ("the university in ruins," in Bill Readings' famous phrase), and of the toll taken by the hours of paperwork required by "audit culture," not only on academic morale but on the overworked bodies and souls of scholars forced to remake their professional subjectivities along more bureaucratized and instrumental lines.[17] However, as Barak Kalir and Pál Nyíri point out, such critiques tend to be unreflexively nation-specific, abstracting and homogenizing as "neo-liberal" the processes they address; in ignoring differing responses to similar pressures enabled by the "highly divergent departure points" of diverse academic cultures, they encourage "a certain fatalism — mostly in Europe and Australia — that mistakes particular managerial fads for the single and inevitable path into the marketized future, whether welcomed or loathed."[18] By editing this volume together, our aim is to provide a set of positive case studies that show — concretely we believe — how energetic groups and movements have been able to create multiple paths towards their own preferred futures across a variety of contexts and circumstances, some of them highly unpropitious.

For example, drawing on a very different natural analogy from that claimed by the patriarchal family, Josephine Ho describes how a group of feminist "parasites" were able from 1995 to establish and maintain a Center for the Study of Sexualities at National Central University in the face of active hostility from both the mainstream women's movement and the traditional disciplines around them in the turbulent political conditions of post-martial law Taiwan. Crucially, they did this in part by seizing as an opportunity the Taiwan government's political need to promote the country's visibility internationally by signifying in Western terms the academic competitiveness and quantifiable research excellence of Taiwan's universities — academic goods that these "parasites" could amply provide, trained as many of those in their generation were in advanced studies at United States- or United Kingdom-based universities. The over-production of refereed articles and books for audit purposes is a coercive feature of new managerialism that today is widely experienced by scholars as an alienating burden; nonetheless, Ho and her "sex-positive" colleagues used their professionalism imaginatively in Taiwan's geo-political situation as an opportunity to make institutional space and create legitimacy for the cause of "marginal subjects" in public as well as academic life — albeit at a high personal cost to scholar activists living in conditions of constant embattlement while producing those refereed publications and social criticism for local newspapers as well. Indeed, Ho's account of what she calls "institutionally embedded activism" concludes that one of the most pressing practical issues in her context is to find viable ways to sustain and reproduce — especially for young scholars — the energy "to withstand the onslaught of disciplinary pressure or conservative retaliation."

Presupposing a long-term commitment to shaping the future through institutional work, this question of sustainability after an initial opportunistic energy burst is addressed, in one way or another, by several contributors. For Kuan-Hsing Chen, the issue for intellectuals involved with social movements anywhere is "how to emotionally maintain intellectual vitality, integrity and intensity" in institutional work, while Stephen Ching-kiu Chan argues that in the ambiguous "post-colony" of Hong Kong today, an ongoing problem for pedagogy is to "release cynical subjects from the trap of negativity" — a trap that the routine practice of cultural critique may simply reinforce. Discussing the difficulties in "brand nationalist" times of popularizing a concept of Japan as a multicultural society, Koichi Iwabuchi wants scholars to become "critical administrators," willing to promote long-term dialogue with media policymakers and the general public; and in the context of Singapore's pragmatic "illiberalism," Audrey Yue argues that maintaining an ambivalent state between complicity and resistance has worked for the country's leading feminist NGO, Aware, as an operational logic, a political resource and a source of longevity for more than twenty-five years.

Josephine Ho's local "survival story" is thus not simply Taiwan-specific, although it is a premise of her contribution and of the book as a whole that the art of the possible in institution-building requires exactly a lucid grasp of what Chen calls "the shifting conditions of practices" in the local, understood relationally as a formation that is multi-layered historically as well as connecting with other places on varying scales of interaction.[19] In his questioning case study of the Inter-Asia Cultural Studies (IACS) project — a movement that has grown over the past twenty years from relatively small, self-constituted gatherings of activists and scholars to generate a refereed journal, a large biennial conference, a multinational network of research centers and now an international consortium project[20] — Chen suggests that Cultural Studies is a useful site for scholars in Asia to compare the diverging circumstances within which we confront similar institutional problems because it can be "the most locally driven" of disciplines in terms of the motivating of research and action priorities but also "the most internationally and regionally linked" organizationally and as a matter of communicative practice. This high degree of multilateral linkage has not emerged because of official university globalization policies (helpful as these are for framing and funding activities), but rather because a distinct form of *solidarity* has emerged in the region over time between those locally engaged scholars who "use institutional space and opportunity to advance critical possibilities."

In other words, Cultural Studies has developed across Asia from the outset as a dialogue between diverse locales and varying modes of local engagement, with the Inter-Asia project acting as a convergence space for reflecting on this diversity and its changing cultural and educational conditions. This dialogue has never been nationally grounded — or indeed bounded by a *containing* "regional" mission. Inter-Asia is an internationalist project, albeit one not based in the West, and scholars from Africa, Australasia, Britain, North America and South America have participated from the beginnings of the Inter-Asia movement with the first "Trajectories" conference (subtitled "Towards A New Internationalist Cultural Studies"), held in Taipei in 1992.[21] Conversely, most of the Asia-based authors in this volume have spent varying periods of time studying and working in other regions of the world, including the Anglophone West. We emphasize Asia in this volume not only because our own lives as teachers and researchers are bound up now with this region, but because we strongly believe that contemporary Asian initiatives in cultural institution-building have over the years developed an exemplary value in the Derridean sense of exemplarity: the accounts in this book of producing spaces for both using and criticizing institutional logics offer us examples that are "without precedent" in the sense that they are inventing a cultural politics as they go along rather than illustrating or replicating a prior model of what a politically and scholastically correct institutional form should look like.[22]

Complexity of circumstance here is a given, and this complexity includes the now extensive international dialogue between academic policy-makers and administrators that adds a new layer of intensity to the need for Western and Asia-based scholars to bring their reflections on institutional experience to the same plane of discussion, as we do in this book. On the one hand, universities across Asia participate strongly in the regime of globalized policy- and posture-sharing that Marginson and Considine call "inter-institutional mimicry, growing marketing dependence and genuflection to content-free generic corporate models."[23] To a degree that nationally isolationist scholars may fail to appreciate, this regime brings a similar audit culture and common problems to institutions around the developed and developing worlds, making it more important than ever to initiate trans-regional as well as transnational discussion of ways to work *through* that culture and those problems. On the other hand, widely differing national education systems and scholarly cultures across Asia, as in many parts of the postcolonial and developing world, must continue to build on the uneven legacies of their colonial and/or revolutionary pasts, while striving to service rapid economic development and respond to the socio-cultural upheaval that such development entails. Necessarily, then, dissimilar intellectual priorities and genre protocols proliferate across a shared plane of discussion about similar problems, sometimes inducing a "difference shock" in participants working from within their own perspectives to establish norms of relevance for deciding the narrative and argumentative "point" of a critical intervention.[24] For some of our readers, the generic mix of essays in this volume may have that effect.

We believe, however, that it is vital now for the discursive and communal *basis* for international debate about the art of the possible in institutions to be broadened (that is, to become more international itself), and we hope that a collection shaped by, but by no means solely "about," locations in Asia may contribute to furthering this. In a famous essay on "Culture and Administration," Theodor Adorno speculates in the course of a highly qualified discussion of "the unique vital force of tradition" (and the best conditions for its negation) that "it is only there where that which was is still strong enough to form the forces within the subject and at the same time to oppose them that the production of that which has not yet been seems possible."[25] As the stories of experiment in this volume suggest, the turbulent collision of historical forces in Asia today throws up rich opportunities for the active constitution of the new and the "possible" in education, as in other areas of life. At the same time, though, this turbulence creates formidable obstacles for institution-builders to overcome, and powerful constraints within which they must work — all the more so in that a great deal of not necessarily hospitable invention goes on around their work in the name of cultural tradition as well as economic development. Along with the five specific program or project case studies with which we open the book (studies of projects based in or launched from the cities of Bangalore, Taipei, Hong Kong and Shanghai), the nationally inflected dimension of the essays by Tejaswini Niranjana (India), Josephine Ho (Taiwan), Stephen Ching-kiu Chan, Dai Jinhua and Wang Xiaoming (China), Koichi Iwabuchi (Japan) and Audrey Yue (Singapore) bring out the complexity of these varying conditions with particular clarity.

However, *how* the often local and fleeting opportunities afforded by those conditions may be seized by critical scholars to create "institutional reality" — sometimes by boldly acting within the constraints as though that desired reality already existed, as John Searle suggests — is a question that frames these stories as of far more than national and regional importance. This book is not an "area" survey of Cultural Studies in Asia, but a work *of* Cultural Studies that seeks to trace the ways in which problems are transformed and solutions translated across differing contexts, in the process enabling a collective invention of new norms of relevance and unexpected zones of commonality. Thus the four essays grouped at the end of the volume explore the potentials of a performative institutional realism in sites where academic work on culture interacts with *other* cultural institutions: fashion, design and the modernist art museum (Douglas Crimp's spiraling memoir of a key moment for the practice of "institutional critique" in late 1960s New York); human rights movements and public law (John Erni); the "gateways" for cultural citizenship formed in illiberal societies by the turn to creative industries (Audrey Yue); and the "metacultural" affiliations of Cultural Studies itself (Tony Bennett) as it seeks to understand the relation between culture, institutions and conduct, and thus the limits as well as the possibilities of its own practices.

Given those aspects of academic globalization that bring new constraints as well as opportunities to locally invested scholars in non-metropolitan sites of intellectual life (for example, the obligation to publish in United States- or United Kingdom-based refereed journals and in English), the multilingual as well as international regional space of Inter-Asia is often much more open to direct engagement with the critical thought and experiences developing in other parts of the world than is the relentlessly Anglophone Western academy. Contributing to the vitality of the institutional initiatives we see taking shape around us, such openness is not in itself a new feature of non-Western and/or post-colonial contexts where the creative local uptake of ideas, values, customs, and institutional forms introduced or imposed from elsewhere is a historically complex practice long reflected upon by scholars engaging with colonial and nationalist histories. As Jennifer Lindsay notes in a study of cultural policy and the performing arts in Southeast Asia, this complexity of uptake allows policy itself to be understood as "part of cultural expression;" governmental structures and practices are not only "superimposed upon indigenous, regional, traditional, infranational cultural forms, but are themselves also formed by the context within which these forms exist."[26]

The essay by Tejaswini Niranjana that opens the volume sets out some of the rich implications for thinking about the potentials of disciplinarity as well as institution-building that follow when we take seriously the variable historical formation of institutions in which "the culture question" is asked. In India and some other post-colonial situations, she argues, critical thinking about culture has always been central to "third world" nationalism, and thus to the very process of creating new and modern institutions. Tracing a genealogy of Cultural Studies in India on this basis, she suggests that the discipline's relationship to institutions there may differ "in a foundational way" from that presumed by many British or US accounts; in India there is little room, for example, for projecting an idealized critical spirit "outside" the institution. However, Niranjana's own story of institutional creativity is enabled by the emergence in the 1970s and 1980s of a *critique* of Indian nationalism, one closely linked to the Indian social movements of the time and that precipitated a break with earlier modes of thought about culture and institutions. Risking a break of her own, she left a major Indian university in the mid-1990s to help establish the Centre for the Study of Culture and Society, a privately funded research institution in Bangalore. Paradoxically, while formally now "outside" the Indian university system, she is asked to intervene centrally in curricular issues across the humanities and social sciences — not only in traditional universities and colleges, but in basic science institutions and schools of management, design, and law.

Niranjana's account of innovation in post-colonial conditions begins a discussion of situated practice that threads through the volume before becoming the main focus in that last group of essays on the "institutional conditions and affiliations" (in Tony Bennett's terms) of Cultural Studies as a discipline. So while we have framed Niranjana's experience as in a sense "foundational" for some of the sorts of questions that we are asking here (what might the potentials of Cultural Studies look like, for example, if Western institutional genealogies were not always used as a default frame of reference in English-language scholarship but shared that frame with others?), it does not follow that we have edited this volume to affirm a charismatic post-colonial, non-Western or inter-Asian "difference" in historical situation and institutional opportunity in the early decades of the twenty-first century. However catchy that might be as a claim pitched to readers in Western public university systems undergoing serious assault in the wake of the global financial crisis of 2007–09, we have precisely not chosen to focus in that way on an exclusively "Asian" experience. Such an appeal to the "doxa of difference"[27] would do more than reiterate tacitly the old division of knowledge production ("the West and the rest") that fictively redraws absolute cultural boundaries that both capital and colonialism have erased. Even more significantly for our purposes here, it would ignore not only the *singularity* of these stories of making institutional space in hard places and times (they differ from each other) but also their *exemplary* value as models of aspiration and realization amenable to creative local uptake elsewhere.

For example, the question of disciplinarity is handled throughout the volume in an active and energetic as well as highly situated fashion. Faced with barriers and discouraging opposition at various levels of their practice, these authors have not simply imported a pre-existing conception of the discipline to their own institutional situations, and then tried to make that conception fit local conditions. Rather, they have worked with those conditions from the outset in a process of imagining and realizing a *project* for Cultural Studies that is capable of working productively *for* the local context and of taking new directions as those conditions change. To put this in another way, they practice a small-scale version of what Tony Bennett here calls (following David Toews) a "compositional perspective" that brings "historically specific 'gatherings' of varied elements … into provisional associations with one another." Happily described by one reader as a "forward-looking coda" to the book,[28] Bennett's essay functions for us as a methodological account of *what happens* in the course of the volume and within its individual chapters. Clearly, this compositional method is not Asia-specific or an exclusive product of post-colonial difference. The method of provisional association does, however, explain why the discipline of Cultural Studies itself looks a little different from chapter to chapter in this volume as local imperatives redefine and extend the discipline's capacities.

Some authors take a historical approach to understanding how the disciplinary project has come to differ from itself over time in particular places.

Thus Douglas Crimp's reflection on the last-minute removal of the artist Daniel Buren's work from the 1971 *Guggenheim International Exhibition* explores a doubly foundational moment for Cultural Studies, one firmly located in New York and at the same time familiar in other forms to many scholars who have come to Cultural Studies from a background in the arts. In one movement of differing in that moment, a critique of institutions predicated on the imagined externality of the critic is challenged by a more nuanced understanding of the subjective and social implication of critical works in those very institutions (as it was by the way Buren's art too powerfully functioned materially as a critique of its own placement in the museum itself). In another movement of differing, the pull of a more popular, "decorative" aesthetic renounced by Western high modernism (but explored in the bastions of that modernism by the works of Buren) begins to up open fields of "critical potential" in architecture, fashion, design and domestic everyday life.[29] In another historically oriented chapter, Stephen Ching-Kiu Chan follows disciplinary transformations unfolding across time instead of those condensed by a single event. His account of the emergence of "pedagogy" as central to both culture and education in Hong Kong between 1989 and 2012 further traces a shift of emphasis from cultural critique to cultural planning and heritage issues for a version of Cultural Studies that remains integrally linked to Hong Kong's geopolitically complex identity debates and vibrant social movements. This too is a turn in Cultural Studies that has taken place in other contexts (Australia and the United Kingdom, for example), but Chan's analysis suggests that it is the critical work of understanding the local reasons for this shift and the stakes involved in participating that gives this intellectual movement its social as well as scholarly rationale.

Other authors focus in a more sociological spirit on how an agenda for Cultural Studies as a university-based project can be shaped by the work of identifying social needs, on the one hand, and analyzing dominant values that must be negotiated on the other. Wang Xiaoming, for instance, meticulously shows how specific theoretical priorities have emerged for the Program in Cultural Studies at the University of Shanghai. Established in response to the massively complex social impacts of twenty years of economic reform in China, the Program's activities have in turn induced a series of "tough questions" for practice and theory to address. Wang's account brings out the way in which the choice of themes for research and of emphases for teaching in the Program is integrally linked to working on major problems such as how to deal with the centralized power of "the establishment" in China's universities;

how an academic discipline that deals with culture can contribute to positive social reform; and how a Cultural Studies embedded in contemporary Chinese experiences might develop a "a sense of care towards the world."

In a third approach to instituting disciplinarity, Dai Jinhua and John Erni imagine the potentials of Cultural Studies in relation to concrete if daunting political tasks that are national and international respectively. Dai discusses the intricate difficulties of translating such keywords as "popular culture" and "mass culture" from English to Chinese, and of doing so in the context of China's "vastly different history and reality." Situating the timing of the arrival of Cultural Studies within the intellectual as well as social upheaval of Chinese globalization and its attendant modes of class stratification and de-politicization (especially of the culture-consuming new middle class), she argues that the promise of Cultural Studies there is to reactivate a politics that "is not only about critique, but reconstruction." John Erni envisages a "relocation" of Cultural Studies in a closer relation to public institutions active in international struggles for social justice. By situating the discipline in relation to formalized "institutional rules of engagement" — in particular those of international human rights law — Erni envisages a metamorphosis of its worldly practice into one that perhaps invests as much in professional training and public participation as it does in critique.

Erni expresses the hope that making such a move towards an area of rights-based activity and a legal space that Cultural Studies has generally avoided or regarded with critical mistrust can "open a door for critical scholarship to flow" (and Niranjana's account of the Law and Culture program at the Bangalore CSCS provides an example of how such a door can open). We believe that Erni's outside-oriented vision of a critical scholarship willing to be transformed as it moves into new areas of practice is shared by the other contributors to this volume, and that this externalizing spirit can generate models as well as stories to think by in other places — perhaps not least in those Western universities now suffering the effects of strategic financial constriction and program demolition. Consistent with this spirit, in preference to talking about the "institutionalization" of Cultural Studies we want to emphasize the active and purposive, fully verbal sense of the term "institution"; this is a book about choosing *to institute* new spaces, practices, and activities.

Tony Bennett noted some years ago an "embarrassing tendency within Cultural Studies for those whose objective position is that of salaried government employees (that is, academics) ... to write of Cultural Studies as if it were somehow outside of or marginal to institutions, and to speak of 'insti-tutionalization' as if it were a looming external threat."[30] Within a Western (and Romantic) cultural inheritance, "institutionalization" can sound like something suspicious and probably unfortunate that happens to you; it has overtones of being confined against one's will or settling down for want of a better choice. The negative nuances are especially tenacious in Western usage when "the academy" is at issue, as though the latter still signifies a mode of professionalism imagined (however implausibly in today's conditions) either as enclosed in an ivory tower, detached from public and political life, or as doomed to a demoralizing state of "collusion" and "complicity" with omnip-otent Powers That Be.[31] To doubt the usefulness of thus devaluing our own workplaces at a time when the struggle to gain access to higher education or to be employed there on livable terms is increasingly harsh worldwide does not require us also to doubt that universities are indeed sites for the production of state and, increasingly, corporate benefits. On the contrary, it is clearly a premise of the chapters in this book that the work of instituting involves a sus-tained and practical engagement with what are often very hostile powers. It is rather the omnipotence of those powers that these institution-builders deny or contest, and they do this not simply by forming arguments about the nature of power in their societies (vital to action as those arguments are) but by forging spaces from which to *implement* their alternative projects and programs.

Implementation requires the formulation of concrete, nameable objectives. We draw from this simple reminder two lessons about the art of the possible in academic life today. First, the studies assembled here suggest that it is not only good in principle but vital for effective practice to have a strong ethical vision of what kind of creativity is worth pursuing in a university context, and why, if change is to be achieved. This contrasts with the fears of those thinkers who, writing in the wake of Adorno's critique of the entanglement of the very idea of "culture" with "the administrative view" ("the task of which, looking down from on high, is to assemble, distribute, evaluate and organize"),[32] see a worrying evacuation of substance from intellectual projects formed in prox-imity to the marketing imperatives and disruptive principles of new manage-rialism in institutions today. For example, reflecting broadly on the "liquid" qualities of "our floating and flowing, fluid modern world," Zygmunt Bauman muses that often "the question '*how* to do it' looks more important and urgent than the query '*what* to do.'"[33] Taking this up in a critique of policy-oriented Cultural Studies, Peter Osborne observes of a conference in the United

Kingdom that it had "no sense … of a theoretical horizon beyond immediate institutional imperatives; no sense of a future any different from the most immediate institutional present;"[34] and in an endnote he restates Bauman's problem: "the critical question remains: 'administration as cultural-political resource' for what project?"[35]

This is a question that makes no sense other than rhetorical provocation without a context to provide materials for a meaningful answer and communities to whom that answer matters. The strength of the local case studies, transformative national projects, personal detours and cross-institutional ventures described in this volume is that they are able to nominate contexts and communities that do indeed give shape and substance to the "what" as well as the "how" of institutional action. Iwabuchi's call to promote more ethnically inclusive ideas of nationality in Japan is just one of the solid and direct answers to Osborne's critical question in this volume. Explicitly taking up Osborne's call for a "pragmatist dispute," Yue's account of sexuality and cultural citizenship in Singapore is another. More generally, each of these authors contests by their writing practice as well as their institutional work the pessimistic suggestion that certain kinds of pragmatic thinking may shrink theoretical horizons and block the imagining of a different future. Concerned as they are with building "up" collective projects, networks, and shared spaces for thought in their everyday practices (rather than "looking down from high" as Adorno's classically vertical trope suggests), a different — and in Erni's terms a more "just" — social and political future is variously projected from the beginning to the end of this book.

The second lesson that we draw from these studies in implementing a vision rather than resting content with melancholically dreaming a dream is that a very strong sense of agency is generated rather than presumed by institutional creativity. Some stories here begin from situations of great social vulnerability or professional marginality; their inspirational force derives precisely from the pragmatic *and* rigorously intellectual ways in which they show exactly how those situations have been transformed. "How" questions matter; the literature on executive leadership and change management in institutions may be as remote from the concerns of most Cultural Studies in the West as the world of human rights law, but it has much to teach us about the impact of the choices made by individual managers in effecting the differing outcomes (in our terms, the varying degrees of livability) that particular universities produce within a common policy regime.[36] Cultural Studies is known for emphasizing consumer and audience agency in the use of commodities and media texts, but we often seem to have less to say (beyond copious citations of Foucault on capillary power and Althusser on our subjectification by "ideological state apparatuses" [ISA])[37] about the concrete modalities within which we exercise agency in the university and what imaginative choices and creative moves we might be able to make in our varying situations and within the constraints that we face.

As editors, we are struck by a special combination of qualities shared by these contributors in their practice of institutional creativity. First, they balance persistence over time with unpredictability in action. On the one hand, these are people who have "stayed the course"; they have been involved in institution-building for a long time, producing knowledge from dealing with failure and generating critiques of their own success. On the other hand, they have eschewed a "holier than thou" approach to institutional alliances; they have forged spaces in unexpected places and achieved some of their goals through forming unusual partnerships. Second, they meld an appetite for risk with a sharp sense of timing in the art of compromise. These scholars are deeply committed to something that goes well beyond narcissistic careerism and narrow institutional reproduction, and they also can talk to and cooperate with a whole range of people. Some have paid a heavy personal price for the risks they have taken, but there is a generosity and capaciousness to the way in which all of them think passionately through their institutional dilemmas that renders their work, in our view, at once effective and admirable.

What we have here, then, is a model of academic activism that is not only inspiring but highly pertinent to the current university landscape in which accountability and relevance (positive values as these should be) are all too often conflated with a grinding version of accountancy and a dispirited or cynical conformity to every management decree.[38] That several (though not all) contributors reflect on their experience through stories assumes a particular importance for us in this context. Whether a story is about a personal trajectory or the development of a center, a journal or a program, the advantage of a narrative approach is that it allows the energetic force of unpredictability and the refreshing effects of sheer, glorious *accident* to enter the space of critical reflection on institutional work. All visions, plans, projects and struggles that face up to a reality test are littered (for good and ill) with mistakes, false steps, strokes of luck and other unforeseen effects of chance. As Simon Marginson points out in relation to the globalizing strategies of entire universities, "not all outcomes are intended. Global creation is not always pre-meditated, and the relation between imagining and practices is not always happy."[39] However, for Marginson these strategies at best are "acts of freedom," and "if the global spatial moves made by universities fail as often as they succeed, in this they are no different to other acts of creation."[40]

That failure may be an outcome of grand university designs will not be surprising to anyone who reads the news, and everyone who has worked with a committee, a collective, a reading group or a network will be well aware that the wisdom of always expecting the unintended also applies to the smaller-scale "acts of freedom" committed in universities by groups of scholars working to create a space that would not exist without their efforts. This is common, everyday knowledge, yet the legacy of critical theory in Cultural Studies does not always encourage us to think deeply about what we know. As Crimp's chapter in this volume suggests, there is a blockage from that legacy around the concept of "institution," and it would be fair to say that debates about cultural policy have not altogether dislodged it — inclined as these have been by the work of Foucault to examine particular institutional forms (the asylum, the prison, the museum) against the powerful conceptual horizon of theories of governmentality.[41]

Problems of theoretical precedent arise if we take "institutionality" as our object instead. On the one hand, Cultural Studies and most other areas of inquiry concerned today with issues of power, subjectivity, identity, desire and the force of social imaginaries have invented themselves, as it were, through a rigorously argued critique of the Hegelian and Scottish Enlightenment idea of human institutions "as products of human action but not of human design."[42] The strength of these areas of inquiry is due in part to their success in identifying social systems of intentionality relative to, say, historical formations of race, colonialism, gender, and sexuality that were invisible to those who merely saw nature or random acts of prejudice at work. At the same time, critical studies in this tradition generally have also chosen to remain at a skeptical distance from the more cheery liberal view that "yes, obviously institutions determine our behavior, but only if we choose to obey them."[43] While Foucault once expressed a similar sentiment, quipping in an interview that "my role — and that is too emphatic a word — is to show people that they are much freer than they feel,"[44] Cultural Studies projects concerned with subjectivity often have more affinity with the dark visions of institutional power as a danger to one's very soul bequeathed to us by Marxist thinkers: Adorno gives us a memorable image of administrative thinking as a parasite or virus that "multiplies within" the "supposedly productive human being,"[45] while Althusser's dystopian — even paranoid — model of ideology is that of an omnipresent voice inescapably booming through the ISAs, "'Hey, you there!'"[46]

Even when stripped (as they usually are) of the qualifications and the sense of difficulty expressed by the argumentatively rich essays in which they first appeared, these dark visions remain compelling, not least because they are often true to significant aspects of our experience in institutions and they link that experience to powerful explanations of large-scale social and political processes. Yet they tell us little that is helpful for understanding the positive values that people find or create as they nonetheless continue to work in institutions, and they do not offer guidance as to how a given institution might be transformed — Althusser, for example, concedes that "the class struggle in the ISAs is indeed an aspect of the class struggle," only to move to a higher level of analysis (the ruling ideology "goes beyond them, for it comes from elsewhere").[47] Sociological or ethnographic accounts of *involvement*, rather than subjection, are more useful for grasping the potentially negative productivity of institutional life as it shapes both action and mentalities. When Hans Gerth and C. Wright Mills acerbically note that "one aspect of learning a role consists of acquiring motives that guarantee its performance,"[48] a large margin is left free for asking what other aspects of this learning might be of value for, say, the sex-positive parasites of Josephine Ho's research center, and for thinking more about the other motives that they bring to the performance of their academic work from "elsewhere" in their social and personal lives.

Through telling stories or anecdotes, people are able to focus analytically on the material force of chance and haphazard events while putting these on the same imaginative plane of discussion as their critique of an institution and their reflection on the latter's transformative effects in their lives. Exemplary of this method here is Crimp's ability to combine a serious account of the issues at stake in the 1971 removal of Buren's work from the *Guggenheim International Exhibition* with two versions of a witty story that he calls "my first job in New York." In one of these versions, the young Crimp wanders into the Guggenheim on impulse to apply for a job and finds himself, improbably, the only person in the vicinity qualified, more or less, for the job that the museum indeed happens to have. We hope that this volume as a whole may contribute to the proliferation of this kind of optimistic spirit as a precondition in difficult times for continuing the work that Kuan-Hsing Chen calls using institutional space and opportunity "to advance critical possibilities."

One of the most eloquent accounts of the reasons for doing this is provided by Mary Douglas in *How Institutions Think*. This book gives us a chilling vision of institutional psychology and the risks of involvement with it that rivals Althusser's scenario in its power to conjure a popular cultural imagery of fear. Douglas accepts the view that "an institution cannot have purposes;"[49] for her, only individuals can intend, plan, and contrive. However, when analyzing the classifying work that institutions do for us and inside us, she also endows them with agency in a passage worth quoting at length:

> Institutions systematically direct individual memory and channel our perceptions into forms compatible with the relations they authorize. They fix processes that are essentially dynamic, they hide their influence, and they rouse our emotions to a standardized pitch on standardized issues. Add to all this that they endow themselves with rightness and send their mutual corroboration cascading through all the levels of our information system. No wonder they easily recruit us into joining their narcissistic self-contemplation … Institutions have the pathetic megalomania of the computer whose whole vision of the world is its own program.[50]

As individuals in Douglas's sense, however, we are capable of formulating other purposes while fashioning other kinds of involvement, and thus we always have open to us the possibility of intellectual independence and resistance. For Douglas, as for Adorno, the first step in such resistance is to discover how "the institutional grip is laid upon our mind."[51] Ultimately, though, "only changing institutions can help. We should address them, not individuals, and address them continuously, not only in crises."[52]

It would be fair to say that Cultural Studies has been involved in practising a great deal of that mental self-discovery entailed by the critique of "institutional grip" over the past fifty years. This book, with its "stories to live by," is about venturing to take the further step of transforming the kinds of classifications that our universities make, not only by refusing their narcissism and megalomania but by forging within them intellectual and pedagogical spaces capable of sustaining more livable social bonds, continuously and on an everyday basis.

Institutional Culture

A Manifesto with Rules

Mette Hjort and Meaghan Morris

The global flow of dubious ideas has taken its toll on many a university, with hyperactive bureaucratic systems increasingly colonizing other forms of institutional culture. In many an institution, time-consuming and ritualized exercises in surveillance and monitoring dissipate the energies of staff. Increasingly required to live according to a bureaucratic clock that segments time in ways that are inhospitable to immersion and flow, teachers and researchers find creativity and real thought more and more elusive. The culture of permanent bureaucratic distractions is instituted at a real cost, for more often than not it brings with it a culture of cynicism that further erodes the collegial norms that market-based principles which favor competitive, zero-sum games also target.

But those who build the institutions that teachers, researchers, and students inhabit do not have to commit to institutional cultures that thwart, rather than promote, academic work environments characterized by creativity, generosity, engagement, and the pleasures of thinking, learning, and collaborating.

It is time to rally around some basic principles. Serio-comic like many of the manifestos that inspire them, the rules listed here are the work not of two disaffected rebels with nostalgic longings for the universities of yesteryear, but of two scholars who believe that the quality of a university's institutional culture is all important and the result not only of government edicts, but of styles of leadership, and of the practices of everyday life to which senior managers — but also those "on the ground" — lend their support.

Let us be vigilant about the colonizing tendencies of bureaucratic systems! Let us resist cynicism! Let us build institutional cultures where terms such as "generous," "creative," "happy," and "fulfilled" have a genuine purchase on reality. To this end, let the following rules be observed.

1. The pursuit of an administrative career path, whether as an academic or non-academic member of staff, shall be conditional on the successful

completion of a summer course devoted to the philosophy of time. One of the (lower level) outcomes of this course will be an ability to understand the relevance to university governance of the basic distinction between bureaucratic (repetitive, meaningless, futile, "dead") time and kairotic (socially significant, creative) time.

2   Persons who enjoy the activity of meeting more than the activities of teaching and research shall be barred from chairing committees, as shall the person who repeatedly shows signs of finding his own voice far lovelier than those of all other colleagues.

3.   Persons who do not understand, or are unable to commit to, the conversational norm of relevance shall be barred from committee membership.

4.   The requesting of a report shall be understood as entailing an obligation to read that report. The phenomenon of unread reports shall be considered an institutional scandal.

5.   The chair of any committee shall be required to calculate the cost of all meetings (salary per hour of all members attending), and to justify the costs of those meetings (in terms of outcomes) in a short report to the president and vice-president.

6.   Administrators who fail to coordinate their report-requesting activities, and who thus request the writing of multiple, overlapping reports, shall be sanctioned, the severity of the sanction being proportionate to the degree of overlap and the required length of the reports.

7.   Academics and administrators who dress like bankers and believe that their sartorial tastes should be adopted by all colleagues shall themselves be required to become bankers (the application of this rule shall make no reference to the current state of the economy).

8.   There is a limit to how many ceremonies research-active scholars can attend without becoming research-inactive. This truth shall be recognized.

9.   Governance by inspiration shall at all times be preferred to governance by fear, sanction, and intimidation.

10.   Administrators shall be required to consider the cost of competition. Administrators who understand the collegial need to constrain zero-sum rationality with other forms of rationality shall not be considered naïve, womanly, or soft.

11.   The university shall clearly identify times of year when it is illegitimate for administrative staff to send academics bureaucratic tasks to perform. At a

minimum, these periods shall include the days before public holidays and public holidays themselves.

12. In the interest of avoiding make-work projects, administrative staff who think academics are "done" once classes end shall be required, as a matter of considerable urgency, to attend a workshop on research and its contributions to the university's bottom line.

13. Anyone caught rumor-mongering with the intent to influence decision-making about university matters shall forfeit the right to apply for an increment and/or to receive a gratuity. Colleagues who fail to exhibit common sense and critical judgment when processing rumors shall be required either to share an office with, or to work for, the purveyor of rumors, as that person's official assistant (any space constraints that might arise shall be seen as part of the fun, and part of the cure).

14. Any head of department who ceases to be able to talk to colleagues without using such terms as "quality assurance," "inputs," "outputs," "deliverables," "performance indicators," "alignment," "graduate profile," "stakeholder," and "evidence-based" shall be required to atone for the pain inflicted on others by performing thirty hours of community art work.

15. Anyone who thinks that increasing the paperwork involved in running a university brings that university in line with corporate practices shall be required to do an internship with a corporation (*any* corporation will do).

16. Universities that are incapable of producing at least ten both serious-minded and happy staff members (academic or non-academic, senior or junior) for the purposes of meeting with the external panel that conducts the annual HA (happiness audit) shall be considered DISMALS (dysfunctional institutions with sado-masochistic alignments). In the interest of protecting taxpayers and their offspring, these institutions shall be seen as meriting the lowest possible rankings in the league tables.

17. League tables that rank DISMALS highly shall be seen as ... dodgy, as shall those who compile them.

1

The Desire for Cultural Studies

Tejaswini Niranjana

My chapter focuses on the new institutional spaces in which the culture question is gaining prominence in the Indian higher education scenario. I begin by providing a sketch of the emergence of Cultural Studies in the Indian context against the backdrop of the crisis in higher education. For the sake of convenience, I will draw on my own institutional trajectory.

Ten to twelve years ago, in the mid-1990s, I was inside the academy, teaching in a mainstream English department of a major Indian university. However, my practice as a cultural theorist was marginal to it, being the target of much hostility and suspicion — whether it was to do with the incursion of what was named as the political into disciplinary spaces or to do with the destabilization of disciplinary canons. Today I find myself outside the traditional academy, located in a privately funded research institution, but invited to intervene centrally in curricular issues across the humanities and social sciences. The intervention is taking place not only in traditional institutions like the universities and affiliated or autonomous colleges, but also in the basic science institutions, the management schools, and the design schools.

What are the factors enabling this change in the Indian higher education scenario? How do we explain what I want to name as the widespread new *desire for Cultural Studies*? Is there an internal churning within some disciplines that are beginning to perceive 'culture' as their blind spot? Are there new pressures on educational institutions to transform themselves? Would an account of these pressures have to deal with the social and political crises that are compelling us to go beyond conventional formulations of culture? What is the relationship between the changes sweeping across the higher education spectrum and the new interest in cultural questions? How do we address these questions in designing new curricula?

Before I offer some speculations on these issues, I would like to suggest that the relationship between Cultural Studies and institutions is perhaps different in a foundational way in India and other parts of the non-Western world compared with, for example, the United Kingdom and the United States. The commonsense of Cultural Studies textbook writers is that it embodies "resistance" and marginality. Even as Cultural Studies curricula take shape in a variety of undergraduate and postgraduate locations, professors who have themselves not obtained degrees in Cultural Studies but teach students who are certainly going to be doing that proclaim that curricularization will be the death of the originary impulses of Cultural Studies. Perhaps this feeling comes from the idea that *criticality* — seen as central to Cultural Studies — resides outside the institution (or, to use the old left word, the establishment).

I argue that in certain kinds of post-colonial situations, thinking about culture has been central to the entire process of institutionalization and the creation of new/modern institutions — whether it is strictly in the educational sphere in relation to the formation of the disciplines or setting the objectives of pedagogy, or in broader spheres like those of democratic political participation. My argument proceeds from two interrelated assumptions about Cultural Studies in India, which are probably generalizable to other non-Western contexts: that Cultural Studies is a new name for curricular initiatives drawing on much older critical engagements with the culture question (which means that contemporary Cultural Studies in India is compelled to take into account these earlier engagements);[1] and that the history of the emergence of Cultural Studies is tied to a crisis in nationalist discourse as well as to a disciplinary and institutional crisis.[2] By nationalism, I mean anti-colonial nationalism of the sort that acquired hegemony in India in the twentieth century, and underwrote the institution-building efforts in higher education — the setting up of universities, research centers, specialized science and technology institutes, management schools, and regulatory and funding bodies for the disciplines.

Tracing the Genealogy of Cultural Studies in India

If we were to ask where the thinking about culture is located, the answer would most certainly have to be that it is central to what used to be called "third world" nationalism (although comparisons with Taiwan or South Korea, where nationalism seems problematic in a very different way, might yield a slightly different perspective). The point I am making here is that there was a critical edge to thinking in that way, and in articulating the culture question in the nationalist framework — although there may have been problems with essentializing culture and with the borrowing of Orientalist frames of analysis.

A major preoccupation of nationalist institutions was the theorizing of culture and the effort to assemble 'national' cultural traditions. In India, culture came to be seen as the antithesis of modernity[3] — as that which was both refuge and weapon, solace and shield from the depredations of the kind of social change colonialism was bringing about. The thinking about culture that emerges from colonialism has as its most significant concern the description and 'fixing' of Indianness, and in this description culture had to be seen in many ways as the 'other' of modernity. This nineteenth-century separation of culture from modernity was to become a key problem for Cultural Studies in India when it emerged as a "field" (and with that name) in the 1990s.

The Culture Question

Let me reiterate that in the third world context, questions of culture were discussed as part of the anti-colonial struggle, where raising the question of culture acquired its own significance and momentum, and where it became important to make cultural claims elaborating the specific connections between culture (seen as that which was our very own) and (Western, Euro-American) modernity. We see this in contexts as different as Africa, South Asia, and the Caribbean in the work, for example, of C. L. R. James, Aimé Césaire, Jawaharlal Nehru, and Jomo Kenyatta.[4] In the formation of the *national-modern*, that which could be named as "our culture" occupied a crucial position. In societies like India, diverse kinds of anti-colonialists in the nineteenth century reached a consensus on the culture claim — that is, the claim to the distinctiveness and continuity of something that came to be called 'Indian culture'. For Indian nationalism, our culture — as opposed to Western modernity — had to be seen as old, with the claim to antiquity underwriting the coherence of contemporary identities.

As sociologist Satish Deshpande points out, there has been a certain ambiguity endemic to the culture claim in India.[5] Culture has been seen as what makes us unique and therefore "special," but also — in nationalist narratives — as what keeps us backward and under-developed. What nationalism had to do, then, was to separate out "ancient culture" (monuments, religious texts, artistic achievements, sculpture) from contemporary problems caused by Indians' sluggishness in becoming modern (allegedly due to superstition, caste, and religious beliefs). The first kind of culture found acceptance as national heritage, while the second was described as something that had to be overcome. Modernity, after all, had to do with transcending "primordial" marks of identity — especially of caste and community.

But nationalist self-esteem dictated that "our modernity" include elements of our specific cultural identity. In asserting this specificity, Indians often drew uncritically on a common nineteenth-century colonial argument that although the past of India was glorious, the present was depraved, requiring Western intervention to restore it to its former splendor. Indians also drew on the work of earlier British Orientalists to define what was truly Indian.[6]

To provide just one example of how nationalists went about defining Indian tradition, I refer to music. The task in the late nineteenth and early twentieth centuries was to create classical traditions that matched up to Western canons. This involved the assigning of pre-colonial textual sources (preferably from the Sanskrit) to contemporary musical practice, the standardization and cleaning up of supposedly vulgar lyrics, and the introduction of notation systems. After Independence, new institutions such as the national and state-level academies for literature, fine arts, and performing arts took up regulatory functions that continued the work of canonization along similar lines.

Cultural Studies as/in the Critical Break

While there is in India at least a century-old history of engaging with the culture question, we do see a break with that history by the 1970s and 1980s, with the emergence of a critique of nationalism. This critique is articulated most power-fully in the social movements of the period (peasant and tribal movements, the women's movement, the slightly later Dalit movement)[7] and in the intellectual initiatives inspired by those movements (Subaltern Studies, feminist scholar-ship, Dalit critiques). The immediate history of Cultural Studies is to be derived from this broad critique.

The crisis of the disciplines (such as Economics, History, English literary studies, Political Science, and Sociology) — also becoming visible in the 1990s — is related to both the larger political crisis and how they were formu-lating their research problems and their pedagogical practices. I refer here to the lack of fit between what they had to account for and the inherited concep-tual frameworks of the disciplines. The problem faced in different ways by the disciplines was the elimination of culture from their various frameworks, or the adoption of analytical methods by which culture can be explained away or de-emphasized.

Let me give examples from four key disciplines: Economics, Sociology, History, and literary studies. Seeing the disciplines in historical perspective might give us a better picture of their inherited burdens. After Independence, the key social science disciplines promoted by the nation-state were Economics and Sociology. Both were seen as providing the information and the strategy inputs for the developmental agendas of the nation. The "data" of both were Indian, but the perspective and objectives were different, as was their approach to the question of culture. Economics focused on theory-building and modeling — the data were presented in terms of numbers. As economist C. T. Kurien says, the link between economic theories and economic problems is not always a strong one. Most economists would like to see their discipline as dealing with goods and services, and with the choice-making *individual*, whereas Kurien argues that Economics is about social relationships.[8] He feels that in claiming analytical rigour, economists actually empty out the substance of Economics itself (that is, they may only look at 'exchange' of goods and not at property *relations*). Here I adopt Kurien's larger perspective to suggest that a Western-derived Economics in India found itself unable and unwilling to look at cultural issues that clearly were central to understanding how economies function.

Sociology, on the other hand, was strongly empirical, and favored qualitative analysis. The focus on culture as distinctive to a population was part of the self-identity of Sociology. In the form of its Indian avatar, Sociology often functioned more like Social Anthropology, which studied non-Western peoples — hence the continuation with Orientalist frameworks, and the effort to account for the specificity of Indians, especially those who were non-modern.[9] Analyses framed by this perspective saw modernization as the erasure or giving up of Indian culture and the adoption of Western values and ways of life. This approach to Indian society created a distance between culture and modernity, so that culture lay in the past and modernity was simply the time-space within which the leaving behind of culture was manifested.

We have a different equation with the culture question in History, which as a discipline in India has early beginnings in the attempt of the late nineteenth-century anti-colonial movements to contest British versions of Indian political and military history; later on, in the twentieth century, History functioned almost like a biography of the Indian nation-state, a situation critiqued in the 1980s by the Subaltern Studies research collective (whose member Gyanendra Pandey made the statement about biography). Subaltern Studies pointed out the continuities between colonialist and nationalist history-writing in terms of how they perceived non-elite populations. Here again, the problems of the discipline may lie in its distinctly presentist attitude: the historian was a modernist, unable in the last analysis to account for phenomena like "communalism" except in culturalist terms. Here we have not the avoidance of the culture question, but the use of it as a last-resort explanation.

Culture has featured in a very different way in English literary studies, which from the time of T. B. Macaulay's proposal to introduce English education into India has been prominent as a discipline at all levels of education. Curiously, the cultural assumptions of English literature were not seen as antithetical by those who fought for Independence from colonial rule. It was only in the late 1980s and early 1990s that the colonial origins of the discipline and its ideal of a universal culture (propagated among others by the nineteenth century critic Matthew Arnold) were brought into question. The argument was that the formation of this universal culture was made possible by various kinds of epistemic violence against the colonized, or against the weaker sections of the colonial society. By the standards of the culture propagated by English literary studies, other cultures came to occupy marginal positions. The critical perspectives of the 1990s represented multiple challenges to literary studies — so much so that the discipline was compelled to undergo transformation.[10] The emergence of Cultural Studies has often been seen as one kind of resolution to the problems faced by literary studies a decade ago. The *work* of Cultural Studies in the Indian academy is something that *renders critical* (to borrow the analogy from physics) *setting*, *discipline*, and *practice*, allowing for new formulations about culture that have a greater purchase on contemporary crises. More about this later.

The Institutions

During the 1950s and early 1960s in India, most of the key educational institutions and statutory bodies for regulating higher education were set up, as well as institutions meant for the identification and recognition of artistic practice. The University Grants Commission, an autonomous body to control higher education, was formed through an Act of Parliament in 1956. The main institutions dealing with the arts — Sahitya Akademi (1954), Sangeet Natak Akademi (1953), and the Lalit Kala Akademi (1954) — were also set up during this period. Shortly thereafter, institutions for training in specific areas were established: the National School of Drama (1959) under the Sangeet Natak Akademi; the Film Institute of India (1960), renamed in 1974 as the Film and Television Institute of India and overseen by the Ministry of Information and Broadcasting; and the National Institute of Design (1961), under the Department of Science and Technology. This diverse set of institutions covered the field of "culture" for the post-colonial state.

Developmental aid from the Soviet Union, the United States and West Germany helped set up the first Indian Institutes of Technology, which were granted recognition as "institutions of national importance" through the *Indian Institutes of Technology Act 1961*. The first management institutions or business schools were set up in Ahmedabad and Calcutta in 1961. The setting up of these specialized institutions further reinforced the *separation of skill-based learning from 'general education,'* a separation that was already evident in the medical, architecture, and engineering colleges from colonial times, which began to grow in numbers following Independence. Interestingly, the management and technology institutes, as well as the basic science centers, had their own investments in "culture" — it was always the additional feature that provided relaxation, entertainment, and spiritual succor, leading to the rounded personality of the Nehruvian technocrat.

Even with general education, a separation between the disciplines was perpetuated. The separation was endorsed by the report of the University Commission (1948), headed by the philosopher S. Radhakrishnan who later became India's president. The report proposed a distinction between facts, events, and values — or nature, society, and spirit (which would be the subject matter of the sciences, social sciences, and humanities respectively). The goal of education was training for citizenship, according to the report, providing a definition of 'general education' that was supposed to include *theoretical contemplation, aesthetic enjoyment,* and *practical activity*. The disciplines fell into place along this tripartite division. Radhakrishnan's emphasis on "general education" was soon replaced by an emphasis on education for the "development" of the nation, especially through the inclusion of "science and technology" or "area (regional) studies," which in turn would inform state policy. However, the model of disciplinary compartmentalization still exists more than sixty years after Independence. Even when there were revisions in education policies — as, for example, in the National Policy on Education (1986), this tripartite division of disciplines based on *facts*, *events*, and *values*, did not change substantially. Cultural Studies' interest in disciplinary legacies needs to take on board not just the colonial formation of the disciplines but also their trajectories in the post-colonial state.

Indian Education System

What is the historical legacy of the institutions, including the educational ones? To gauge the possible institutional impact of Cultural Studies interventions, we should take a look at the structure of the Indian education system — which is a massive one, 'recognised as the second largest system in the world.'[11] This includes over 300 universities including deemed-to-be universities. With the Private Universities Bill an impending reality, and the Foreign Universities Bill waiting to be cleared by Parliament at the time of writing in December 2009, in the immediate future this entire system will have to prepare to face the consequences of globalization.

Some statistics may not be out of place here. Each university has about fifty affiliated colleges; in some instances this number can go up to 300. About 8–9 per cent of the relevant age group of the population has access to higher education. (To provide a contrast, the Asian average is 11 per cent.) Women represent 40 per cent of all students. Roughly two-thirds are enrolled in arts and science programs (45 per cent in arts, 20 per cent in science), 18 per cent in commerce and management, 7.5 per cent in engineering and technology, and 3.25 per cent each in law and medicine.

The rate of growth of higher education has been about 13–14 per cent every year since the 1960s. One-tenth of the students in higher education are doing postgraduate work, and 88 per cent are undergraduates in colleges. Some 50 per cent of the postgraduate students are also in colleges (rather than on university campuses). An important fact is that 80.5 per cent of higher education is still subsidized by the government, with most private-sector investment in education being in professional education. Another fact that could be important for Cultural Studies is that in the Institutes of Technology and the law schools, 15 per cent of the coursework is supposed to be devoted to the social sciences/humanities.

Cultural Studies

By raising questions about the objects of study conventionally associated with specific disciplines — as, for example, in the Radhakrishnan report's tripartite division allotting nature to science, society to the social sciences, and spirit to the humanities, or the distinctions between professional and non-professional education, or even between market-oriented disciplines and the others — Cultural Studies has made significant curricular innovations. The focus has been on issues and problems rather than on specific kinds of objects of inquiry.

Cultural Studies has evolved within the context of the Indian education system as an interdisciplinary field that has engaged critically with (a) older formulations about the place of culture and (b) specific disciplinary histories. As explained above, the earlier formulations centered around culture's endorsement of the nationalist project in terms drawing from Orientalist descriptions of Indian "difference," whereas Cultural Studies today is not only critiquing both the description and the endorsement, but also challenging the separation between culture and modernity. Cultural Studies has also interrogated the disciplinary frameworks (English literary studies, History, Sociology-Anthropology) in which culture was embedded, and questioned the absence of the cultural in disciplines such as Economics or Political Science.

Knowledge Interventions: The Domain of Cultural Studies and Cultural Studies Initiatives

I will now move to a brief discussion about the institutionalization work of the Centre for the Study of Culture and Society (CSCS) in Bangalore that I helped to establish. The center is an independent academic research organization launched in 1998 as an experiment in institutionalized research excellence in inter-disciplinary humanities and social sciences. It is itself a higher education institution, but one that was born out of a diagnosis of the crisis in Indian higher education; thus it has continued to reflect on the implications of the crisis and the possible role of institutions like itself at such a moment.[12]

In March 2001, three years after its inception, the CSCS launched a PhD program in interdisciplinary Cultural Studies, the first and only one of its kind in the country at the time. It also launched its own online Master's program, something of a pioneering experiment in higher education in the social sciences. Both these programs are unique in the field of humanities/social sciences teaching at these levels in India.

As is well known by now, Cultural Studies emerged in the 1980s in Britain, Europe, and the United States, and in numerous Asian countries, as something of a response to crises in the humanities and social sciences. These crises were reflected in the difficulties of bringing into teaching practice the kinds of cultural phenomena that were becoming increasingly relevant, for example, to definitions of politics, to people's everyday experience, and to issues of human rights. Relevant to these phenomena were larger issues such as growing religious intolerance, the emergence of new modes of communication, and the rise of new social-political movements.

Such a field has come to be recognized today by the distinctive manner in which it selects the objects it analyzes and by the methods it employs. While there are a number of key texts — international as well as Indian — that would be seen as seminal to the discipline as we would define it (these texts are taught at our PhD and diploma levels as part of mandatory courses), it must be added that Cultural Studies also includes substantial resources of previously invisible writing and cultural production — such as autobiographies, oral testimonies, legal documentation, early efforts by political practitioners of various leanings to develop theoretical models, human rights documentation, the popular press, the cinema, and previously unexplored traditions of performance or visual expression — that would earlier have been either unteachable or seen as irrelevant to the concept of "teaching culture," but which are now becoming an increasingly crucial resource for cultural theory.

It is therefore important to see Cultural Studies on at least two levels. The first constitutes the recognition and teaching of the field and its achievements, its landmarks, and what we would see as its key texts, produced as much in India as elsewhere. Most leading academic publishers in India (such as Oxford University Press and Sage) have used Cultural Studies as a library classification category for some years; coupled with locally produced books and essays from anthropology, history, political science, literary and film studies, this material clearly has by now established a respectable body of local literature that would need to be taught alongside Western "classics" in the field, but that is still yet to enter most arts-related classrooms, except in sporadic form — mainly through the initiative of individual teachers. Second, the more difficult contemporary process into which the CSCS ventured — that of thematizing culture as a possible *field of inquiry* — was reflected as much in innovative ways of institutionalizing the program as it was in course content. In this latter instance, there were neither some trademark Cultural Studies objects and questions, nor "master texts" to be "explained" and assimilated. Instead, any domain — be it the political, ethical, or (to shift to the epistemic side) scientific, psychological or cognitive — had to be seen as either directly "cultural" or relevant to the understanding of culture. To take a few examples of such fields, *visuality* (or the ways in which visual forms inhabit our lives) would become an object of inquiry that both included and went beyond specific forms like painting, cinema, or architecture, asking instead how these might relate to each other. Likewise, the interrelationship between *caste* and *democracy* constituted for us a possible research area where the discipline of Sociology or Social Anthropology would itself form part of the investigation. Issues of *gender* and *modernity* also formed another key area of concentration, and included investigations into the discourse of gender employed by, say, development institutions. In this wider sense, the focus was on the institutions and practices of our modernity.

Some issues followed from the latter contention. This program included work across a number of disciplines, extending its appeal to students trained in, or wishing to work in, fields ranging from Anthropology, History (including and especially Art History), and Literature to Political Science, Sociology, Communications, and Media. The student body today includes people with backgrounds in medicine, architecture, market research, religious studies, psychology, and urban studies. The general curriculum, as well as individual courses, is devised according to the specific interests of students, and is dependent on our seeking out and securing the participation of visiting faculty in the areas shaped by student demand, since the CSCS core faculty is a small one. Such syllabi need a diversity of resource materials, and therefore the support of many institutions, since no single institution could conceivably possess all the resource materials that potentially would be of interest. CSCS also organizes workshops, conferences, and consultations that supplement the regular courses. Such a curriculum is defined in its implementation, and such implementation would by definition include the need to document both the data and the process by which syllabi are assembled, taught, and researched so that the process can be replicated elsewhere.

However, while our center is impacting the mainstream university and college systems through the online MA in Cultural Studies or through our undergraduate diploma in Cultural Studies, it is in our more unconventional interventions that the challenge for the future seems to lie.[13]

Below is a quick overview of some of our key curricular interventions in partnership with other institutions:

Law, Society, and Culture

The Law and Culture program at CSCS was introduced with the aim of developing new and critical interdisciplinary research on some of the crucial social-political issues of our time. The original conceptualization of the program emerged through a long history of interaction with faculty and alumni from the National Law School of India University (NLSIU), some of whom are currently members of the Alternative Law Forum, Bangalore. Among other issues, the dialogue — which extended to a year-long seminar — has addressed intellectual property rights, questions raised by the Uniform Civil Code, and questions of human rights and public-interest litigation, as well as larger issues of popular justice, alternative dispute resolution, and indigenous and colonial histories of the law. The seminar paved the way for subsequent teaching of courses at the PhD and other levels, and helped conceptualize a broad-based program on law and culture.

Teaching Interventions

CSCS has made progress in actively involving itself with a range of core and peripheral educational initiatives in the area. Most importantly, a course titled "Law, Rights and Culture" has been offered every year to the PhD students of CSCS since August 2004. The course is cross-listed as an optional seminar course for the final-year students of the NLSIU. Besides the CSCS PhD and diploma students, the course was picked up by seven students in 2004 and thirteen students in 2005 from NLSIU. At the postgraduate level, a course titled "Law and Culture" was developed for the MA online degree program in the 2004–05 academic year (for the curriculum, see www.cscsarchive.org). A fifty-hour optional course on media law was also taught as part of the CSCS undergraduate Diploma in Cultural Studies at Christ College, Bangalore.

It is expected that eventually all these teaching interventions will be institutionalized as a PhD program in "Law and Culture." Although it is to be housed at CSCS, it eventually could become a prototype for such courses in law schools.

Science Institutions: Integrated Science Education

Since 2006, CSCS has been working with the Indian Institute of Science, Bangalore, one of the oldest science research centers in the country, to offer a sixteen-week course premised on the need for the integration of knowledge, forms, and practices. The course, titled "Production of Knowledge in the Natural and Social Sciences," has been offered twice in the last few years. The course is offered at the postgraduate level, and is open to students from all the science institutions in Bangalore, college science teachers, and CSCS PhD students. It covers a range of issues — including those of *representation*, *interpretation*, and *analysis* — that can be approached from natural and social science perspectives. A related course, titled "Natural and Human Sciences: Arguing about the Two Cultures," was taught at the PhD level at CSCS in 2009. The Higher Education Cell at CSCS is currently incubating five research programs at the Indian Institute of Science Education and Research at Pune, which eventually will result in taught courses that integrate the human and natural sciences at the undergraduate level.

Design and UG: The Artists' Program

This project is designed to create a context that introduces the student to, first, a different understanding of "arts practice," and second, a new set of questions about culture. The plan is to conceptualize a specific set of activities around which a new kind of interaction between the student community and the arts practitioner becomes possible. The artist will be encouraged to familiarize herself/himself with the courses taught by CSCS, and to use the intellectual resources available at the center. Interaction will be with undergraduate students from collaborating institutions. The interaction could be in the form of a course, an activity with students and faculty of the institution (such as an installation/performance), or a research project. Cultural Studies has questioned the distinction between "fine arts" and the popular forms of arts by asking questions about representation, by speaking about conditions of production of art objects and art practices, and by studying the role of the "symbolic" in popular art practices and representations. We expect the artist–student interaction to take place under these conditions of critique. The institutional collaborations will be with Srishti School for Art, Design and Technology — a long-time CSCS partner — and a handful of undergraduate colleges.

Cultural Studies Today

What our different interventions in diverse institutional locations have shown us is that Cultural Studies is poised to emerge as the critical space in the interstices of the humanities and the social sciences. The work coming out of this space, through enabling interactions between researchers, teachers, and students across disciplinary boundaries, is likely to lead to (1) the raising of new questions that address culture; (2) an interrogation of institutional priorities; and (3) the reconceptualization of the disciplines themselves.

My argument is that Cultural Studies can help revitalize the social sciences and humanities so that they can not only attract more engaged students but also create better opportunities for the students who end up there by default because they lack the academic credentials to get into professional courses. Cultural Studies has evolved within the context of the Indian education system as an interdisciplinary field that has engaged critically with both older formulations about the place of culture and specific disciplinary histories. As explained above, the earlier formulations centered around culture's endorsement of the nationalist project in terms drawing from Orientalist descriptions of Indian "difference," whereas Cultural Studies today is not only critiquing both the description and the endorsement; it is also challenging the separation between culture and modernity.

For us, undergraduate colleges have been a significant location for the testing out of new curricular ideas. Exploiting the interest in certain kinds of colleges to "add value" to their courses, Cultural Studies — in experiments carried out by CSCS, for example — has moved from being the extra-curricular course to become the for-credit course. With the new move towards autonomy (from the traditional affiliating university), colleges will be allowed to determine their own courses and syllabi, and come up with their own methods of evaluation. The indirect impact of changes in the college's pedagogic and evaluative structures will be felt at the university level, and eventually at the research institute level as well. Ironically, this might reverse the trickle-down effect often advocated by educationists, where the university is seen as the standard-setting and syllabus-devising authority. The implications of the General Agreement on Trades and Services (GATS), including the entry of foreign universities, will no doubt contribute to creating a context for higher education where the old models of pedagogy and research — already in crisis for some decades — will need to be seriously re-thought.

While the immediate field of intervention might be the undergraduate college, crucially the preparation for this has to be at the level of the research institutes — and maybe even the universities. The idea is to have significant interdisciplinary research in different social science and humanities disciplines energize the re-visioning of undergraduate curricula, and in turn to have the products of colleges — with a far richer general education than the older system could provide — become stronger participants in the emerging knowledge economy at all levels, whether it is in journalism and the media, in civil society groups and in NGOs, or in more specialized research locations.

The CSCS vision for the next decade, as we identify it, is to explore the interface between research, teaching, pedagogy in a larger sense, the market, and social policy. We intend to undertake this through our research programs, which currently include interests in law, society and culture; higher education; cultural diversity and cultural policy in Asia; and culture, subjectivity, and psyche. The understanding of interdisciplinarity with which CSCS works and that it envisions is a more foundational weaving together of disciplines to produce new fields of investigation and inquiry. The Integrated Science Education Initiative of the Higher Education Cell, for instance, is working with science institutes like the Indian Institutes of Science Education and Research (IISERs) to produce new fields that can be researched and taught in natural science and social science institutes — areas like "cognition" or "bio-diversity." The Law, Society and Culture program, likewise, would produce areas of inquiry like "legal history," which would figure in both the law school and the arts and humanities college/university. These programs have emerged organically over the previous years out of our interdisciplinary reflection (for instance, thinking about law not in isolation, but in relation to society and culture) and our commitment to building an integrated institutional structure — for example, our partnerships with other institutions.

Each of these initiatives applies and takes forward the agenda of Cultural Studies as imagined in the first decade of the existence of CSCS. The view is to deepen the capacity of Cultural Studies as an interdisciplinary field of research and pedagogy by creating an interface with the market, society, and public policy, through applied research. Each research program evolves its own framework of research and pedagogy, and pursues its implementation, through partnerships and fundraising projects that converge with the intellectual goals and objectives of the program. Each program thus has its own partnering institutions — which may be civil society organizations, NGOs, other educational institutions (national and international), and funding agencies that have a stake in policy and implementation.

Cultural Studies initiatives in India have helped imagine new models of institutions of higher education, as in the CSCS example, and to craft innovative forms of collaboration between older and newer institutions. The larger challenge for the set of interventions Cultural Studies can initiate would be to transform the disciplines as well as the institutions. What is at stake is nothing less than envisaging afresh what higher education in the non-Western world might mean.

2

Social Movements, Cultural Studies, and Institutions

On the Shifting Conditions of Practices

Kuan-Hsing Chen

Drawing on my own involvement over the past 20 years, in this essay I pinpoint the shifting dynamics between social movements, Cultural Studies and institutions. My initial observation is that, in the late 1980s and early 1990s, the driving forces and inspirations for Cultural Studies in Asia came from engagements in social and political movements; the institutionalization (in quite diverse forms) of Cultural Studies from the late 1990s onward has redefined the field as both an intellectual movement and a set of institutional practices. This shift is over-determined by the aggressive power of a neo-liberal economy, the disenchantment with political democracy in the region, and the inability of professionalized academic disciplines to respond to the new conditions; it is in the fluctuation of these forces that Cultural Studies finds interstices to carve out spaces on university campuses, based on the spirit and credibility established in the earlier moment of social involvements. In what follows, I focus on the *Inter-Asia Cultural Studies* journal project to bring out issues for discussion.[1] Although it is not clear whether it is premature to do the reflexive work, since many projects and practices are still ongoing, thinking critically together might give us a sense of the shape, strengths and weaknesses, and possible directions of Cultural Studies as an intellectual movement in the region and beyond.

Thinking retrospectively, the Trajectories project, made up of two conferences held in Taipei in 1992 and 1995, and resulting in a book titled *Trajectories: Inter-Asia Cultural Studies*,[2] was instrumental in the process of international regionalization. Strangely enough, unlike other academic fields, Cultural Studies is perhaps most locally driven but most internationally and regionally linked. For the established disciplines — such as literary studies or Sociology — academics in Asia go to the MLA or American Sociological

Association for academic conferences, but they seldom interact in the region. In the case of Cultural Studies, we seem to have met all the time, and for ten to fifteen years friendship, trust, and solidarity have been built. In our circle, I have never sensed competition among ourselves, only mutual support. Do you think the signing of a Memorandum of Understanding between eleven Cultural Studies institutions in Asia could happen overnight?[3] This form of solidarity has to do with our habitus evoked earlier: we use institutional space and opportunity to advance critical possibilities.

Looking back, the *Inter-Asia Cultural Studies* journal project was started by a group of "living fossils," by which I mean a generation of people who, though living apart in different places, somehow shared certain political commitments that have now been abandoned in the contemporary era of neo-liberal professionalism. The late 1980s, particularly the years 1987 and 1989, represented an era of radical transformation. The first generation of intellectuals and scholars operating in the name of Cultural Studies was involved locally in social, political, and cultural movements. In that earlier moment, what might be termed "cultural criticism movements" (in the form of writing for the popular newspapers) were an integral part of that great transformation, at least in most of the East Asian cities — Seoul, Tokyo, Beijing, Shanghai, Hong Kong, and Taipei. At that time, the prioritized concerns were never in academia, but always already in the social and political arena. Some of us, located in the capitalist bloc territories, could not identify ourselves with the dominant right-leaning political forces. Instead, we were more sympathetic to the emerging progressive social movement, and saw ourselves as the intellectual and discursive side of the movement.

Though no longer part of the age of revolution in this region, this is the generation that does intellectual work with the imagination (in all senses of the word). Intellectual work is embedded in and directly connected with the society in which one lives; it is driven by larger concerns and has impacts that extend well beyond the academic context. One thinks and works beyond the boundaries of the academic institutions. This committed belief did not come out of the blue as a political dogma, but was constituted by that moment of history when the struggle for democracy and for liberation from the melancholia of political control had become a political and social movement (in the wider sense of the word). The priority in life at this point was to engage in the organizing work behind political rallies and demonstrations, rather than to undertake "research and teaching." Somehow this local experience of organizing later became the precondition for the Inter-Asia movement. Without that era of grounded struggle, there would have been no way to build an international network anchored in the local, and there would have been no way to mobilize our own experience to understand the conditions of others in different locations; without that period devoted to organizational work, we would not even have known how to organize ourselves across the region as we would not have had a clear sense of what might and might not work. It is also that deep involvement that prevented us from flying on air. Thus, from its inception, we all knew that we were not simply working for ourselves but for the local communities within which each one of us was only an element. We imagined ourselves as undertaking some sort of internationalist endeavor — the idea being to work beyond the territory in which we each lived and to reach out for a larger vision. We looked for the counterparts to ourselves, here and there, for partnerships involving not being an isolated individual but someone who is connected to different groupings, often mediated through local journals or NGOs.

What we did not realize was, first, that this involvement would become part of our "habitus," and would later condition our work within the academy; second, that these productive activities in the form of writing and networking would somehow translate into the accumulation of cultural, if not academic, forms of capital; and third, having occupied spaces within various academic institutions, we would become part of a movement and would change the meaning and shape of both "institutions" and "social movements."

The sub-title of the journal, "Movements," carries the "legacy" and spirit of an era. If I recall correctly, we wanted to emphasize "Movements" and to place the term before "Inter-Asia Cultural Studies," but the press came back to us, indicating that libraries would not know how to catalogue the journal. So we gave in but insisted that the term be there somewhere. In fact, I went to my cover designer friend, Huang Mali, and she suggested putting different Asian words for "movement" on the side of the cover. This positioning of the journal as part of the larger intellectual movement (to change the world!) has become constitutive of the necessary tension we have to confront all the time: How do we balance scholarly and academic rigor with intellectual concerns and forms of practice? Interestingly enough, the challenge never came from the side of the "movement" but from the academic institution. Besides support from the Japan Foundation for the first three years of international editorial meetings (mediated through Chua Beng Huat from the National University of Singapore

end of things), the journal's managing editorship received support from the
National Science Council (Taiwan, ROC) until 2008. I take special note of the
adventurous support from two of the earlier directors in charge of the humanities and social sciences division, Huang Rung-tsuen (a NTU psychologist
who later became the Minister of Education and who is now the president of
the Chinese Medical University) and Wang Fansen (an intellectual historian
with Academia Sinica who later became a member of the Academy). These
were liberals who were willing to take a risk, the IACS project being the first
international journal they had ever supported, and without any assumptions
about controlling its direction. Later, nationalist politics came into the picture
and the rules now state that a journal can only get support if more than one-
third of the editorial board members are Taiwanese; that was the end of our
relation with the National Science Council. During the nine years of support,
the editorial office had to put forward applications every year and to respond
to criticisms from the reviewers every time. Each year, it was a matter of "living
dangerously" for the office staff (Su Shu-fen, Mon Wong, Zheng Sheng-xun,
Oiwan Lam, Grace Wu, and then Emma Liu and myself). The question was
always: What will happen if the National Science Council does not support
us this year? Every time, when the final result was announced, everyone felt
great relief. In one of the early years, the challenge from the reviewers took the
form of pointing out that the journal was edited and organized by a group of
"academic activists" (read: suspect individuals). Another reviewer stated:

> IACS is not a pure academic journal. Its editorial direction is defined to
> promote the Inter-Asia. This idea is similar to the Asian Confucian ideal
> as universal value of Asia, except that it starts out as leftist thought, which
> diverges from our Confucianism and also differs from our purpose.

If you think about what it meant to be constantly evaluated — and in all likeli-
hood by neo-Confucianists — you will get a sense of the paranoia that we felt,
and of what I mean by the idea of living dangerously! To win academic credibility, from the outset we developed a rigorous and productive referee system
(in practice this became an Inter-Asia process of reading others' work from
different locations), to enable authors to sharpen and tighten their writings.
Activist work (such as Hanasaki Kohei's (2000) piece published in the first issue
of the journal)[4] went into this process. However, working on the ground, you
begin to realize that this system cannot be taken for granted as universally valid.
Working on the South Asia Special issue with Ashish Rajadhyaksha (one of our

core members and the special issue editor),[5] I realized that the referee system relied on many assumptions, including the power structure of the academic regime, and that those working outside the academic system — journalists, artists, and writers, for example — would feel offended by this blind review process. As a result, the operating principles of the referee system have to be deployed cautiously, and have to be continuously revisited and revised.

To further the attempt to interact with the social movements sector, we invited regionally connected and respected intellectuals such as Muto Ichiyo to join our editorial board. Our involvement of Muto in the work of the board was by no means accidental. The journal has its main purpose, which is to publish, and activist thinkers like Muto are actually quite rare. Muto is a thinker, a writer, a teacher, a translator, an eloquent speaker, and an organizer. It was through Muto that the journal could link more effectively with ongoing movements — such as the regional peace movement among others. By late 2001, we felt the board had become too big to discuss issues effectively and that it was too slow to reach decisions, so we restructured the organizing body by adding an executive committee to deal with the journal's daily operations. This was also the moment when we invited activist scholar Cho Heeyeon to join the committee, as someone who was able to mediate between academic and activist work. No one could have predicted that, in alliance with ARENA, Heeyeon would go on to build an Inter-Asia Graduate School of NGO Studies on Sung Kung Hoe University campus in South Korea (the school was officially launched in February 2007). Nor could anyone have predicted that this program would become more than a NGO Study program, and would go on to become a base for activist retreat in the region (with fifteen full fellowships a year). We slowly discovered that the tension between academic and activist work had become productive: the journal network is an integral part of the movement towards regional integration, with the journal concentrating on the level of knowledge production within an emerging division of labor. The journal has become an intellectual movement, operating not in isolation but as an activity that is organically linked with different sectors of critical forces across the region. Other contacts, projects, groupings, and so on spin off from the network.

A critical issue remains: Are we able to develop a new mode of knowledge through the tension and interaction between the activist and academic work? In the 1990s, we tried to formulate this problem as a dialectical attempt "to theorize movement and to movementize scholarship." After a period of fifteen to twenty years, the uncertainty is still with us, but now the problematic appears in a new light. To recast the problem, it appears that, as a result of engaging with the social through organizing and mobilizing work, activists have accumulated a body of knowledge that allows them to understand how society works. And is this not precisely what a well-grounded social analysis (academic or otherwise) is supposed to achieve? However, immersed as they are in daily life struggles, activists do not have enough space and time to reflect on the body of knowledge that they have acquired through practical engagements. Without a sense of urgency, they cannot quite fully articulate their insights into analytical knowledge (which is absolutely central to the advancement of the movement itself). Academics, by contrast, however involved they may be in the activist arena, are bound by the logics of institutions, and their knowledge of the social is also constrained by the daily struggles of the teaching and research institutions within which they work, not to mention the mode of knowledge in which they have been trained; "field work" or shorter periods of participant observation cannot develop the new form of knowledge that is needed. In other words, I strongly believe that the current crisis for both movement and intellectual work has to do with the mode of knowledge being instituted. Unless a new mode of knowledge emerges to break away from the conditions of knowledge in which we are caught, it is difficult to envision the work that could be carried out in the future, not to mention the desire to change the world. I do not have the answer to the issue of whether the journal has achieved any progress in this regard, but in the longer run we have come to know more and more about what sorts of knowledge are grounded and closer to the real, and which ones are imposed from the outside by a system of knowledge.

This leads me to the second set of tensions constantly confronting the Trajectories project. The journal is a regionally based, transnational project. In reality, most of us are driven by the immediacy and urgency of our local work, and moreover, the notion of local specificity is Cultural Studies' epistemological assumption. So how does the journal connect to the local without losing its own identity and subjectivity? How does it negotiate the local and the outside? Very early on, in 2001 during the Beijing editorial meeting, a consensus was reached to commit ourselves to the priority of the local (not in the narrow sense but in the wider sense, sometimes to mean the Asian region as a site of the local). The resulting editorial policy has been that the journal publishes work which addresses problems internal to the local formation; deploying an abstract conceptual apparatus from the outside and imposing this on the local is not our intellectual mission. Given all these considerations, theoretically the project needs to be simultaneously localist, internationalist, and regionalist. In practice, the journal created a layer of imagination, one demanding extra time and labor with which to engage. If you go to the Centre for the Study of Culture and Society (CSCS), in Bangalore, India, and look at it with a sensitive eye that does not treat it as a regular university space where administrative structure is taken for granted, you will realize just how much work is involved in setting up an independent institution, with its own library, computer and accounting systems, and the basic infrastructure needed to operate. In addition to the countless tasks that this process involves, there are the courses training PhD students and the research and writing that allow the center to maintain its reputation as one of the most productive academic units in India and South Asia. With this scenario in mind, one understands what it means to ask our core members from CSCS or elsewhere to help with the editorial work, the reviewing and soliciting of papers, the organizing of conferences and panels, the editing of special issues, and so on. The commitment to the local sometimes ends up competing with the requirements of the regional and international. Thus the journal has to minimize the demands made, or to try its best to fit these demands into the agenda of its members. By July 2009, we had organized six larger-scale conferences (in Taipei, Fukuoka, Bangalore, Seoul, Shanghai, and Tokyo) since 1998. All of these had to create intellectual concerns that were locally situated. One rule that has been put into practice is to provide translations so as to include the local audiences as much as possible — though we do understand that translation is an impossible process.

I still remember vividly how at the 1998 Taipei Conference, when we had just started, we did not have enough budget to buy any equipment. So we brought in guerrilla radio station friends to set up several channels (Chinese, Korean, Japanese, and English), and asked participants to bring their own portable radios to adjust to the airwave channels. Meanwhile, friends with the ability to translate undertook voluntary work to help. At the 2000 Fukuoka Conference, translation was done not simultaneously but continuously, which doubled the regular time for the presentations (and Muto had to take over the work of translating Sun Ge's presentation in Chinese-accented Japanese into comprehensible English). The 2004 Bangalore conference was a miraculous encounter between South Asia and East Asia. Our South Asian friends could not really understand the (non-grammatical) English of Northeast Asians, and the latter could not fully guess the diverse accents of the former. But it was a memorable historical encounter — radically so relative to our experiences with communication in English. By the time of the 2005 Seoul conference, we had finally managed to purchase some portable receivers to help with the translation process. By the 2007 Shanghai conference, the first open-call forum, the translation rule was no longer sustainable beyond the plenary session. For parallel sessions, we could only encourage panelists to provide English PowerPoint presentations and to ask capable friends to help with onsite translation. The point is that we asked ourselves from the beginning: Is the project only talking to people who speak English? Or do we need to connect with those who are central to the local formation and who share the intellectual concerns of the project, regardless of the languages they speak? We have thus made some effort to prioritize our relation with the local. All board members are locally situated, and a significant number of us — from, say, Korea, Japan, and China — are mainly locally trained intellectuals.

We built a list of affiliating journals, which are locally based, to facilitate mutual translation; at the 2000 Fukuoka Conference, we brought the editors together in a large roundtable discussion (a network of journals then formed a basis for further meetings in Seoul in 2006 and Taipei in 2008).[6] We did a certain amount of translation work (though not enough) to bring the local work to an international readership in Asia and beyond; given the nature of the work, we had to largely rely on the "labor of love" (an expression I learned) or the friendship of solidarity (we have constantly called on Lee Kenfang, Peter Liu, and Zhang Jinyuan, and they have become our frequent contributors of translations). Meaghan Morris once said in private: "You cannot think that if it works for Inter-Asia, it will work in other instances, because Inter-Asia works through solidarity, not by interest." Over the past decade or so, what we have achieved is to build a translocal network in the region. With limited institutional support — such as the Asia Research Institute (ARI) — some younger scholars were able to do research outside their home territory and gather together here and there; some graduate students were also able to move around and study on an exchange basis. For some of us, this movement across locales has fundamentally transformed our own intellectual work; we have left behind the old formula of "the local versus the West" to slowly build alternative systems of reference. Once again, the extent to which this trend is able to constitute a new mode of knowledge and whether we have accumulated enough to see any emerging logics are issues that remain to be debated and reflexively discussed.

Over the years, through the experience of setting in motion and implementing a regional project, I have been excited by the discovery that if the globe is
made up of all the world's regions and globalization is constituted by regional
routes, then to be in the regional network is always and already to be in the
global circuit; the regional is the global; the global without the regional and the
local is simply a form of empty imagination. Of course, this is not to disguise
the uneven organization of the world. The "rise of Asia" as a globally recognized structure of sentiment should not encourage us to bury ourselves in a
self-indulgent triumphalism. As the editorial statement documenting our collective analysis in 2000 states:

> Since the 1980s, a pervasive rhetoric of the "rise of Asia" has come to mean
> more than the concentrated flow of capital into and out of the region: it
> has come to constitute a structure of feeling that is ubiquitous, yet ambigu-
> ously felt, throughout Asia. Historically, this feeling of the "rise of Asia" is
> complicated by the region's colonial past. While Asia's political, cultural
> and economic position in the global system will continue to fluctuate,
> there is a need to question and critique the rhetorical unities of both the
> terms "rise" and "Asia." Wealth and resources are unevenly distributed
> and there is no cultural or linguistic unity in this imaginary space called
> "Asia."[7]

Ten years later, this structure of sentiment has not faded. With India and
China becoming giant economies and exercising greater power in global
politics, we will need to connect more with the less powerful parts of the region
and beyond, forging links with other parts of the developing world — Africa,
the Caribbean, Latin America, and so on. This "Third Worldist" desire has
been on some of our minds, but once again with an uncertain tension: Have we
built a sufficiently solid subjectivity in our own neighborhood before making
the next move to connect with other parts of the world? In ten years, we are
more solidly connected in some parts of Northeast, Southeast and South Asia.
The phrase "some parts" boils down to meaning our contact points in urban
centers. Over the years, we have begun to sense the limits of the project when
it comes to establishing links. We have come to realize that the production
of papers, essays, or reports is materially grounded — not only in the sense
of material wealth, which sustains institutional support for the generating
of knowledge, but also in the sense of material history and traditions of per-
ceiving the value of learning and writing. Taking all the material conditions
together, not to mention the specificity of what "Cultural Studies" *critically*

enables or disenables, we are only able to work with intellectual populations, and moreover those who have the desire to work with us. As we have indicated elsewhere,[8] we have been quite eager to reach our counterparts in West and Central Asia, but still cannot quite connect; we will continue to try. We were lucky a couple of years ago, for example, to be able to publish an essay by Carolyn Cooper, the first piece out of the Caribbean, and we hope to publish more such powerful work out of other parts of the developing world.[9]

Let me finally come to the project's tension with "institutionalization." Before moving to National Chiao Tung University in August 2008, I devoted most of my energies to the Center for Asia-Pacific Cultural Studies (established in 1992) at National Tsing Hua University, which has by now been recognized as one of the first Cultural Studies institutions in Asia. In the early 1990s, the dean of the College of Humanities and Social Sciences wanted to promote collaborative and interdisciplinary work outside the existing departments, and four proposals were approved. At that time, the College had just moved to a new building, since physical space was available. Each of the four centers was allocated a physical office space, but even today the center is without an annual budget and stable operating allocation. Nevertheless, it has been a powerhouse of activities. In the early 1990s, it organized the monthly cultural criticism forum over a period of two years in a public space in Taipei; it organized international gatherings, such as the two Trajectories conferences in 1992 and 1995; it housed the secretariat of the Cultural Studies Association, Taiwan, during its founding period between 1998 and 2000; it organized the first Inter-Asia Cultural Studies conference on "problematizing Asia" in 1998, and then housed the editorial office of the *Inter-Asia Cultural Studies* journal from 2000 to 2008; and it created a chair in Thoughts, History and Culture, to recognize leading Asian thinkers such as Partha Chatterjee, Mizoguchi Yuzo, and Paik Nak-chung. It did not take long to realize that the lack of a regular budget could also mean freedom. Free from bureaucratic meetings and free from the control imposed by academic structure, organizing work could be done at our own will. The center was able to operate solely on the basis of project funding; however, unlike other research centers which, in order to survive, have to go out of their way to cater to funding initiatives that may have nothing to do with their intellectual agenda, the center was lucky enough to be able to concentrate on its own work.

I thought I had discovered a secret place in the university where I could do intellectual work. But when I looked around, I realized that other friends were doing similar things. With no steady budget, Josephine Ho and three colleagues started the Center for the Study of Sexualities at the National Central University in 1995. Since then, the center has done all the pioneering work on, and has been involved with, the women's movement, sex workers' movement, queer movement, and trans-gender movement. Now the center is internationally recognized as one of the most productive research centers on gender and sexuality.

Taking these two small centers together, we find the lingering mood of the 1980s and 1990s in places like Taiwan, where the energy of social transformation was widely and strongly shared and the legitimacy to do critical work on university campus was established. With no sense of accumulating capital within the academic regime, the productivity of these units nevertheless became highly competitive when entering the neo-liberal era, with its requirement that scholarship be internationalized. What are these possibilities? Let me come to the instance of Lingnan University in Hong Kong. Stephen Ching-kiu Chan left the Chinese University of Hong Kong for Lingnan in 1998, and set up the BA in Cultural Studies program in 1999. Why did they want him? Because of his track record in the early to mid 1990s organizing the Hong Kong Cultural Studies project. Then Stephen and Meaghan Morris teamed up, and in the course of ten years, the Cultural Studies Department has become a landmark, not only for Lingnan but for Hong Kong as a whole. Now when you bump into younger, fresh PhDs coming back to Hong Kong, they all want to join Lingnan's Cultural Studies Department. But how many jobs can you create? The reputation of the program was won through its huge commitment to teaching — and particularly teaching disadvantaged students. Fair enough: teaching is a responsibility we all have. But the Cultural Studies Program does more than just acquit itself of this basic, shared responsibility. The Cultural Studies Department started a self-funded Master of Cultural Studies (MCS) program in 2003, with school teachers, social workers, and cultural practitioners as its students; this enables a movement mediating through teaching to engage the larger society. In 2005, in the larger context of educational reform, the department opened another special program, the Postgraduate Diploma in Liberal Studies (PDLS), aimed at high school teachers.

So can or should an intellectual movement be institutionalized? In a similar vein, the question can be asked: Can or should Cultural Studies be institutionalized? This is not a politically correct issue; it concerns how to emotionally maintain intellectual vitality, integrity, and intensity. For many of our generation's living fossils, our relation with the institution has never been an easy one. The two successful stories are the Centre for the Study of Culture and Society (CSCS) in Bangalore and Lingnan University's Cultural Studies Department. CSCS was formed by a small group of intellectuals, based on earlier friendships, with the intent of coming together in order to break away from the institutional constraints of the university by setting up their own independent institution. Lingnan University's Cultural Studies programs, from the BA to the PhD, were made possible at the right moment by a smaller university, which often tends to be more flexible. In both instances, a huge amount of work was involved — work related to negotiation, self-financing, and the infrastructure of buildings. In both instances, too, special talents and personalities were involved — individuals with the capacity to "manage" on all levels of operation. When it comes to the journal project, how would one institutionalize it? We were lucky to have a free office housed in the Centre for Asia-Pacific/Cultural Studies, which has never been a formal unit of the university, with an annual budget and regular staff. Usually, in the context of Taiwan, an "institutional" journal operates under a department or is owned by the university (as is the case, for example, with the *Tsing Hua Journal of China Studies*). IACS was neither affiliated with a department nor owned by a university. Given the nature of the project, and given the track record of zero institutional loyalty, we knew from the beginning that the journal would not be institutionalized and had to live an unstable life. The advantage was that no one could tell us what we could and could not do, and we have enjoyed the freedom of being left alone with the activities that we have wanted to organize.

When the IACS Society was first discussed at the 2004 Bangalore meeting, we knew that it had to be a loose organization and that it needed to be flexible enough to make things work. I learned a lot from the experience of organizing the Cultural Studies Association, Taiwan, which was formally registered as a NGO and financially supported purely by membership; it requires a bi-annual election to change offices, and so on. This is roughly how things work locally in different places. I was also involved in setting up the Association for Cultural Studies, which had ambitions to be global; because ACS was constituted under Finnish rule, I learned how formalism works within Northern European bureaucratic culture and came to understand that this simply would not work in our part of the world. Moreover, just collecting membership fees would be a huge task and the electronic election of ACS chairs was already a big enough headache. How was it possible to set up an effective society to get work done without bureaucratic blockage? Is this form of quasi-institutional-ization viable? Unlike other academic associations, which have become sites of power struggle, the IACS Society is imagined as an interface for organizing events for the younger generations, who are not yet in a position to organize for themselves. Kim Soyoung, film director, feminist scholar, and core member of the journal, took up the burden, with the support of other Korean members of the network (including Yoo Sunyoung, Paik Wondam, Cho Heeyeon, Shin Hyunjoon, Kang Myungkoo, Cho Haejoang, and Kim Hyunmee) to start the IACS Society in Seoul around 2006. As the division of labor was envisioned, all IACS related activities would be conducted in the name of the society. The first summer camp for graduate students from the IACS network was held in July 2007, and the second one was scheduled to take place in July 2010.

Alternative forms of institutionalization have also been imagined but have never taken off. In 2001, with the support of Kuan Chung-ming, economist and member of the Academy and at the time the director of the Research Centre of the Social Sciences (NSC), we carried out a Nexus project, attempting to get together groupings, programs, and small institutions in the network to imagine the formation of a regional institution. This concept is now being taken up again, with plans to officially form a Consortium of Inter-Asia Cultural Studies Institutions, with a secretariat housed at Sung Kung Hoe University in Seoul, in collaboration with the Centre for the Study of Culture and Society from July 2010. In December 2006, we organized the Globalizing Academic Production in Asia conference, bringing together major critical publishers in Asia and the United States to imagine the possibility of working together, forming a mecha-nism to channel Asian-language publications into the global circuit. Not all of these imaginings have materialized; all of them require strong institutional back-up and infinite levels of negotiation with partners involved, and all need a visionary person who has a business mind, and a capable manager who will be able to get things off the ground. But it is only in the process of articulating these imaginings — failed or otherwise — that we have discovered the limits of what can be done and, if you wish, the limit of history. In other words, whether to institutionalize or not is not a choice to be voluntarily made by a group of living fossils. I am certain that elements of these imagined projects are being implemented in organic ways linking with nodal points in the network, and other parts will emerge again in the future when we will find ourselves sur-rounded by new conditions of possibility and at a new threshold of history.

3

Life of a Parasite

One Survival Story in Cultural Studies

Josephine Ho

Opening the Cultural Studies and Institution conference at Lingnan University in 2006, Meaghan Morris described Cultural Studies as a "gadfly," as "something inconsequential and not taken seriously, though both deadly and charming" — certainly an apt description of the role of Cultural Studies as it irritates by challenging accepted frames of mind and established structures of power.[1] Here I use another organism also known to be a persistent irritating nuisance —"the parasite" — to help explain the existence and operation of certain critical gatherings of Cultural Studies within Taiwan's institutions of higher education.[2] Though almost always precarious, such existence penetrates deep into conventional disciplines and may, when the conditions are right, work to reorient the host departments beyond their original disciplinary boundaries. Of course, the precariousness of such "parasitic" existences also keeps the groups on their toes, striving to maintain their professional credibility within prevailing academic conventions while continuing to initiate unconventional intellectual activities as well as social activism. Our own Center for the Study of Sexualities at National Central University may serve as a good example here.

Feminist "Parasites"

The emergence of the Center itself marked the tumultuous developments in the Taiwanese feminist movement in the trajectory of the post-martial law "democratization" process.[3] Women's groups had been somewhat insignificant among the new social movements pushing for democratization in the 1980s. Yet, as the lifting of martial law in 1987 opened up political terrain for contestation, gender increasingly was taken as a potent social division that could become politically pivotal at election times. After all, rapid social change had already exacerbated existing and emerging social "problems" — domestic violence, divorces, extra-marital affairs, teenage rebellion, and so on — fanning anxieties that could easily be configured into election platforms, eventually not only mobilizing women into becoming concerned voting citizens but also enlisting women's organizations as social service franchises in post-election governance. The prospect of mainstreaming and power-sharing quickly tapped into latent differences in class orientation among feminists, polarizing them through a successive string of debates in the mid-1990s over, respectively, female sexuality, lesbianism, sex work, pornography, surrogate mothering, teenage sexuality, and most recently sexual information and contact on the internet.

Differences in opinion had been commonplace within the feminist camp yet, as sex-related issues tended to attract intense media attention, the stakes suddenly became higher when sex-positive feminist discourse on the subject of female sexuality sparked social controversy in the midst of an ongoing sex revolution in Taiwan in 1994.[4] Fearing that the hard-won respectability of the women's movement would be compromised by such controversy, mainstreaming feminists made the public announcement at a press conference in 1996 that feminism had nothing to do with such a stance of sexual emancipation. The statement at that historical moment amounted to no less than a disfranchisement that would deprive sex-positive views on female sexuality of any significance for gender empowerment, and leave them easily relegated to the morally questionable and subjected to social condemnation. Such a political gesture would furthermore annihilate the legitimacy and credibility of sex-positive feminists as they tried to speak on a variety of women's issues. Faced with this venomous disavowal and its consequent disinheritance, sex-positive feminist scholars had no other recourse than to seek support elsewhere — most readily from the legitimacy of the education institution to which most of them rightfully belonged. After all, aside from the women's movement, academic gender/sexuality studies can still command social respect and credibility due to its elite status in the social hierarchy, and was thus able to provide the platform the renegade feminists needed.

As all the leading sex-positive feminist scholars happened to be teaching at National Central University, we decided to set up a Center for the Study of Sexualities and Difference (nicknamed the Sex Center) in 1995, under the umbrella of the English Department, which afforded the most liberal atmosphere and to which most of us belonged.[5] Though our science and engineering-oriented colleagues could not see the connection between English and gender/sexuality studies, gender happened to be becoming a state issue at that moment, and a new gender equity education was just being brought into place at the urging of public outcry against rising rates of crime against women in 1996–97.[6] The rush in state policy created huge demands for so-called "gender specialists" and, oblivious to the division within the feminist camp, the university was somewhat elated that some of its female faculty members rose to the task "out of their own initiative" to set up a center that the university could showcase as part of its own gender initiative. The Center was thus favorably received at this initial stage, and succeeded in reconfiguring the marginal and unorthodox stances of our research and teaching into timely and creative responses to ordained state gender policy. In the following years, such innovative transformation of policy-induced institutional demands into self-determined forms of action would prove to be quite instrumental in the Center's continued survival and its function as a potent platform for gender/sex non-conformity.[7]

As history would have it, gender/sexuality issues and feminist discourses served as the terrain upon which conservative and progressive voices contested to shape social values and political power in Taiwan, with the sedimentation amounting to no less than a schism within the feminist camp toward the end of the 1990s. On one side were the state-oriented mainstream feminists who, in an effort to make the feminist agenda palatable for national politics, chose to maintain a safe distance from any issue or stance — starting with lesbianism within the feminist groups — that might cause social controversy or stigmatization. On the other side were the non-conformist feminists like us — insidiously referred to as the "sex liberation faction" — who, in response to emerging marginal sexual subjects and communities, worked to promote sex-positive views and question, or even dismantle, the existing gender/sexual deployment of power. The schism revealed its ferocity in two purges of the non-conformists from the feminist camp: in 1994 over the issue of female sexuality, and again in 1997 over the issue of female sex work.[8] As the social activism of the non-conformists continued to formulate and articulate feminist positions on marginal gender/sexuality issues and subjects from newly forged locations of resistance, such efforts were entangled in direct and open conflict with mainstream feminists who aligned with the state in the latter's effort to purify social space for "the protection of women and children." Worried that the public was becoming confused about the starkly contrasting and contesting feminist positions in the dead-heat of the female sex work debate in 1998, one prominent "state feminist"[9] tried once and for all to expunge the non-conformist feminists from the women's movement:

> The sexual liberation movement and the [part of the] women's movement that emphasizes gender politics have continuously come into conflict since 1994 … the two [camps] inhabit the same political space and have struggled over the interpretation of the same and shared issues … the sexual liberation faction will not create its own organizations, and instead, puts all expectations in women's movement organizations — especially the Awakening Foundation — hoping that these organizations will provide material resources and symbolic authorization for the sexual liberation movement. Therefore, the sexual liberation camp's politics of sexuality and desire has closely stuck to/glued itself to the gender politics women's movement organization, seeing in the latter a *host-body*.[10]

Women who had fought side by side since the 1980s and 1990s to open up social space for discussions of women's issues and women's rights were, according to the mainstreamers, actually two separate movements — namely the feminist/women's movement and the sexual liberation movement. Ostracized to the outside of the women's movement, the non-conformists would no longer have any rightful claim to any credibility and legitimacy that they may have won for the earlier women's movement.

In terms of mainstream feminist institution/organization, the non-conformists might have been expunged; however, in terms of political stance we were not about to give up what we had begun with — as feminists. From our professional posts, we would continue to articulate sex-positive feminist discourses to feed into the developing LGBTQI movements.

Institutionally Embedded Activism

If professional academic status came to our rescue as we struggled to maintain our feminist presence and action, our efforts to conduct social activism from our posts in the academy, in the meantime, began galvanizing other tensions.

To begin with, we belonged to a generation of scholars who had completed their advanced studies at United States- or United Kingdom-based universities at a time when Cultural Studies was establishing itself as the exemplar of interdisciplinarity in various humanities and social sciences departments on university campuses. The paradigm shift allowed us to acquire ample training in Cultural Studies, not to mention familiarity with Marxist thought.[11] As we returned to Taiwan at the post-martial law moment in the late 1980s, most of us found employment in local universities — albeit teaching in departments that still abided by traditional disciplinary boundaries. The post-martial law social milieu was volatile yet promising for cultural intervention and social change. Aspiring to become what Gramsci had termed "organic intellectuals," many of us began writing social criticism in local newspapers and journals to intervene in whatever developing phenomena captured our attention.[12] The fresh and provocative approach of such writings created a new cultural force that swept up a whole generation of young and restless minds, resulting in a critical mass that prompted the establishment of the Association of Cultural Studies in Taiwan in 1999. In the years that followed, the Association's annual conference grew bigger and bigger while the more traditional disciplines saw the attendance at their conferences dwindle. Understandably, the stark contrast resulted in anxieties that would make the path toward institutionalization of cultural studies more treacherous.

The active and broad involvement of cultural studies in social issues naturally ranged beyond our original areas of academic specialization, and often landed us on controversial turfs unfamiliar to the public and even to our colleagues in the English Department. The Sex Center in particular has been active in engaging Taiwan's specific formation of knowledge production and academic professionalism in the area of gender/sexuality studies. As we often found ourselves drawn into various marginal movements and coming into contact with marginal subjects through social activism, we also began taking the initiative to expand and build upon new research areas, and new conceptions and orientations. From queer politics to sex work to trans-genderism to sado-masochism to body modification, it was the issues and subjects rising from actual social struggles that helped us reframe our understanding of the feminist and the social. Our work has been driven by the emerging needs of emerging marginal sexualities, and whatever insights we were able to develop were made possible precisely by learning from the lives of such marginal subjects; in return, our academic research and teaching also lent support and legitimacy to such marginalities as they struggled for social presence and legitimation.

Sadly, as our own departments and off-campus research funding agencies still functioned within disciplinary boundaries, we sometimes found our most vibrant research and teaching efforts frustrated by colleagues and reviewers who saw our work as deviating from or even betraying the department as well as the field. For example, our applications for funding to host conferences on gender/sexuality issues suffered repeated scrutiny, if not interrogation, not only in our own department meetings but also in the university funding review committee in the late 1990s. We were openly questioned about whether gender/sexuality issues constituted proper subjects for the English Department or for academic research as a whole.[13] Disciplinary boundaries provided easy ground on which our efforts could justifiably be scrutinized and then curtailed.[14] Our individual efforts in academic accumulation fared no better. At the height of the prostitutes' rights debate in 1998, sex work-related research proposals drafted by members of the Sex Center and our allies in other universities received scathing reviews at the National Science Council, a major funding agency for academic research. The proposals written by the three most outspoken supporters of prostitutes' rights were flatly rejected for being "biased" by reviewers whose comments revealed their own blatant anti-prostitution stance. Fortunately, two out of our three rebuttals for repeal were approved and we eventually won back funding from the NSC.[15] Such hostile and revengeful peer reviews were not rare at all: the obstacles concretized not only reprimands from various levels of existing disciplines, but also retaliations directed at our efforts to link the academy with social movements. All in all, our clear identity as "the Cultural Studies people" in our departments and schools and fields often left us in an awkward position, a nuisance to the allegedly apolitical academic institutions.

As our involvement in Taiwanese gender/sexuality politics grew deeper and wider, and efforts to contain us within the academic field were not always successful, retaliations moved to the arena of legal action. In 2001, when one of the pages on our sexuality website featured articles and records of panel discussions that we had organized to criticize and satirize police entrapment of net citizens who were merely trying to seek companionship through the internet, the Catholic Good Shepherd Sisters sent in a complaint to the Ministry of Interior that the Sex Center's web page included "wrong-headed" discussions of the popular practice of *enjo-kosai* ("compensated companionship" in Japanese), which may "mislead" youngsters into occasional sex work. The Sisters demanded that we be reprimanded and possible litigation considered for our alleged breach of the child-protection law. Under pressure from the ministry, but fearing further social controversy, the university decided to let us off with a slap on the wrist by demanding that our web databank be removed from the university academic network. The conservatives thus at least succeeded in forcing us to use precious funding to purchase commercial space in the business domain in order to keep our website on line. More directly in 2003, a total of eleven conservative religious, censorship, and parent-oriented NGOs jointly brought litigation concerning the "dissemination of obscenities" against the Center's Coordinator, Josephine Ho, for including on the zoophilia webpage in our sexualities databank two hyperlinks that could lead to overseas pictorial zoophilia websites. The conservative groups were hoping that the demonization and indictment that followed upon the litigation would once and for all discredit and silence the Center and its sex radicalism. The university, instead of actively defending freedom of information and research within the academic domain, decided to leave everything up to the judicial system. Thanks in part to the concerted support efforts by local academics and activists and a widespread international petition drive, as well as to the valiant discursive defense line put up by the defendant and her allies, the case received a not-guilty verdict both in the District Court and the High Court in 2005. The vibrant mutual penetration between the academic and the activist was kept intact.

As our experiences have shown, institutionally embedded activism has its advantages: in this case, we were able to use the legitimacy of the institution to strengthen and defend marginal issues and positions. Yet the precarious and fragile existence of such activism-oriented academic gathering is also quite clear: both disciplinary boundaries and conservative retaliations work to jeopardize our continued existence and operation. In the end, we were able to stay in the game only because the nature of the game was changing at the time as a result of the conjuncture of several important factors, and consequently it wanted to retain those of us whose academic performance suited its needs, as I shall explain in the next section.

Comprador Professionalism and Its Localization

After twenty years of economic prosperity on the back of the manufacturing industries, Taiwan suddenly found itself hard-pressed to upgrade its industrial production in the 1990s so as to develop a new competitiveness in the rapidly globalizing economy.[16] This time the scale of upgrading was not limited to the economic sphere only: education and research geared toward the international scene came to be regarded as possible vanguards in boosting national pride and global standing for a prospering economic body with a problematic nation-state status.

Academic production and performance that could lay claim to international visibility thus suddenly took on nation-state significance. The National Science Council — the government agency in charge of promoting academic research — began to provide travel funds for paper presentations at international conferences held overseas, as well as funding for international conferences organized and held in Taiwan.[17] Generously subsidized visiting positions or lectures were offered to established scholars in the West.[18] Integrated research collaboration ventures across national borders were highly desirable and well supported. All of these measures have afforded an unprecedented influx of funding for those of us who are capable of carrying out international exchange, and willing to put in extra effort to make it happen. Consequently, our Sex Center was able to bring in world-renowned activists/scholars for our conferences on such heavily closeted topics as homosexuality, sex work, or trans-genderism. We were also able to travel to conferences overseas as a team, or to pool our research resources together to support the need for staff for the Center. All in all, as long as we remained productive and competitive, we fared quite well in the general trend of professionalization.

As research rose above teaching as the key criterion in university reviews, new sub-disciplines were created to encourage faculty members to devote themselves to research. "Cultural Studies" was finally recognized as a sub-discipline. A separate "Gender Studies" sub-discipline was also created — because, as one top official disclosed at a meeting, other advanced countries had presented very strong performances in gender-related research and Taiwan certainly could not be absent in that area, especially when gender issues made up an index of a nation's status on human rights. Having felt out of place for quite a few years in their original disciplines or institutions, many practitioners of cultural studies began to breathe a sigh of relief as they now could opt for the new sub-disciplines, and have their work reviewed by peers who might be more receptive to the interdisciplinary approach. As the pragmatic policy of the national funding agency valued academic output over disciplinary boundaries, it helped remove some of our obstacles within the university. For if we could out-produce our critics and were more active on the international scene, our research topics — though marginal and problematic in the local context — could still enjoy some legitimacy, for we were, among other things, making valuable contributions to the competitiveness of our university.

Ironically, though it originated out of nation-state interests, this over-valuation of academic output may still work for the benefit of marginal subjects. Kuan-Hsing Chen and Sechin Y.-S Chien have written about the impact of the Cold War on Taiwan's academic scene,[19] where the formation of the Cold War structure after World War II, the Chinese civil war between the Nationalist Party and the Communists, and the former's dependency on the United States to maintain political stability have all helped to make the United States the sole dominating force in Taiwan's academic and cultural frame of reference since the second half of the twentieth century. In this academic hierarchy, United States-trained scholars would rank higher than locally produced scholars, and ideas and theories imported from the West would be considered more convincing than locally produced ideas and theories. Despite its colonial connotations, this favoritism actually provided some shield of protection for scholars of marginal or difficult topics so long as the topics could be demonstrated to be academically viable in the context of the West. If sexuality studies is now the newest and the hottest field in the US academy, and also considered to be related to human rights, then it is hard to dismiss it in Taiwan where keeping pace with world trends and maintaining a good record in the area of human rights are key to the desired nation-state image. Academic professionalism, exemplified in sound research and published papers, still seemed to afford some degree of legitimacy that could resist moral panics. What had once been considered "comprador scholarship" was thus transformed into a useful structure under which marginal topics could still find some room for development (The reality, of course, is never that simple, as I have demonstrated in the last section on the threat of litigation. The delicate tug-of-war between academic freedom and existing moral imperatives is ongoing and constant.).

This protection, however fragile, is vital for our survival in a sex-phobic context such as Taiwan. As members of the Sex Center had already established impressive academic credibility in the field of Cultural Studies before getting entangled in local feminist debates, our track record offered some staying power as moral panics flared around our unconventional views on sexuality. As the new state policy of gender education worked only to ensure that changing sexual values and practices as well as emerging gender variance were met with the most stringent response and reaction, we were keenly aware of the importance of building up the gender/sexuality studies area in the most broad-minded fashion. So the Center has organized more than a dozen major conferences since 1996 with themes that continued to broaden the scope of local gender/sexuality thinking, with papers drawn from local scholars as well as activists, with invited international speakers whose lives and theories demonstrated the possibility of alternative thinking and practice in gender/sexuality matters,[20] and with a friendly milieu that eventually made the conferences famous occasions for empowering come-out confessions. The conferences not only fostered a critical community for marginal thinking, but also cumulatively helped forge the Center's visibility and power of influence, which eventually consolidated the Center's status as the most vibrant research collective in the gender/sexuality field in Taiwan. The Center also published more than twenty volumes of ground-breaking books on gender/sexuality issues, amounting to more than five thousand pages and three million words. With four active core members, no steady budget, and limited resources, the Center achieved the virtually impossible: challenging the public health-oriented hegemonic discourse on sexuality, producing sex-positive discourses to defend various sexual minorities, winning a continuous string of research grants from national agencies, and intervening on almost every single issue that threatened to rigidify sexual and social space — all while its members maintained outstanding teaching records and assumed various administrative duties.[21]

While professionalization may have provided some legitimation and support for marginal-minded academics, the cost of such neo-liberal accountability is also quite high. The pressure to publish and produce according to prescribed criteria, the endless paperwork that accompanies every sum of subsidy, and the need to make seasonal reports and presentations all took up more precious time and effort. In the early 1990s, many progressive academics regularly contributed to the literary supplements or other sections of local newspapers in order to join in critical discussions on various post-martial law socio-cultural phenomena and ideas, thus creating a vibrant atmosphere for critical practices in cultural studies. But now, fewer and fewer intellectuals can afford to write on topical issues for the public. For one thing, such writing would not count toward academic credit at all — it might even compromise the professional status of the academics for "taking sides" on an issue rather than remaining "objective." Consequently, such discursive productions are now first and foremost written in the academic format, which effectively insulates them from a wider readership and wider influence.[22] Structurally speaking, it is increasingly difficult for activist-minded young academics to devote their time and effort to social movements — unless they can devise ways to package such activist involvement in academic clothing.[23]

Institutionalization/Reproduction

Pockets of Cultural Studies on various campuses more or less live with similar kinds of opportunities and frustrations, but it has become increasingly clear that we need to move in the direction of institutionalization and reproduction if we are to sustain the momentum Cultural Studies has accumulated over the past decade in Taiwan. If nothing else, we need a more concentrated channel for reproduction, and we need to create a more favorable professional environment for those younger scholars and students who may not yet have the staying power to withstand the onslaught of disciplinary pressure or conservative retaliation.

The process of creating this mechanism for reproduction has again illuminated our status as annoying parasites. Since 2003, Cultural Studies scholars from three (four since 2010) geographically proximate and strategically allied universities within the University System of Taiwan have been trying to build a cross-campus cultural studies graduate program.[24] We are presently affiliated to different academic programs, including, to name a few, Social Research and Cultural Studies, English, Chinese, Hakka Studies, Sociology, and General Education, but we have made repeated appeals to our universities, telling the decision-makers about the importance of interdisciplinary collaboration. The universities — all well known for their performance in the science and engineering fields — are only receptive to the idea of a limited non-degree-conferring program in Cultural Studies that they could easily cite to demonstrate their devotion to the humanities and social sciences, but could just as easily ignore or drop without much cost. The Cultural Studies people, on the other hand, would not accept such easy erasure. We continued to work closely in developing exchange and collaboration so as to build up a broad basis for cultural studies throughout Asia, and to exert more pressure on the universities to listen.[25] We had finally persuaded our universities to let us submit a proposal for a degree-conferring graduate program in cultural studies to the Ministry of Education at the end of 2009, after getting sixteen different departments from these universities to approve the collaboration agreement in their departmental meetings. The Sex Center, likewise, sent in a proposal for a PhD program in gender/sexuality studies at the same time that it pulled together the efforts of five different programs from two different colleges in National University. Unfortunately, such collective efforts were not appreciated by the ministry: both attempts at building up sites for intellectual reproduction failed. Again, the affirmation of existing institutional structures and hierarchies served as grounds for refusal.

New developments in 2011 are more encouraging. The Cultural Studies people within the University System of Taiwan regrouped again and took a different strategy toward institutionalization. This time, instead of coming together to create one program and submit it through the only university that has a social research and cultural studies program, we wrote up one collaborative proposal and sent it through the due process of approval in all four universities, and then the package was submitted to the Ministry of Education. We are hoping that the weight of four universities working in unison to promote Cultural Studies will send a forceful message to the Ministry. The final verdict will come toward the end of April of 2012.

Michel Serres has described the parasite as something that disrupts a system of exchange and exclusion by forcing the simple system to a new level of complexity and thus creating the diversity and complexity so vital to human life and thought.[26] At this moment, whether our bid for institutionalization succeeds or not, we embrace the upbeat realization that marginal parasites work best when they work as parasites, not aspiring to infest the host too much, but sticking/gluing ourselves to whatever institutional hosts are available, and always maintaining a vibrant life force to keep ourselves alive and procreating — which is what we continue to do today.

Acknowledgment

This is a significantly revised version of a paper written for the Conference on Cultural Studies and Institution, Lingnan University, Hong Kong, May 26–28, 2006. The struggles and continuous developments in our bid for institutionalization have since then added many twists and turns that will extend beyond the story told here. Thanks to Kuan-Hsing Chen and Meaghan Morris for their continued encouragement and generous support.

4

The Assessment Game

On Institutions That Punch Above Their Weight, and Why the Quality of the Work Environment Also Matters

Mette Hjort

Increasingly required to demonstrate their relevance to society, their fitness for purpose, and their ability to justify the allocation of public monies to their sector, universities have become more or less willing players in a high-stakes game called Assessment. There are variations on this game, of course, for it can be played on a purely national level, on a global scale, on a voluntary or required basis, and with players variously pre-selected in terms of key traits. Quality assurance and research assessment exercises are examples of the game of Assessment being played on a national level, but with reference to global trends, and on a non-voluntary basis. International rankings such as those published by the *Times Higher Education Supplement* and the Shanghai Jiao Tong University of Higher Education are instances of a far more global game, with players included on the basis of their status as comprehensive institutions, among other factors.

I am particularly interested in a new variant on the game of Assessment, one initiated by *The Chronicle of Higher Education* and Modern Think LLC in 2008.[1] Designed "to recognize higher education institutions that have created exceptional work environments," the "Great Colleges to Work For" initiative is potentially promising. By emphasizing the quality of higher education institutions, *qua* places to work, the ranking brings human resource factors into the Assessment game in a serious way. The costs associated with some versions of the Assessment game can be very high in human terms, with pervasive cynicism and a widespread loss of morale being some of the most frequently cited negative consequences of the use of performance-based models in Australia and the United Kingdom, and increasingly Hong Kong. What is interesting about the "Great Colleges to Work For" initiative is that it effectively establishes a context for beginning to think about the correlations between quality teaching and research — which are both allegedly measured and thus encouraged by any number of the Assessment game's variants — and institutional culture. As an initiative that is clearly an intervention with a critical dimension, the new survey invites us to think about the impact that an institution's practices, as a form of institutional culture, has on the very people who are charged with carrying out the core activities of teaching and research. Practices ranging from the codified and mandated to the informal are all constitutive of various kinds of institutional culture. Far from providing a purely neutral framework for the core activities of teaching and research, these institutional cultures encourage or even require modes of sociability and interaction that may be seriously at odds with the stated goals of quality and excellence — at least insofar as these terms retain some of their traditional meanings.

The "Great Colleges to Work For" initiative invites thoughts that are well worth pondering. For example, if teachers and researchers are best able to pursue what they see as their core activities — teaching and research — in the context of a quality work environment, might they not also actively be motivated to seek out such environments, even if these are to be found in sites not traditionally associated with prestige and excellence? Given that top-performing teachers and especially researchers enjoy mobility, and given that mobility these days extends well beyond the boundaries of any particular national system, a systematic disregard for the "cultural" entailments of an institution's codified or merely habitual practices could turn some of the more hard-nosed efforts to achieve excellence into internally inconsistent, self-defeating exercises. For example, a failure on the part of senior managers to think carefully about the social and cultural ramifications of the administrative or regulatory practices that they impose could well have the unintended consequence of motivating a preference for "exit" on the part of top performers — hardly the intended outcome of a politics of "quality" or "excellence."

Whereas well-performing academics were once drawn to magnets of established excellence in the West, there are now powerful magnets elsewhere in the world. Robin Wilson's article "Globe-Trotting Academics Find New Career Paths" cites the example of Mary Kathryn Thompson as indicative of a new trend. With a doctorate from MIT and employment opportunities at top-tier US universities, Thompson opted for a position at the Korea Advanced Institute of Science and Technology following an exchange with Nam Pyo-Suh, then Head of Mechanical Engineering at MIT and soon to be dean in Korea. A key point made by the article is that Thompson sees herself as having "more opportunities [in Korea] than she would in the United States."[2] Certain universities outside Europe and North America are increasingly seen by top-performing academics with global mobility as offering work environments that are highly enabling and motivating. Such perceptions may be based on any number of factors. Universities in Asia employ very large numbers of support staff, who are virtually without exception competent, hard-working, responsible, and committed to seeing their universities thrive. As a result, these universities can offer very high levels of IT and administrative support to academics, which in turn frees up academic energies not only for research and teaching, but for a whole range of related activities: conference organization, teaching innovations requiring IT support, and the curating of teaching- and research-relevant art exhibitions, to name a few possible examples. High levels of competent administrative and technical support also allow top-performing academics to commit to institution-building, and to a more capacious conception of the academic's tasks and roles in a changing (academic) world.

In addition to noting such factors as administrative and technical support, it is relevant to point out that global recruitment strategies in Asia and the Middle East are creating work environments that are highly energizing and inspiring, on account of their cosmopolitanism and the opportunities they provide not only to learn about new cultures but to work with academics who have a higher tolerance for risk and uncertainty than is the norm, and who make for creative and flexible team players as a result. In some cases, visionary university leaders at ambitious universities located outside the traditional centers of excellence are creating work environments fueled by a motivating and inspiring sense of drive and mission, which is simply unavailable within the non-local academic's "home" context.

The point is that universities must now compete globally, not only for students but increasingly for academics. Institutions that demonstrate a reflexive awareness of the social and cultural implications of their management or regulatory practices — an understanding, that is, of these practices as having cultural entailments — enhance their chances of competing successfully for academic talent. By offering the sorts of quality work environments to which the "Great Colleges to Work For" initiative draws attention, universities enhance their chances of recruiting and retaining the most promising PhDs, just as they enhance their chances of recruiting not only top performers with global mobility, but mid-career academics on the cusp of consolidating the results of years of consistent hard work. Institutional culture, in short, genuinely matters and has clear implications for an institution's ability to compete in terms of the more established performance indicators.

Institutions That Punch Above Their Weight

The more conventional variants on the Assessment game — research assessment exercises, quality assurance audits, and the ranking of universities in terms of research impact (Shanghai Jiao Tong) or holistically in terms of reputation (THES) — would appear to favor certain players. That is, as in any game, there are players who would appear to be better prepared to play these variants on the Assessment game than others. And the results are indeed often, if not always, unsurprising. In some instances, the surprising nature of the results has to do with the way in which the rules of the game change from one year to the next. In "Rankings Ripe for Misleading," Simon Marginson describes the catastrophic impact on the University of Malaya when the rules of the THES game no longer allowed Chinese and Indian students to count as international.[3] Malaysia's oldest public university dropped from 89 to 169 in the 2004 THES ranking, with dire consequences not only for its Vice-Chancellor (who failed to be renewed in 2006) but for the university's "reputation abroad and at home."[4] Given that the University of Malaya had not actually declined in terms of its performance, the 2004 ranking was (among many other things) surprising. In addition to the surprises that poor methodological thinking produces, there are surprises that take the form of a particular player quite simply performing far better than expected, given the received wisdom about the institution's capacities. An example of this far less disconcerting, and in many ways inspiring, kind of "assessment surprise" is Lingnan University's performance in the 2006 RAE. In this competitive game aimed at measuring the research performances of Hong Kong's UGC-funded tertiary institutions, Lingnan placed immediately after the research-intensive universities (University of Hong Kong, Chinese University, Hong Kong University of Science and Technology) and ahead of Hong Kong Baptist University, City University, and Hong Kong Polytechnic University. "The research indexes of all of [Lingnan's] three panels" were above "the sector-wide average," with Business Studies and Economics achieving an index of 84.14 per cent and a ranking of second. Equally surprising was Lingnan's "institution-wide research performance index," which had doubled to 76.35 per cent, compared with 38.85 per cent in the 1999 RAE.[5] While a comprehensive study of Lingnan's performance in the 2006 RAE would have to take into account a whole range of factors, Lingnan's institutional culture clearly played a decisive role, making it possible for academics to achieve research results that would have been unthinkable, even with lighter teaching loads, in more divisive, cut-throat institutional environments.

There are institutions that punch above, and institutions that punch below, their weight, and these are the institutions that are of particular interest in the context of discussions about institution-building. For if we are to understand the deviations that warrant explanation, we must look to the question of institutional culture, to the forms of sociability that are created by these institutions' regulatory practices and habits. We must ask, for example, whether these institutional practices create the conditions for trust, fairness, inclusiveness, and cooperation, or whether, on the contrary, they promote distrust, nepotism, opacity, and divisiveness, among other undesirables. What the punching image from the world of sports is intended to capture is the distinction between two kinds of institutions — those that are able to overcome serious obstacles, at times by transforming such obstacles into the very conditions of possibility of success, and those that evidence a kind of "inverted Midas touch," a capacity to waste opportunities arising (typically) from a wealthy and powerful donor base, from a favored position within a given government's scheme of things, and from a "persistent prestige" phenomenon derived from *ancienneté*. There are lessons to be drawn from institutions that ultimately disappoint, but there is no need to articulate them, or to dwell on them, here. Those lessons are best left implicit here, as the flip-side of a positive and constructive narrative focusing on institutions endowed with a far more inspiring alchemical touch.

But why should we be especially interested in the universities that achieve above expectation? After all, their institutional magic does have limits, and few — given their constraints — can be expected ever to be amongst the absolute top performers in those variants on the game of university assessment that would appear to matter the most. The short answer is that universities that excel against serious odds have much to teach us about the implications that two key phenomena have for institutional culture: scale and leadership. It is my intention in what follows to focus on Lingnan University in Hong Kong, an institution that has managed to overcome considerable odds, to the point where reflection on the enabling conditions that its institutional culture provides becomes pertinent. While some of the inspiration that is to be derived from this particular case will be of interest primarily to institutions grappling with similar constraints and obstacles, much of it is, in my view, of far more general interest. Embedded within the practices of institutions such as Lingnan, we find insights into the ways and means of developing institutional cultures that have the qualities needed to *motivate* and *enable* teachers and researchers to perform to the highest level possible.

Lingnan: Some History

Lingnan's history is a remarkable one, shaped by the drama of larger historical forces, as well as by the loyalty, tenacity, commitment, and courage of its staff and alumni. The university traces its roots back to the Qing dynasty, and to Guangzhou in mainland China, where it was originally known in 1888 as the Christian College in China. The College "disassociated itself from the American Presbyterian Church" in 1893, and was subsequently governed by "a board of trustees based in New York."[6] With the government becoming increasingly suspicious of its activities, the College relocated to Macau in 1900. In 1903, "it changed its English name to Canton Christian College," Lingnan Xuetong in Chinese. While it was located in Macau, there was talk of having the College move to Kowloon, but instead it "returned to Guangzhou in 1904." In 1918, "15 renowned universities, including Harvard, Yale, Columbia, Stanford and Toronto, announced that Lingnan's graduates would be eligible to apply for their postgraduate programmes." When the Nationalist government passed a new regulation (in 1926), prohibiting foreigners from running universities in China, Lingnan — now known as Lingnan Xuexiao — appointed "a predominantly Chinese board of trustees."

In 1938, when it became clear that the Japanese would take over Guangzhou, Lingnan moved to Hong Kong. When Hong Kong fell to the Japanese in 1941, Lingnan's faculty and students were taken "to Shaoguan in northern Guangdong," which was outside the zone occupied by the Japanese. Due to the vicissitudes of war, Lingnan "was forced to move once again, this time to Meixian, east of the Pearl River." When the Japanese surrendered in 1945, Lingnan University was able "to return to its Guangzhou campus," where President Lee Ying-lam, followed by President Chen Xujing, provided exceptional leadership. A "proponent of Westernisation" and "himself a well-known academic," Chen recruited academics from leading institutions such as Tsinghua, and also appointed such "literary giants" as Chen Yinke, Wang Li, Liang Fangzhong, and Rong Geng, "thereby consolidating Lingnan University's leading position in the humanities field." In 1952, following the Communist takeover in 1949, the "former Lingnan campus became the campus of Sun Yat-sen University, while the programmes or faculties of Lingnan University were merged into other institutions in Guangzhou."

Lingnan University was re-established in Hong Kong as a result of the remarkable efforts of the alumni of Lingnan College in Guangzhou. In 1967, the new Lingnan College, located on Stubbs Road in Hong Kong, opened its doors to students. It was "officially recognized as a post-secondary institution" in 1978, and given permission to offer degree programs in 1991. In 1995, Edward Chen Kwan-yiu became president of Lingnan University, moving the university to its present campus in Tuen Mun, in the New Territories and close to the border with the People's Republic of China. In a context requiring role differentiation amongst Hong Kong's tertiary institutions, Chen advocated liberal arts education as Lingnan's defining mission, and laid the foundations for Lingnan (which achieved university status in 1999) as we know it today. Chan Yuk-Shee became president in 2007, following Chen's retirement that same year, and in 2008 Jesús Seade became vice president.

The Art World, Small Nations, and Universities: What Are the Connections?

A question worth asking at this point is what makes me think that I, a scholar with research and teaching interests in such areas as cognitive film studies, theatre history, and environmental aesthetics, might have anything insightful to add to the already voluminous and still burgeoning literature on universities? As a citizen of a small country (Denmark) who has spent much of her life in countries that are classifiable as small on account of their colonial histories (Kenya, Hong Kong), the marginality of certain national tongues (Danish, Dutch), and geographic as well as demographic factors (Denmark, Holland, Hong Kong, Switzerland), I have been particularly interested in understanding the ways in which various measures of scale correlate with cultural achievement and the dynamics of its (mis)recognition.

I have devoted quite some time to understanding the contributions made by cinematic practices that involve visionary artists devising artistic projects with the capacity to turn conditions traditionally seen as impediments to creativity into the very bases for creativity, and this in a way that benefits a larger collectivity. The manifesto-based film movement known as Dogma 95 is a case in point, as is the Scottish "Advance Party" initiative.[7] In exploring these artistic initiatives, my aim has been to shed light not only on constraints as a basis for creativity, but on what I think of as "gift culture." "Gift culture" is a term that picks out projects and practices that reflect a deep belief in the kind of social magic whereby 1 + 1 becomes not 2, but 3 or 4, as a result of the effects of generosity. The very antithesis of the zero-sum games that construe one player's gain as some other player's loss, practices warranting description as forms of "gift culture" reflect agents' understanding of the extent to which the gains of collaboration can outweigh the gains of competition.[8] A number of especially astute film artists have taught other film practitioners, scholars, and — far more importantly — politicians and policy-makers that under-performing film industries can be revived, and even made to thrive, through a careful and consistent attunement to the nature and dynamics of gift culture. It is my conviction that the same is true of universities, and that this truth goes to the heart of the phenomenon of universities punching above their weight. Inasmuch as creativity is a good with intrinsic value, an acknowledged source of pleasure and positive self-concepts, and a crucial factor in quality teaching and research, a perspective on university culture that is attuned to the kinds of artistic practices to which I am drawing attention here may help to define what might count as an exceptional university *work* environment. Such a perspective may also prove suggestive with regard to the role that such an environment plays in fostering the types of excellence that research assessment exercises and quality assurance audits measure.

Creativity and Academic Activism is designed, among other things, to provide academics who have long been committed to institution building with an opportunity to reflect on the factors that either thwarted or enabled their institution-building efforts over the years, and on the lessons that might be drawn from the "thick descriptions" that such first-person narratives provide. Inasmuch as the emphasis in this chapter is on the conditions that enable rather than those that thwart, my discussion is informed by my experience, along-side colleagues, of building the Visual Studies Program, now Department, at Lingnan. The program was launched in 2005, in response to the Hong Kong government's call for capacity-building in the area of visual studies, through programs offered by Hong Kong's tertiary sector. This call — which reached Hong Kong universities in the form of a brief paragraph in a so-called "start letter" from Alice Lam, then chair of the University Grants Committee — was itself a response to the Hong Kong government's decision to transform the city into an arts hub. More specifically, the invitation to develop new programs was linked to the envisaged West Kowloon Cultural District. To be located on a 40-hectare waterfront site overlooking Victoria Harbour, the West Kowloon project has been described by the Office for Metropolitan Architecture (OMA), which is led by five partners, including Rem Koolhaas, as "a project of such scale and ambition that it could define the nature of the public realm in the 21st century."[9] The WKCD project has also been described in less flattering terms — as a cultural theme park, for example — and has generated its fair share of controversy, with cultural activists and artists locking horns with government representatives and the developers who are seen as likely to hijack and profit from it. At the time of writing, the most recent noteworthy event in what increasingly is seen as the saga of West Kowloon is the resignation of the project's internationally respected executive director, Graham Sheffield. The former artistic director of the Barbican walked away from a HK$3 million-plus annual salary after only five months in the job, citing health reasons. The widespread assumption is that Sheffield's declining health and resignation were the result of what I have been calling "institutional culture" — in this case, a hyperactive government bureaucracy.

The decision to launch Visual Studies at Lingnan, initially under the auspices of the Department of Philosophy, was made possible by support from the Faculty of Business, and by contributions from several departments in the Arts Faculty. The Faculty of Business agreed to transfer some of the resources that would be needed to recruit academic staff and students for the new program from Business to Arts, while the Departments of History, Philosophy, English, and Cultural Studies developed courses that could serve as Visual Studies program electives during an initial period of hiring and institution-building. Visual Studies achieved stand-alone department status in 2009 and now has six full-time faculty members, an artist-in-residence program that recruits two visiting artists per year (one of them non-locally), and a main office staffed by two clerks.

Visual Studies at Lingnan brings together analytic aesthetics, cognitive film studies, and art history, and integrates these sub-disciplines by means, among other things, of a cross-disciplinary emphasis on such priority areas as Chinese art, art and well-being, and environmental aesthetics. The department has sought to integrate conceptual, historical, and experiential learning through the provision of opportunities for students to engage in "research expression," the exploration of research questions through artistic practice. Visual Studies now offers credit-bearing internships, opportunities to study abroad at such partner institutions as the Emily Carr University of Art and Design in Vancouver, and the possibility of engaging in "service learning," with students "learning to serve, and serving to learn" through integration into hospital environments where art practice is put to therapeutic uses.

The process of instituting Visual Studies at Lingnan has focused on hiring and curriculum development, as is to be expected, but considerable effort has also been put into the forging of an institutional culture that favors trust, inclusiveness, transparency, generosity, frank and open discussion, a capacity to see constraints as creative opportunities, and collaborative rather than competitive practices. The sense throughout has been that getting the institutional culture right was just as important as the other tasks on the agenda. Lessons learnt from the art world and having to do with "gift culture" and the gains of collaboration, and with "creativity under constraint," have informed thinking about departmental protocols, about the implications of these protocols for collegiality and motivation, and about how best to achieve longer-term departmental goals.

I believe that we have managed to develop an institutional culture that is consistent with our aspirations, and that the existence at this point of a robust culture of trust and mutual support has made it possible for us to do more, and to perform to a higher standard, than would otherwise be the case. Trust, for example, makes it possible to acknowledge mistakes promptly and openly, and this in turn facilitates continued improvement in any number of areas. A culture of trust allows teachers to take risks and to explore new ways of teaching, but it also encourages acknowledgment of both the failures and successes of pedagogical innovations, which itself allows for ongoing adjustments in the area of teaching and learning. Trust, together with the mutual liking that it fosters, allows us to work quickly and effectively on various administrative tasks as they arise, which in turn produces an energy-giving sense of group efficacy that allows teachers and researchers to return to their research projects with the peace of mind that serious thinking often requires. If it is fair to say that Visual Studies at Lingnan performs well — as I hope it is — then one of the reasons for this is that careful and consistent thinking has gone into not just curricular planning and recruitment, but the articulation of administrative and communicative protocols that yield a quality work environment for both staff and students.

I do not wish to suggest that departments at Lingnan are at liberty to invent all their own protocols or to forge their own institutional cultures unconstrained by university-wide parameters. Departmental protocols clearly have to articulate with university-level protocols. But this articulation is to an important extent what my narrative about Lingnan, as an example of an institution that punches above its weight, is about. My colleagues and I have been able to develop the kind of enabling and performance-enhancing institutional culture that now exists in Visual Studies at Lingnan because the larger institutional environment — that is, the university's institutional culture more generally — provides conditions that either do not thwart our departmental aspirations or actually support it. University-level protocols, for example, do not require me, as Chair Professor and head of department, to play trust-eroding zero-sum games with my colleagues at the departmental level, nor do they require me, on a recurring basis and as a matter of business as usual, to compete in collegiality-eroding zero-sum games at the faculty level.

However, the absence at Lingnan of the kind of thoroughly competitive framework that pits departments and colleagues against each other at the turn of each administrative screw does not mean that competition is entirely removed from the institutional picture, even at the level of our departmental culture. Research postgraduate allocations to departments are, for example, made on the basis of a formula that measures departments' relative performances in the most recent RAE, as well as their track records in securing internal, direct grants, and external grants allocated by the Research Grants Council. In this instance, performance-based institutional rewards are a matter of transparent criteria that are not easily manipulated and that do not as a result encourage attempts to win by means of divisive power politics and coalition-formation. Furthermore — and I speak now as a head of department — the criteria governing the allocation of the rewards are such that they encourage a sense of shared purpose at the departmental level. They also help to motivate academics at the level of middle management to put effort into properly nurturing the research potential of all staff. Competition at Lingnan is, quite simply, kept in check by core elements of the university's institutional culture, and governed by a properly institutionalized conception of fair play. As such, it serves to motivate and reward academics, and does not serve to institute the kind of culture of fear and mutual distrust that can only dissipate the energies of teachers and researchers. What is absent, then, is the phenomenon of low morale that is likely to play a central role in any explanatory account focusing on universities that punch *below* their weight. Unlike contexts where one person's contract renewal entails (or is perceived as entailing) non-renewal for someone else, competitive arrangements at Lingnan do not thwart stable, long-term collaborative partnerships, nor do they discourage the kind of sharing of talent, knowledge, and networks that ultimately drives a university's "gift culture."

Lingnan's institutional culture is of interest because it helps us to pinpoint the significance of scale and leadership. I will focus most of my comments on the question of leadership, but do not wish to neglect the matter of scale entirely. Scholars who work on the specificity of small states have argued that limited scale need not be a problem, and can on the contrary make it easier to develop practices that are perceived as intimately tied to social and political goods. Thus, for example, Björn Olafsson argues that "the citizen of a small state has a better possibility to influence decision making than a citizen in a large state."[10] There is no question that the culture of trust that we have worked hard to institute in tandem with Visual Studies' development as a department has been an achievable goal partly on account of the particularities of scale with which we were operating. For example, the kind of flow of information that makes for an inclusive institutional culture, and thus fosters trust, is less of a challenge in the context of a department of six than it is in the context of a department of forty. Furthermore, our small department is one of many small departments, and they in turn are part of a university that itself is small, with around 2400 students.

The limited scale of individual departments encourages cross-disciplinary cooperation, as in the case of Lingnan's integrated Social Sciences program, and also in the case of Visual Studies, which owes its initial viability to the contributing efforts of colleagues in other departments. The citation from Olafsson's work on Iceland (as an example of a small state) is more than suggestive, for it helps to pinpoint the basis for the inclusiveness that is a vital feature of Lingnan's university culture more generally. Lingnan's members of staff, whether academic or non-academic, are known to senior managers, who choose, and are also actually able, to remember their names and their achievements.

There is also the question of access, another key issue that scholars with a special interest in small nations and states tend to foreground. Lingnan's president and vice president can afford to be accessible, and can in fact be counted on to provide prompt responses to inquiries of all kinds, and to meet with colleagues about matters of concern, among many other things. A recurring theme in the literature on small nations and states is that it is important to identify the challenges of limited scale and just as important to be attuned to its advantages. It is my firm conviction that many of those who choose to work at Lingnan, especially at the more senior levels where involvement in university management is expected, have thought hard about questions of scale, and are of the persuasion that the advantages of being small outweigh the challenges. As I see it, one of those advantages is the opportunity to develop the kind of quality work environment that allows an institution to punch well above its weight.

The Globalization of Dubious Ideas: Its Implications for University Leadership

While no doubt traditionally a critically minded group, many academics today seem to be especially gloomy about their institutional lives. Many of the reasons motivating common complaints about university life are well known, having been identified and discussed by the countless authors and journalists who have contributed to the still-burgeoning literature on enterprise universities, corporate universities, research assessment exercises, performance indicators, quality assessment audits, and any number of other phenomena.[11] As Mok Ka-ho puts it, with reference to some of the Australian practices that are now being imported to Hong Kong: "With more weight given to 'quality' measured by crude performance indicators of research output and teaching performance, educational practitioners and academics in Australia feel very demoralized and substantially deprofessionalized."[12] Caught up as they are in what we might think of as the "globalization of dubious ideas and dismal policies" — many of them traceable to Tennessee, to Margaret Thatcher's United Kingdom, and to John Howard's Australia — academics increasingly find themselves working according to bureaucratic dictates that they consider meaningless, counter-productive, wasteful (in terms of money, energy, and time), demoralizing, and ultimately in real tension with the core activities that they are still expected to carry out, and to ever higher standards of performance.

Not everyone is disgruntled, however, as my remarks about Lingnan suggest — and that, of course, is one of the points of this intervention, which seeks to underscore that intelligent leadership at the highest level of a university can affect the impact that the globalization of dubious ideas has on a particular institution. While government policies and global tendencies necessarily shape a university's institutional culture, the decisions that are made internally, within a given university, are just as important, if not more so. Policies and tendencies do not have *necessary* entailments, and as a result the ability of powerful decision-makers to make wise decisions, and this within the context of the institutions that they oversee, becomes crucial. Between government edicts (in response to global tendencies) and the implementation of new policies within a given university, there is always "wiggle room," a space where practical wisdom, or the capacity to make appropriate and judicious decisions, comes into play, and in ways that are decisive for institutional culture.

For example, while the UGC is requiring, at the time of writing, Hong Kong's tertiary institutions to implement an Outcomes Based Approach to Teaching and Learning (OBA), it does not seek to specify completely how a given institution chooses to implement OBA. Uptake and implementation will always be a matter of interpretation, and the quality of a university's institutional culture *qua* work environment will be shaped by the quality of the reasoning that informs the relevant interpretive processes, by the extent to which decision-makers understand the social and psychological implications of the practices they mandate, and by the resulting costs and gains. University leaders, and those who work for them, are necessarily involved in the articulation of an institutional culture, whether or not this is properly acknowledged. It will not do to blame the poor quality of a university work environment on government edicts or global trends — although these do make a significant difference. Even in the context of the globalization of dubious ideas, a university's institutional culture is shaped, to a very significant degree, by choices that are made *within* that institution.

Leadership

The literature on university presidents makes a distinction between transactional and transformational leadership, with proponents of the transactional position likening "decision making in a modern academic institution to a highly complex 'garbage can' over which the president, in the last analysis, has little control," and transformationalists contending that "presidents with vision and energy can and should make a great deal of difference."[13] While I acknowledge the descriptive force of the transactional narrative in some cases, my sympathy lies with the transformationalist position — especially its normative dimensions. Part of the difference that university leaders can make stems from an intelligent grasp of institutional culture, from an understanding of the ways in which the protocols, regulations, preferred practices, and persistent habits of an institution affect the motivation, creativity, and involvement of academics.

Howard Gardner's ground-breaking and well-known work on multiple intelligences helps to bring some of the central capacities that we might look for in university leaders into focus. When he first developed his theory of multiple intelligences, Gardner identified seven "separate intelligences" — linguistic, logical-mathematical, musical, bodily-kinesthetic, spatial, interpersonal, and intrapersonal — and since then he has entertained the possibility of other intelligences, such as moral intelligence and spiritual intelligence.[14] In a chapter entitled "The Intelligences of Creators and Leaders," Gardner identifies the forms of intelligence that are "crucial to leaders" as follows:

> First, they are gifted at language; they can tell effective stories and often can write skilfully, too. Second, they display strong interpersonal skills; they understand the aspirations and fears of other persons, whom they can influence. Third, they have a good intrapersonal sense — a keen awareness of their own strengths, weaknesses and goals — and they are prepared to reflect regularly on their personal course. Finally, the most effective leaders are able to address existential questions: They help audiences understand their own life situations, clarify their goals, and feel engaged in a meaningful quest.[15]

The profile that Gardner sketches refers to what he calls "voluntary" leaders, "the men and women who succeed in making changes without coercion," and who do so "primarily by telling stories and by embodying those stories in their own lives."[16] The contrasting idea here is that of coercive leadership, "as in the case of a tyrant or an authoritarian regime [where] ... leadership is only as effective as the force that grasps the trigger."[17]

Keeping Gardner's various intelligences in mind, I would like to share some suggestive anecdotes about Edward Chen, the president who, for over a decade, played a decisive role in creating the Lingnan we know today. An Oxford-trained pro-Keynesian economist with a special interest in Asian economic development, Chen taught Economics for many years and was Chair Professor and director of the Centre of Asian Studies at the University of Hong Kong, the territory's oldest university (if we discount Lingnan's history in Guangzhou) and its most highly ranked (twenty-fourth in the 2009 THES). During the period 1992–97, he was a member of the 'Cabinet' (the Executive Council) of the last colonial governor, Chris Patten. Chen's contributions to Hong Kong have been considerable and wide ranging.

In his speech at a farewell dinner organized by Lingnan in his honor on the occasion of his retirement, Chen recalled his decision to accept the Lingnan presidency, and did so by referring to different kinds of institutional culture. In some contexts, he argued, a university's institutional culture is like hardened clay, making it impossible for a president, however gifted or motivated, to pursue his or her goals successfully. His assessment of Lingnan, however, as he made his decision to accept the presidency, was that its institutional culture was more like putty, still malleable, and thus amenable to being shaped along certain lines. He further remembered having thought about the size of Lingnan, and what might be achieved by a strong-willed individual in the context of a small institution. Speaking to an audience comprising staff from Hong Kong, from the People's Republic of China, and from many other countries — including Australia, Singapore, Denmark, France, Canada, and Croatia — Chen chose to highlight the issue of recruitment as a particularly crucial element in his approach to institution-building. Aware that Lingnan could easily have become a kind of satellite to the most established university in Hong Kong, his guiding idea was to work with an inclusive approach to hiring and retention that emphasized attitudes and values in addition to achievement, and this in a way that did not favor particular institutions or even countries. Thoughts about the relation between scale and institutional culture, about the university's mission and the kind of sociability that would be required to achieve it, were all clearly in the picture when Chen took over at Lingnan in 1995. Viewed with the eyes of Chen, Lingnan's putative shortcomings — its lack of institutional muscle in the Hong Kong scheme of things, its status as a non-comprehensive university, and its small size — all became opportunities rather than constraints. Absent from the Lingnan context was the institutional baggage of the most established, but still in many ways colonial, institution in Hong Kong, and the intra-institutional marginalization of arts and social sciences so typical of comprehensive universities, with their faculties of Medicine, Science, and Law.

Chen was (and still is) a gifted storyteller. I have participated in several staff inductions over the years, and the one at Lingnan was memorable on account of the stories that Chen shared with his new staff members on that occasion. Told with conviction and passion, and exhibiting a crystal-clear understanding of the audience's likely worries and fears, Chen's stories brought linguistic, interpersonal, intrapersonal, and no doubt other forms of intelligence into play. Unforgettably, Chen began his introduction to Lingnan, as an institution with clearly defined goals and values, with a reference to the effects of its institutional culture on staff and students. "At Lingnan," he claimed, "you will find happy staff, and happy students." Some four years earlier, I had attended a staff induction session at another institution. On that occasion, the (now retired) Vice Chancellor (a dentist by training) introduced new staff to the person charged with handling contract terminations in the Registry. He also indicated that there would be those amongst the inductees who would "get the rewards" and "those who would not," all depending on their performance within a competitive, and apparently zero-sum, set-up. In any context of comparison, Chen's willingness to take the very phenomenon of institutional happiness seriously would no doubt be striking. In one allowing for a contrast between leadership by intimidation and leadership by inspiration, the willingness to commit to something as "soft" as happiness was more than merely striking.

The next part of Chen's introductory story about Lingnan was no less noteworthy, for it involved identifying the various discursive moves that new members of staff were likely to encounter on account of their willingness to work for a small and, within the Hong Kong scheme of things, still emerging university. Fully aware of the moves that can be made within the prestige game, Chen evoked some of the more predictable ones, before going on to outline a series of counter-moves. References to Lingnan's relatively recent status as a university could be countered, he emphasized, with historical knowledge of Lingnan's remarkable role in the provision of quality education in China as early as the nineteenth century. Remarks about Lingnan's putatively peripheral geographic location could be countered in various ways: by referring to its location on an efficient transport system, and by highlighting the sheer cheek of simply dismissing Tuen Mun, a town with over 500,000 people, as peripheral. Much like the Vice Chancellor in that other induction session, Chen also entertained the thought that not all new recruits would remain at Lingnan, but departure in his speech was framed as a matter of choice, rather than forced removal: "Lingnan staff love students. If you don't love students you will either leave because you will find that you don't fit in, or you will change and come to love students."

Over the years I would hear Edward Chen tell many stories, and together they articulated a strong sense of institutional purpose, one informed by clear social and moral values, by a commitment to fairness — for example, to community and community outreach, and to social transformation through education. The message conveyed by these articulate stories was often amplified by the story that Chen himself embodied. Chen was a "teaching president" throughout his years at Lingnan, and much loved by the students. He promised every student at Lingnan that he would have breakfast with them at least once during the course of their studies, and the president's breakfasts were to become a well-known feature of Lingnan's institutional culture. Each year, Chen would attend the inaugural ceremonies and annual dinners organized by the many student societies at Lingnan, a staggering commitment of time. Chen would remember the names of not only the students he taught personally, but of most of the students with whom he engaged. All of these commitments of time and energy contributed to a strong sense of community, one based on robust social bonds. A masterful orator, Chen was particularly adept at framing the university's goals and achievements in terms of "we-intentions." In his speeches at the annual Chinese New Year Party — always a well attended, wonderfully noisy, and highly gregarious occasion — Chen would highlight Lingnan's central accomplishments in the preceding year, and would never fail to point out that these achievements were the result of teamwork, of Lingnan's staff pulling together as a community oriented by we-intentions. Chen scrupulously avoided taking credit for Lingnan's achievements, referring always to what "we have achieved together."

I have been building a case for seeing Lingnan's institutional culture as an example of what intelligent leadership can accomplish in order to make the point that if we are to be coherent in our insistence on rankings and quality, then the quality of the work environments that universities provide cannot be ignored. I have been suggesting that to be seen as offering a quality work environment, a university would need to develop an institutional culture that, in addition to being enabling and supportive, provides a context in which many forms of academic work (including administrative tasks) can be seen as pleasurable and meaningful, and as offering a sense of fulfillment.

I have been suggesting all along that the rejection of zero-sum thinking contributes to an enabling and supportive environment in which work can be carried out with the kind of focus, sense of flow and involvement, and conviviality that make certain activities genuinely pleasurable. What has yet to be broached is the question of why the kind of institutional culture that Lingnan has developed might stand a better chance than some of also offering a sense of fulfillment — not punctually, in relation to specific tasks, but in the long run and as a result of the institution's mission. Before I conclude on a personal note, then, I wish to say a few words about Lingnan's commitment to community engagement.

Community Engagement and Social Relevance

With "Serving to Learn, Learning to Serve" as its motto, Lingnan qualifies as what is sometimes called an "engaged university." In a consultation document entitled "Engagement as a Core Value for the University," produced by the Association of Commonwealth Universities in 2001, "engagement" is defined as implying thoughtful:

> interaction with the non-university world in at least four spheres: setting universities' aims, purposes, and priorities; relating teaching and learning to the wider world; the back-and-forth dialogue between researchers and practitioners; and taking on wider responsibilities as neighbours and citizens.[18]

By virtue of its core mission, guiding values and commitments, and history, Lingnan has never been part of the "ivory tower" phenomenon. Committed as it is to education as a transformational process that creates opportunities for those without inherited economic and cultural capital, Lingnan has not had to reinvent itself in order to meet the growing demand, from governments and society at large, that universities be responsive to society. If anything, the demand for social relevance has created a tertiary sector that is far more hospitable to the kind of institution that Lingnan is. Whereas some universities have opted to understand "relevance" primarily in terms of market demands or the needs of business, Lingnan has aimed consistently to engage communities with little or no economic or political clout, and not only in Hong Kong. *Uniting Social Capitals for the Global Society*, one of the annual reports published by Lingnan's Office of Service Learning, provides a detailed picture of how the university seeks to "produce a positive developmental impact on student learning and growth" through community engagement.[19] Included in this report are accounts of such engagement — for example, of a three-year pilot project, supported by Deloitte Touche Tohmastsu, that involves students contributing to the sustainable development of a remote village in the mountainous region of Yunnan province on the Chinese mainland.

The point is that the legitimacy given to community engagement at Lingnan has far-reaching implications for its institutional culture. At Lingnan, students and staff (whether administrative or academic), live their university lives in an environment that is shaped by various social and political concerns, and by the many concrete projects that colleagues have devised in response to them.

Posters announcing events and opportunities for involvement, and public talks and exhibitions, all articulate the commitments of Lingnan as an engaged university, but so does the presence of non-traditional learners. For example, with its aim of fostering inter-generational solidarity in Hong Kong, Lingnan's Elder Academy enables "elderly people with different educational backgrounds" to audit courses at Lingnan, and thereby to contribute, among other things, to the experiential richness of the university's learning environment.

As an engaged university, Lingnan's institutional fabric is one that articulates what Canadian philosopher Charles Taylor would call "a story one can live by." That story is one that brings those who engage with it into contact not only with the better selves that they also potentially are, but with the "moral sources" that allow life choices to be made with genuine moral discernment.[20] What we have here are some of the possible conditions for a life lived meaningfully, and with a sense of genuine fulfillment.

Conclusion

Intelligent university leadership no doubt comes in different forms, with some leaders exemplifying some of the necessary traits to a significant degree, and other leaders other traits. Which of the traits are to be especially preferred may be a matter for debate, or even a question of cultural preferences. My aim here has not been to settle these issues, nor has it been to suggest that Lingnan or its former president provide some kind of model of perfection. What Lingnan does provide is one example of a context where the concept of institutional happiness, far from being unthinkable or neglected as naïve or soft, has been part of the actual process of institution-building, at least according to the self-understanding of one of its most central former decision-makers. This reflexive awareness of the social and psychological implications of what less remarkable leaders often think of as mere institutional infrastructure is the first step towards a quality work environment. And if we are going to embrace the Assessment game, then we cannot afford to ignore the lessons that are embedded in the institution-building efforts of such figures as Edward Chen. One such lesson is this: the Assessment game is best played in the context of the kind of work environment that is most likely to produce success, namely a *quality* work environment.

Having worked at Lingnan for many years, the phenomenon of the institution that punches above its weight is no longer puzzling to me. Some universities provide institutional cultures that are profoundly enabling and inspiring, and capable as a result of fostering a profound sense of gratitude in those who inhabit them. And gratitude is a powerful motivating force that has yet to be properly recognized by many a senior manager. That I am grateful to Lingnan for providing a quality work environment in the context of Hong Kong's tertiary sector will be clear to anyone who has read this far. As a film scholar, I am grateful for the university's very genuine interest in, and commitment to, arts and humanities. As a non-local scholar, I am grateful for Lingnan's cosmopolitanism and cultural capaciousness. As a woman, I am grateful for the university's refusal — currently but also historically — actively to embrace or quietly to endorse patriarchal arrangements and practices. As a mid-career academic with a strong commitment to institution-building, I am grateful for the opportunity to build a new department, one with an institutional culture favoring trust, friendship, and happiness. As a survivor of cancer, I am grateful to the university for having had the humanity knowingly to hire me at a time when the prognoses about recurrence and survival were just that, mere prognoses. More than anything else, I am grateful for the opportunity to work for truly remarkable university leaders, and to be part of an institutional story that cannot be a source of regret, or of a sense of a life squandered.

5

Three Tough Questions of Cultural Studies

The Case of the Program in Cultural Studies at the University of Shanghai

Wang Xiaoming

Cultural studies as an academic and intellectual activity only began to flourish in the Chinese mainland near the end of the 1990s and at the beginning of the new millennium, thus lagging at least ten years behind Hong Kong and Taiwan. In the mid-1990s, several keen scholars such as Dai Jinhua were adopting research methods similar to Cultural Studies in their research on film and urban popular culture, and there were those like Li Tuo who openly advocated the development of Cultural Studies. These efforts did not generate widespread echoes at first. However, when Cultural Studies finally arrived it quickly gathered enormous momentum. By 2004, universities around the country — especially those in Beijing and Shanghai — were busy organizing open lectures and courses, translating and publishing Cultural Studies works from Europe and the United States, starting different research projects, and establishing special institutes for the teaching and research of the subject. These activities combined into a so-called "cultural studies fever" that continues in China today.

There were two driving forces behind this phenomenon. The first was a need generated within the academic and university establishment. From the early 1980s, the academic establishment in China became a faithful follower of European and US academic trends. This narrowing of international focus was relatively new: while the Chinese intellectual world has been influenced by the West since the late nineteenth century, until the 1940s "the West" was understood to encompass more than simply "Europe and the USA," and in the early 1950s there was even a mood for upholding the Soviet Union and downplaying the importance of Western Europe and the United States. However, the fascination with the United States became even more pronounced after the mid-1990s, and by that time Cultural Studies was the only Euro-American "popular discipline" that had not been introduced systematically to the Chinese mainland. Therefore, from the perspective of academic knowledge production (or an academic politics that was eager to create a new dominant discourse), Cultural Studies seemed to be very important and attracted much attention.

The second and more complicated driving force was a need stimulated by social reality. After twenty years of "reform," China's society (especially in the southeast coastal region and in many middle- to mega-size cities) has changed tremendously, to an extent that now renders it unrecognizable. This transformation has elicited different interpretations among scholars of the humanities and social culture. Some have argued that, as China entered the era of consumer society and popular culture, Western capitalism became the dominant force shaping society. There was therefore a need to introduce theories from Cultural Studies — mainly American theories developed after the 1970s — in order to affirm this new reality. Others were not so optimistic. They were, in contrast, disturbed by the great change in Chinese society. China is utterly different from what it was in the period from the 1950s through to the 1970s; politically and economically, it is no longer the old "socialist" society, certainly, but over the past twenty years it also has not come much closer to the model of European or American capitalist society. The Chinese government still practices collective authoritarianism; it still controls the media; and it has even become more corrupt. It seems that China is following a path that is still very much beyond the scope of current human understanding.[1] Where is China going? What will it become? What kind of impact will this changing China have on the world? These big questions puzzled this particular group of scholars.

Under these circumstances, the members of this group initially were resistant to taking an optimistic view of China's present and future reality, instead choosing to look at reality critically. Second, they thought the most urgent task was to begin the study of social reality, as only through such study could we achieve an understanding of this great change. Third, these scholars believed that this kind of study should cross the boundaries of current academic arenas, not only to analyze cultural reality in a holistic and comprehensive manner but also to combine the study of culture with that of politics and the economy, given their internal linkages with cultural life.

It was with this understanding that those in this second group of scholars found their way to the Birmingham School of Cultural Studies. What attracted them most to the Birmingham School was the kind of critical social studies they encountered there. However, given China's unique situation, in which the rigid binary theoretical divisions beloved of the Chinese intelligentsia in the 1980s (modern/traditional, socialism/capitalism, project economy/market economy, communist authoritarianism/liberal democracy) had ceased to be effective, what they needed apart from new theoretical resources was a new name under which to work. They thought that "Cultural Studies" was the name they could borrow, although they were cautious about not following the mode of post-1990s Cultural Studies in the United States, which had become too entrenched in academic institutions and gradually lost its influence on society.

I was one of those who felt puzzled. Against this background, I became involved in Cultural Studies research and teaching activities that began to flourish in Shanghai, accompanied by the development of supporting institutions. In 2001, Shanghai University established the first Cultural Studies institute in mainland China, the Center for Contemporary Culture Studies (CCCS). In the following four years, institutes of a similar nature mushroomed in different universities in the city, such as Shanghai Normal University, East China Normal University, and Tonji University. These attracted scholars from different disciplines, such as Literature, History, Sociology, Anthropology, and Media and Film Studies, who were interested in pursuing Cultural Studies research. The academic faculty working at different institutes sometimes overlapped — for example, the staff of the Cultural Studies sub-division of the e-Institution of Urban Cultural Studies at Shanghai Normal University are mainly from CCCS. In turn, CCCS contains not only full-time scholars from Shanghai University itself but also more than a dozen scholars from other universities who work in the center as part-time researchers.

These research institutes began initiating their own research projects, and those organized by CCCS were on the largest scale. In 2003, a five-year research project was launched with the overall title "A Cultural Analysis of the Shanghai Region in the 1990s." It included eight sub-projects involving topics such as media (television), the real estate market and its advertising campaigns, visual images of the street, "workers' new villages," the cultural history of factories and workers, literature websites, urban new spaces, and fashion. Research arising from these sub-projects has been published in monograph form by CCCS and Shanghai Bookstore publishing house since 2008. In that same year, CCCS started another, even bigger, ten-year research project, "An Analysis of the Contemporary Cultural Production Mechanism." The project was again divided, this time into two parts: "An Analysis of the New Dominant Cultural Production Mechanism" and "An Analysis of China's Socialist Cultural Problems."

In Europe, the United States and some Asian countries (for example, Japan and South Korea), Cultural Studies scholars have been reluctant to subordinate the subject to the agenda of the prevailing academic establishment. In China, however, there was an urgent need for Cultural Studies to expand its teaching space in universities. In the second part of this article, I consider the major reason for this, but here is a minor reason: relative to the vastly ambitious mission of Cultural Studies, there are simply too few young people in mainland China (including active regions for Cultural Studies like Shanghai and Beijing) who are capable of undertaking any kind of Cultural Studies research. In this context, university education is an effective channel for training students. From 1999 on, several universities in Shanghai (such as East China Normal University, Fu Dan University, Shanghai University, Shanghai Normal University, and Tonji University) introduced elective courses on Cultural Studies for senior undergraduates. In 2002 and 2003, the Department of Sociology and Department of Chinese at Shanghai University enrolled PhD students who proposed to do research on Cultural Studies. Then in 2004, Shanghai University set up the "Program in Cultural Studies," which was the first teaching and research institute on Cultural Studies in mainland China.

In 2006, Cultural Studies scholars from five universities or institutes — Shanghai University, East China Normal University, Shanghai Normal University, Fudan University, and the Literature Research Institute of the Shanghai Academy of Social Sciences — joined forces to establish a joint Masters degree program in Cultural Studies. The program, which is still running, consists of a variety of courses (such as "Literature/Video Text Analysis," "Selected Readings in Cultural Studies Theories," "Cultural Problems of Chinese Socialism," and "Reform and Problems of Chinese Modernity"), and each of these courses has its own special discussion forum on the "Program in Cultural Studies" website (http://www.cul-studies.com) to enhance discussions among students, teachers, and interested individuals.[2]

Joint-school teaching programs and related exchange schemes on a larger scale followed. Let me take Shanghai University's Program in Cultural Studies as an example of this kind of cross-institutional activity. In 2007, the department organized a summer seminar on "Cultural Studies in the Chinese World"; eleven experienced Cultural Studies scholars came from Beijing, Hong Kong,

Taiwan, and Shanghai to spend five days discussing their work with more than thirty young teachers and PhD students from Hong Kong, Taiwan, and mainland China.[3] Then, in 2008 and 2009, the department worked with the Institute of Chinese Literature and Culture at Waseda University in Tokyo to create discussion platforms among PhD students from both sides. Starting from 2010, the department is taking part in the planning of a multilateral regional Asian Cultural Studies postgraduate program in "Inter-Asia Cultural Studies." Further, it is organizing a two-part summer seminar on "Cultural Studies Methodology," with the first meeting taking place in August 2010 in Haikou, capital of Hainan Province, and the second projected for summer 2011 in Harbin, capital of Heilongjiang Province.

These activities have induced a series of difficulties, or "tough questions," in both practice and theory. Below I elaborate three of these, still using the Shanghai University program as an example.

Cultural Studies and the University Establishment

Historically, to be anti-establishment is one of the basic standpoints of Cultural Studies. But in contemporary China, where centralization of state power is still the norm, nearly every major social resource is in the hands of "the establishment." If Cultural Studies did not enter the established university order and utilize its resources (for example, the means to circulate information and secure financial help), it would have no hope of surviving. On the other hand, school education plays a heavy role in a mature modern society, where unequal social structures may have an intensified impact on students through the formal education process. In China today, children from the lower income stratum are experiencing a severe "intellectual retardation." Schools have become the major sites for reproducing, instead of breaking down, unequal social structures. In literary education, for example, there has been a decline in subjects such as "Modern Chinese Literature," "Literature Studies," and "Comparative Literature" that played an outstanding role in the 1980s in nurturing critical thinking among students; in the 1990s, one by one they became rule-abiding and lost their luster. At the same time, the viewpoint that university is merely a place to gain a ticket for high-paid jobs is becoming more popular. After the mid-1990s, the sharp rise in tuition fees and an emphasis on so-called "quality education" led to a more frightening phenomenon: children from low-income families are finding it increasingly difficult to study in universities. Under these circumstances, how could Cultural Studies abstain from the university education system, which defines the future of society?

However, there are risks to consider. When you try to make use of the establishment, the establishment has its own agenda for making use of you. When Cultural Studies gradually entered the university system and set up departments, we had to ask whether it would face the same fate as, say, the Comparative Literature that was introduced to China thirty years ago but subsequently faded as a critical and socially active discipline. As Cultural Studies reluctantly struggled into the university establishment (not an easy task),[4] our corresponding strategy was to remain fully alert to the risks involved and to try to develop and maintain the subject's inter-disciplinary characteristics. In 2004, when Shanghai University's Program in Cultural Studies was in preparation, we upheld one key principle: Cultural Studies is not a specific profession or discipline like "Modern Chinese Literature." It is more like an approach, a research method towards culture and society, or a broad vision that must be free of rigid disciplinary boundaries.

There are different ways to implement this principle. First, the department doesn't offer undergraduate programs in Cultural Studies; only undergraduate elective courses are offered.[5] We encourage students to receive a systematic academic training in a particular profession or major before they pursue the programs in our department. Second, our Masters and PhD programs are not offered under one discipline but under many different disciplines.[6] From 2008 on, the department opened a core course, "Introduction to Cultural Studies," for first-year Master's students from a variety of majors. In this way, it is treated as a kind of general education unit — for example, we opened a general education course on "Cultural Studies and Problems of Chinese Modernity" for first-year Master's students from five streams of the Department of Chinese ("Chinese Modern and Contemporary Literature," "Chinese Ancient Literature," "Literature Studies," "World Literature," and "Comparative Literature"). In future, the department is going to come up with further diverse arrangements, and let our postgraduate students continue to break away from their monotonous specialist training.

In order to match up with its "multidisciplinary" characterization, the Program in Cultural Studies maintains a comparatively small full-time faculty. Thus, in September 2009, the department had only three full-time professors with PhD research areas in, respectively, Literature, Sociology and Gender Studies. Eleven members of the department committee, including the department head, are from five different departments or schools of the university: the Department of Chinese, the Department of Sociology, the Department of Video and Art, the Department of Media, and the School of Intellectual Property. We hope that this structure can overcome the tendency towards narrow professionalization that is common practice in China's university education system.

Finally, the department continues to push Cultural Studies education beyond the physical boundaries of the university and to enable it to enter the expansive social sphere. Alongside our participation in the joint Master's degree program and the "Inter-Asia Cultural Studies" postgraduate program mentioned above, the Cultural Studies forums on the "Contemporary Cultural Studies" website (http://www.cul-studies.com) also have great potential for further development. At the time of writing, there are ten BBS forums for ten Cultural Studies courses (mainly postgraduate courses, although some are senior undergraduate courses) offered by different universities.[7] Excellent discussions are uploaded to the website's major forum ("*Re Feng*") as soon as possible in order to reach a wider readership and attract more criticisms. Through this method, the Cultural Studies education based in a particular school can link up with a global readership. That expands the openness of Cultural Studies education.

These initiatives are all arrangements secured within the teaching system, but these alone cannot completely resolve an even tougher question: if one wants to establish an independent working area for Cultural Studies in the university system, then Cultural Studies needs first to be accepted as an independent discipline. In order to gain this status, it is necessary to confirm that Cultural Studies has its own specific research topics that cannot be grasped by other disciplines, and to provide corresponding analytical theories and methods. To say "cultural studies is an approach" cannot fulfill these requirements. In my opinion, this may be the trump card of the university establishment. It forces us to solidly define the academic content of Cultural Studies as an independent discipline, and it is exactly during this process that the establishment tries to tame it. The university's demand to make Cultural Studies a subject is closely related to the pressure of the so-called "manpower market." When they ask "What is the academic content of Cultural Studies?" they are in effect asking "What kind of jobs can Cultural Studies graduates do?" As teachers, we must pay attention to the employment prospect of students. It is not an easy task to fulfill this need and at the same time avoid Cultural Studies becoming another manpower-production profession under the double pressure of the current university establishment and the Chinese-style market mechanism. Therefore, we must choose for Cultural Studies a specific academic content that serves two purposes. On one hand, it could — at least partially — fulfill the formal requirements of the establishment, but at the same time it could preserve or even develop a kind of potential energy that can break through this formality.

Two decisions were made with respect to this problem. The first was indeed to confirm the basic research object of mainland China's Cultural Studies. One important aspect of the great social change over the past thirty years has been the formulation of a new dominant culture that is utterly different from the "Maoist thought" entrenched from the 1950s to the 1970s. Based on a highly idiosyncratic mechanism for formulation, operation, and dispersion, the new dominant culture has saturated nearly every aspect of the society, from the value system to material life, and it has become the major channel for the reproduction of the whole society. It is worth paying attention to the relationship between this new dominant culture and "socialist" history during the period from the 1950s to the 1970s. If the latter did not exist, it would be difficult to conceive of the formation of the current phenomenon. In a sense, the current culture is the product of the socialist phase. On the other hand, one of the key functions of today's dominant culture is to control the public understanding of the past era (no matter whether someone has experienced that past or not). From this perspective, the "socialist" history now in the minds of numerous Chinese is to a large extent a product of the new dominant culture.

In the light of this understanding, we affirmed both "the production mechanism of the current dominant culture" and "the relationship between this culture and 'socialist' history" as the major objects of Cultural Studies in the Chinese mainland today. These objects, or a full outline of them, could only be scrutinized clearly through the window of Cultural Studies as we understand it. We do not even hesitate to say that it is this window of Cultural Studies that gives form to these objects. We believe that no researchers who bind themselves within a singular discipline (including Cultural Studies) can have an adequate insight into these research objects. It is only when they determine to cross over the boundaries between disciplines and borrow from different trains of thought that they can really move forward.

The second decision was to confirm the outline of a methodology for mainland China's Cultural Studies. The basic purpose of Cultural Studies in China not only rests on the critical analysis of the cultural situation in the society and the oppressive mechanism behind its production; there is another mission that is at least equally important — to enhance the possibilities for a positive reform of the society and the cultural situation in general. This purpose is based on a judgment: while a new social structure that is seriously twisted has already taken shape in China today, it is still not totally stable. Turbulence continues in the economy, politics, and culture, and is delaying the settlement and self-perfection of this new structure. Reality is worrying but not without hope: if there are enough positive elements ready to intervene, the society may change in a positive direction. Based on this understanding, a bilinear structure is used to outline the methodology of mainland Chinese Cultural Studies, one in which "critical analysis" and "proactive intervention" are undertaken at the same time. To borrow a pair of political concepts from the 1950s, it involves "destruction" and "construction" at the same time; these work together and survive reciprocally. Hopefully this methodology can help Cultural Studies to continue its breakthrough work, not only among different disciplines but across academic circles, the wider society and culture, and even social movements.

This formulation of the academic content of Cultural Studies should work with the teaching strategies described above to fight against the strong assimilationist power of the university establishment.[8] However, the results are not yet clear.

Cultural Studies and Positive Reform of Society

Another tough question follows: If Cultural Studies is not to be equated only with research activities in universities but also wants to intervene and change reality, then it is necessary to consider the potential forces for positive social reform. In present-day China, urbanization is taking place at a rapid pace, and "winner takes all" becomes the norm under severe social stratification; where, then, are these potential social forces for positive reform? Outdated theories of revolution cannot provide an effective answer. We must do the analysis ourselves.

At present, scholars in the Cultural Studies circle suggest two answers. The first points to the middle-income stratum (not "the middle class") in the cities. This stratum is a very complicated one, and a large part of it — for example, the white-collar management staff of industrial and commercial enterprises and the many below-middle-level civil servants — is deeply influenced by the dominant culture; these people think of themselves as the lucky ones who continue to benefit from the "market economy reform." Therefore they choose, consciously or unconsciously, to stand beside the "new rich," a new stratum that appeared together with a "lower stratum" during China's social stratification over the past thirty years. At present, the majority of the new rich consist of three types of people: the so-called "civil entrepreneurs," the "middle to upper level civil servants," and the senior management staff of different industrial and commercial enterprises. (In fact, this stratum has become the ruling class of today's China.) But there is also a group of people in the middle-income stratum who understand their real social position and have a certain amount of cultural and economic power. They are the ones who have the will and energy to reform.

The second proposed answer is that the major force for reform can still come from the lower income stratum in cities and villages, mainly the poor city dwellers, migrant workers, and poor farmers who live in villages (the majority of the rural population), because they are the most oppressed people. According to Maoist thinking, one finds the biggest resistance where there is the greatest oppression.

Currently, I am inclined to agree with the first answer. In a highly modernized society like that of contemporary China, it is not possible for the public to retain their own political, economic, and cultural space, and people from the lower stratum have been deprived of their powers in many respects. In this situation — although they are indeed facing huge oppression — they lack the energy to resist, and their many vigorous actions do not actually constitute a strong disruption of the present social structure. For this reason, I am afraid the lower stratum cannot be a major potential force for reform.

However, the dispute between these two answers generates further analysis of the corresponding political, economic, and cultural conditions of the urban middle-income stratum and the lower income stratum. At the same time, it also stimulates reflection on the teaching methodology of Cultural Studies. The question is whether Cultural Studies education in mainland China today should focus on the middle-income stratum through university programs, newspaper articles, websites, lectures, and academic papers, or on the lower-income stratum through non-regular educational means such as night schools, schools for the children of migrant workers, and village construction campaigns.[9] It is difficult to choose between the two. However, since we are in the city, the teaching activities of the Program in Cultural Studies have been following — at least until now — the middle-income set of educational means.

The second answer may not be correct, but there is no reason to overlook it, as it brings out another important related issue: the relationship between Cultural Studies education and the Chinese village. Despite pervasive urbanization and 200 million migrant workers working in the cities, villages still occupy the biggest part of China and the majority of the Chinese population are still farmers. However, at least up to this moment, mainland Chinese Cultural Studies basically focused on "cities" — to such an extent that there is little difference between Cultural Studies and "urban cultural studies." There are many reasons for this, one being a near "innate" theoretical restriction: European and US Cultural Studies theories were generated in the social conditions of highly urbanized societies, and when these theories were introduced into China they naturally led research to focus on the cities. There is also the real stimulus that, while China can still be treated as an agricultural country, it is dominated by cities and if you want to see China clearly you cannot avoid those cities. Moreover, Cultural Studies scholars usually work in universities and live in cities, and they are also bound to their own life experiences. However, the lack of understanding of rural reality in Cultural Studies circles, and the wide range of false imaginings derived from this lack (for example, the idea that most Chinese villages still retain a 'village' culture that is clearly distinct from urban culture) are worrying. How should we teach Cultural Studies in this situation? Is it reasonable to simply evade the rural area and its cultural conditions, and talk about the cities alone?

Over the past six to seven years, a considerable proportion of the postgraduate students in Cultural Studies programs have come from the rural area, or had teaching experience in village schools beforehand. They had first-hand experiences of contemporary rural reality, and this is true not only of Shanghai University but other universities as well. However, to have lived in the village does not mean that one understands the village; rather, the key is how to learn from one's life experiences. For example, villages in the east of the country have long been absorbed by the urban dominant culture. Young people there are classified legally as farmers, but their perceptions of themselves and their lifeworld are mostly "urban." They are eager followers of urban popular culture, and during class discussions we found that those who came from the village were more attached to urban popular culture than students who actually grew up in the cities.[10] Villages in China today have long been incorporated into the social network led by big cities; therefore, both ends of the domination chain actually form part of the one urban–rural system. It follows that if Cultural

Studies education only focuses on cities and overlooks the villages, it is no different from restricting one's horizon or seeing things with one eye shut. Teachers with their eyes shut cannot train students to perceive and grasp the full picture of a society.

So how can students use Cultural Studies methods to discuss rural cultural issues in the classroom? In 2004, under the influence of nationwide discussions on "the three-dimensional rural issues" (agriculture, rural villages, and farmers), we started to organize students — mostly postgraduate — to work as volunteer teachers (*zhi jiao*) in villages — for example, in poor regions in Shandong and agricultural regions in Hubei — and to do cultural and social surveys at the same time.[11] Some of the students also went to teach in schools for migrant workers' children in the Shanghai suburbs until 2007, when the Shanghai municipal government began allowing the children of rural migrant workers to study in local schools and at the same time closed all specialized schools for these children. These activities had good effects on our students. For example, when students acquired a direct understanding of the reality of rural culture, it usually helped them to understand better the working mechanism of urban popular culture; some students even stepped forward to help set up specialized organizations and planned long-term involvement in the reform of rural cultural conditions.

Nevertheless, there were many obstacles and difficulties. Local officials tried to obstruct students from doing surveys, the headmasters of village schools exploited the "teaching volunteers" for their own benefit and, in some cases, even the national security authorities stepped in. The biggest problem, though, is that without the full support of relevant research resources we have to ask whether it is really an effective way to open up the village dimension of Cultural Studies education through these short visits. From one perspective, to work in the village is a trial to test the validity of the second answer to the above question about the potential forces of positive social reform (remembering that as early as the 1950s, and as part of the "education revolution" advocated by Mao Zedong, many universities organized students to go to villages and even have classes in the fields). From another perspective, though, the practice itself is immature; it is no different from building a bridge without having a deep foundation on both sides (i.e. university and village) — the bridge built will surely be unstable and unsafe. A great deal of work is necessary if we really want to open up Cultural Studies to village experience and explore the issues of rural culture. It is still very difficult to tell how the teaching of Cultural Studies can become part of positive social reform.

The "Glocal" Sensibility of Cultural Studies

A reality confronts us. On the one hand, after a process of "passive moderniza-tion" that lasted for 150 years, China is now deep in the massive current of modernization/globalization. Nearly every corner in this country is closely linked to that current. On the other hand, China remains a unique country for many historical reasons (of which four of the most important are its huge population and territory, its geographic position, the timing of its encounter with the imperial West, and the sheer historical momentum carried by 5000 years of uninterrupted civilization), and its modern history and current social situation clearly differ from those of the West. Therefore, Cultural Studies in the Chinese mainland should develop "glocal" characteristics to accommodate this complicated reality. "Glocal" here means developing an intellectual horizon or a comprehension ability capable of combining the "global" with "China." This would be a capacity capable of simultaneously identifying both the Chinese influence on the world and the global elements active in China, for only if it is equipped with this glocal awareness can Cultural Studies in the Chinese mainland develop both a real and effective global horizon and a sense of care towards the world. In effect, one of the reasons that we chose "Cultural Studies" to name ourselves is that the subject has developed a strong politics of locality.

So how can this glocal sensibility be developed? The first thing necessary is to confront the daily experiences of contemporary Chinese. We have achieved this in two ways at a teaching level. First, starting from 2006, the content of the introductory Cultural Studies class was adjusted so that it no longer began with the conventional history and concepts of Cultural Studies as these presuppose a lot of European and North American social conditions and include theoreti-cal terms that are far removed from the students' life experiences. The course now begins with their everyday lives as contemporary Chinese: their past, their current sources of stress, their worries and hopes. Then the conditions of Chinese society are introduced in general terms, and these become the basis of their life experiences. Later, we raise the challenges that this reality poses in and for our critical intellectual lives: What major issues does the reality of Chinese society impose on intellectual circles? Finally, Cultural Studies is introduced as an important way for Chinese intellectuals to respond to this reality. The course then also introduces some of the historical and theoretical resources that Cultural Studies inherits, and the basic strategies for analyzing reality. While this introductory class limits the content of theories coming from

Europe and the United States, it clearly strengthens the students' understanding of the local significance of Cultural Studies, and in turn this understanding can encourage their later participation.

Second, we simultaneously restructured the Cultural Studies theory class. Apart from offering selections from important theoretical works, there is now a series of courses called "theory and practice," targeting postgraduate students of different types and different grades; the courses have different titles, but all contain the words "theory" and "practice." The class template has two parts, the first being a special introduction to current cultural and social studies theories — mainly from Europe and the United States — while the second part is an analysis of cases taken from mainland Chinese Cultural Studies. If the situation allows, lecturers invite related researchers to share their ongoing or newly finished research with the class.

If it works well, a theory class that includes practical analyses can be beneficial to students in two ways. Combining "theory" and "practice" in this context is similar to bringing the idea of "Europe and the United States" together with "the glocal." From the sites and situations in which these two formations work well together, we can understand the universal conditions of the contemporary world, and from those where the two conflict with each other, we can grasp the crucial importance of local reality and perhaps find a breakthrough point for future theoretical development and practical analysis. This is therefore a good way to enhance the development of local characteristics in Cultural Studies at a teaching level. Mainland Chinese Cultural Studies has a short history; there is a lack of well-tested examples, and this hinders the development of broadly similar courses. However, some rough frameworks are in place right now and the development continues.

There is another rich resource that a glocalizing Cultural Studies in China can provide: Chinese revolutionary thought and the history of revolutionary practices. China began its modern history and developed its modern ideas under the pressure of invading Western imperialist powers. In these circumstances, China's modern ideas were developed from the perspective of the oppressed. Chinese thinkers strongly expressed the view that China did not accept the modern order's "law of the jungle," and should seek to create a more democratic social structure than that of the West. From the end of the nineteenth century to the mid-twentieth century, this broadly speaking leftist ideal dominated modern Chinese thought. This same ideal inspired different parts of society, and generated social reforms and liberation movements that lasted for at least half a century. This is what I mean by the "Chinese revolution."[12]

After reflecting on present reality and reviewing modern Chinese history, we have come to believe that *this* "Chinese revolution" represents a most precious tradition for Chinese intellectuals today, providing both spiritual resources and a social legacy that is still traceable in real life. Over the past twenty years, it has seemed that the revolution has been driven underground but, as Lu Xun once wrote, its flame has not died out but still burns somewhere in the dark as a "subterranean fire."[13] In fact, the academic activities of the self-proclaimed "cultural studies" circle are among the results of this subterranean fire. Marxism and the different Western critical theories and practices of the Birmingham School give us important intellectual resources but, comparatively speaking, the Chinese revolutionary tradition is the spiritual pillar that is at once more substantial and closer to us.

From 2007, the department added a new core course to the Masters and doctoral programs: "Special Topics in Modern Chinese Thought."[14] The results so far are not bad: students have discovered many new details of intellectual and social history and widened their understanding of such common constructs as "modern China," "Chinese revolution," and "socialism." More importantly, their capacity to focus on and envision our reality becomes more substantial with the guidance provided by that part of our history, and they are less misled by a superstitious belief in Western theories. This is very important if the new generation is to develop an ability to produce precise analysis and to intervene in real situations. In fact, over the past decade we have noticed a global shortcoming of critical thought and intellectual activities: it is difficult to develop new paths, new concepts, and new methods apart from the commonly circulated canon of critical theories from Europe and the United States. The development of Cultural Studies in the non-Western regions is already enveloped by theories from Europe and the United States to varying degrees. Despite advances in concrete analysis, the development of theories, concepts, and research methods is falling behind, and sometimes is not even visible at all. As a result, the theoretical education offered in the name of Cultural Studies in these regions easily slants towards the Euro-American canon. Of course, structural factors may have a role to play here — perhaps it is not that regions beyond Euro-America are lacking distinctive developments in critical theory, but rather that — due to the structural imbalance in global knowledge production and circulation — these developments cannot easily be shared by Cultural Studies scholars in different places.

In this context, the mainland intelligentsia's emphasis on "Chinese experience" is particularly meaningful. "Chinese experience" is a wide-ranging term that can be claimed by different parties — including right-wing forces such as narrow-minded nationalism. But this term also provides a spacious area for in-depth Cultural Studies research, and for simultaneously more introspective and more expansive contents. The boundaries of this space have not yet been determined, and because they are still changing all the time, the contents of the space may be rewritten and supplemented — it is a space full of new possibilities. So what is "Chinese experience?" It is to confront people's feelings towards daily life, to inherit the rich memories of Chinese revolution, and to look into the internal oppressive structures active in our reality. Once "Chinese experience" of this type becomes public on a broad scale, the "glocal" characteristics of our Cultural Studies will come along with it.

6

Doing Cultural Studies

Critique, Pedagogy, and the Pragmatics of Cultural Education in Hong Kong

Stephen Ching-Kiu Chan

As a context-specific project, Cultural Studies in Hong Kong takes shape within a set of frameworks defined by the post-colony's proximity to the dynamic social and cultural changes in mainland China, as well as the accessible networks linking it to parallel developments in the Asia-Pacific region, where humanities education, cultural economy, and cultural citizenship all encounter new challenges under neo-liberalism.[1]

What can we learn from the teaching of culture as an institutionalized critical project? As I raise this rather mundane question, I am concerned about how the intellectual and educational project that grows in the name of Cultural Studies has allowed us to learn over the years about the role of critique, pedagogy, and pragmatics in the field of culture and education. While critique remains the basic task for all Cultural Studies practitioners, pedagogy becomes an increasingly indispensable part of its critical work in a variety of contemporary contexts, as the project defines and organizes itself into diverse programs for the effective reordering and affective reinvention of the ways we do culture today.

My discussion is organized around three crucial, formative moments and contexts framing my two decade-long career as a Cultural Studies scholar and teacher in Hong Kong: first, the context of academic work in which the progressive institutionalization of *critique* (even dissent) is subject to various social, economic and political changes throughout the late colonial and the post-colonial period since the 1980s;[2] second, the disciplinary context in which the growing needs and challenges of *pedagogy* interact with shifting institutional parameters and the relocation and reproduction of Cultural Studies as an interdisciplinary nexus of scholarship and applied practice (including its education) grounded in local history;[3] and third, the complex relationship between the ordinary practice of critical pedagogy in higher education under the trends of neo-liberalism, the constant evolvement and articulation of identity imaginaries among the local people, and the *technologies* (in Foucault's sense) of subjectivity and citizenship in the course of Hong Kong's quasi-democratic transition from a colony to a post-colony. As we consider the relevance of these contexts for the project of Cultural Studies, I want to highlight the functions and potentials of critique and pedagogy in cultural education today by outlining our *pragmatic engagements* with "the cultural" as work *useful* in the collective move toward a sustainable, critical intervention into the status quo under the new global order that has been shaping the social body on the ground.

The Moment of Critique

The first moment that concerns many of us is that of *critique*, generally taken to be the primary work of Cultural Studies. Indeed, it cannot be over-estimated how important its work and function have been for Cultural Studies. I begin by sketching the relevant socio-historical context for *doing* critique of the contemporary identity imaginary and the shaping of political subjectivity that is entailed by this work, which involves both the teaching of critique and the process of learning to engage in it.

Hong Kong's concern for its own political and cultural identity in relation to British colonial domination and Chinese national sovereignty can be traced back at least to the 1960s and 1970s. This was a period of rapid economic growth and gradual social reforms without democracy, when the colony could boast a rather rosy image of itself as one of the most prosperous cosmopolitan cities in Asia, thanks to the drastic changes on the Chinese mainland in the post-war era, the global Cold War, and over a century and a half of British colonial rule (1842–1997). Throughout the 1980s and 1990s, Hong Kong people developed through their everyday practices a contemporary, local set of identity imaginaries quite distinct from that of other Chinese urban centers. Ironically, at the time the younger, locally born generations — primarily children of the first refugees/migrants who had fled communism to come to the territory — would readily recognize the colony as their unlikely home caught in between a range of local, national, and trans/post-national positions. These hybrid articulations led to the shaping of a set of unique cultural sensibilities and dispositions peculiar to this contextualization of coloniality in East Asia, a result that is not matched in the history of Chinese modernity. It is through a critical discursive reconstruction of such complex social events and experiences that the specific and meaningful contexts can be laid out for the historical analysis of the production of subjectivity under the post-colonial condition. As the early works of Hong Kong Cultural Studies reveal, not only was the subject formation here deeply concerned with the form and substance of a new identity discourse and cultural sensibility, but it also became increasingly dependent on the transfiguration of a remarkable array of social movements and imaginaries — something that has become typical of Hong Kong's status as a "post-colony."

Only toward the closure of their colonial regime after 150 years of rule in the southern Chinese *entrepôt* did the governing British masters initiate a long-overdue process of democratization amidst the threat of "brain-drain" in the pre-Handover Hong Kong after the Tiananmen massacre of 1989. On June 4 that year, over a million Hong Kong people put down their habitual pragmatic and cynical masks and took to the streets in the central avenues of the city in demonstration against the tragic violence done in Beijing by the state against its young dissenters, whom the whole of the colony's now angry, petrified, and desperate people considered their own contemporaries and compatriots. Thereafter, during the 1990s, as the countdown to the 1997 Handover was anxiously anticipated in the colony — then newly branded as "Asia's World City" — the Britain-led last-minute call for democratization in Hong Kong was intensely resisted, furiously interrupted, and strategically contained by the Chinese authorities in Beijing — still an autocratic regime led by the Chinese Communist Party (CCP). As a result, Hong Kong people's high, collective expectation before 1997 for democratic political reform was unable to materialize. Added to the sentiments lingering behind the Hong Kong government's inability to address the full range of social demands generated by the neo-liberal policies, this widespread culture of frustration, cynicism, and despair has served to consolidate the rapidly politicized social discontents well beyond 1997 into an increasingly powerful anti-hegemonic force in the post-colony. Soon the outburst of energies negative and positive against the suffocating socio-political condition in the post-Handover era was triggered further by such external factors as the Asian financial crisis and the global SARS epidemic, and culminated in the unforgettable spectacle of the people's pro-democracy march on July 1, 2003, during which half a million people turned out in loud but solemn public demonstration of that very anxiety, discontent, and anger on the day of the establishment of the Special Administrative Region (SAR) government. As the dominant political institutions of the SAR cannot cope effectively with the growing populist demand, an unmistakable trend and sentiment of *dissent* prevailed, targeted at the widely visible proliferation of institutionalized injustice, as well as the obvious inadequacy of the half-baked representational political system specific to Hong Kong's post-colonial realities.

This set the stage for the emergence of Cultural Studies in the local context, which allows us to see the significance of dissent and understand the work of negotiation of cultural-ideological differences rooted in radical sources of identity, affect, and sensibility. Here was where such notions as hybridity, cultural translation, negotiation, contradiction, and social imagination gradually became attractive, almost *useful*, conceptual tools in the socio-political condition during the 1990s. Supplementing this sketch with a chronology of some of the major events in the last two decades relevant to our discussion of context here, let me offer a rough timeline for ease of reference (see p. 109).

Local Identity and Cultural Politics

Based on this chronology, one might consider how the subjects/citizens of Hong Kong have been made a people as they witness this tiny piece of homeland transformed from a somewhat alienating colonial haven to the ambivalent, semi-autonomous zone known as the HKSAR under the unprecedented "One Country, Two Systems" design. Traces of identity mixing, matching, and blending work together toward a changing cultural landscape, resulting in new configurations having to do with who we are, who I am, what you want, and why we care amid the rapidly evolving socio-political maelstrom in which the reordering and reinvention of the lived culture of people have materialized in the territory today.

Elsewhere I have outlined the contemporary cultural formation in Hong Kong through three modes of identity representation registered respectively in the local, the national, and the transnational imaginaries.[4] I try to map the politics of identity onto the trajectory, beginning with discourses of the local in the 1950s and 1960s which had developed coextensively with a regional culture of (Southern) Chineseness bearing as yet limited traces of distinct Hong Kong identity. What the local signifies has since undergone a major transformation with the tragic course of the Great Cultural Revolution on the Chinese mainland and the advance of the "glocal" mass media and an irreversible public sphere in the so-called Crown Colony. But the 1980s also saw the complex hybridization of the local through its rearticulation with a changing national,

#1	1989	June 4, Tiananmen, Beijing; massive demonstrations, Hong Kong
#2	1989	Hong Kong University (HKU): new Department of Comparative Literature
#3	1990	*Tiananmen Review* published
#4	1991	Hong Kong (colonial) government "rose garden" projects
#5	1994	The Chinese University of Hong Kong (CUHK) Department of English (Graduate Division in Comparative Studies): first MPhil thesis in Cultural Studies (on "The Uses of Sam Hui")
#6	1994–97	CUHK Program for Hong Kong Cultural Studies: first inter-institutional University Grants Commission-funded project in Cultural Studies
#7	1995	Lingnan College: Tuen Mun campus opened
#8	1997	Hong Kong Special Administrative Region (HKSAR) under China established following the end of British colonial rule
#9	1998	Asian financial crisis
#10	1999	Lingnan University: BA in Cultural Studies program launched
#11	1999	CUHK Department of Modern Languages and Inter-cultural Studies
#12	2000	Lingnan University: Department of Cultural Studies established
#13	2002	Lingnan University: first batch of BA Cultural Studies graduates
#14	2003	Lingnan University: Master of Cultural Studies program
#15	2003	SARS; July 1 anti-government people's march for democracy
#16	2004	CUHK: Department of Religious and Cultural Studies reorganized
#17	2005	Lingnan University: Postgraduate Diploma in Liberal Studies; Donald Tsang as the second Chief Executive; World Trade Organization meetings in Hong Kong
#18	2006	HKU: reconstitution of the various arts departments
#19	2007	Star Ferry demolished; resistance movement
#20	2008	Queen's Pier demolished; resistance movement
#21	2009	June Fourth twentieth anniversary memorial in Hong Kong
#22	2010	Anti-Hong Kong–Guangdong Express Rail Link demonstration
#23	2010	Lingnan University: tenth anniversary of Cultural Studies Department
#24	2012	Four-year university system to be instituted in Hong Kong

political *unconscious*. For most of the academics and intellectuals associated in one way or another with the early uptake of a Cultural Studies label and project in Hong Kong universities, this marginal but suggestive cultural-discursive space had opened up and multiplied in a context where people's subjectivity was shaped by the emergent political imagination and social struggle that grew following the bloody crackdown on the Beijing student movement at Tiananmen Square in 1989 (#1, *Timeline*). And once the handover of its sovereignty in 1997 was over with the first SAR government put in place (#8, *Timeline*), the end of the twentieth century led us on to a critical stage where *the local* — as the emergent, post-colonial cultural construct — transformed into something lurking in between the transnational and the post-national, thus shaping a social imaginary that unsettles the dominant discourse (and the political promise; #4, *Timeline*) of a "Hong Kong ruled by Hong Kong people."

In this light, for the local scholar interested in tracing the trajectory of the disciplinary development in the 1980s and 1990s (#2, 5, *Timeline*):

> Cultural Studies in the universities emerged in the form of a social practice in Hong Kong, linked on the one hand to the examination of social welfare, poverty, consumption, the urban/rural divide, domestic life, distribution and allocation of social and cultural resources, and so on, and on the other hand to the attempt to think through educational issues clustering around the promises and pitfalls of various curricular formations and their ideologies.[5]

To take the project with which I was associated as an example, *Cultural Imaginary and Ideology* and *Whose City?* were two such early attempts to deal with the politics of the local through the reinvention of the Hong Kong people's destiny in the form of critical narratives of the city.[6] They formed a part of fifteen titles in the series of projects organized and edited by the Program for Hong Kong Cultural Studies (HKCS) at the Chinese University of Hong Kong (CUHK) and published by Oxford University Press (China) in Hong Kong between 1994 and 1999 (#6, *Timeline*). As Director of the HKCS Program, a five-year cross-institutional research project aimed at initiating the critiques of local cultural politics and heritage, I was naturally aware that it had possibly been the first such collective work in Hong Kong Cultural Studies to be supported by the University Grants Committee, the major public funding body for higher education fully appointed by the government during the last few years of British colonial rule. Directly adopting the label of Cultural Studies, the project drew attention from the public through the mainstream media as

Hong Kong approached 1997. Critics were sensitive enough to note that any serious scholarly attempt to make the case for a critique of the imagination and formation of "Hong Kong cultural identity" was seen as a significant political practice in the relevant historical context.[7] In this light, the desire for Cultural Studies as a project was closely tied to the new intellectual endeavor to open up a discursive space for the exploration of cultural perspectives on the questions Hong Kong has had to face.[8]

Thus, when a minor work such as *The Practice of Affect* was popularly received, as it drew on a collaborative project in the cultural critique of local popular music by a group of graduate students based at the English Department of CUHK and affiliated with the HKCS program between 1994 and 1997,[9] our research involved working through cultural forms — such as the literary and filmic text — of the local in order to identify their textual and contextual links to social discontent, ideological regression, and political stagnancy of the time, thus isolating a certain critical twist in the dominant hegemony — the "status-quo" condition of Hong Kong. In a similar way, readings of local writers (Xi Xi, Wong Pik-wan) and filmmakers (Stanley Kwan, Wong Kar Wai) were significant exercises in critical textual practice associated with Hong Kong identity politics.[10] Artistic representations of the changing urban space, sensibility, memory, and identity were critiqued for their contemporary relevance to the local cultural formation. Several research projects in Cultural Studies were undertaken in between or at the margins of academic disciplines and departments during the 1990s. Putting this in perspective, Ma's account of the local institutionalization of Cultural Studies provides the following summative observation:

> Since the late 1990s, Cultural Studies has been formally incorporated into academic institutions as departments offering undergraduate and postgraduate degrees. The process of institutionalization demonstrates an interesting pattern of complicated struggles with mixed imperatives. There are three major institutional initiatives to build Cultural Studies programs in local universities [HKU, #2, *Timeline*; CUHK, #11, *Timeline*; Lingnan University, #12, *Timeline*], and they are directly or indirectly related to English departments.[11]

In short, while searching for the "limits" of critical cultural thinking and imagination, we address the question of relevance with a discourse that intervenes through the work of textual and contextual analyses. But as the practice of textual critiques proliferated with progressive programmatization, we began to ask what indeed Hong Kong cinema and its "cultural studies" could show or offer us, as part of an institutionalized critical apparatus. One answer lay in the way in which local films of the political "transitional period" (1984–97) were deemed capable of evoking, intellectually, the chaotic, formless condition of life under post-coloniality.[12] Films such as those making up the fantasmatic genre of *wuxia* (swordplay) were read as "unorthodox social investments that are irreducibly creative in responding to changes in our history, politics and social attitudes"; allegorical reading, or the textual strategy of "reading otherwise," was highlighted for its critical function in managing our imagination for our past, present, and future.[13] Again, the scholarly focus is on a certain political logic ("unconscious"), if not necessity ("imagination"), in most works of cultural critique.

The gradual opening up of a range of local orientations for Cultural Studies had in the meantime prompted comparative work in the field of humanities (Chinese-based comparative literature, English-based literary/cultural criticism) to look for new meanings, new directions, and a new mission. Since the 1970s and 1980s, literary comparatists like myself were tempted to bring to the field of cross-cultural studies readings of various cultural traces in a wider range of texts, particularly as these had been disciplined in the changing discursive and sociopolitical conditions of Hong Kong (#5, *Timeline*). Both the cultural critic and the academic reader would want to analyze "texts" of one kind or another — from *Dream of the Red Chamber* to Lu Xun, and from Xi Xi to Ann Hui or Stephen Chow — against the shifting contexts of communication mediating everyday Hong Kong cultural experiences. In retrospect, I think such scholarly initiatives and intellectual efforts, together with the difficulty, limitation, and frustration that often accompanied hard disciplinary negotiations and confrontations (if not combats), has driven some to seek to put forth programs with alternative critical approaches and long-term institutional objectives.[14] Hence, on the ground, the degree of intervention of any critical attempts in the contemporary reading of culture must be appreciated in relation to both the institutional context and the socio-historical formation concerned — such as, for instance, in the case of the English Department conflict at the Chinese University of Hong Kong where I taught from 1988 to 1997 (#5–6, *Timeline*). The department had no doubt pushed Cultural Studies into a dissenting project in which disciplinary constraints and institutional red tape served to contain the research initiatives and intellectual energies that produced the critiques of the local to which I referred (Research personnel involved in the HKCS Program based at CUHK at the time, including Wing-Sang Law, Po-Keung Hui, Siu Leung Li, and Iam-Chong Ip, were years later to join the Department of Cultural Studies at Lingnan University — see #6, 7, 12, *Timeline*).

Dissent as Context: The Turn to Pedagogy

Significantly, in Hong Kong dissent has continued to grow in a social context that poses challenges to the city's cultural-political position in contemporary Chinese history. Since 1997, the flows of people and their ideas, beliefs, and sentiments have moved in an increasingly fluid pattern. With an ever-changing logic and momentum, a series of spectacular events have left major marks on the formative phase of post-coloniality in the city, leaving traces on the fabrics of the social body. The Asian financial crisis (1998; #9, *Timeline*) and the SARS epidemic (2003; #15, *Timeline*) were no doubt critical moments of traumatic social spectacle, in which the fluidity of life underscored the context for the growth of the local people's new collective bonding. Rarely in Hong Kong — a unique polity and social body in history ruled by an institutionalized network of "collaborative colonial power"[15] — would people from all walks of life be allowed to come together in sharing a chain of life-threatening and life-shocking experiences under the specific post-colonial condition. A certain pattern of crucial "disjuncture" has now intervened in the social fabric.[16] This collective cultural experience carried rare historical significance; it also brought lasting social and political implications, resulting in transformation of the way the cultural dynamic of civic life works. Thus, amid the still-evolving global economy in the twenty-first century, the order of things moved uneasily back to the regular mode of operation as the post-1997 SAR struggled to recover from the growing impacts of the disjuncture the local people had come to experience.

Meanwhile, within the initial institutional set-up of Cultural Studies as an undergraduate degree since 1999 (#10, *Timeline*), one motivated by the desire to articulate the rather young project to a concrete educational program, we ask questions of pedagogy on the ground: How can we teach all that is implied by the discipline to our students? In developing the degree of Cultural Studies, to what extent have we been able to teach the students the gist of what we want to accomplish with a "critique?" A certain tendency toward social insensitivity and resistance to radical changes became the prominent focus of public discourse, especially in the years leading up to the 1997 Handover and the period immediately following it. At the core of post-colonial governance is, crucially, an issue of cultural change.

Historically, under colonialism, generations of Hong Kong students had an obscure sense of their cultural relationship with modern China because the British-led local government had excluded Chinese texts (literature, art, films) from 1911 to 1949 from the local school curriculum for decades, up until the 1990s. For young people to acquire a sense of identity, they need to have a firm hold of how Hong Kong has become what it is today *culturally*. This is so because we have not had that component in our education or in our social memory for a prolonged stretch of time.[17] Hence the approach to culture goes beyond simply the work of ordinary as well as dissenting voices (text) and their histories (context), and encompasses these as they have been manifested and become embedded in concrete local cultural practices that take the form of linguistic, literary, aesthetic, filmic, popular, economic, political, as well as other significant modes of representation. Through diversely shaped social experiences, organic intellectual practices and academic Cultural Studies were drawn to each other, thereby creating overlapping social spaces for cultural critique. These practices became mutually influential and, in some cases, closely tied together — as the cases of the post-June Fourth Hong Kong alternative intellectual project *Tiananmen Review* of the early 1990s (#3, *Timeline*), and that of the HKCS Program of the mid-1990s would testify (#6, *Timeline*).

Since 2000, however, people have been frustrated by the slow pace of social and political reform, and discontented with the government's incompetence in handling the deep-rooted problems in our civil bureaucracy, governance and democratic development. Few could see how, in the ways the existing system works, any fundamental change in the dominant practices can occur to solve the problems. People have been trained to live according to the status quo fixed by the elitist, technocratic system of governance, including that of the educational institution as an effective arm of the state. Hui has discussed this changing context of dissent in terms of populism and cynicism.[18] It is clear that when governance becomes ineffective, negative impacts change the way people identify who they are as members of the community. Public consciousness and cultural subjectivity dwell on how a critical stance on governance could embody what people think, and help to shape and articulate what they want. Their acute critique of the dominant hegemony helps define who they are, what they want, and how they would choose to act at the level of the local community.

This explains why the recent social movement triggered by the heritage preservation and urban activism surrounding the government's demolition of the
Star Ferry in 2007 (#19, *Timeline*) and the Queen's Pier in 2008 (#20, *Timeline*)
have taken on momentum through the latest currents in the civil society on
issues directly related to people's livelihood (such as urban renewal and town
planning), culminating in the strong protest over the Guangdong–Hong Kong
Express Rail Link plan in 2010 (#22, *Timeline*) with crowds of young people
(including many graduates and students of Cultural Studies) demonstrating at
the forefront. The movement has taken off through the way the young people
articulate into their activist agenda how people's local identity and community
values are threatened by the dominant currents in the city's socio-economic
development.[19]

Now with the colonizer removed from the scene, the equation in which *the
self* is articulated and defined in relation to *the other* must be reconsidered. We
need to understand the effective alienation of the local community during the
1980s and 1990s, after the signing of the Sino-British Joint Declaration in 1984.
There has been no shortage of social, cultural, and ideological crises during the
transitional period between 1984 and 1997. The mainstream pro-establishment
discourse remains conservative, and the government's judgments differed substantially from those of the local community, whose commitment to heritage
conservation has evolved through engagement with such critical issues as local
identities (their cultural significance and historical value) and the location of
those *community-based* identities (their actual social situation and specific
spatial coordinates within the community). Even after colonialism, the local
Chinese-Hong Kong subjects have not necessarily identified themselves as part
of an integral community, whether taken as the once colonized, or as the newly
decolonized. Hence those adopting the hybrid perspective on the changing
local culture and history continue to express themselves through a variety of
cultural forms, such as literature, theatre, dance, music, film and video, comics,
mixed media, exhibition, installation, happenings, and so on. Many look at
1997 and what comes after with ambivalent anticipation and hope, as well as a
deep sense of discontent and disorientation (#8, 15, 21–22, *Timeline*).

If the problem for Hong Kong is indeed culture, as the recent trends in
social discontent and struggles reveal, the issue for Cultural Studies is not so
much "critique" itself as its relevance — or better, its *uses*. With implications
for the shaping of post-colonial subjectivity, the work of critique at the socio-
political plane of operation is called into question. The heritage-driven social

movement since around the mid-2000s has grown in the form of a challenge to existing ways of heritage conservation and cultural management, but also as a test as much of social representation and cultural identity as of political institution.[20] The power transition in 1997 gave rise to a drastic crisis in *subjectivity* and shift in *sensibility*.

This crisis has become increasingly evident in the public space, as contemporary cultural practices have set in with sharper socio-historical consciousness since the Handover. In this light, one begins to appreciate the specific difficulty in the *negotiation* of cultural and ideological differences rooted in deep sources of identity and subjectivity. This marks the changing social context of dissent for Cultural Studies today, with our critical subject reconfirmed in both senses of the term: as object of critique, and as the subject (the student as much as the teacher) of that same act of critique. The so-called "post-80s" generation — that is, young people born in the 1980s — has become deeply interested in the critical issues of identity,[21] such as: Whose heritage is it (with reference to the issue of access to the rich resources of our culture)? Who has the authority when it comes to defining the cultural and historical significance of the built environment and lived cultures in our community? Who has the right to claim ownership on matters of culture and heritage? The struggle over the preservation and management of heritage, framed in the material condition of the built urban space of Hong Kong — where land premium and real estate prices are inevitably high — reaches deep down to the roots of Hong Kong's colonial history and culture of governance. The logic of history is revisited today with increasing critical insights drawn from the changing social visions, cultural values and community aspirations of our time after colonialism.

These concerns reveal the social impact and political relevance of the heritage-driven social movement: a growing discontent but also engagement with the dominant trends of urban imaginaries and redevelopment policies in Hong Kong. They also focus our attention on the way urban and cultural projects are tied up with the work of heritage management and cultural planning. They return us to the fundamental questions raised in the emergent social context of dissent: What is culture for Hong Kong? How is culture formed through the historical moments and trajectories its people have experienced? What is the process in the cultural production and circulation of meaning throughout various historical stages? While, institutionally, Cultural Studies helps to shape the discourse and legitimize the practice of Hong Kong culture in the academy

[#24, *Timeline*], with the emphasis on the representation of dissent at the core of its educational project, its intellectual thrust is pointed firmly at the hegemonic forces working to contain the very liberating cause that distinguishes the initial moments of Cultural Studies. Since the late 1990s:

> [T]he major form of expression of Cultural Studies in Hong Kong has been the convergence of Cultural Studies with Hong Kong Studies. Cultural Studies has been appropriated … to legitimize indigenous culture … Furthermore, the process of developing Cultural Studies into a program offering degrees suggests the unavoidable differentiation between a body of theoretical knowledge (cultural studies) and a topic of inquiry (Hong Kong Studies) … [C]ultural Studies will continue to be a project which valorizes local culture, but there will be a new thrust to transform Cultural Studies into an education project for *local university students*.[22]

At this point, we may try to reorganize the crux of our question thus: What specific mode of teaching is involved in the kind of cultural critique we do as a program in Cultural Studies? What does it mean for our students in the local contexts to have to learn — and to have learnt — to "do critique" as a part of their training and education provided in the name of this emerging discipline? For substantially local cultural critiques have added up to "a declaration of *dissent* against any official discourse of 'success' (ill-)promised for Hong Kong by both the departing colonialists, the coming nationalists, and the circling globalists." Now we can learn from the lesson of pedagogy as we rethink how the challenge for our project was in part to identify a "shared secular idealism that pulsates critique and hope at the same time."[23]

Critique as Pedagogy: The Lingnan Project

In *Culture: A Reformer's Science*, Bennett examines two crucial issues: first, the suggestion that a pedagogic "turn to Cultural Studies" presumes a commitment to nurturing student resistance; and second, the implied "danger" in the continuous institutionalization of Cultural Studies.[24] He foregrounds the contextual linkage between two crucial social roles in Cultural Studies education: the student (the novice scholar) on the one hand, and the (mature) critical intellectual on the other. Borrowing his insight, I want to stress that cultural mediation is a key function of the Cultural Studies project, seen as part of an effective Foucauldian program — that is, an instituted machinery with its pragmatic work in academic knowledge production and pedagogic subject formation:

> Cultural Studies raises questions about the kinds of knowledge and
> training that are to be imparted to students; about the occupations these
> will equip them for; about the roles they will play as future intellectu-
> als; and about how these roles will stand in relation to the role played by
> intellectuals trained in adjacent fields. These are vital questions, and if
> Cultural Studies is to have a worthwhile future, they are ones that need to
> be answered clear-sightedly, taking into account where Cultural Studies
> students are likely to be recruited from, what their career destinies are
> likely to be, and what roles they can intelligibly be expected to play as
> intellectuals in diverse fields of governmental and private employment.[25]

Yet, as the prospect for a post-colonial Cultural Studies looks uncertain in
Hong Kong, can we usefully handle the kind of "secular idealism" believed to
be driving the project, and make the best out of the shared ambivalence of hope
and critique in the Cultural Studies *classroom*? More importantly, what would
it mean to our students to have learnt what we thought we had taught them
through the work of critique? And what did *that* critical process of mediation
do to them, and what did that make them *do*?

Itself the exemplification of a complex socio-pedagogic process about ways
of doing culture, Lingnan's BA Cultural Studies is a curriculum that examines
the ordinary but complex teaching and learning process in the inter-generational and trans-disciplinary transfer of cultural literacy and knowledge in the
pragmatic contexts of schools, artistic groups, NGOs, and creative enterprises,
as well as the academy.[26] The Cultural Studies Department at Lingnan has
become a distinction of some sort for the university, which has positioned itself
as a liberal arts institution with a focus on undergraduate teaching and "whole
person development" since it moved into the Tuen Mun campus in 1995 (#7,
Timeline). But the department is known also for its clear and close alignment
with dissent as a social position in the Hong Kong civil society and social
movements, not least among the "post-80s" generation,[27] with its programs
"uniquely tailored to the need for producing an intellectual — and dissenting — class sensitive to cultural and political matters in Hong Kong, China,
and the world."[28] These emphasize "transdisciplinary" work that involves the
development of socio-political analysis, cultural and aesthetic sensitivity, as
well as intellectual currents and historical consciousness. Let me reiterate that
in our field today, as we engage ourselves routinely in multi-layered mediatory
work when we teach and do research, we negotiate constantly with others, often
through efforts that deal with the various ideological and social differences
channeling the many sources of identity, affect, and sensibility we encounter

inside and outside of our work, our office — and, more importantly, inside and outside of the classroom in which we try to transfer knowledge, demonstrate what critical acts are, and generate impacts on the student about *how* critique works.

There is no doubt that in Hong Kong we have yet to come to grips with the form and implication of decolonization, if only in its specific cultural-pedagogic mode. For here, the general features that are significant in the educational environment at large include (1) the hegemony of educational policies as symbolic policies, (2) the over-emphasis of pedagogical approaches in the local educational reform, and (3) the reinforcement of cynicism and cynical practice.[29] Under such conditions, one of the Lingnan department's strengths is the capacity of its unique positioning and innovative curriculum to attract a highly dedicated faculty (#12, *Timeline*). It has a strong concentration of expertise in locally based Cultural Studies, with teaching and research organized around textual and contextual issues on the ground. The interdisciplinary curriculum creates synergies between these fields of expertise and activity, and a crucial unifying force of the program is the shared commitment to undergraduate teaching and community engagement, as well as to the ideals of some radical version of "liberal education" (#7, 10, 24, *Timeline*). Indeed, with the Lingnan project, Cultural Studies is realized in:

> an always-institutionalised set of practices whose functioning has, in part, to be assessed in terms of their role in organising a new set of relations between educational institutions and new generations of students who have either lacked, or been unreceptive to the value of, traditional forms of cultural capital.[30]

It is here that we ought to bring into perspective the issue of student learning and seriously reconsider the pragmatic question of (student) subjectivity from the vantage point of Cultural Studies pedagogy, beyond the approach adopted by the usual teacher-centered mode of exposition through exemplary forms of cultural critique. What the moment of pedagogy has presented for our BA Cultural Studies program is as much a pragmatic as a theoretical question. For in approaching the local cultures of modernity and post-modernity, Cultural Studies is about understanding ways of shaping subjectivities in the future, of remembering and representing the kind of local history or popular memory with which local people have grown up, and of rethinking the status of the contemporary cultural production and reproduction. Organized as a set of critical practices grounded in discursive, material, and socio-historical contexts,

Cultural Studies plays a key role in shaping the students' understanding of self, identity, community, and the contexts of their cultural significance. With a context-specific pedagogy, the Lingnan program emphasizes a student-centered approach to doing Cultural Studies, in a field where high value is placed on the interfaces between the intellectual program, engagement with the social world, and critical intervention through practices of the self. Here, the access to and understanding of context allows the individual learner to shape the relevant condition of learning. In attempting to engage in a specific critique, for instance, the novice scholar would begin to realize how learning takes place within and around the self, in relation to the context at issue. Any context can be useful pedagogically — whether it relates one to the cultural industry, cultural policy, or community dynamics; or to school, family, or popular culture as a social platform for subject-formation. A key principle behind such ideals, I suppose, is to nurture *in practice* a sense of engagement by the students in the pedagogic process through such projects as the Student Internship program, an innovative scheme involving student placement in community, media, and professional organizations. Another example is our participation in the market-oriented self-financed programs of study — the Master of Cultural Studies (#14, *Timeline*), or later, the Postgraduate Diploma in Liberal Studies (#17, *Timeline*) — with both programs allowing working cultural practitioners to take up Cultural Studies as a project alongside their ongoing career tracks in the areas of media, education, and community work. It is true that our students have much more to learn (about cultures, about themselves) through these interfaces with the real-world contexts of cultural practice. Likewise, I believe we have learnt much ourselves from this experience about the demands of our times on Cultural Studies as an educational project.[31]

The Pragmatic Outlook: Agency, Education, and the Sustainability of Culture

For the Cultural Studies community generated through the Lingnan project, nurturing local culture (its talents as well as industry) becomes a strategy many would adopt to meet the challenge of the global "knowledge economy" today. This offers us, in the new area of urban cultural policy and creativity studies, two specific perspectives: first, to take culture as *symbolic resources* embodied in the material form of cultural *products* and *practices*; and second, to take culture firmly as the *way of life* and *civic process* embedded in the people-driven, *lived* community world of experience. Post-colonial Hong Kong would definitely need to ask how pragmatic it is for us to help bring culture, with all its knowledge, perspectives and strategies, to our students for the preparation of new vocations, thus contributing to local cultural changes and developments.[32] Through our daily interface with the social and governmental practices rooted in their discursive, material, and institutional contexts, Cultural Studies becomes *more*, not less, productive in its pedagogic mode of operation — that is, in its effective facilitation of the subject's coming to terms with "identity," "subjectivity," "sexuality," "community," and so on, as well as the contexts of their hegemonic functions. As such it tends to favor a student-centered approach in its pedagogy, so as to help engage the subject concerned *pragmatically* with the challenges of our diversely contextualized social hegemonies, under which *governmentality* works, *learning* takes place, and the individual's *subjectivity* takes shape. Often by phases, the "self" is made and remade as a "critical" agent, possibly targeted and energized by the pedagogy that introduced the individual to the work, role, and agency of critique in the first instance.

Thus, approaching the condition of the "practicable" in the fields of local social engagement — under which students, regardless of their class and social identities, will learn to do critique — I refer to the issue of social agency in light of critical cultural practices in ordinary pedagogical set-ups, and offer to change the context so as to develop a pragmatic politics for what we do. My own strategic goal is to explore Cultural Studies projects as a *useable* option in cultural education (#13–14, 17, 24, *Timeline*), thus addressing pedagogy as a key to understanding our roles and functions within the present institutional set-up, in schooling as in all sorts of post-secondary programs available under academic capitalism. I would like to suggest how the analysis and engagement of students' pragmatic problems would pose crucial questions for Cultural Studies as a locally grounded critical intellectual project across geo-political borders. To be pragmatic — or to be engaged with a "prosaic politics" (in Bennett's words) — means to be concerned "with practical consequences" in matters pertaining to "the affairs of a state or community,"[33] or to any social programs that embody the technologies of subjectivity and citizenship. Teaching Cultural Studies today, we work with many collaborators, through interfaces between the disciplinary apparatus (operating at the moment of pedagogy) and real-world cultural engagements (realizable only at the moment of pragmatics). By articulating Gramsci's hegemony project to Foucault's project of intervening within the field of "governmentality," our critical and pedagogic work is mediated through and for the community and professional networks concerned, covering areas ranging from citizenship initiatives, novel concepts of global peace, and school curriculum reform to cultural policy strategy.

Hence Cultural Studies can be organized as a materialist, pedagogic project in cultural mediation with a pragmatic outlook on the relation between power and culture. But how does one teach *articulation* not just as theory, but as a model of practice? Indeed, how does one teach *intervention* as a strategy to foster the subject's engagement with culture? How can we enable students to come out of the pedagogic process capable of changing their context for the better? To put this in a contemporary local setting, Hong Kong governance under post-colonial capitalism tends to reduce public commons to the efficient abstraction of space. As our accessible public places are fast disappearing, they give way to the dominating work of finance and real estate speculation. This privileging of property managerialism in our social fabric encroaches into the public life of communal cultural imagination. Moreover, Hong Kong is in the midst of putting in place the massive West Kowloon Cultural District plan, while the community expects the mega-project to focus on the development of culture, allowing for mixed land use for commerce, entertainment, residence, and tourism. Accordingly, critical projects in policy research and development become urgent and practical for the advancement of an effective strategy in urban cultural planning. Our critique and pedagogy ought to be effective in allowing the students to be able to deal with the relationship between the globalization of culture and the changing roles of civil society, as well as the tension between consumption, social justice, and cultural citizenship — and all this through a perspective on the sustainable development of people's culture.

The kind of post-colonial subjectivity to which I alluded earlier must be contextualized in terms of the politics of resistance, which opens up the pedagogical space — a space for engaging with the culture and politics of dissent — and leads to social agency shaped by a governmental interest in the cultural management of the population. This subjectivity has been reshaped through the formation of a new "locality" for Hong Kong. The time has come for the Cultural Studies project to take on the pragmatic challenge to engage productively with the exercise of power in relation to such a cultural formation. And the destiny of Cultural Studies thus allows "everyday life and cultural experience to be fashioned into instruments of government via their inscription in new forms of teaching and training."[34] From the perspective of pedagogy and the continual need for critique to inform, and be informed by, the politics of pedagogy, we must work to make *sustainability* a key in our institutionalization process over the long run. For it is not enough to plan to achieve "outcomes" — or indeed "excellence" — in this or that domain; we need also to ensure that teachers and students alike have the time, the support, the resources, the energy, and the morale to act upon any such plans.[35]

As researchers involved in the production and circulation of meanings, we are fully aware of and critically concerned about the institutional nature, function, and structure of the kind of knowledge we help put in place via our research. Indeed, we want to argue that getting to know the process and intervening (by playing a pragmatic, mediatory role) in it *is a critically sensitive and productive way of participating in the process itself* — as this is the case in the curriculum set to run as classroom practices within the educational reform. As discussed by Chan and Hui, in the interdisciplinary work of Cultural Studies, our pragmatically oriented action research involves the analysis of the cultural process, through which we investigate the production and circulation of meaning among the various "stakeholders" in the educational reform. In our case, the various processes of *knowledge-formation* are contextualized in the classroom, the curriculum, the social process of pedagogy, and the institutional condition for the educational reform (via the school subject of Liberal Studies).[36] One key intellectual reason is to transform the whole pedagogic practice from a teacher-centered to a student-centered mode, thus allowing the student to engage proactively with learning, and to own the learning process. Hence, if there is no guarantee that the "teaching-related" work is relevant and aligned with the educational objectives, it is conceivable that coordinating extra-curricular activities, performing administrative duties, and communicating more interactively with fellow teachers, parents, and employers may be useful in improving the overall environment and generating more positive learning opportunities for the students. For that, the teacher might just need to coordinate and negotiate more effectively with the relevant parties in the process. This involves a lot of specific mediatory work normally not regarded as education related (#23, *Timeline*).

During the course of this self-reflection, I have referred to the historical, institutional, and intellectual factors that shape Cultural Studies as an alternative field and program of disciplinary studies, initially addressing the issues of cultural identity/politics. In the spirit of reflexivity, I underscore the problems in the current uses of culture for Hong Kong during the last two decades, from the point of view of Cultural Studies as a critically inclined disciplinary (*teaching*) apparatus (#16, 18, 23, *Timeline*), against the context in which hope has become a scarcity. The proliferation of cynicism is no doubt the "outcome" of the repetition of routine and ritualized practices in the education system (in our schools and universities alike). Indeed, it is under such conditions that cynical subjects are produced, at both ends of the pedagogic process. The pressing task for critical intellectuals is therefore to create the condition for new pedagogic practices that could release cynical subjects from the trap of negativity, and to free them from the destructive emotions that perpetuate the hegemony within which it is extremely hard for people to think differently about the world, its possibilities and its accessibility.

At the end of the day, I would like to think that there is opportunity still for the pragmatic realization of our project, however discontinuous or non-effective it might appear in light of the existing condition of knowledge production and educational practice in which we must survive. Cultural education in the new times — like history for Nietzsche and Foucault — must be radical enough in combining discontinuity and effectivity, and in reshaping despair and hope into an intellectual and pedagogic project. In such a reordered perspective, all teachers and students of Cultural Studies will have a *pragmatic* role to play in allowing this knowledge project to reinvent itself effectively as a viable formation of dissenting positions in the contemporary context, via a program of critical, affective education.

7

Coordinates, Confusions, and Cultural Studies

Dai Jinhua

The Arrival of Cultural Studies in China

In the course of the 1980s, Cultural Studies emerged as one of the most popular of the humanities and social science disciplines in Europe and the United States. It is regarded as having waged a cultural war on the globalization of capitalism and the neo-liberalist/Washington consensus. However, ironically enough, the route traveled by Cultural Studies in regions outside Europe and the United States coincided with the spread of globalization. In fact, the introduction of Cultural Studies into China occurred simultaneously with the process of China's involvement in globalization.

During the post-Cold War period in the 1990s, Cultural Studies was introduced to the Chinese-speaking territories.[1] In light of the social realities of mainland China, Taiwan, and Hong Kong during that period, it could be argued that Cultural Studies arrived at the right time. When the West triumphed over communism and capital investments flowed rapidly into the non-capitalist "virgin land," an Americanized mass culture and corresponding cultural industry were born. In mainland China, Cultural Studies began at the same time when media corporations and consumer culture were expanding rapidly, and when Hollywood as a symbol of multinational (cultural) corporations embarked on recovering the "lost territory" in China. Cultural Studies was just in time, and in the right position, to explain and respond to these new developments. However, it could also be said that Cultural Studies arrived at the wrong time. This claim could be made because in the different Chinese-speaking territories Cultural Studies started to flourish just when the global structural basis of critical or leftist cultural practices disintegrated. Neo-liberal political practices construed "culture" as insignificant, in the name of the market. On the other hand, the expansion of cultural and creative industries led the way towards a consumerist lifestyle, which allowed the agenda of the Cold War winners to be maintained, but in an apolitical guise. In the 1980s, culture did play an important role during the so-called "period of great social change," as is evidenced by mainland Chinese campaigns such as "Reflections on History and Culture" (歷史文化反思運動) and "Cultural Fever" (文化熱). But Cultural Studies only really emerged when all these specific and effective political practices of culture had disappeared.

Today, the meaning and significance of "culture" have changed completely. When the battlefield of social and cultural criticism retreated to the universities and assumed the form of specialized discussions and the production of equally specialized knowledge, the vision of culture as social was buried by mass culture. The rise of a "knowledge economy" and of a "creative industry" allowed capitalists to engulf the vitality and creativity of culture at an unprecedented speed. It is also useful to mention post-modernism, which was introduced to the mainland slightly earlier than Cultural Studies, and ended up becoming the cynical theoretical background for developments in the post-revolutionary and post-1989 era. Cultural Studies tried to respond to all these phenomena, but first it needed to find a way out of the local reality, which was full of obstacles and winding paths.

Keyword Confusion

In major European languages, the word "Culture" is a huge and complicated signifier. Cultural Studies, which emerged in the United Kingdom at the beginning of the Cold War, needed in the first instance to face the word "culture" and actually benefited from its rich meanings. In mainland China, when Cultural Studies encountered the reality of mass culture (*dazhong wenhua* in Chinese) and the cultural industry, the first complicated keyword to be evoked was *dazhong* (大眾, literally "the people"), with its specific local historical background. The growth or rebirth of Chinese mass culture in the global context occurred at the edge of a cleft between history and reality, and what links the two, and illustrates the social change in the keywords that have been used all along. According to the premises of Cultural Studies, the term *dazhong wenhua* (大眾文化) in Chinese corresponds at once to the English "popular culture" and "mass culture" (both keywords in Cultural Studies). The integration of "popular culture" and "mass culture" in *dazhong wenhua* departs from the basic position of Cultural Studies, at least in its British variant, which opts for "popular culture" rather than "mass culture" as a means of identifying certain research targets. The point of opting for "popular culture" is to highlight (working-)class issues, the subjective actualization of the people in the act and process of cultural consumption, and the opening up of the discursive arena of culture to daily life — especially as it is lived by workers. Chinese Cultural Studies researchers made an effort to draw a distinction between "popular culture" and "mass culture" by translating "popular culture" into *liuxing wenhua* (流行文化) or *tongsu wenhua* (通俗文化). Yet these translations just led to more confusion, because while *liuxing wenhua* or *tongsu wenhua* illustrate the characteristics of "popular culture," they efface the meanings of "of the people, for the people and by the people" carried by the word "popular." Moreover, when we translate "popular culture" as *liuxing wenhua* or *tongsu wenhua*, we also cut off all the resonances with "populism," another word that has been key in terms of understanding the history of modern intellectual and social movements. The debate surrounding "cultural populism" constitutes an important chapter in the history of British Cultural Studies.[2] On the other hand, when we use *dazhong wenhua* to translate "mass culture," the historical background carried by the word "mass" disappears.[3] At the same time, what also disappears are the multiple discourses and myths of "mass society," all of which offer probing criticisms of a newly developed capitalist society from an aristocratic standpoint. These intellectual backgrounds form the basis of Leavisism, which is directly related to British Cultural Studies.

Sometimes the above meanings lost in translation can be slightly recaptured in the Chinese term *dazhong* (大眾) and related terms like *laoku dazhong* (勞苦大眾, toiling masses) or *gong nong dazhong* (工農大眾, factory workers and farmers), but the vastly divergent history and reality of China resulted in very different and complicated cultural and social practices. In fact, in modern Chinese *dazhong* carries fewer negative connotations than the word "mass" does in English. Twentieth century Chinese history made *dazhong* a term of unquestionable virtue, as is reflected in current usage. This is the case in spite of the connotations of *zhong* in a Chinese Buddhist context. As a word of foreign origin *zhong* (眾, mass) is sometimes understood as the opposite of *fo* (佛, Buddha) and can be derived into negative terms like *yong zhong* (庸眾, the vulgar people) or *wu he zhi zhong* (烏合之眾, a mob), which means something like "masses" in English. The sense of virtue that is associated with the term *zhong* mainly stems from the adoption and spread of the term by Marxism and (especially) from the historical practices of the Chinese communist revolution. The term appeared everywhere from the 1950s to the 1970s. The term *dazhong* signified the idea of the master of society and of the historical subject (*laoku dazhong* or *gong nong dazhong*). It was sometimes used interchangeably with *gong nong bing* (工農兵, workers, peasants and soldiers), more of a Maoist term. *Zhong* was placed in the middle of the spectrum of terms used to describe people, which ranges from *renmin* (人民, which is entirely positive) to *qunzhong* (群眾, which is relatively negative). Thus, in the theory of socialist humanism (or revolutionary humanism), *dazhong* became synonymous with "the overwhelming majority" and had unquestionable legitimacy. When the term *dazhong* was used in relation to culture, it was mobilized in debates on the popularization of art and literature aimed at defining their functions in modern society. Another debate on the "language of the masses" (大眾語, *dazhong yu*)[4] was a major event in modern cultural history, and illustrated the controversial nature of modern Chinese/colloquial Chinese. This debate brought to the surface a specific issue concerning the reception of cultural products, for as Mao Zedong declared in his "Talks at the Yan'an Forum on Art and Literature," "[To be] loved by the masses is the basic criterion of Literature and Art criticism."

Interestingly, when *dazhong wenhua*, characterized by commodities, consumption and amusement, arrived in mainland China in the 1990s, the modern history of the term *dazhong* and the absolute standard of "loved by the masses of people" provided the discursive support for its legitimacy. What belongs to *dazhong* must be just, what is "loved by the masses" must be good. Ironically, the mass culture products that were first imported into China were all reproductions of US mass culture sold at relatively high prices. On account of this, the first receivers/consumers were not, and could not be, the majority of "urban China," let alone the whole country. As a result, the first prominent mass culture products to come under the scrutiny of Cultural Studies were those enjoyed by only a minority group. These products included Hollywood movies, Hong Kong *mo lei tau* culture, fashion, advertisements, mega-cities, pubs, cafés, lofts, magazines introducing luxurious lifestyles, and computer games. The consumers in question consisted of the Chinese new middle class who were once given the title "petit-bourgeoisie"; they mainly lived in Chinese first-class cities (Beijing, Shanghai, and cities around the Zhujiang delta). They were young, well educated, and worked in foreign corporations or famous state enterprises. Most of them belonged to the first generation to have grown up under the one-child policy. They were the winners or survivors of a Chinese examination-oriented educational system. They shared and enjoyed the individualistic culture characterized by consumerism. When the term *dazhong wenhua* was used inaccurately to refer to the consumption practices of a minority culture, the result was the suppression of the real *dazhong* (majority of the people) and their local mass culture: traditional newspapers, especially evening papers; popular magazines targeting second- or third-class cities or middle-to low-income groups (for example *The Reader*, *The Girlfriend* and *The Family*); TV series, especially those that were not circulated through the internet and had no talking points; and films mainly screened in villages. None of these cultural products was given priority by members of the Chinese Cultural Studies circle who worked on *dazhong wenhua*.

The phenomenon of "minority culture" being mistaken as *dazhong* did not occur only in China, for many newly modernized countries experienced something similar when they became caught up in globalization. In the 1990s, the Chinese concept of *dazhong wenhua* was based on Western, or more accurately US, mass culture. In a sense, the globalization of culture was equivalent to Americanization. Of course, Hong Kong and Taiwan — both places where the development of mass culture was relatively mature — served as an important window too. In these exporting countries or regions of mass culture, the middle class is the major consumption group and also the overwhelming majority in society. It was during the Cold War and the era of financial capitalism that this middle class-dominated social structure took shape. While the established social structure was seen as "just," it was in fact based on an increasingly unjust pyramidal global structure.

It is important to point out that the mass culture of developed countries is destined, when reproduced in developing countries, to become a minority culture. Consumers belonging to a minority group bestow a sense of elite culture, or a standard of elite taste, on these products of popular culture. This phenomenon of mass culture becoming minority culture demonstrates the hegemonic position of Western — or, more accurately, American — culture. Globalized capital and the mobilization of the elite class combine to create the imagined identity of "world citizen" and a culture of consumption that works everywhere in the world. What this process demonstrates is that the new Chinese middle class finds the basis for its self-identification and self-imagination in the construction of mass culture in the era of globalization. But apart from this, it needs to be emphasized that the new Chinese middle class has a natural affinity with Western mass culture. The reason for this is twofold:

on the one hand, members of the new Chinese middle class identify themselves with the status and order established by globalized capitalism; on the other, in this unified capitalistic world, members of the young and new Chinese middle class actually occupy a position in the social structure that is similar to the one occupied by the mature American middle class in the United States. As a result, they are able to share essentially the same representational value system, the same form of self-regulation, and the same everyday lifestyles.

The relationship of the term *dazhong* with communist history gave *dazhong wenhua* an entry pass into mainland China, yet paradoxically the arrival of *dazhong wenhua* also symbolized the end of a political era. As the subject of "literature and art for the workers, farmers and soldiers" in the 1950s to 1970s, *dazhong* provided a justification on the discursive level for the cultural industry and the *dazhong wenhua* of the 1990s. However, the deeper reason motivating the acceptance of this new *dazhong wenhua* was that it practiced a new agenda of apolitical cultural politics. In this new trend, entertainment took the place of politics, while marketing took the place of propaganda. These substitutions explain why Chinese commercial cinema was once dubbed "amusement film," and why various elite intellectuals took the initiative to promote *dazhong wenhua*. In this context, the Chinese term *dazhong wenhua* usually was used interchangeably with the term "civil culture" (*minjian wenhua*, 民間文化), which is different from folk culture. *Minjian* (民間, civil) was a keyword in the 1990s for the Chinese intelligentsia. The term finds its roots in the discourse of the public sphere and civil society, and its meaning is the opposite of "official." To arouse the idea of justice embedded within the term *minjian* as the underlying message of *dazhong* in a new social imaginary was to utilize the confrontational characteristics of *minjian* against what was specifically official.

The Role of Chinese *Dazhong Wenhua*

It was in the context of all these complications about keywords that Chinese *dazhong wenhua* made its appearance at the beginning of the 1990s. The timing of its arrival was by no means a coincidence. In fact, between the tragic end of the 1980s and the flamboyant arrival of the 1990s, there was a blank period that lasted almost three years. *Dazhong wenhua* appeared quietly in that period to fill in all the "blankness." It then continued to expand, to the point of dominating the cultural horizon at the turn of the century. This "blankness" refers to the gap between two grand narratives. The period in question was marked by the 1980s coming to an end, and by the end of the Cold War. It was also a time when a feeble Chinese society and equally feeble Chinese culture lost their anchor, a time defined by an ideological vacuum. The dominant discourse of legitimacy was seriously challenged, to the extent that it no longer functioned. At the same time, the confrontational discursive system of the 1980s was operative at a subterranean level, but unable genuinely to break through. As a result, the Chinese cultural arena at the beginning of the 1990s was full of "delirious aphasia," but the stage was empty. When Chinese *dazhong wenhua* finally stepped on to the stage, it had to take up many important tasks: to vent social misery, but also to assuage it; to use cynicism to alleviate the sense of trauma and aphasia; to reconstruct human desires and rewrite the principles and standards of social lives; to cover up the exacerbated class divisions and social conflicts; and, finally, to identify and calm the hatred in society by manipulating the logic of the dominant narratives of the past. At that point, the country's image that had reached such a low point rose up again. In the 1980s, Chinese intellectuals endeavored to promote *dazhong wenhua* with the aim of confronting authority through an apolitical agenda; in the 1990s, *dazhong wenhua* successfully utilized its apolitical image at full capacity, to implement a cultural politics reflecting the risks of the times. By the beginning of the twenty-first century, *dazhong wenhua* had in effect assumed responsibility for constructing the new mainstream ideology. Its most significant function has been to fill in historical gaps imaginatively, to dismiss real differences, and to provide a new discourse of legitimacy.

One effective method along these lines was the activation of different mechanisms of forgetfulness for the purposes of displacing memories. In this context, many popular versions of historical stories were brought into the spotlight. Viewed in terms of the heights of their achievement, the Qin, Han, and Tang dynasties were narrativized. As such, they became substitutes for the late Ming and late Qing dynasties, and carriers of contemporary metaphors for reality — the representational vehicle for China's self-imagination. The dramatic representations of history (including modern and contemporary history) in the form of TV series and films provide imaginary solutions to conflicts that are real. Interestingly, it is popular culture — though not high culture — that supplies the new mainstream culture with an effective way of evading the bloodiness of history, of healing the multi-layered wounds of modern China, of "overcoming" the confrontations of the Cold War era, and of "achieving" (impossible) reconciliations between history and reality. Up until now, I have been discussing a part of China's *dazhong wenhua* that circulates among the majority of the population. It is now time to look at another part of it, one that circulates among members of a minority.

The element of minority culture that is attached in this instance to mass culture entered China through different channels in the second half of the twentieth century, but it only became genuinely popular when the internet was properly established in China in 1997. It was then transmitted throughout society by means of traditional media, in the form of stylish texts or "petit-bourgeois classics." This part of China's *dazhong wenhua*, which once circulated only among members of a minority, remained anonymous within society for a long time. The reason for this anonymity was that many of the relevant texts were introduced into China through informal channels from the other side of the Cold War. These types of cultural consumption, which were outside the horizon of mainstream cultural criticism for some time, actually nurtured a whole generation of urban Chinese youth during the period, which was marked by great social change and by an ideological vacuum. Pirated Hollywood films on DVD (especially action, science fiction, and disaster films), Hong Kong martial arts fictions (featuring Jin Yong and Gu Long as the masters of the genre), Eileen Chang, Japanese and Korean TV series, American TV series, Hong Kong and Taiwanese pop music (Taiwan singer Lo Da Yu has a special position in this category) provide the basic texts in the family tree of this minority part of *dazhong wenhua*. Other essential components include Japanese and Korean animations and comics, TV games, Hong Kong movies (*mo lei tau* or Stephen Chow, John Woo, or crime and gangster movies, post-modernist aesthetics or Wong Kar Wai). To be added is a stack of petit-bourgeois "must reads": apart from Eileen Chang, who is an enduring priority, there are Jorge Luis Borges, Italo Calvino, Hakuri Mirakami, Marguerite Duras, Yu Hua, Wang Xiao Bo, and so on; and "petit-bourgeois classic movies" — Andrei Tarkovsky, Krzysztof Kieślowski, Eric Rohmer, and Pedro Almodóvar, among many others. In recent years, the list has included the books in the *Harry Potter* series, the *Lord of the Rings* trilogy and Asimov's science fiction.

To draw up a list of popular culture items — especially those circulated amongst members of a minority group — is not a clever gesture, because the speed of change is simply so high in the post-modern internet era that this year's popular works become next year's classics, only to be entirely forgotten soon afterwards. The aim here is not only to recapture that one-off moment of popularity, but also to visualize the traces of a specific era. In fact, apart from Yu Hua and Wang Xiao Bo, all of the people on the list were from "the West," in terms of both cultural geography and ideology — that is, they were from what was the Western camp during the Cold War, compared with the Socialist East. When we look at the list from this perspective, then it becomes not only the "symptom of the schizophrenia of our era," but also an occasion for noting the logic of a certain internal integration. This internal status of "unanimity" testifies in a subtle way to how Chinese social culture was seized by the logic of the Cold War in the last twenty years of the twentieth century: the normal order was reversed while at the same time the whole society was led in a single direction. It also illustrates how a strange cultural "takeover" succeeded in Chinese society. Furthermore, when we look at the list from the perspectives of contemporary history and reality at that time, it appears to be "history without an axis" and "reality without a context," like an enclave. This "cultural recipe" that has nurtured a whole post-Cold War and post-revolutionary generation actually wipes out the memories of modern history. Furthermore, it white-washes the traces of twentieth century Chinese culture, cuts off many foreign texts from their historical background, and presents itself as something pure that is far removed from the actual bloodiness of the Cold War. In this pure enclave — one forged out of the pollution of politics — the depths of twentieth century history become some fragmented bloodstains, some soul-less textbook passages, or some indistinguishable interludes in the vast history of civilization. One of the major symptoms of mainstream neo-liberal culture in the global era is the disappearance of the depth of history, and this enclave actually helps to realize the construction of this global mainstream culture.

On this family tree of minority culture, there is an unidentified group of pre-modern Chinese literary texts, none of them apparently stylish or fashionable. It includes mainly poetry (*shi, ci, fu*), drama and informal essays (sometimes historical texts). This partly hidden and partly visible Chinese element does not change the characteristics of the Chinese minority/mass culture enclave. All foreign components of the enclave originate in some distant place, in terms of spatial geography or political geography; the elements in the Chinese category are also distant, in a temporal sense — that is, they are from before the 1919 May Fourth Movement. The pre-modern Chinese literature in question looks like an old Chinese pagoda inside a cultural theme park belonging to the age of globalization.

However, this under-current of minority culture, which ran parallel to the mass culture of traditional media, was not only an illustration of the rich leisure class's stylish consumptions. When this culture finally became prominent as a result of its dissemination through the internet, a profound social reality was evident: the generation nurtured by this minority version of mass culture has become the core of society in the new political and economic structure. Its members constituted the new elites in the political and economic arenas. The cultural fast food on which this group was raised determined the boundaries of its cultural horizon and became the source of its value system and self-imagination. In September 2000, white-collars and "gold-collars" in their thirties flew in chartered planes from Beijing and other cities to Shanghai to attend Lo Ta Yu's live concert, with the media describing the event as "the 80,000 people's altar of youth." This spectacle provides a footnote to this narrative, aimed at understanding the social functions of the Chinese majority/minority dimensions of mass culture. This reality, which has a context, is also a floating bridge. It floats on the phenomenon of the Cultural Revolution having come to an end, and indeed on its having been buried; it also floats on the disruptions of the end of the 1980s, and offers a route for sending people and social security to the frontline of global capitalism. There is another profound symptom that is also a reminder: Western mass culture and post-modernism arrived in China at the same time, and the latter lent legitimacy (although not in any necessary and sufficient way) to the former, through elitist cultural criticism. Paradoxically, from the end of the 1980s to the moment at the outset of the 1990s when mass culture and post-modernism arrived, members of the new elites did not engage in criticisms or confrontations but rather became a constructive force supplementing mainstream political culture. On the one hand, these new elites ended the elite culture that in fact had been brought to a standstill by political violence earlier; on the other, they also participated in the establishment of the new system of economic or political elitism.

The Merging of Majority and Minority Culture, or the Creation of Hegemony

In the second decade of the twenty-first century, Chinese mass culture and the minority culture that is an aspect of mass culture are no longer separate. The new Chinese middle class that grew up with the minority version of mass culture became the dominant consumer group. Members of this class started to

develop their own tastes, values, and morality, and they influenced the production of local mass culture. In the singing contest *Super Girl's Voice*, organized
by Hunan Province's Entertainment Channel in 2004, what has been referred
to as "China's biggest fan club"[5] mobilized supporters via the internet. In the
final round, 3.5 million people voted for a female singer (with an androgynous
or bi-gender style) and "pushed" her to the championship and even to the
front page of *Time Asia* magazine as one of "Asia's Heroes 2005," for allegedly
representing "the mechanism of democracy in China."[6] However, it was no
secret to anyone that the crucial element in her victory was her supporters'
comprehensive economic power as subjects of cultural consumption. Directors
of multi-national corporations provided an effective business model: *Super
Girl's Voice* enabled China to become the newest part of the global media production chain, and demonstrated that cultural enterprises have the capacity to
earn huge profits. This success story illustrated the power of members of the
minority/new middle class in their capacity as consuming subjects, and linked
the mass media to the consumption practices of a minority. At this point, the
dazhong of *dazhong wenhua* is no longer related to mass society or to society's
majority, for the term no longer identifies "the audience" in a general sense,
but picks out a group that has become an important and organic component of
the chain of "capital/(cultural) production/(cultural) consumption." What this
means is that those who have little or no power to consume are left behind by the
market. What we see here is how confusion about keywords became the origin
of a social screening system. The Chinese characteristic of this phenomenon is
that when the majority became negligible in a statistical sense — on account of
its lack of any power to consume — it nonetheless remained very much present
in the mass cultural arena. The majority was simply constituted as a mere
"audience" — as the voiceless receivers of mainstream ideology. It might be the
view of some that although the relevant minority culture successfully occupied
a place in the mass media, those who consume it remain a minority in the
context of China's huge population. However, with their growing power to
consume, and growing demand for stylish cultural products, these people (who
were a cultural minority in the past and now make up the new middle class) are
qualified to negotiate with the cultural institutions and cultural enterprises of
the state. New interactive and collaborative relationships have been created as a
result. These people established subject positions reflecting patterns of cultural
consumption and a sense of moral consciousness based on belonging to a new
class. This group went from enjoying the subject position associated with the

"drifter generation"[7] to trying to occupy the vacant space in China's "civil society," and from believing in cultural cynicism based on consumer-oriented individualism to getting involved in social issues driven by common interests. As a result of these shifts, this group was motivated on occasion to identify and join forces with the middle and lower classes. Practices exemplifying the shifts can be found in the little theatre phenomenon (a format typical of minority culture). In 2007, there was a famous stage production directed by National Theatre of China's director Meng Jinhui, *The Life Opinions of Two Dogs*, which ran continuously in major cities in China until 2009. Through the production's staging of self-mockery and self-pity from the standpoint of the middle class, members of the various audiences were offered an opportunity to reconcile themselves with certain realities. What was new about this production was the friendly and comical depiction of "migrant workers" on the stage of minority culture. What needs to be noted, however, is that the effect of petit-bourgeois audiences in the large cities identifying with this comical representation of the lower class is more appropriately described as an instance of hegemonic con-solidation than as a process of social reconciliation.

If we compare *The Life Opinions of Two Dogs* with another hugely popular TV series, *Shi Bing Tu Ji* (Soldiers' Raid), of the same year, we achieve further insight into the more general context. *Shi Bing Tu Ji* was only one of many TV series that featured lower class people and soldiers' lives and brotherhood, but it was the only TV series that achieved a rapidly growing popularity without much media hype, to the point even of breaking through the boundaries that usually contain TV series and into the arena of social discourse. Elite intellectuals, petit-bourgeois/new middle class and migrant workers were all unanimous in their praise for it. Much as in the case of other popular texts, *Shi Bing Tu Ji* attracted the attention of a large number of people on the internet, and many fan clubs devoted to the series were set up. A wide spectrum of audiences praised the series from quite different perspectives; the popularity of this TV series demonstrated just how important a role mass culture plays in the construction and spread of hegemony. As Chinese writer Han Shao Gong put it: "This is the triumph of a particular worldview and view of life, this is an effective presentation of our 'core values.'"[8] If *The Life Opinions of Two Dogs* illustrates the way in which the petit-bourgeois/middle class implemented a downward-looking process of social identification and integration through a minority culture format, then *Shi Bing Tu Ji* demonstrates how mass culture co-opted members of the petit-bourgeois/middle class who normally looked down on local TV series.

Antonio Gramsci's idea of "hegemony" is used here to describe a series of social phenomena after 2007 — phenomena such as the emergence of a comprehensive form of social identification, the merging of cultures, and the reconstruction of the imagined community. In Gramsci's theory, "cultural hegemony" emphasizes the idea that domination in an area of thought is not achieved through violent conquest; in contrast, it is achieved by winning the hearts and minds of the majority. For this to happen, concessions need to be made to the exploited people in society through certain social/political negotiations, and these same people have to be afforded a space of personal identification.

Louis Althusser's theory of ideological state apparatuses claims that the seamless operation of mainstream ideology depends on the provision of a series of mirror images that allow various people in society to identify with the subject position, which is also a social position, of "I." When people gave their comments on the TV series, some concentrated on its apparent critique of the prevalence of pragmatism, utilitarianism, mammonism, and consumerism in post-revolutionary times, and on the resurgence of idealism, sacrifice, and altruism; some were encouraged by its message of perseverance;[9] some were intrigued by the story of brotherhood and even saw hints of an alternative erotic practice in the narrative; some were angry about the disciplinary violence depicted in the series and saw it as promulgating conformism. Although the world of the series abides by "winner takes all" dictates, the "master soldier" or working ant still has his/its social value.

The point that requires reiteration is that when people within and outside the People's Republic of China cheer the triumph of "civil society" and "democracy" (though sometimes it is "rule of thumb democracy," or grand events built up with capital) over and against the "authority" and "centralization of power" in the arena of mass culture, and when the national audience ratings of popular TV series get close to or sometimes even surpass China Central Television's "News Simulcast" program, there is quite simply a failure to recognize the extent to which mass (minority) culture has been merged with capital and the ways in which mass culture is undergoing a process of restratification. Mass culture's social function has also changed, for whereas it once filled a certain vacuum and provided a certain reality without a context, it now contributes to a deliberate process of establishing the new mainstream ideology that is to be operative until such time when the new social cultural hegemony matures. After thirty years, a grand and bizarre historical metamorphosis is close to completion.

In fact, it is the unrivalled importance of Chinese *dazhong wenhua* that determines the position of Chinese Cultural Studies: if we admit that during the twenty years before and after the turn of the century, Chinese *dazhong wenhua* occupied a position that was essentially that of mainstream ideology, then Cultural Studies is destined to become the most important of intellectual battlefields. If we admit that in the course of society's restratification, Chinese *dazhong wenhua* has become the major engine of the new mainstream discourse and effectively equips the machine of power with its legitimizing discourse, then the deciphering work of Cultural Studies provides an alternative path for society and culture. If we admit that the mainstream social culture that mass culture represents functions through anti-politicization or depoliticization, then the attempt at repoliticization that Cultural Studies offers is not only about critique but reconstruction. Although Cultural Studies in China and Asia lagged behind the West and arrived belatedly, it occupies a specific intellectual, cultural, and academic position, and has a whole range of tasks to take up. These include responding to a whole range of social and cultural realities, confronting the poverty of the humanities in the post-Cold War era, participating in the process of repaying the "historical debt," and trying to discover and develop new intellectual resources and visions for the future. Cultural Studies is somewhere between social and cultural history, history of the cultural industry and intellectual history; somewhere between academic production and social involvement. Cultural Studies should become — indeed must become — an effective practice of alternative cultural politics.

8

Uses of Media Culture, Usefulness of Media Culture Studies

Beyond Brand Nationalism into Public Dialogue

Koichi Iwabuchi

Often, Cultural Studies is criticized for its over-politicization of culture. Rather than deeply appreciating culture's aesthetic value or its tranquil presence in people's everyday life, researchers tend to be preoccupied with analyzing and comprehending it in terms of their own aspirations to engage with cultural politics. However, since culture as a form of meaning construction and a process of communication is ubiquitous in all social activities — which necessarily are power laden — culture extends its relevance and strategic usefulness to spheres beyond itself. As George Yúdice argues, culture has become an expedient "resource" that allows various social actors to pursue their own political, economic, communal, and activist interests.[1] Various social actors, including marginalized persons and NGOs, have engaged in identity politics and become involved in new social movements by resorting to the expediency of culture. That said, the media and culture industries have especially been attuned to the instrumental value of culture, having used it most effectively and aggressively for commercial purposes. Recently, states have also shown a strong interest in using such media and popular cultures for the promotion of national interests, politically to enhance national brand images and economically for developing service sectors in which creative/content industries play a significant role. While the national policy of using culture in the pursuit of national interests is not new, the recent development signifies a new collaborative relationship between the state and media cultural industries, and between culture, economy, and politics.

This chapter discusses these issues in the Japanese context by critically examining the recent development of what I call "brand nationalism." My focus will be the Japanese government's growing interest in recent times in using media culture for the promotion of national branding in the international cultural arena. I argue that the resulting institutionalization of the expediency of media culture has had the effect of significantly thwarting the development of media culture's capacity to promote hitherto marginalized voices and cultural expressions in the public sphere. The relevant process of institutionalization also encourages a neglect of crucial cultural issues that are raised by the market-driven evolution of globalization. In the age of brand nationalism, when — to appropriate Adorno's well-known words[2] — "whoever speaks of administration speaks of culture, whether it is in his/her interest or not," we need to consider seriously how critical researchers of culture might make an effective critique.

"Cool Japan" and the Rise of a Soft Power Policy Discussion

While the spread of Japanese media culture into the United States and Europe has been a gradual and steady phenomenon since at least the 1980s, it has intensified in the new millennium, so much so that we have recently witnessed the rise of a "cool Japan" discourse, which discusses the global spread of Japanese media and consumer cultures in a celebratory manner. It is the attention devoted to this phenomenon by Euro-American media that gives credence to the concept of a "cool Japan."[3] Several commentators have attested to Japan's growing cultural influence in the last several years: "During the 1990s, Japan became associated with its economic stagnation. However, what many failed to realize is that Japan has transformed itself into a vibrant culture-exporting country during the 1990s";[4] "Japan's influence on pop culture and consumer trends runs deep";[5] "Japan is reinventing itself on earth — this time as the coolest nation culture."[6] Coining the term Gross National Cool — or GNC — some journalist even announced the rise of Japan as a cultural super-power in the international arena.[7]

At least since the early 1990s, the rise of Japanese media culture in the global audiovisual markets has engendered the emergence of a "soft" nationalism in Japan — that is, a narcissist discourse on the global (i.e. crucially including Europe and the United States) spread of Japanese media and consumer culture. The recent diffusion of Japanese media culture in the world has further inspired a social and personal lift in Japan, as it contrasts strikingly with the long-standing Japanese economic slump. However, this time Japanese embracing of "cool Japan" is not just limited to a celebratory nationalistic discourse.

It is also accompanied by the active development of national cultural policy discussion and implementation aimed at further enhancing Japan's cultural standing in the world. And a key term is "soft power."

The term "soft power" was first coined by American political scientist Joseph Nye. In 1990, Nye argued that "soft co-optic power" was a significant factor in the attainment of the global hegemony by the United States; he defines this as the power to get "others to want what you want" through such symbolic resources as media and consumer culture: "If [a dominant country's] culture and ideology are attractive, others will more willingly follow."[8] The US use of media culture for advancing public diplomacy is not new. Indeed, the US policy of disseminating the image of liberty, affluence, and democracy through media and consumer culture to win the Cold War is all too well known. Nye considered it imperative that the US government further develop a soft power policy, the point being to make strategic use, in the post-Cold War era, of a globally diffused media and consumer culture, of symbolic icons and positive images and values associated with the United States.

A decade later, the concept of soft power attracted renewed attention in the context of the Bush Administration's hard-line policies, especially after 9/11. This time, soft power was discussed not just in connection with the United States, but also in relation to other parts of the world, including Japan. When he first advocated "soft power" in the early 1990s, Nye dismissed Japan's soft power as negligible. His contention was that Japan was a "one-dimensional economic power," with its consumer commodities — no matter how globally spread — still lacking an associated "appeal to a broader set of values."[9] However, more than ten years later, Nye has come to acknowledge Japan's cultural influence in the world:

> Japan's popular culture was still producing potential soft-power resources even after its economy slowed down. Now, with signs of a reviving economy, Japan's soft power may increase even more.[10]

This is another welcome endorsement of Japan's soft power by the US authority. Nye has been invited by the Japanese government, think-tanks, and mass media to confirm the rising soft power of Japan to the Japanese populace, through lectures, translated publications, and media interviews. The Japanese government also began to announce its policy orientation towards the enhancement of soft power publicly. For example, the 2003 Japanese Cultural Agency's gathering for discussion about international cultural exchange states:

> In the twenty-first century, "soft power," which is the capacity to attract
> foreign nations by the appeal of lifestyle and culture of the nation, is
> more important than military power. Japan as the nation rich in attrac-
> tive cultures is expected to make an international contribution through
> international cultural exchange and actively display the 21st century model
> of soft power.[11]

The Japanese government is particularly interested in the development of
content business and in the promotion of cultural diplomacy, with the aim of
enhancing the international images of Japan through media cultures. Since the
turn of the century, many committees focusing on the promotion of Japanese
media and culture have been established by the government and by think-
tanks, especially under the Koizumi government, including the Head Office
for Intellectual Property Strategy (2002), the Committee for Tourism Nation
(2003), the Committee for Info-communication Software (2003), the Research
Committee for Content Business (2005), the J-Brand Initiative (2003), the
e-Japan Strategy (2003), the Council for the Promotion of International
Exchange (on the Strengthening of Cultural Dispatch) (2006), and so on.
Many Japanese universities have also established programs that aim to train
professional creators by inviting prominent film directors and animation
producers, including internationally renowned film directors Kitano Takeshi
and Kurosawa Kiyoshi. Indeed, the significance of utilizing media cultures to
enhance Japan's soft power has been widely discussed in the new millennium,
and related practices have been institutionalized.

From Soft Power to Brand Nationalism

It should be noted that Japan's soft power turn is symptomatic of the internationalization of soft power. In the last two decades, many countries other
than the United States have significantly developed the capacity to produce
media cultural texts and symbolic images, thanks to the development of digital
communication technologies and glocally adoptable cultural formats, and
the expansion of media culture markets in previously less developed regions.
While Nye was deploring the decline of American soft power under the
Bush administration, other states began to pursue the idea of exploiting the
economic and political utility of media culture to win the international competition more aggressively — although the term "soft power" was not necessarily used. "Cool Britannia" might be the best-known policy and practice of

this kind, but in East Asia too, Korea, Singapore, China, Taiwan, and Japan are keen to promote their own cultural products and industries to enhance political and economic national interests. Most famously, the Korean government has actively promoted Korean media cultures overseas since the 1990s, thereby contributing to the sweeping popularity of Korean media cultures, known as the Korean Wave.[12] Motivated by Korea's success, the Japanese government has also become active in developing the policy of promoting Japanese media cultures internationally in the twenty-first century.

While media culture is now publicly recognized as a useful resource for promoting political and economic national interests, the internationalization of soft power does in fact diverge from Nye's original argument in some significant respects. One such divergence has to do with the uses of media culture as a resource in the context of an international image politics. According to Nye, media culture is just one of three possible resources for the enhancement of a nation's soft power, the other two being respectful foreign policy and attractive democratic values established in the relevant society.[13] In particular, he clearly warns against conflating the international appeal of media cultures with soft power, stressing that soft power will not be enhanced if the other two resources are not properly developed. What is striking, however, is that this kind of conflation is actually a prevalent operational principle of cultural policy discussions in many parts of the world. Key figures, it turns out, are more preoccupied with largely effortless pragmatic uses of media culture for the purposes of enhancing an international image and boosting the economy, the key term here being branding. International relations scholar Peter van Ham,[14] for example, argues for the significance of the state's role in branding the nation, and does so in terms of international politics and the economy:

> Branding acquires its power because the right brand can surpass the actual products as a company's central asset. Smart firms pour most of their money into improving their brands, focusing more on the values and emotions that customers attach to them than on the quality of the products itself ... Smart states are building their brands around reputations and attitudes in the same way smart companies do.[15]

Thus the state should be determined to play an active role in the production of attractive national cultural odor in the age of global image politics.[16]

Likewise, the idea of national branding was strongly advocated by a former Japanese foreign minister (who became prime minister in 2008). Aso's 2006 statement regarding the significance of media culture for the policy of public/ cultural diplomacy is as follows:

> We want pop culture, which is so effective in penetrating throughout the general public, to be our ally in diplomacy … one part of diplomacy lies in having a competitive brand image, so to speak. Now more than ever, it is impossible for this to stay entirely within the realm of the work of diplomats … what we need to do now is to build on this foundation [the fact that Japan already has achieved a good image] and attract people of the world to Japanese culture, whether modern or that handed down from antiquity.[17]

The flippancy of this kind of cultural diplomacy through national branding was clearly revealed in its failure to engage with unresolved historical issues of Japanese colonialism and imperialism in other East Asian countries, especially China and Korea. Referring to the 2006 BBC survey of national images, Aso actually boasted about Japan being amongst the most favorably perceived nations in the world, and proposed to promote national brand power further by exporting more attractive Japanese media cultures (especially manga and anime). However, he completely neglected the fact that in the survey two countries — China and Korea — showed quite negative responses to the images of Japan. While the Koizumi government tried to promote cultural diplomacy policy quite aggressively, it actually escalated anti-Japanese sentiments in China and Korea over the issues raised by history textbooks, long-standing territorial disputes, and Prime Minister Koizumi's relentless official visits to the Yasukuni Shrine. Nye points out that unresolved historical issues with other Asian countries are one of the crucial weaknesses of Japanese soft power, besides the lack of a migration policy (in spite of Japan's ageing population) and the cultural-linguistic particularism that indicates the extent to which "Japan's culture remains inward-looking."[18] Nye publicly criticized Koizumi's repeated visits to the Yasukuni Shrine[19] on account of its negative impact on Japan's soft power. While the Koizumi government emphasized the importance of widely disseminating Japanese media cultures for the purposes of establishing harmonious relations with other countries, it actually seriously damaged relations with neighboring countries by closing down dialogue.

Furthermore, the idea of cultural diplomacy tends to rely on a naïve assumption about media culture's capacity to improve Japan's reputation abroad, and to transcend the problematic and historically constituted relations between Japan and other East and Southeast Asian countries. The cultural diplomacy policy

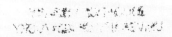

of the post-war era was institutionalized in the 1970s as the so-called Fukuda doctrine. The possibility of improving Japanese images in the region through the introduction of various Japanese cultures attracted serious attention from the state when anti-Japanese sentiments were aroused in Southeast Asian countries due to economic exploitation. While traditional cultures such as the tea ceremony and kabuki have been the main objects of cultural exchange, media cultures became significant in the 1980s. The popularity of TV drama series — especially *Oshin*, which became a phenomenal hit in many countries — attracted more attention to media cultures on account of their capacity to enhance the international understanding of the "liberated" and "humane" faces of post-war Japan. The thought was that these media cultures could help to overcome disapproving historical memories of Japanese colonialism and the negative image of the country's economic exploitation of the region.[20] The significance of disseminating Japanese media cultures was even more urgently discussed with the intensification of anti-Japanese demonstrations in China and Korea in the early twenty-first century. However, there was a tendency to assume naïvely that the spread of Japanese media culture would easily efface lingering antagonistic sentiments regarding Japan's history of imperialism and colonialism. When Aso was appointed Foreign Minister in 2005, he allegedly stated that Japan's relationship with China should be unproblematic inasmuch as many young people in China were reading Japanese manga. Also, the 2005 White Paper produced by Japan's Economic and Trade Ministry clearly states that "without the spread of Japanese pop culture, anti-Japanese sentiment would be much stronger in Korea." Here too, it is assumed that Korean young people who like to consume Japanese media culture will feel more tolerant towards Japan, and that increased exports of media culture to Asian markets thus automatically serve Japan's cultural diplomacy. However, the reality is far more complicated than such reasoning suggests. In Korea and China, many of those who are happy to consume Japanese media culture actually consider historical issues separately, and critically.[21] The coexistence of thoughts such as "I love Japanese comics" and "I cannot forget what Japan did to our grandparents" within the same person's mind is by no means ruled out. Even if a favorable consumption of Japanese media cultures might positively change the images of contemporary Japan, it does not erase the past nor people's memories of it. Historical issues need to be dealt with continuously, and on their own terms.

Significantly missing in the discussion of cultural diplomacy through the export of media cultures is what images and ideas of "Japan" are to be promoted, how their reception is complicated by the nature of various audiences, and how the circulation of media culture is to be located in a comprehensive cultural policy that aims not just at the betterment of national brand images but at the advancement of transnational dialogues among citizens. The recent discourse of cultural diplomacy, as shown above, does not promote but rather thwarts a sincere engagement with "historical truthfulness," which can only be fostered through transnational dialogues involving various citizens' views of the past.[22] As I will discuss later, media cultural flows in East Asia have facilitated mutual understandings in an unprecedented manner. However, what cultural policy needs to consider is how the consumption of media culture might be used as the impetus for citizens' further and possibly conflict-laden dialogues. Far from assuming that media culture has the magical power to overcome historical issues, it should be a matter of thinking carefully about how it might contribute to such a project.

Thus, in the course of the internationalization of the idea of using media cultures as part of a national foreign policy strategy, the soft power argument has been replaced by a shallow policy discourse on the enhancement of international images. As a result, soft power is not so much being misunderstood and misappropriated as used to bolster a quite different logic at the level of cultural policy governing national media cultures. A good term for the relevant phenomenon is "brand nationalism," for the aim is opportunistically to administer media culture for the purposes of promoting national political and economic interests in the international arena by way of branding the nation. This is not to defend soft power discourse; Nye's soft power argument shares with brand nationalism the basic principle of using media culture for the enhancement of a narrow and focused set of national interests. The two do not take seriously cross-border dialogue amongst various citizens, since attracting others and making others follow are both instances of unidirectional communication. However, brand nationalism needs to be critically interrogated in terms other than soft power inasmuch as what has been widely institutionalized is not just opportunistic discourses on the uses of media culture but also a highly market-centered vision of cultural policy.

Brand Nationalism and Its Ideological Closure

Some would question the idea that brand nationalism is effective in enhancing certain national images, as policy-makers contend that it is, and this is not merely because the Japanese government's way of dealing with historical issues is obviously contradictory and unconvincing. Furthermore, any close research on how Japanese media culture is received and consumed in the world would easily reveal the intricate ways of an inter-cultural image politics that betrays the naïve expectations of those who advocate cultural diplomacy. After all, as brand nationalism — and soft power — disregard the complexity of uneven cultural globalization in terms of production, representation, and consumption, the suspicion is very valid. Nevertheless, precisely because of this disregard for the relevant complexity, we cannot easily dismiss the rise of brand nationalism as an unsubstantial and fallacious policy discourse. As a dominant social discourse, it has a wide public impact in terms of material institutionalisation and fiscal funding, and as a way of comprehending the pragmatic usefulness of (national) culture. Furthermore, the impact of this discourse is non-trivial inasmuch as it disregards crucial policy questions concerning who the beneficiaries of brand nationalism are and whose culture and voice are being neglected. What matters is less the effectiveness of brand nationalism than its ideological closure, for it is the latter that effectively suppresses all serious discussions about the uses of culture in the service of wider public interests.

While it is claimed in a Japanese cultural policy statement that the advancement of international cultural exchange, rather than the uses of hard military power, will be key to the creation of a peaceful world where cultural diversity is mutually respected, and celebrated and multilateral understanding and dialogue promoted,[23] brand nationalism actually aims to promote a particular kind of cultural diversity and intercultural dialogue, and to hinder other kinds. I have already argued that cultural diplomacy in tandem with national branding does not promote the ideal in question, and even works to suppress any sincere commitment to transnational dialogue about historical issues. Moreover, brand nationalism's pursuit of narrowly focused national interests has a drawback when it comes to any serious engagement with socio-cultural democratization of the kind that does justice to hitherto marginalized voices and differences in society. Its impact is equally negative with respect to the promotion of public dialogues — locally, nationally and transnationally — about those imperative issues that are engendered by the advancement of market-driven cultural globalization. These points are related to another crucial difference between brand nationalism and soft power, one that ultimately reveals a damaging shortcoming in Nye's argument. While Nye clearly distinguishes between culture as soft power and economy as hard power, a clear separation of economy and culture is untenable if we are to understand the power structure of a market-oriented globalization, as recent discussions of creative industries and content business would suggest. While discourses supporting brand nationalism as well as soft power stress the national interest being furthered by the smart uses of media and popular culture by the state, it needs to be noted that the rise of brand nationalism is not so much initiated by the state's policy implementation of using culture for the promotion of political and economic national interests in the international arena as it is basically organized by the logic of capital.

Brand nationalism, then, is not just an opportunistic nationalist policy discourse on the uses of media culture; I would suggest that it legitimizes, and is facilitated by, the rise of a neo-liberalist mode of internationalism. In order to comprehend critically the rise of brand nationalism in Japan — and other countries too — we need to look at the wider context of globalization processes where media cultures are circulating as nationalized commodities, in the "inter-national" arena where the marketing interests of media culture industries endorse, and are endorsed by, the pragmatic interests of various states. It is widely accepted that globalization is, in fact, constantly giving rise to cultural diversity, which is governed by the logic of capital.[24] As demonstrated by the prevalence of the television format business, globalization does not destroy cultural differences, but rather brings about a "peculiar form of homogenization" while fostering difference in a particular manner.[25] The world is becoming more diverse through standardization, and more standardized through diversification as a result of a sharing of globally disseminated cultural formats. This process is first and foremost organized and promoted by transnational corporations, most of them based in the developed countries, and most of them committed to the pursuit of profits through a tailoring of glocal cultures in every corner of the world's markets, through transnational tie-ups and partnerships. What is crucial here is that the national has functioned as one of the most profitable local markets, as a unit of commercialized cultural diversity in the world. National images are increasingly constituted by global mass culture formats that provide the basis for the expression of national specificity. As John Urry argues:

> Nationality gets more constituted through specific local places, symbols and landscapes, icons of the nation central to that culture's location within the contours of global business, travel, branding … nation has become less a matter of the specific state uniquely determining the nation.[26]

This process has accompanied the institutionalisation of what Urry calls a "global screen," a site through which national culture is mutually appreciated and global cultural diversity enjoyably consumed. Since the 1990s, we have witnessed a substantial increase in global media spaces through satellite and cable broadcasting, and audiovisual internet sites, as well as through international media events and opportunities to come together — such as sports competitions, film festivals, music awards, food expos, and tourism. In all these cases, cultures from many parts of the world are exhibited and introduced, and compete with each other in the "inter-national" arena. This is the context in which national branding has attracted growing attention and in which states have become keen to promote branding in conjunction with media culture industries.

Capital has no loyalty to national borders, but fosters the national as the local market unit while also requiring state regulation and control in order to make profits through a neo-liberal mode of cultural globalization.[27] States, for their part, are complicit in this process, for they work with it rather than regulating and controlling it for the public good, embracing two exclusive forces simultaneously: one linked to the dynamics of the market, the other to the policing of national boundaries. In advancing the market-oriented administration of national culture, brand nationalism does not give due attention to the issues of power relations, domination, and marginalization that are generated by transnational cultural flows and industrial collaboration, especially at the site of production and cultural labor. While the development of creativity in the production of internationally appealing culture is emphasized in favor of developing creative industries or content industries, there is little or no emphasis on critical assessments of how cultural production actually operates in the wider socio-economic context in which transnational media and cultural industries dominate the production and distribution of culture.[28] We need to discuss the market-oriented policy agendas cautiously in terms of such issues as the high concentration of ownership in a handful of global media conglomerates, their monopoly on copyright, and the international division of new cultural labor.[29] As Naomi Klein eloquently argues, brand exploits![30]

Aso's speech, mentioned above, was delivered to would-be creators who were learning creative skills related to the production of digital cultures at Digital Hollywood in Akihabara. Aso praised the creativity of Japanese animation and manga, which significantly elevates Japan's brand image, but he was not concerned at all with the actual working conditions of animation subcontractors in Japan. Those conditions are infamously poor, and there is no sign of improvement. Exploitation of cultural labor is not just a domestic issue but a transnational one. Japanese animation companies have long sub-contracted the basic work of animation production to other parts of Asia.[31] Korea and Taiwan used to provide key production sites, but as the cost of labor increased there, there has been a shift to China, where wages are lower. When McDonalds ran its Kitty dolls campaign in 2000, it was reported that children from rural parts of China worked at the factory in Shenzen for fifteen hours a day and for the extremely low wage of 21 yen per hour.[32] What is urgently required is serious public discussion of whether and how the profits of branding the nation actually return to media-factory workers and to the society, both domestically and abroad.[33] There is an expectation that the pro-moting of content industries will benefit the relevant content creators and will help new kinds of cultural creativity originating in Japan to flourish. Yet, as Otshuka and Osawa point out, without fundamentally changing the current structure of profit-taking through distribution and copyright, which currently are controlled by global media and culture industries, many creators' working conditions and the structure of uneven profit distribution are unlikely to be much improved.[34] As the frameworks for global media production and distri-bution are restructured by alliances and partnerships amongst multinational media corporations, brand nationalism might very well lend itself to strength-ening the global media conglomerate oligopoly's strong control of distribution networks and intellectual property rights, the most significant issue of cultural domination under globalization.[35]

The national government should seriously tackle these issues of domestic and transnational unevenness and cultural domination by media culture indus-tries, given that there is no effective international political institution to take up the tasks. What we see instead, though, is a government that is highly moti-vated to attract transnational capital, and thus inclined to endorse and advance the unevenness and resulting domination through collaboration with private corporations. The public good increasingly is being made to serve business in the name of putative national interests.

Banal "Inter-nationalism" and Missing Links with Marginalized Voices

Another issue that is excluded from public discussion by the workings of brand nationalism, especially its institutionalizing of an international mode of cultural exhibition, encounter, and consumption, concerns marginalized voices in the nation-state. Michael Billig argues that national feeling is more often than not facilitated and displayed by means of such mundane practices as casually showing the national flag in the city.[36] The banality of national belonging is further promoted by an increase in encounters with people, goods, and images from many parts of the world. As stated above, there has been a rapid development of various kinds of international events and spectacles that require people to purchase a ticket to enjoy a given event by displaying a particular national emblem. Consequently, a plethora of mundane occasions emerge in which "banal nationalism is increasingly consumed by others, compared and evaluated, and turned into a brand."[37] Urry sees this process as involving a "move from banal nationalism to brand nationalism in the new global order."[38] However, brand nationalism does not differ fundamentally from banal nationalism in terms of the centrality of the national framework, and even intensifies it. The growing emphasis on a collaborative discourse, and on policy implementation that involves the state and media culture industries in a process of branding media cultures, engenders "banal inter-nationalism," which reinforces the premise of methodological nationalism among the general public. Methodological nationalism has been criticized seriously in social science, as it unambiguously and uncritically regards the national as the principal unit of analysis, thus disregarding the diversity and differences within the national and the transnational connections that are actually constitutive of people's lives in society.[39] With the growing salience of international media cultural spectacles and the rise of an associated policy discourse on the pragmatic uses of media culture for the purposes of national interests, the exclusive notion of national belonging has become even more pervasive in society, as has the idea of the nation as the basis for global cultural encounters. Banal "inter-nationalism" self-evidently associates culture with the national, essentializing the ownership of national cultures with the indication of cultural DNA. At the same time, transnational and cross-cultural encounters are understood in terms of mutually exclusive inter-national encounters that are highly commercialized and more spectacular than ever.[40]

Banal inter-nationalism makes the questions of who is excluded and whose voices are suppressed in society irrelevant, and further hinders paying due attention to postcolonial and multicultural issues within a given national society. In early 2006, for example, the expansion of international broadcasting services had begun to be seriously discussed in Japan, and the services commenced in February 2009 with the purpose of enhancing Japan's national image in the world for the promotion of political and economic interests. However, discussion of the service first started when foreign nationals residing in Japan complained to then Prime Minister Koizumi about the lack of broadcasting in Japan in languages other than Japanese. So what was at stake in the beginning was the failure of the Japanese broadcasting system to provide due public service to people of diverse ethnic and linguistic backgrounds who were residing in Japan. The question of the broadcasting system's publicness, in the sense of doing justice to the diversity of citizens whose voices and concerns are not well reflected in the mass media, is indeed an urgent one inasmuch as Japanese society is becoming more multicultural. In connection with my own research, I have also often heard similar complaints from foreign nationals resident in Japan. However, in the Cabinet meeting a few days later, the concerns were translated into a strategy aimed at the enhancement of national images in the world by developing an English-language international broadcasting service. Brand nationalism clearly suppresses a vital cultural policy engagement with the task of bringing the hitherto marginalized voices and concerns of various citizens into the public sphere, and of ensuring that they are heard.

The increasing dominance of the inter-nationalized framework in global cultural encounters has also put a significant limit on the development of cross-border connectivity via the consumption of media cultures. It tends to promote particular kinds of cultural diversity, cross-boundary connections, and dialogues through the practices of inclusion and exclusion, at the same time reinforcing social marginalization within the nation-state. The question of identifying who is left out of the newly emerging inter-nationalized connections is a crucial one.

Since the mid-1990s, regional media culture flows and consumption have been encouraged in East Asia. Close partnerships within the sphere of the media industry have been formed as companies pursue marketing strategies and joint production ventures spanning several different markets. Media cultures from places like Japan, South Korea, Hong Kong, Taiwan, and China are finding sympathetic acceptance in the region, leading to the significant advancement of cross-border conversations and a level of mutual understanding that is unprecedented.[41] However, it is important to caution against naïve celebration. Together with the rise of the state's concern with national branding, the emerging commercially orchestrated connectivity tends subtly to emphasize the national boundaries, and to disregard and suppress the issues of existing differences, marginalization, and inequality within each society in terms of gender, sexuality, ethnicity, race, class, age, region, and so on. It needs to be remembered that what is being promoted is the exchange and dialogue between cultures that are dominant and popular within each nation-state context. If we take cross-border dialogue engendered by media cultural flows seriously, we should go beyond the national framework and consider how the complicated transnational circulations of people, capital, and media texts intersect with and are shaped by local multicultural and postcolonial issues.

Japan's embracing of the Korean Wave (a term used to refer to the popularity of Korean media cultures), and the relation between this process of affirmation and the social recognition of resident Koreans, is a case in point. The consumption of Korean TV dramas has led to vigorous post-text activities such as learning the Korean language, visiting Korea, and even studying the history of Japanese colonialism. What this shows is that Korean TV dramas help to create certain dialogic possibilities, by fostering the inclination among (mostly middle-aged) female audiences to seek out active post-text encounters with Korea in ways that encourage a changed understanding of Korea and a more self-critical conception of the history of Japanese colonialism. If we are to take cross-border dialogue engendered by the Korean Wave in Japan seriously, however, we should examine how the complicated transnational circulations of people, capital, and media texts intersect with local multicultural and postcolonial issues. In this regard, the examination of how the Korean Wave has impacted on the social positioning and recognition of resident Koreans in Japan — most of whom are the descendants of expatriates under Japanese colonial rule and who have long been discriminated against as second-rate citizens — would be a crucial touchstone in the consideration of transnational cultural dialogue.

As I discussed elsewhere,[42] the impact of the Korean Wave still tends to be constrained by the dominant attention that is given to the international relationship, which overpowers serious concern with resident Koreans. The sense of frustration is often expressed by resident Koreans themselves, who note the extent to which Japanese people have embraced the Korean Wave while leaving the structure of social discrimination and indifference intact. The social recognition of resident Koreans has improved, as the Korean Wave does help to create a more positive image of Korea. Yet this process tends to facilitate an ahistorical recognition of resident Koreans, one that understands their existence in relation to the contemporary culture and society of the nation-state called South Korea. This is clearly shown in the representation of, and audience responses to, a popular Japanese TV drama series that features resident Koreans as the central protagonists. The drama was significant in that it was the first to deal with socio-historical issues concerning resident Koreans, and to be shown during prime time. Nonetheless, it failed to cast light on the historically embedded experiences of resident Koreans. Their historical trajectory, suffering, and identity-formation are instead effortlessly associated with and understood through the culture and people of present-day South Korea. Audience responses to the drama series on the web included critical comments insisting that resident Koreans were living together with "us" in Japan, as citizens constitutive of Japan, rather than of South Korea. However, many viewers were inclined to praise the drama series for further improving the relationship between Japan and South Korea and to perceive resident Koreans as South Korean nationals living in Japan, at the expense of serious understanding of the complexity of resident Koreans' experiences and social positioning in Japanese society. This example points to yet another way in which postcolonial and multicultural issues are subsumed under the framework of banal inter-nationalism.

The point is by no means simply to dismiss media culture's potential to stimulate transnational dialogue. Certain kinds of media culture have actually promoted new forms of mutual understanding and new connections in East Asia, especially as the flows have become multi-directional. However, there is a limit to these positive effects, and if we take media culture's potential seriously, we need to think carefully about how to develop and foster the transnational dialogue that it to some extent has initiated. Furthermore, cultural policy should play an active role in this too. Yet, as is also the case with cultural diplomacy regarding the issue of historical reconciliation with other East Asian nations, such priorities cannot easily be accommodated within a narrowly focused brand nationalism.

Towards Democratic Uses of Media Culture

Raymond Williams draws a distinction between cultural policies proper and cultural policies as display,[43] as McGuigan reminds us.[44] Cultural policy proper is concerned with social democratization in terms of support for art and media regulation designed to counter the kind of penetrating market forces that tend to marginalize unprofitable cultural forms and the expressions of minority groups. Additionally, social democratization encompasses efforts aimed at the construction of open and dialogic cultural identities that go well beyond the constraints of the national imaginary. Cultural policy as display is "the public pomp of a particular social order."[45] This form of cultural policy is typically put on display by a given national event and ceremony in order to achieve "national aggrandizement." Yet cultural policy as display also takes the form of an "economic reductionism of culture" that aims to promote domestic business opportunities and economic growth. While cultural policy can no longer effectively be developed without considering the role played by commercialized cultures in the public sphere, the two forms of cultural policy as display have been well integrated inasmuch as the state is trying to claim its regulating power by collaborating with private corporations.

The nationalist strategy of promoting political and economic power through a branding of the nation is one-dimensional and has only a very limited scope. This strategy is neither concerned with the complexity of cultural connections, nor with the dynamics of political and economic power relations in the realm of culture. Furthermore, the discursive formation focusing on the use of culture to enhance national interests conceals rather than reveals more imperative issues to be tackled within the era of globalization. These issues include social democratization aimed at making marginalized voices heard, and at making the nation more inclusive, and the promotion of cross-border dialogue over transnationally shared issues.

There is an urgent need to generate dialogue across various divides and boundaries in connection with these cultural issues, but also in connection with the uses of culture in the construction of an egalitarian inclusive society involving various local, national, regional, and global levels. I suggest that critical scholars of media Cultural Studies should engage, now more than ever before, with the creation of alternative visions and practices regarding the uses of media culture. This requires us first to take a broad view of cultural policy "in the sense of disputation over cultural issues"[46] through the active involvement of a wider public, which includes governments, mass media, intellectuals, and NGO/NPOs, not to mention the diverse groups and individuals concerned. In Japan, for example, we have set up a research centre for media and cultural citizenship whose aim is to open up academic knowledge and university spaces to a wider public. We have organized various workshops with the intent of sharing concerns and promoting dialogue — on the issue of the publicness of media cultures and on multicultural questions in Japan — among media producers, artists, students, activists, various citizens, and researchers in order to go beyond the exclusive notions of nation and identity, and to popularize the conception of Japan as a multicultural society. While we academics might share the view that we have overcome such issues through theory, we have failed to translate the argument into actual practices in everyday life. Serious engagements with public pedagogy have been fundamentally under-developed. Only by collaborating with non-academic people and by being involved with non-academic practices will academics be able to learn the practical means of convincing the critical mass of the relevance of academic critique for the purpose of making society more democratic and caring.

As Adorno expressed his hope at the end of an influential essay: "Whoever makes critically and unflinchingly conscious uses of the means of administration and its institutions is still in a position to realize something which would be different from merely administrated culture."[47] Cultural Studies scholars should play a key role in producing such administrators — not just as policy experts but also as critically minded ordinary citizens. These scholars also should themselves take up the task of being critical administrators who are committed to coordinating public dialogue and collaboration. They should be determined to promote and institutionalize more egalitarian and dialogic uses of media culture.

9
Way Out on a Nut

Douglas Crimp

> If, by an additional turn of the spiral, some day, most dazzling of all, once every reactive ideology had disappeared, consciousness were finally to become this: the abolition of the manifest and the latent, the appearance and the hidden? If it were asked of analysis not to destroy power (or even to correct or to direct it), but only to *decorate* it, as an artist?
>
>   — Roland Barthes, *A Lover's Discourse*

In his conversation with Daniel Buren at the Guggenheim Museum in conjunction with Buren's 2005 exhibition, *The Eye of the Storm: Works in Situ*, art historian Alex Alberro raised the question of color in Buren's work by suggesting that Buren's palette seemed very French — related to, for example, Matisse.[1] The comparison to Matisse's palette was mentioned again in a panel discussion two weeks later about Buren's work, *Couleurs Superposées: Act IV*, performed at the Guggenheim on the opening weekend of *The Eye of the Storm*.[2] I suppose the reference to Matisse in both cases was meant to bring to mind that artist's late, decorative works, such as the cutouts, or perhaps such earlier work as the décor of the 1920 Ballets Russes production of Stravinsky's *Le Chant du rossignol*.

Buren said nothing to Alberro about Matisse. He did say that color was extremely significant for him — that it very directly and purely constitutes the visibility of his work — but he also insisted that the experience of color is absolutely subjective and indescribable:

> When I say red, I have no idea if the color that I have in my mind is the same as the one that comes to your mind. Even if I say strawberry red or cherry red, I don't know if what I mean means the same to you. Moreover, I don't know if the red I see is the red you see.[3]

Buren also said that, in spite of how essential color is to his work, no intention-ality and no taste is exercised in his choice of colors; the particular color that he uses in any given situation makes no difference to him. He said he chose the color of the gels used on the skylight for his work in the Guggenheim's rotunda, *Around the Corner*, simply because that happened to be the color that was available in sufficient quantity when he sought out the material for the gels two weeks before the opening of *The Eye of the Storm*.

New York Times art critic Michael Kimmelman described the skylight gels of *Around the Corner* as magenta and the parapet stripes as kelly-green.[4] I wasn't sure why *kelly*-green. Maybe Ellsworth Kelly? I thought: Kelly-green, like International Klein Blue? I looked up "kelly-green" in the *Oxford English Dictionary* and found that its first recorded appearance in the English language was in a *Mademoiselle* magazine ad for sweaters in 1936.

So then, magenta and kelly-green. Or just purple and green. I will use a few more examples of this color scheme — all purely coincidental — to frame my discussion.

- An ad in a Sunday *New York Times Style Magazine*.[5] Buren's green and white stripes translated to limited-edition Illy espresso cups. And a purple FrancisFrancis! espresso machine. Purple and green.
- A photograph of me sitting in my office at the Guggenheim Museum about the time we were preparing for the *Sixth Guggenheim International Exhibition* in 1970 (Figure 1). If you can take your eyes off the gorgeous rear end of Ultra Violet on the poster behind me, you can see the colors of my very 1970s fashion choice: purple and green — pale purple sweater, pale green corduroy pants.
- And finally, speaking of fashion, a work of couture: a purple and green cabana-striped silk taffeta evening mantle designed in 1937 by Charles James, photographed for *Vogue* by Horst P. Horst.[6]

The question of color and how it matters and doesn't matter in the work of Buren raises another, related question — that of design. In classical art history, color and design are opposed — as, for example, in the opposition of Venetian to Florentine painting, or of the Baroque to the Renaissance. But in Buren's work, color and design are linked in what Buren calls the "proposition," or the "visual tool" — which, in his words, consists of "a minimum or zero or neutral composition," and "all colors used, without any order of preference, systematically."[7] This reduction, which makes it possible to identify the appearance of 8.7 centimeter stripes, alternating color and white, as "a Buren," runs the risk — which Buren openly embraces — of decoration (Figure 2). "In all of my in situ works," he writes, "the question of the frontier between the decorative and the non-decorative is posed, because the thing that is applied to the wall becomes the wall. Here, one encounters another problem: this would seem to suggest that the wall itself is decorative!"[8]

Figure 1 Douglas Crimp at the Guggenheim Museum, 1970 (photographer unknown)

Figure 2 Daniel Buren, Photo-souvenir: "Peinture-Sculpture," work in situ, in *VI Guggenheim International*, Guggenheim Museum, New York, February 1971 © DB.ADAGP Paris. Photo: Marzot.

One unremarked aspect of this risk of decoration is revealed as early in Buren's career as the letter to *Studio International* written by minimal sculptor Dan Flavin in the exchange of letters about the last-minute removal of Buren's work from the 1971 *Guggenheim International Exhibition*, a removal that Flavin was known to have instigated. Flavin's final paragraph adds what he would like his readers to believe is an after-thought:

> Oh by the way weeks after opening day of the *International* Bob Morris happened to mention to me that he had heard that *he* had led the artists' opposition to the French drapery. 'There will be wars and rumors of wars.' Ah, but what a beautiful day, and the Yankees are winning well in Oakland. It must be a sinister American 'petit-bourgeois' 'imperialist' plot to please me.[9]

Thus Flavin scoffs at the Guggenheim's exclusion of the work by the artist he calls "little Buren" and his own role in it. Flavin's peculiar means of dismissing the critique of American imperialism in the *International Exhibition* in Buren's own letter to *Studio International* after his work *Peinture/Sculpture* was removed is certainly worth mentioning here.[10] Flavin's making light of charges of imperialism by inserting the line about "wars and rumors of wars" from the *Book of Matthew* seems especially careless for that moment in history, for in doing so Flavin appears to condemn anti-Vietnam War politics as little more than apocalyptic silliness.

But I am also struck by a different tactic of Flavin's scorn: his reference to *Peinture/Sculpture* as "French drapery." Curator Alison Gingeras notes, in one of her contributions to the catalogue of *The Eye of the Storm* and in her essay in *Parkett* about Buren's large-scale exhibition at the Centre Pompidou in 2002, the tendency in some quarters to disparage Buren's recent work as merely decorative and thus to fail to comprehend the "decorative strategy" in Buren's work from the beginning. Such an operation, Gingeras claims, "epitomizes a model of reception … that bifurcates artists' careers … into an early (pure) phase and a late (decadent) period" (Gingeras cites as an example Benjamin Buchloh's *Artforum* review of the 1997 Münster Skulptur Projekt, in which he disparages Buren's contribution as "fun-fair decoration").[11] In Gingeras's view, this critical model holds artists to the terms and standards by which their work was judged in its initial moment of reception, whether or not those terms and standards continue to apply — or indeed were entirely appropriate at the time.[12] In this, I think Gingeras is right — except that by locating the animus toward Buren's decorativeness only in the work of "moralizing academic critics" (her words) who repudiate the artist's later career as decadent, she overlooks the fact that the animus toward the decorative was as much present from the beginning as was the decorative strategy of the work itself. The animus was already firmly in place in 1971 when Flavin referred to *Peinture/Sculpture* as French drapery.

And, in my view, the precise meaning we are meant to take from the sneer at Buren's *Guggenheim International* work as French drapery is secured by Flavin's simultaneous pronouncement of himself a Yankees fan.

Moreover, the vocabulary of scorn for the decorative is continued in the present not only by "academic critics" but also by journalists such as Kimmelman, who wrote in his *New York Times* review of *The Eye of the Storm*, concerning *Around the Corner*:

> There is not much to the work, phenomenologically speaking, beyond the initial, kaleidoscopic effect of its mirrors. The museum's ramps are empty. Alternative planes of the circular skylight are colored with magenta gels, making a kind of checkerboard pattern, at certain times of day the sun splashing patches of purple onto the upper part of the Guggenheim's bobbin. This is pretty. Short kelly-green stripes of tape are stuck below the outside rim of the rotunda's parapet. They too reflect in the mirrors, like sprockets of an unspooled film, or like decorative fronds of ivy over the balconies of a hotel atrium. These are not attractive.[13]

Having damned *Around the Corner* as merely producing effects — some pretty, some not attractive — Kimmelman makes his next predictable move: "For years Buren has been a particular darling of the art theorists, beloved for what is perceived as his conceptualist *élan*."[14] Clearly Kimmelman doesn't much keep up with the "art theorists" for, as we've just seen, at least some of them have long since abandoned Buren because, it seems, his *élan* has trumped what they thought were his initial conceptual art commitments.

The Guggenheim Museum invited me to look back at one moment of that initial reception because they knew that I had experienced the 1971 *Guggenheim International Exhibition* at first hand.[15] I gladly accepted their invitation, but I was wary of the implied mandate to tell what "really" happened. Because my subject was, broadly, my memory of first encountering "conceptual art," one model that suggested itself to me was Silvia Kolbowski's *Inadequate History of Conceptual Art*, an art work — indeed, a conceptual art work — of 1998–99 that complicates contemporary accounts of conceptual art by, as Rosalyn Deutsche writes in her essay on Kolbowski, "introducing memory — and with it, the unconscious mind — into the writing of history." The "inadequate" of Kolbowski's title, Deutsche reminds us:

> describes the condition of all cultural histories, since history is a

representation of — a narrative about — the past and therefore unequal to reality. It does not correspond to things as they were. And narrativity is inadequate for another reason: it arises from desire, a desire, as Hayden White says, introducing the problem of subjectivity into the writing of history, "to have real events display the coherence, integrity, fullness, and closure of an image of life that is and can only be imaginary."[16]

I often tell the story of my first job in New York. I had come to the city in 1968 after graduating from college with a degree in art history. I lived in Spanish Harlem, and one day I set out to go to the Metropolitan Museum, where I planned to apply for a job. As I walked down Fifth Avenue from 98th Street, I came upon the Guggenheim, and thought to myself, "Here's a museum, I might just as well try this one." I inquired of the first person I encountered in the lobby of what was then the administration wing about applying for a job. His immediate reply, to my surprise, was to ask, "Do you know anything about Pre-Columbian Art?" "Yes," I answered, "I studied it extensively at college." And so, after very little further discussion, I was offered a job. Entirely fortuitously, just at that moment the Guggenheim was getting ready to install a large exhibition of Pre-Columbian Peruvian art; however, Thomas Messer, the Guggenheim's director at the time, had quarreled with the show's guest curator, Peruvian textile expert Alan Sawyer, and ordered him out of the museum. Whereupon some 800 art objects arrived from Lima, and no one on the Guggenheim staff — all of whom were trained as modernists — knew a Nazca pot from a Moche pot. So it was thought that I might be able to help out with the installation and later work on the information desk. Subsequently I managed to convince the Guggenheim administration that my real field of expertise was modern art, and so I was kept on staff as a curatorial assistant.

I've told this story so many times over the years that I no longer know how much of it is simplification in the interest of narrative design, and how much is embellishment in the interest of making it amusing. I certainly remember working on the installation of the exhibition *Mastercraftsmen of Ancient Peru* in the fall of 1968.[17] More vividly, I remember the black-tie opening, particularly the fact that some of the guests seemed to wish to compete with the exhibit. I was dazzled by socialite Doris Duke's very large ancient Peruvian necklace, and even more dazzled by seeing art collector Ethel Skull — famous for her portrait by Andy Warhol — who, evidently having no ancient Peruvian jewelry to wear, instead carried with her a small pillow on which rested a gold jaguar figurine. It was the wrong Pre-Columbian culture, but it made an impression — and all the more so in that she wore a matching gold-lamé pantaloon jumpsuit. I remember, too, that Pisco sours — cocktails made with a Peruvian brandy — were served at the opening. Also, in those days the Guggenheim always served giant boiled shrimp as hors d'oeuvres at their gala openings. A year or so into my brief tenure at the Guggenheim, a group of us tried unsuccessfully to organize the museum staff to join a labor union, one of our arguments being that the budget for these private parties was way out of proportion to the budget for the pitifully low staff salaries (My starting salary in 1968 was $4200 a year.).

Still, I was pleased to say that I worked at the Guggenheim. It was a famous museum — one of the most famous — because it had a famous building — also one of the most famous — and that made my first job seem very glamorous. My memory of how glamorous it felt was recently sparked when I saw, at the Museum of Modern Art's exhibition *The Museum as Muse*, a photograph by Garry Winogrand of the Guggenheim's tenth anniversary party in 1970.[18] Typical of Winogrand's shoot-from-the-hip aesthetic and wry social commentary, the fancy dress-clad dancers in this picture compose a neat diagonal from the three blurred fingers of a hand cut off by the frame at the lower left to an outstretched arm at top right, punctuated by the corner of a machine-aesthetic pastiche painting by Roy Lichtenstein. You'll have to take it on faith that the blurred hand on the left edge of Winogrand's picture is mine. I was dancing with the woman in the white gown so vividly caught in Winogrand's flash. Her name is Nicole, and her port de bras, even while dancing the frug, confirms what I remember best about her: that she came to New York from France to study with Martha Graham.

After all these years, I still enjoy telling people the story about my first job in New York, working at the Guggenheim Museum. But the story isn't true — that is, it isn't true that my first job in New York was working at the Guggenheim. I have another story of my first job in New York, but I tell it more selectively, because it entails a different sort of glamor.

It was 1967, not 1968, and I had left college before finishing my degree. In my final semester at Tulane University, I was too worried about being drafted during the Vietnam War to concentrate on my school work. Or rather, what preoccupied me was how I would escape the draft. In order to be classified unfit to serve, I told the army at my induction physical that I was gay. So I quit school and moved to New York, where I got my first job. In the summer of 1967, I was hired by Charles James to help him organize his papers for the purpose of writing his memoirs.[19] At the time, James was nearly destitute and living in a squalid suite of small rooms at the Chelsea Hotel. My job with him didn't last long at all, in fact only a couple of weeks. I resented having to do menial tasks like walking his beagle around Chelsea. I wasn't happy that he was slipping amphetamines into my morning coffee. I couldn't tolerate his tantrums. The final straw was his telling me that instead of paying me for my work he would open a charge account for me at Barney's. All told, I just wasn't ready for Charles James. Even so, I love being able to say that my first job in New York was working for Charles James, which I tell shamelessly in some circles — circles where it has even greater cachet than saying that my first job in New York was working at the Guggenheim Museum.

But who, you might ask, is Charles James? Charles James is the designer of the purple and green evening cape. He is a cult figure in the fashion world, where he is generally regarded as America's greatest couturier.

James' career spanned the 1930s, 1940s, and 1950s. He was the dress-maker of choice of many well-known society women of his era — Babe Paley, Millicent Rogers, Lee Radziwill; of other fashion designers — Coco Chanel, Elsa Schiaparelli; of opera divas Lily Pons and Risë Stevens, ballerinas Alicia Markova and Tamara Karsavina, movie stars Gloria Swanson, Marlene Dietrich, Jennifer Jones, even Janet Gaynor, who hardly needed a dress designer, since she was married to Adrian. Unusual for a fashion designer, James was highly regarded in the art world; he received high praise from Museum of Modern Art director Alfred Barr. James' work was the subject of a solo exhibition at the Brooklyn Museum while he was still in his thirties.[20] Artist Lee Krasner and art patron Dominique de Menil were clients. Indeed, James not only made clothes for Mrs. de Menil but he also decorated the interior of her modernist house in Houston, designed by Philip Johnson in his early Miesian phase in 1949–50. James' art-world connections explain my getting a job with him. Another of his clients, Jeanne Bultman, the wife of abstract expressionist painter Fritz Bultman and the mother of friends from college with whom I came to New York, knew that James needed an assistant and suggested me.

James was venerated by these people not only as a fashion designer but as an artist, a sculptor in cloth. At the beginning of his career, James billed himself as a "sartorial structural architect."[21] He was famous for draping fabric directly on to his clients' bodies in the initial process of constructing clothes. Richard Martin, the late curator of the Metropolitan Museum's Costume Institute, described James' dresses as "monumental sculptures in fabric."[22] A James dress, he wrote, "could very nearly stand on its own, so filled was it with material, but the picturesque effect was that of a dream walking. Some James dresses are reportedly nearly fifty pounds in weight."[23] *Bombast* would be an accurate adjective for many of James' gowns; the literal meaning of *bombast* is "padding for clothes." In spite of the discrepancy between bulky structure and gossamer appearance, James was considered by some to be a true modernist, and the following recollection by one of James' clients reads to me like a wonderful parody of the subject–object relations entailed in ideas of modernist autonomy:

> He was sometimes so entranced by the shape he was 'sculpting' over one's own shape that when the dress arrived finished it was impossible to get into it. It existed on its own. Much time was then spent in discerning the proper relationship between shapes.[24]

I like to picture this scene in the lady's dressing room: unable to get herself into her new gown, she simply positions herself somewhere near it and contemplates it as the self-reflexive work of art it surely must be. In the face of such transcendent "presentness," who's to complain? Or think of oneself? Compare Anne, Countess of Rosse, another James client:

> But — the wearer if she wanted to enjoy his creations had sometimes to be sacrificed for the designs! To begin with, there could be a mystery as to how to get into the clothes when they arrived! Or which was the front or the back, which he might have altered at the last moment! With some, walking might be difficult — or sitting down tricky! But an appreciative wearer would gladly cooperate.[25]

That modern forms do not necessarily follow function was one of the lessons of the Fashion Institute of Technology Museum's 2004 exhibition titled *Form Follows Fashion*, which featured James as presiding genius.[26] James was given the Coty American Fashion Critics Award in 1950, cited not for the mystery of how — or whether — a dress was to be worn but for the "great mystery of color and artistry of draping."

With that citation — "great mystery of color and artistry of draping" — I'll return to the business at hand: to Daniel Buren, the 1971 *Guggenheim International*, to what Dan Flavin called "French drapery," to my other first job in New York.

I worked at the Guggenheim Museum from the fall of 1968 to the spring of 1971, most of that time as the curatorial assistant to Diane Waldman, one of the two curators of the *Sixth Guggenheim International Exhibition*, and the curator who decided to remove Buren's work from the show. As Waldman's assistant, I dealt with the day-to-day details of many aspects of the exhibition and its catalogue. I remember very well Buren's instructions for his contribution to the catalogue, which I carried out. I most likely remember the details well because Buren's contribution was unlike any other, and it was difficult at first for me to comprehend. The catalogue had a unique design. It was a silver-colored box containing, first, a 42-page staple-bound booklet with a preface by museum director Thomas Messer, essays by each of the show's curators, Edward Fry and Diane Waldman, a general bibliography, and a number of black and white illustrations; and second, fold-out sheets of four, six, or eight pages for each artist in the show.[27] The general scheme for each of these was a cover page with a brief biography and a photograph of the artist, followed by photographs and drawings of their works, and an exhibition list and bibliography. The artists had some say in what would be included in their individual pages. Buren asked the museum to print his usual 8.7 centimeter stripes — red in this case — 8.7 centimeters apart, on the recto and verso of a six-page fold-out sheet. At the bottom of each page, a printed caption read: "Daniel Buren: Detail in Actual Size of a Work Executed in 1966," "Daniel Buren: Detail in Actual Size of a Work Executed in 1967," and so forth, up through 1971. That was all. No photos or drawings, no biography, exhibition list, or bibliography. Buren's pages varied from the formula for the individual artists' pages more completely than did those of any other artist, and his instructions were absolutely precise.

I have little doubt that Buren's instructions to the museum for his work *Peinture/Sculpture* were as clear and detailed as they were for his allotted catalogue pages, which would contradict Waldman's allegation in her *Studio International* statement, "The Museum Responds," that Buren had kept his intentions vague until the last minute.[28] But I do not have as clear a memory of my dealings with Buren about the work as I do of that about his catalogue pages, and I regrettably didn't take copies of my own files with me when I left the museum the following summer. I do remember the installation of the indoors portion of *Peinture/Sculpture* on the day before the opening of the exhibition (the outdoors portion was, of course, never installed). The very complicated rigging that was required to hang the 32x64 foot striped canvas from the top ramp of the Frank Lloyd Wright rotunda took almost all day, a day filled with the on-the-spot working-out of technical problems that these sorts of installations entail. But finally in the late afternoon, there it was. How to describe it? I feel a certain pressure here. I was one of only a very few people who actually saw the work. The trouble is, I've also subsequently seen photographs of it, over and over again. Buren took a number of his *photo-souvenirs* on the day the work was installed, and the Guggenheim staff photographer also photographed it, and these photographs have been published widely over the years.

Buren's work for the *Guggenheim International* was what he called a work "in situ," or what we now call site specific. While a number of other artists in the *International* made or adapted work for particular locations in the museum, only a very few of the works could be characterized as site specific, and none had the site-specific force or meaning that Buren's did. Buren wrote at the time in *Studio International*:

> The demonstration I tried to make at the Guggenheim incorporated among other things a certain use of the space which revealed both the place itself and the attraction which diverts attention away from the spiral ramp on which the paintings are hung; the architecture renders what is exhibited obsolete and peripheral ... As soon as the architecture appears so powerfully in its own right, the work of art (intended for a cubic, classic, customary setting) disappears. This is what happens with the Guggenheim Museum, and it is for this reason, among others, that any work that brings out this fact ... creates an unexpected commotion.[29]

I think everyone who saw Buren's banner was astonished by it. Its enormous size and placement in the center of the Guggenheim's rotunda exposed — in both senses of the word: it laid bare and it showed off — Frank Lloyd Wright's architecture more dramatically than could have been foreseen from drawings and measurements, and in doing so it fully demonstrated what Buren understood as the subjugation to that architecture of any work of art that does not contend with it. With Buren's work in place, for example, when you looked down from the museum's upper ramps onto Richard Serra's steel-plate prop piece, *Moe*, on the floor below, it looked like a miniature, a maquette for what, in the context of its more usual placement in a white cube gallery space, would be a massive and threateningly precarious-seeming work.

The story of what happened next has been often told and is highly contested. No sooner had the work been installed than it was taken down, so that by the time the *International* opened the following evening, Buren had been expelled from the exhibition. I was sorely disappointed. I had been exhilarated by the work's imposing presence; its absence rendered what was left of the exhibition uninteresting to me — or perhaps I should say that the loss of Buren's work was all that I could experience. I had worked more directly with Buren than any other artist in the show, and we had become friends. Without question, my recognition of the implications of this work, delayed and indirect though they were, reverberated through my critical work on contemporary art practices and the institution of the museum during the 1980s.[30]

Why was the work removed? In his thoroughly researched essay about the event, "The Turn of the Screw," Alex Alberro locates the censorship of Buren's work in the context of what he calls a "massive wave of reaction" in American politics in the early 1970s, during which, he argues, the museum felt forced to uphold a compromise position, a liberal version of avant-gardism that presented new art as critical only of previous art trends, not of the institution of art as a whole. "The museum had erred in interpreting Buren's proposal," he claims, because they failed to understand the radical politics that informed his work. This, he continues:

> became all too clear when Buren made unequivocal the critique developed by his installation by providing a political language outside of his work. Speaking to *New York Times* reporter Grace Glueck, who had come to preview the *International*, Buren insisted that he not be referred to as an artist and proclaimed that "both artists and museums in the traditional sense are obsolete." Inasmuch as in and of themselves the banners at the zero degree of form did not offer any information whatsoever to the viewer, their message was completely overdetermined by the critical metalanguage Buren provided outside the frame of the paintings — metalanguage that rendered unavoidable not only the installation's critique of the function of the other works in the show but also its *détournement* of the museum itself. It is likely that more than anything else it was this statement, which appeared in the largest daily newspaper in the United States the day before the opening, that led Guggenheim officials to decide that it was in their best interests to censor Buren's work.[31]

Alberro's assertion that it was "political language outside the work" that necessitated the Guggenheim's action separates the meaning of Buren's work from its material, visual presence, and in so doing reduces the meaning of "a zero degree of form" to a purely textual meaning. In this, Alberro repeats the error of Buren's first US critics. In 1973, for example, Roberta Smith wrote:

> The work, already nonvisual enough, tends to be a little overwhelmed by [the texts], becoming some kind of illustration for the ideas ... Buren is interesting and important for the criticisms he makes, for the discussion he precipitates, but ... it is a discussion more precipitated by reading than by looking.[32]

In "Why Write Texts, or The Place from Where I Act," the preface to his *Five Texts* published in 1973, Buren warned against this reduction of his work to a concept, or simple content:

> The importance of the texts should not be exaggerated, and the reader should beware of the facility and illusion which they may engender, the facility that would permit one who has read the texts to feel exempt from looking at the painting, thinking them explicit in the texts, and forgetting that the painting explains and inspires the texts.[33]

In addition to reducing the work to a textual content, Alberro goes much further than Buren when he seeks to amplify Buren's simple statement, quoted by Grace Glueck in the same *Times* story, that "The Guggenheim Museum really kills a piece of art, primarily because it is a work of art itself." Alberro writes that because "the museum is constructed along an extended spiral ramp, the installed works are not spatially distinguished from one another," which "produces a confusing jumble of signs, resulting in the uniqueness of the spectacular building itself becoming the most significant work of art." Moreover, "the architectural order of the building is essentially authoritarian in nature" because the spiral ramp imposes "sequential perception" that "allows the spectators no real choice as to how they will view the works." And finally:

> The museum is itself a spectacle. The works on exhibit are in constant competition with the grandeur of the omnipresent gaping vortex. This effect is amplified by the Guggenheim's continually spiraling walls, which, like the curvilinear motion of a whirlpool that is directed toward the center of the axis of rotation, attract the viewer's eye inward toward the void where the building celebrates itself.[34]

In 1962, during his tenure as curator at the Museum of Modern Art, the beloved New York School poet Frank O'Hara viewed the then-relatively new Frank Lloyd Wright building far more charitably. In one of his Art Chronicles he wrote:

> It may be worthwhile, or at least different, to say something nice about the building ... From long before construction work started on it, it had been a controversial thing, and it stayed so throughout the work on it, its opening, and its first several shows — every detail of its design was discussed everywhere from the newspaper to The Club, and rumors that its then-director might quit because he hated the floor, or the wall, or the dome, or the lighting, or even the elevator, were circulated ... The museum is, of course, worthy of all this attention, and it has many merits not shared by other institutions of similar or identical nature ... it's wonderful

looking from the outside, and when you enter the flat exhibition space on the ground floor the effect of the works near at hand, the ramps and over them glimpses of canvases and then the dome, is urbane and charming, like the home of a cultivated and mildly eccentric person.

O'Hara enjoys a downward stroll on the museum's ramp, which for him:

is enhanced by the glimpses you've been sneaking … at the pictures on the lower ramps, and you get lots of surprises: things that looked especially inviting or dramatic from a partial look turn out to be totally uninteresting and others you hadn't bothered to anticipate are terrific (though the operation isn't invariable).

He also likes the ramp because, in his view, "it almost entirely eliminates galley-going fatigue." "Anyhow," he concludes this short musing on the museum:

I like the whole experience, the "bins" where you come around a semi-wall and find a masterpiece has had its back to you, the relation between seeing a painting or a sequence of them from across the ramp and then having a decent interval of time and distraction intervene before the close scrutiny: in general my idea is that this may not be (as what is) the ideal museum, but in this instance Frank Lloyd Wright was right in the lovable way that Sophie Tucker was to get her gold tea set, which she described as, "It's way out on the nut for service, but it was my dream!"[35]

The well-known photographs of Frank Lloyd Wright's building by such modernist architectural photographers as Ezra Stoller and Julius Shulman seem to want to awaken Wright from his dream by reducing the building to the rationalism of pure abstraction. That reduction of modern architecture to abstract iconicity would, in turn, appear to be the subject of Hiroshi Sugimoto's recent series of photographs of canonical modern buildings, including the Guggenheim Museum. The effect of blurring in Sugimoto's pictures makes visible the fact that our images of modern architecture are by now mnemonic, even dreamlike, and in so doing hints at modernist architecture's own unconscious.

Dare we call it the decorative unconscious? And could this unconscious, produced by repressing modern architecture's deep affinity with fashion, as Mark Wigley has convincingly argued in his book *White Walls, Designer Dresses*,[36] be what Charles James wished to expose when he undertook the interior decoration of Philip Johnson's residence for the de Menils in 1950? Certainly James' design could not have been more perfectly suited to the French-born Houston collectors, whose impeccable high modernist taste, rooted in their primary devotion to Surrealism, could incorporate a wildly eclectic array of art — from Cycladic figures and Byzantine frescos to Mark Rothko and Andy Warhol. Johnson's austere modernist house — which appears from the street as a plain cream-colored brick wall punctured only by the small apertures of the kitchen windows and the glass-door entrance — is adorned inside with an equivalent eclecticism, but in this case the eclecticism of a flamboyant decorator. As a *New York Times* story on the De Menil house restoration put it:

> James swept down from New York prepared to cause a little trouble. He took one look at the plans and insisted that the ceilings be raised 10 inches. He designed and built distinctive new furniture, including an oversize octagonal ottoman and a chaise longue in wrought iron and chartreuse silk.
>
> In an audacious deviation from the white walls prescribed by devout Modernism, James anchored the living room with a striking gray wall and made the hallways vivid pink, crimson, and tobacco.[37]

The moment you enter, you face an acid-green velvet upholstered Victorian settee, a signal of the fact that the furniture throughout will be a hodge-podge of periods, cultures, and styles and include, among James' other creations, his *Butterfly Sofa*, inspired by Salvador Dali's 1936 *Mae West's Lips* couch. This is décor gone berserk. If design is a crime, as we have recently been lectured, then this must be a lurid sex crime.[38]

Of course, Frank Lloyd Wright was hardly a modernist in the sense that Phillip Johnson understood and practiced modern architecture at mid-century. Wright polemicized against what he called "the box," never banished ornament, never painted a wall white. The Guggenheim Museum is *off*-white.[39] This great spiral museum, commissioned from the 76-year-old Wright in 1943 for what was then called the Museum of Non-Objective Painting, would cap a long career that began in the nineteenth century. Wright died before the building was completed in 1959.

When Barbara Reise asked Guggenheim director Thomas Messer in an interview for *Studio International* following the Buren debacle whether he thought Wright "was possibly forcing some questions upon the character of what a museum, as an institution, could accept or … ratify as art," Messer replied, correctly in my estimation, "No … I think he probably had in mind a highly static situation in which a great collection assembled by a particular family would be shown permanently …"[40]

I doubt whether Wright could have understood Reise's question at all, since it is asked from the historical perspective of 1971, a perspective opened up by work such as Buren's. By 1971, the Guggenheim Museum was rarely used as Wright had expected it would be, as the repository of the "non-objective" paintings collected for Solomon Guggenheim by the Baroness Hilla von Rebay, protégé and proponent of Kandinsky. It had subsequently become an exhibition venue for very different kinds of art. For example, in 1970 the spiral ramp was entirely given over to the work of Carl Andre.

Thirty-four years later, the ante had again been upped. The lessons of Buren's censored work of 1971 had been learned, even by his antagonist Dan Flavin, who remade and extended his *Guggenheim International* work to occupy the entire museum ramp in 1992. In addition, he installed a floor-to-skylight column of pale pink fluorescent light in the center of the museum's rotunda. He titled the work *to Tracy, to celebrate the love of a lifetime*, and he and his love were married there. A few years later, in 1998, Guggenheim director Thomas Krens also made an exhibition dedicated to his lifetime love — in this case, motorcycles — and he got the most celebrated of contemporary museum architects, Frank Gehry, to design the installation.

It is in these changed circumstances that Buren returned to the "eye of the storm," to present *Around the Corner* and other works. "French drapery" is apparently no longer adequate to the circumstances. Now "the proposition," "the visual tool" for exposing Wright's museum as itself a work of art, is — in addition to the purple and green, the magenta gels and kelly-green stripes — an imposing mirrored structure whose corner is dead center in the grand sky-lit rotunda. As we circle down the ramp, that structure continuously reflects the rotunda and our own spectatorship of it, except when, again and again, six times over, we enter into the relative darkness of the mirrored wall's verso side. Unlike a Charles James garment, this is a structure that we can get into. As a visual tool, though, it has all the ostentation of a James evening gown. Like the Guggenheim Museum itself, like Sophie Tucker's gold tea set, it's way out on a nut for service.

10

Who Needs Human Rights?

Cultural Studies and Public Institutions

John Nguyet Erni

Reframing Cultural Studies

My goal in this chapter is to attempt to bring about an articulation between Cultural Studies and public law in order to better understand the changing and complex political context that continuously shapes contemporary ethical debates. More specifically, I am trying to forge a closer relation between Cultural Studies (especially the social movement bent of the field) and human rights (especially critical legal theory as well as the pragmatic practices of the field) — seeing that both share a commitment to social justice work — at a time of enormous global uncertainties and egregious erosion of liberties. I know this is a tall order, so I'd like to keep this project modest by focusing on the way in which we may reconceive human rights and international public law — including the assumptions, institutions, relations, and practices of the rights discourse, as it is imagined politically and legally — in order to remap the ethico-political commitments of Cultural Studies from *within* a "rights imaginary." This will require a perspective that will enable us to embed the practice of Cultural Studies inside the legal space of, the institutions associated with, and social movements connected to human rights.

Cultural Studies and human rights practices have different genealogies. Whereas the former is grounded in anti-foundational philosophy, critical sociology, critical theory in the humanities, and interpretive social sciences, the latter are influenced profoundly by Kantian philosophy and ethics, natural law, positivist law traditions, and social movement work. While there are philosophical incompatibilities between the two, there are also intellectual and political synergies. To date, however, interdisciplinary dialogue or institutional collaboration remains rare across the two domains.

Without having to put together the list of wars, killings, brutalities, and all forms of social and economic exploitations that we see today in national and international contexts, it is nonetheless possible to mark this current conjuncture as, in David Luban's words, "the end of human rights."[1] At the same time, it is equally possible for us to note a sense of ethico-political renewal of global human rights accountability that has been raised by problems of acute poverty, extreme environmental crises, and deep ethnic and religious conflicts, to name just a few. In this context, how are the concurrent ideas about the "death" and "renewal" of human rights related to Cultural Studies? I ask this question assuming that Cultural Studies is still a project committed to analyzing the changing contemporary conjuncture, and is still supposed to be self-reflexive about its vocational objectives. Political theorist Jean Cohen observes that as capitalist expansion becomes more and more globalized, she conceives of two choices we have in dealing with a possibly obsolete international human rights system. We could either work to strengthen human rights legal institutions and norms by updating them — that is, by cosmopolitanizing them — or seek to suspend consensually established global rule of law in the name of "saving" human rights from "rogue" nations and fringe groups with the underlying intent of restoring the neo-liberal order of "empire."[2] We know full well which of the two options the Bush–Blair regime from 2001 until 2008 took toward the United Nations and the entire global rights discourse. What does Cultural Studies have to say to this at the moment when basic rights are seriously under threat, and when the discourse of human rights has been hijacked to serve the agenda of the imperial powers?

I am trying to think through how Cultural Studies can be *relocated* to meet the current challenges in social and political struggles worldwide, and thus to remap the context for the field itself.[3] Is human rights law a viable political practice that can address what Nancy Fraser calls redistributive and recognition justice?[4] My hope is to take Cultural Studies somewhere from which it has largely stayed away — the domain of formalized institutional rules of engagement in general, and international human rights law in particular — and in so doing, open a door for critical scholarship to flow. To this, Rosemary Coombe's reminder in her article entitled "Is There a Cultural Studies of Law?" seems useful: "Although legal texts, legal forums, and legal processes have been analyzed as cultural forms, no substantial body of work demonstrating the methodological commitments, theoretical premises, and political convictions that characterize the interdisciplinary field of Cultural Studies has yet appeared with respect to law."[5]

In the last chapter of his 1992 book, Larry Grossberg gave a biting critique of the American left's failure to mobilize an anti-war struggle in the wake of the first Iraq War.[6] There is an interesting section of the chapter that reads, "Politics as the Art of the Possible."[7] Referring to the dramatic dismantling of Apartheid in South Africa, Grossberg argues that what the progressive movements did to help bring Apartheid to an end was to "mobiliz[e] popular pressure on institutions and bureaucracies of economic and governmental institutions."[8] He addresses the American left:

> The Left too often thinks that it can end racism and sexism and classism by changing people's attitudes and everyday practices … Unfortunately, while such struggles may be extremely visible, they are often less effective than attempts to move the institutions … which have put the economic relations and Black and immigrant populations in place and which condition people's everyday practices. The Left needs institutions which can operate within the systems of governance, understanding that such institutions are the mediating structures by which power is actively realized … The Left does in fact need more visibility, but it also needs greater access to the entire range of apparatuses of decision making and power. Otherwise, the Left has nothing but its own self-righteousness.[9]

Grossberg's call for an increased institutional visibility of the left, which he made at that time in response to Reaganism, is entirely relevant — if not more so — today in an era shaped by a global regime of military and economic aggression bolstered by an ever-expanding neo-liberal cultural order, even in the Obama years.

Cultural Studies and Ethics

In recent years, many have expressed dissatisfaction about the relevance of Cultural Studies. The myriad forms of intellectual and political interventions that have been made under the broad rubric of Cultural Studies, it has been said, have promulgated at best a discourse of general dissent, but at worst a space for self-reproduction.[10] Whatever "success" there is for Cultural Studies in engendering new intellectual formations in and outside of universities, it is generally tainted by a nagging lack of clarity or ethical force. Joanna Zylinski puts it this way:

> [W]hile the more overtly articulated political questions shape the Cultural Studies agenda, ethics seems to be its hidden, unrecognised and

uncalled-for other. Whenever ethics does make an appearance in Cultural
Studies, it risks being reduced — even if mainly by press commentators
and supporters of the traditional model of "excellence" in education — to
either moralism or "victim recognition."[11]

In ethico-political debates today, is Cultural Studies that which one cannot not
want?

I still remember being profoundly struck by a lecture Stuart Hall gave at
the 1990 Cultural Studies Now and in the Future conference in Illinois, when
he talked about the marginality of critical intellectuals in "making real effects
in the world."[12] At that time, Hall spoke in part in response to the HIV/AIDS
crisis in the United States and worldwide. If the crisis, at its deeply despairing
moment in 1990, both biomedically and politically speaking, ushered in Hall's
own despair (when he said, "Against the urgency of people dying in the streets,
what in God's name is the point of Cultural Studies?"[13]), then what are the
choices for Cultural Studies today when confronted by all of the political violations we see in front of us? If Hall explicitly refuses to let Cultural Studies off
the hook (of its political and theoretical obligations), this cannot be explained
by any reluctance to recognize the innovations Cultural Studies has brought to
the political field and the enterprise of theory, but it can be explained perhaps
by the urgent need to metamorphose the very notion of Cultural Studies as
a type of practice in the world. Put more explicitly, I think the problem is in
part how to recharacterize Cultural Studies *after* the exuberant proliferation
of its own spaces. In academic corridors at least, is Cultural Studies a newly
remodeled humanities discipline, a consciousness-raising flagship operation
on behalf of politics in the streets, or a new form of applied research? Or can
it be a reformulated type of discipline built on the advancement of pragmatic
justice through a tripartite investment in critique, professional training, and
public participation? I am certainly not the first person to ask this kind of con-
stitutional question about Cultural Studies,[14] but I have in mind a specific way
of (narrowly) posing the question, which is this: In the (re)turn to both dis-
tributive and recognition justice, how will Cultural Studies clear a space for a
parallel intellectual and political engagement with human rights law as a global
professional, interdisciplinary, and pragmatic humanitarian practice?

I came into contact with human rights debates through an interdisciplinary
program at Columbia University. In 1999, I held a Rockefeller Fellowship that
enabled me to participate in Carol Vance's then newly established Program
on Gender, Sexuality, Health, and Human Rights.[15] The program was an

intellectual enterprise established by Vance to engage with the multiple forms of social, political, cultural, and postcolonial wars against non-normative genders and sexualities. This enterprise culminated in the weekly seminars, which saw participation from feminists, representatives of community groups, critical-minded staff and graduate students, and human rights advocates, analysts, and practitioners. While very few of those participants directly allied themselves with Cultural Studies *per se*, the discussion in the weekly seminars intersected tacitly with it by means of a shared critical sensibility, a more or less common academic vocabulary drawn from a broad Marxist, feminist, subalternist, and postmodernist ethos, and finally, a crypto-critique of the relevance of Cultural Studies itself. As our discussion began to take shape around a complicated set of concerns brought about by theories of gender and sexuality, the various forms of public health practices that contoured international body politics, and the community-based activist-oriented critique, the discussion was also frequently dominated by a human rights legal perspective. A rights-based discourse in formal legalistic terms, as well as in the more informal terms of oppositional critique of law, was not only leading our discussion, it effectively colonized it. I mentioned earlier the presence of a crypto-critique of the relevance of Cultural Studies. The inadequacy of Cultural Studies in using its analytical tools to speak about the problematics at hand became a tacitly agreed-upon fact among the participants. The "shame," if you will, was subtly cast in the form of Cultural Studies' lack of institutional knowledge of, or strategic political capital in, either rights-based discourse or legal-based intervention. The tacit or hidden agreement about the seeming irrelevance of Cultural Studies, while not manifesting in any direct attack on Cultural Studies, nevertheless silenced it. To me, the experience was one of intellectual reinvigoration via a strange form of (self-)silencing. I found myself troubled by a certain kind of theoretical as well as political reductionism in an intellectual atmosphere dominated by human rights discourse and international law. In this particular context, are human rights discourses and international law that which one cannot not want?

Mostly, I remember feeling very uneasy about a certain kind of self-assurance of political certainty. I felt that human rights were too easily taken as a rallying point to either express various modes of injury or to attack various forms of nationalism that inflict those injuries. Yet at the same time I was immensely seduced by the rights discourse and international law. I felt that those were clearly blind spots in Cultural Studies' whole theoretical apparatus for thinking through questions of power and politics. That a complicated

engagement through an oscillation between skepticism and seduction was conducted via (self-)silencing, convinced me that Cultural Studies somehow must
render itself more "relevant" without sacrificing its anti-reductionist stance.[16]

Facing the problem of Cultural Studies' apparent lack of relevance, we may
be compelled to ask what is *after* Cultural Studies as we know it today, by aban-
doning those elements of the field that lead to mere self-reproduction, thus
relinquishing a certain barrier to other critical impulses. Larry Grossberg has
continuously called for a necessary "relocation" of Cultural Studies in relation
to the pressing conjunctural struggles. To do so, he argues, would require us:

> not only doing Cultural Studies conjuncturally but also reinventing
> Cultural Studies itself — its theories and its questions — in response to
> conjunctural conditions and demand. It is for this reason, I think, that
> Cultural Studies (along with many other critical paradigms and practices)
> has had surprisingly little to contribute to the analysis of the very signifi-
> cant struggles and changes taking place within many national formations
> as well as on a transnational scale. Without an understanding of what is
> going on, Cultural Studies cannot contribute to envisioning other scenar-
> ios and outcomes, and the strategies that might take us down alternative
> pathways.[17]

Refiguring Human Rights

Let me now briefly sketch an integrated framework of analysis that serves to
redirect Cultural Studies toward a symbiotic convergence with human rights
political and legal practices. This is a framework underscored by the notion
that human rights is, simply put, "a site of legal-cultural struggles." By this I
mean three critical dimensions: (1) a conceptual reorientation of human rights
as a political representation of modernities-in-struggle; (2) a perspective of
human rights as a nodal point of transnational social movements; and (3) a
utilization of human rights as a global legal apparatus with notable impact on
the discourse of public social justice.

Human Rights as Modernities-in-Struggle

The genealogy of the modern human rights regime suggests that not only were
distinctive states engaged in a search for a common humanity, they were also
in search of a common modernity. Those were at least the expressed motivations for constructing a new and peaceful international community in the

early twentieth century. The price for peace and stability took the form of an enactment of a moral-juridical discourse of universal rights buttressed by the rational science of international relations. However, in this embryonic stage of industrial modernity, there were already two signs that suggested the fragility of that universalist project. First, the League of Nations formed at the end of World War I instituted a series of minorities treaties as soon as a remapping of territoriality was underway in Europe. It was realized that the redrawing of state borders and the creation of new states necessitated the creation of minorities treaties and declarations to protect displaced ethnic groups, especially those in Eastern Europe. This was the first sign of a nascent but localized particularism in the world conception of human rights. But a more serious threat to universal rights came in the contentious debate over the question of slavery. The reluctance of many members within the League to abolish slavery, needless to say, seriously called into question the moral foundation of the rights discourse. Despite efforts to address the question of slavery, such as the 1926 Slavery Convention, the notion of a unified modernity was breaking at the seams. With that, the property-based conception of human rights looked all too suspect, and the concern for the plight of workers felt all too phony. Yet at a deeper level, this second sign that punctured the universalism in human rights revealed a larger problem, which is the question about modernities-in-struggle.

What the modern system of human rights exposes is a competition of modernities, manifested through rivalry among immutable colonial powers as well as recognition of vestiges of cultural differences around the globe. Western nations formed their own power bloc in order to proffer Enlightenment ideals of human emancipation, while continuing to advance their imperial interests around the globe. Meanwhile, pre-industrialized African nations banded together to formulate what an appropriate rights regime might look like for their indigenes. The League of Nations was widely perceived as a failed revolutionary project, since it succeeded neither in banishing armed conflicts, nor in inaugurating a new modernity of equality and human emancipation.[18]

The history of human rights leading up to the current moment continues to annex a history of encounter between industrial and post-industrial modernity of the West and alternative visions of modernity embodied chiefly by the colonized others. Agrarian modernity, Islamic modernity, Confucian modernity: these are but provisional notations gesturing toward visions of humanity and of rights that are *excluded* from, or made *secondary* to, colonial modernity. It is therefore not by chance that the modern human rights structure under the United Nations saw a stratification of rights into primary and secondary rights, or successive "generations" of rights. The second and third generations of rights are those rights that are most closely relevant to non-Western nations, including development rights, cultural rights, indigenous rights, and various forms of social and economic rights. Meanwhile, the imagination of primary or first-generation rights coincides with the political imperative of protecting industrial interests, processes of marketization, Judeo-Christian rights, and the development of the legal architecture of modern governance.

To date, the most visible and controversial retort to the hegemonic discourse of primary rights linked to Western liberal models of democracy has come from industrialized East Asia. With the 1993 Bangkok Declaration on Human Rights, an apparent consensus was reached to oppose the universalizing norms in the Western conception of human rights. The Bangkok Declaration attempted to reframe human rights as a question of sovereignty defense by Asian nations — a kind of putative regional rights platform to plan their own alternative future without interference from the West. Article 6 declares that "all countries, large and small, have the right to determine their political systems, control and freely utilize their resources, and freely pursue their economic, social and cultural development." Here, an ethno-national argument is clear, when elevated to the status of a political consensus for a regional right of self-determination, emboldening Asian governments to achieve hegemony over an ostensibly "alternative" polity. The consolidated tag of the "Asian values" debate in fact exposes the chauvinistic nationalisms of industrialized East Asia, which in many ways mirror the colonial nationalisms of the industrialized West. In fact, right after the Bangkok meetings, in barely three months' time, the Vienna Declaration in 1993 saw many NGOs from the developing world, including those from Asia, *reject* the "Asian values" push. Many of the groups still wanting to work toward establishing local human rights commissions in their countries nonetheless refused to let the ethno-nationalism of the Bangkok Declaration go unchallenged.[19] Pheng Cheah takes this kind of sentiment one step further by arguing that the polarization of modernities masks an underlying hegemonic order:

> [W]hat is at stake in the elaborately media-staged skirmishes between states over international human rights [at the Bangkok meetings] is not really Western or Northern imperializing universalism versus Eastern or Southern cultural difference. The two poles of that binary opposition are complicitous. The fight is between different globalizing models of capitalist

accumulation attempting to assert economic hegemony. The coding of this fight in terms of cultural difference diverts our attention from the subtending line of force of global capital that brings the two antagonists into an aporetic embrace *against* the possibility of other alternatives of development, feminist or ecological-subalternist.[20]

Here, Cheah strikes a cautionary note on any sense of statist alterity that captures "culture" as simultaneously a defense and a mask. What is ultimately excluded is the possibility of an autonomous politics of human rights in the Global South, the site of a range of emergent modernities that have variously been called indigenous, post-developmental, or post-socialist. The human rights system as a whole has not adequately responded to these emergent modernities that, despite their marginality in the global geopolitical sphere, must struggle with all forms of political and economic violence brought about by global capitalist expansion. We must ask: How does the modern human rights system move forward to address post-Enlightenment and post-capitalist rights by considering the rights discourse's own postcolonial condition? How do we reconceive of an outside to the modern human rights regime, by thinking from *within* the regime's configuration of modernities?

To work through this conundrum, some international lawyers from the Global South have sought to reconceptualize a new, and perhaps more genuine, conception of universalism in human rights. They argue that international law must be "decolonized," without threatening the universal applicability of international law itself. They have called for a new international economic order and the establishment of the UN Conference on Trade and Development.[21] They believe that colonial history has already enabled an exchange between the West and the colonized nations over the value of humanity, rights, and indeed universalism. Some human rights law scholars propose that human rights reform entails both an excavation of hidden sources of positive value in the occidental universal value system — a kind of appeal to Kantian peace[22] — and an injection of *multiple universalisms* drawn from different world traditions and epistemological systems into international law itself.[23] Both strategies involve only a partial repudiation of the universalism of international law because they maintain that the universal applicability of international law is essential for the human rights system as a whole. But more importantly, such approaches contend that subaltern cultures in emergent modernities are equally entitled to inform universal values, and even more interestingly, that the process by which cultures were subalternized already involved a colonial exchange that had historically shaped what we now take to be universal values.[24]

What results from our discussion thus far is that human rights and international law together form a political representation of modernities-in-struggle. The articulation between a continuous analysis of the colonial origins of rights and the global applicability of international law ensures that no one modernity will forever dominate the rights discourse. At the heart of human rights and international law, there is thus a sense of a productive ontological instability. Among other things, this ontological instability means that we shall continue to have to struggle with universalism and its paradoxes in human rights.

Human Rights as Transnational Social Movements

Human rights constitutes an axis in a transnational range of social movements. The mass organizations today are more likely than their predecessors in the Cold War era to form an intricate collectivity capable of transforming the traditional fixed positions, whether it is the position of the peasant, the unionist, the woman, the black, or even the intellectual. With "horizontal networking" as its *modus operandi*, this collectivity strives to link up various scales of social movements from different locales and regions, generating both planned and impromptu events to lend support to people and groups that have been unjustly treated by the state, raise popular consciousness, oppose repressive policies, and stage direct actions.

In the horizontal networks of social movements, human rights occupy a productively ambivalent position. It is true that some social movements are organized to precisely oppose the liberal logic and a perceived vertical power structure that underpin human rights organizations. Indeed, we must not forget that tension often exists between the broad civil society sector and human rights groups over where to put the appropriate focus of their efforts (for instance, humanitarian, welfare-based, or treaty-based),[25] and what kind of relationship they should maintain with the state organs (that is, whether it is more or less desirable to acquire legal recognition by the state). Moreover, for a long time, a vast part of Latin America saw no organic connection whatsoever between their struggles and human rights, seeing the complicity of, or at least an unfortunate connection between, human rights bureaucracies and state-based power.[26]

Yet, despite the ambivalence, social movements have never strayed far away from the political ethos of rights. The interconnection of rights as a fundamental principle can provide an important political strategy for articulating social movements as a differentiated but interrelated field. International human rights law provides a sufficiently decentered conception of the political sphere to imagine not only individual rights, but increasingly also collective rights. For instance, when rights are viewed as always already "inter-rights," a notion that demands a rigorous juxtaposition and balance among various forms of justice claims, they can become a productive locus for moving beyond individual rights to analyze how best to strategize collective claim-making. In the 1990s, a conception of inter-rights protection was in fact a basis for promulgating in international law a new principle of "legal intersectionality," which began to demand innovative combinations and realignments of rights claim-making in order to redress the blind spots inherent in any singular human rights instrument. Originally conceived on the basis of individual rights, the principle of intersectionality can nonetheless be conceived to refigure violence as violence against differentiated but connected groups. In other words, it is a principle that can be expanded to cover both *intrinsic intersectionality* (for example, in the case of a multiply positioned individual seeking rights) and *extrinsic intersectionality* (as in the case of a whole group seeking a multitude of interrelated rights).[27]

There is an important realization behind the articulation of a technical legal intersectionalism and global social movements, which is the fact that human rights create interpretive communities. A majority of social movements — especially from the global South — emerged largely as a response to the new, harsh forms of global economy. Yet the same social movements are never contented with a mere economic analysis of their miseries. Social movement actors scrutinize the role that human rights play in people's everyday struggles and, in turn, the impact of those struggles on rights-based politics and law. A scrutiny of rights can indeed open up an analysis of the dynamics between institutional forms of power and "extra-institutional" aspects of resistance at the global and national levels.[28] Collective mobilization occurs at one level based on a reading of interconnected forms of everyday struggle and dissent to form what Rajagopal calls "texts of resistance."[29] Interpretive acts by individuals and groups in social movements can help to clarify issues of rights; they can also enact contestation to the legal language and practice of rights. To configure social movements as interpretive communities is, first, to repudiate any conception of unitary agency in movement struggles, given the plurality of subject positions and pragmatic motivations behind social movements and, second, to identify actors in non-state and extra-judicial spaces who are either the perpetrator or the recipient of all forms of violence. This radically contextual understanding of social movements has the potential to forge a new conception of human rights discourse that takes into account the complex relations between its institutional, legalistic, and even ostensibly elitist tendencies on the one hand, and its lived effects as an outcome of non-universalizing and even anti-rationalist consideration of everyday struggles on the other.

Human Rights as a Global Legal Apparatus

Social movements politicize and humanize the discourse of rights by paying attention to the life spaces of peoples and their everyday struggles. However, this does not erase the importance of the institutions of law that impact upon those very life spaces, nor does it suggest that social movements are always and everywhere opposed to the tools of law to effect change. Before we consider the specificity of international human rights law, we need to first reconcile common assumptions, especially among left intellectuals, about law as the hegemonic center of modernity. No doubt it is important to keep a critical stance toward all restrictive forms of power that deny recognition of differences and promote an ideology of state neutrality. On this latter item, it is important to recognize that the kind of authority that can impose its own will on how social, economic, and cultural resources are distributed in society while claiming a transcendent position of neutrality is the kind of authority that must be demystified. Commonly, many of us share an understanding that law isn't the same as objectivity, objectivity isn't the same as neutrality, neutrality isn't the same as fairness, and fairness isn't the same as justice. Yet in liberal societies where many of us live, most people, as if in a permanent suspension of belief, accept the law as a more or less coherent process or protocol.[30] Many of us are willing to risk our cultural security so as to trade it for the possibility of justice and empowerment. And this applies to people of different ideological orientations. Sufficiently numerous liberals and conservatives, including the left and right intelligentsias, invest in the general idea of a judicial process that will produce "legally correct" results.[31] As to whether this blanket investment in law will lead us to a strengthening of legal competence to effect social change or to a kind of political banality is an open question.

What is important, though, is for us to recognize the over-determined nature of legal reasoning and the legal process itself. This necessitates rethinking three problematics. First, we need to recognize that the question about the site of legal knowledge, or the assumption that the courts, law schools, and law societies are the singular formation or site of legal knowledge, needs to be replaced by a recognition of the multiplicity of legal consciousness and uses of that consciousness by people that form the social origin of law. It is here that the study of law connects strongly with Cultural Studies' commitment to the problem of the politics of "the popular." Second, the problem of doctrinalism — or the assumption that legal principles are the essence of law, or its only source of value — needs to be replaced by an understanding of the radically contingent nature of legal interpretations in real litigation situations. This connects with the tradition within critical legal studies of "liberal constitutionalism" in which activist liberal law professors, judges, and public-interest lawyers argue that legal interpretivism is something *already* built into law itself, especially in the provisions guaranteeing rights of various kinds.[32] Third, the question of legal essentialism, or the assumption that there is a stable and universal distinction between legal and non-legal practices and relations, needs to be replaced by the recognition that legal relations are always partly discursive or relationally produced. Here, the "non-legal" means at least two things. It means all aspects of life that neither express themselves through law nor embody law. But it also means that which is fundamentally important to human life, and therefore will be incorporated into law and policy. Both meanings of the term render any fixed distinction between law and non-law untenable, thereby returning us to the anti-reductionist ethos of Cultural Studies.

In short, the legal determination of the social totality is not any simpler or more monolithic than any other levels of determination — be it economic, political, or cultural. The modernist roots of law do not and cannot negate the fact that law is radically contextual and historically contingent. The power exercised by law, it must therefore be insisted, is a matter of conjunctural struggle, whereby the admittedly absolute constituting power of law enters into an intricate negotiation with the site upon which it is supposed to constitute its own power. It bears reminding that, for instance in Foucault's theory of governmentality, the power of law is never conceived of as a total or totalizing sphere (Foucault's famous phrase about cutting off the king's head), but as a network implying an intricate interweaving of many micro-events of power and counter-power. As Rosemary Coombe reminds us, "If law is central to hegemonic processes, it is also a key resource in counterhegemonic struggles."[33]

The international regime of human rights law exhibits exactly such a field or network of legal entities. Indeed, when we consider human rights law as consisting of a set of actions — fieldwork, consultation, diplomatic negotiation, drafting of covenants, monitoring, responding to violations, exerting pressure, prosecuting — then the whole *system* of human rights presents itself as a critical "apparatus" in the Gramscian sense. It is an apparatus that opens on to a multiplicity of overlapping and contradictory geographies, histories, institutions, and even cultural standards of morality. This global human rights legal apparatus embeds scales (domestic, regional, supranational, international), actors (states, individuals, groups, international civil society), processes (documentation, protocols, making of institutions, debating principles and values), and relations (legal, political, diplomatic, military). To quickly illustrate, take any legal provision in an international human rights treaty — say, Article 5(a) of the Convention on the Elimination of All Forms of Discrimination Against Women, which reads:

> State Parties shall take all appropriate measures to modify the social and cultural patterns of conduct of men and women, with a view to achieving the elimination of prejudices and customary and all other practices which are based on the idea of the inferiority or the superiority of either of the sexes or on stereotyped roles for men and women.

Putting aside the liberal bias of the provision (which arguably fails to enshrine any substantive form of resistance available to women), it nonetheless is important to note how the provision encodes an entire apparatus consisting of legal actors (including state parties and ordinary citizens in public and private domains), social institutions (including family and educational institutions), and policy processes (such as legal, educational, technical assistance, even reconciliation protocols) that together act to repudiate the nexus of customs and traditions that subjugate women. More importantly, this encoding of the apparatus sets in motion a whole range of processes for legal redress, processes that are built in through (1) the state parties' self-ratification procedure, (2) the establishment of a specific treaty body within the United Nations to monitor the condition of women's rights among the state parties, (3) a complaint mechanism, and (4) an investigative procedure. In other words, international law acts to dis-embed forms of prejudice and violence from the social, and re-embed it with a legal safeguard based on consensual agreement over common moral principles and appropriate forms of legal remedies. Of course, there is no fixed apparatus prescribed here. Any response from the apparatus would also require a rigorous contextual analysis. Yet one thing is clear from the provision: change is *mandated*.

A theory of apparatus is coextensive with a theory of articulation, both pointing to the complexity of a conjuncture. Larry Grossberg reminds us that a conjuncture is "always a social formation as more than a mere context — but as an articulation, accumulation, or condensation of contradictions."[34] Seen in this way, the international human rights regime, as epitomized by the UN structure (though it cannot be reduced to it),[35] exhibits precisely a contradiction of different mechanisms, procedures, and jurisdictions, each carrying different aims and a wide range of levels of enforceability of international norms. Nonetheless, a common unifying goal is to produce a shift in the conjuncture. Far from guaranteeing human rights as the achievable result, the UN regime in fact strives to create a contingent space for the multilateral geopolitical struggle for rights in a legal environment. Most importantly, it is an *actionable* space.

Conclusion

In this chapter, I have suggested that I see law as the aspirational space opened up by the processes of human rights reasoning, legislation, and prosecution, which could be a space for Cultural Studies to theorize the questions of rights, intersubjective claim-making, the performativity of the legal subject in judicial processes, and most importantly to theorize the attainment of justice within a formalized institutional setting. My aim is to strengthen our conception of human rights and international law by making explicit the relations between rights and the questions of modernities, of social movements, and of legal cosmopolitanism. The integrated framework of analysis proposed above, I hope, will not only show us the axes around which human rights and Cultural Studies intersect, but also reinvigorate an engagement with a range of international debates about, and critiques of, human rights from a critical institutional perspective. It is time for us to consider the advantages, limitations, and paradoxes brought about by the theoretical and strategic possibilities of inserting human rights legal discourse into Cultural Studies. Specifically, we may:

- consider how rights can be promoted, and violations monitored and challenged, through an analysis of the institutional arrangements and procedures that give rise to various forms of political identities, actors, events, and outcomes

- theorize the notion of "normative power" and its associated benchmarkable standards of justice, which might be put to pragmatic use for the benefit of the injured
- remap the various institutional sites of power that influence rights, and thereby expand our scope of analysis to include the police, the courts, constitutions, and comparative law
- consider how we can work with those sites of power to open up a space for a counter-hegemonic challenge, for building up capillary power in Foucault's sense
- envisage critical work that orients more toward the advancement of cases rather than projects — in other words, how can we bring cases of injustice to somewhere relevant? Can Cultural Studies find its way into institutional spaces where cases can be heard, and not merely critiqued and deconstructed?

It is counter-productive to separate the intellectual political project of Cultural Studies from the institutional infrastructures of human rights. A separation would even be an epistemologically untenable assertion, given their shared political commitment to a critique of statism, nationalism, and colonialism, their iterations of identity-based cultural politics, and their shared vision of achieving some sort of social transformation. The task is not to imagine Cultural Studies and rights philosophy as external to each other, or to position the political project of the former and the legal project of the latter as if they were mutually antagonistic. In short, it is worthwhile to ask: How can cultural critique as a political exercise move us to an intellectual condition for an advancement of *actionable justice*, backed by institutional analysis and participation? Or to put it more pointedly, how can we move from projects of *resistance to* to cases of *resistance for*?

Acknowledgment

This project has benefited from financial support from the Research and Postgraduate Studies Committee of Lingnan University, Hong Kong Special Administrative Region, China (Project #: DR09B2).

11

From Gatekeepers to Gateways

Pragmatism, Politics, Sexuality, and Cultural Policy in Creative Singapore

Audrey Yue

Introduction: The Aware Saga

On May 2, 2009, more than three thousand people, mostly women, attended a four-hour-long meeting at a convention hall in Suntec City in downtown Singapore. They had come for an extraordinary general meeting called by the old supporters of the country's foremost feminist non-government organization (NGO), the Association of Women for Action and Research (Aware), to vote out a group of female corporate Christian fundamentalists who had earlier taken over the executive running of the organization. As both sides debated and tactics of all sorts were put out on display, these highly charged hours saw #awaresg, the Twitter channel for the organization, peak as one of the top three global trends, on par with topics on the HINI flu and the theft of the *Wolverine* rushes. By the end of the evening, with the votes counted, the status quo had prevailed and supporters of the old guard were restored as the unanimous victors. This win affirmed the values of "openness, transparency, inclusiveness, diversity and secularism," and rejected "dishonesty, non-transparency, exclusiveness, intolerance, divisiveness and oppression/bullying."[1] It marked a "defining moment of liberalism"[2] in the nation-state, and was hailed as "a coming of age for the civil society."[3] For a moment, Singapore showed itself to be a diverse society less divided by race than multiple world-views.[4]

The issue behind Aware's leadership tussle is the educational content of its Comprehensive Sexuality Education Program, delivered to thirty secondary schools. The Christian new guard claimed they were motivated to run for the executive because they were concerned that the content, by teaching safe sex and same-sex sexual practices, promoted homosexuality. Four days after the old guard's historic win, the Ministry of Education suspended Aware's sex education program. It found the guide "too explicit and inappropriate, and convey[ed] messages which could promote homosexuality or suggest[ed] approval of pre-marital sex."[5] Although Aware had won the battle, it had lost the war.

I begin with the Aware saga, as this event has come to be called, to highlight three positions inherent in the mobilization of pragmatism in Singapore. The first is the commonsense notion of economic practicality that has structured the country's developmental logic. The suspension of Aware's sexuality education program — one the government had earlier endorsed as a paid external education provider — is at best and at its most colloquial, a pragmatic move to appease the dominant status quo, a generation of which has grown up with the logic of family values firmly entrenched in the fashioning of their everyday lives. At odds here is not the extreme fundamentalism of religion, but how Christianity, as an imported faith, affirms the legacy of British colonization and promotes the Westernization of its followers.[6] Rather than the focus on religion, the state's intervention privileges the institutions of education and sexuality. The former are seen to build moral conduct while the latter are seen as destroying it. Sexuality, along with the symbolic economies of "woman" and "gender," has become the "limiting boundary by which the principle of democracy is usurped by the sociological reality that communitarianism actually is."[7] That it should end like this should not come as a surprise; homosexuality, after all, is still illegal in a country that has yet to repeal its draconian Victorian laws.

Underpinning this rationale is the second utility of pragmatism as a mode of instrumentalism in the governance of policy. In a small country with no natural resources, which has to rely on the quality of its human resources, education presents economic benefits rather than intrinsic cultural value.[8] In this positivistic tradition, the civilizing aims of education are valued more for collective and individual well-being than for their humanizing and therapeutic functions. To suspend an optional school program that potentially may sanction what the status quo would stereotype as deviant conduct befits this pedagogy.

Notwithstanding the hijacking of sexuality by religion and education, the Aware saga also reveals the potential of pragmatism to create new subjectivities that will transform its civil society. In a country where protests and the forming of non-government community groups are banned, and where any gathering of more than five people in a public space requires official registration, the coming together of such a large group of people speaks volumes about the changing values of the public sphere. Since this event, large-scale grassroots gatherings of this nature have surfaced. One of these is the Pink Dot Day, which has now become the first officially registered annual event for the Gay, Lesbian, Bisexual, and Trans-gender (GLBT) community and their supporters, including family and friends, to come together to celebrate the freedom to love. At the first gathering in the aftermath of the Aware saga in May 2009, more than 2000 people, dressed in pink, turned up at Hong Lim Park in Chinatown, to form a pink dot. Participation doubled in 2010 in a carnival of performance and speeches. When the 2011 campaign video by award-winning Singapore gay auteur Boo Junfeng was released on May 17, 2011, in the month leading up to the annual event, it garnered 34,000 views within thirty-six hours of its launch. Clearly, while pragmatism has driven neo-liberal economic growth, it has also shaped the ethical self-fashioning of a new generation of its citizens. Pragmatism of this nature is a political resource that is creative, democratic, and action-oriented.

These three mobilizations of pragmatism coalesce around the instrumental-ization of sexuality, which is governed not only by censorship and consensus, but also for its economic capacity. Most at odds here ultimately is that, despite its illegality, homosexuality (like the knowledge institution of education) is appropriated by the government as a pragmatic move to 'catch up' in the new knowledge-driven creative economy. Such an economic impetus is evident in recent years, which have seen cultural liberalization result in the develop-ment of creative industries and the inclusion of culture as a driver for fuelling the economy. Liberal policies, such as the employment of gay people in the civil service in 2002, allowing gay people to migrate as foreign talent in 2003, the social campaign of sexing up the city in 2005, and the government's tacit endorsement of gay spaces in 2007 following the community's unsuccessful petition to repeal the anti-gay law 337A, have seen sexuality used to leverage the new cultural economy. This move has prompted some critics to suggest Singapore is "more likely to be known as the gay, rather than the creative, capital of Asia."[9] Elsewhere, I have called this the practice of using sexuality as a technology for policy to refer to the relationship between the state and the sexualizing of culture.[10] In a country that still criminalizes homosexuality, gov-erning the business of culture has also inadvertently provided the conditions for the self-fashioning of new sexual subjectivities.

This chapter will develop critically the three positions of pragmatism described above to historicize the relationship between pragmatism and culture. It begins with the first two views on pragmatism and the way these have shaped the development of cultural policy and the creative economy in Singapore. It problematizes the "catch-up" discourse dominant in studies of Asian creative industries, and uses the example of the film hub to show how cultural institutions in the creative economy are better defined as gateway clusters rather than traditional gatekeepers. It concludes with the third view of pragmatism to show how cultural citizenship is an example of a gateway institution that has emerged as a pragmatic response to the instrumentalization of culture. Using the Aware saga as a case study, I show how "doing" sexuality has enabled gays and lesbians to make claims to cultural citizenship. While pragmatism shapes culture as an economic resource for ideological and neo-liberal legitimacy, it is also a political resource for critical action.

Pragmatism as Ideology and Policy

Pragmatism exists as an ideology that has supported the conceptual structure of post-colonial governance. Chua Beng Huat provides an historical materialist understanding of the aims of nation-building from the 1960s by showing how this ideology privileges the economic over the cultural because economic growth is seen as the best guarantee of social and political stability necessary for the survival of the nation.[11] It is evident not only in making domestic conditions favorable to multinational foreign investments, but in all aspects of social life, including the promotion of education as human capital, meritocracy, population policy, language, and multi-racialism. Pragmatism, Chua argues, rationalises policy implementations as "natural," "necessary," and "realistic": "in everyday language, [it] translates simply into 'being practical' in the sense of earning a living."[12] It has enabled popular legitimacy because it has sustained the nation's "performance principle."[13]

What is unique about pragmatism is that governmental interventions are "contextual and instrumental" rather than "in principle" — that is, they are "discrete and discontinuous acts, in the sense that a particular intervention in a particular region of social life may radically alter the trajectory that an early intervention may have put in place,"[14] so that a rational intervention in one special area of social life may turn out to be quite irrational when the totality of social life is taken into question. Key to this technique of governance is the concurrent operation of the forces of liberalism and non-liberalism, rationality and irrationality — what can be described as the ambivalence of illiberalism.[15]

As a practice of intervention, pragmatism has resonance in Anglophone cultural policy studies in the West. An early seminal criticism by Tony Bennett of Raymond Williams' conception of culture as a way of life is relevant to situating the governance of culture in Singapore. Bennett suggests that Williams provides a loose anthropological definition of culture and misses the narrower aesthetic definition used as a means of social regulation. Bennett stresses that culture is constitutively governmental — that is, culture must be conceived of as "a field of government;"[16] government is not seen in its narrow sense of the state, but as the fields of "social management," as a material inscription for forms of behavior.[17]

Bennett's engagement with the pragmatics of culture has prompted Jim McGuigan to consider policy as a "practical engagement with *a politics of culture*."[18] McGuigan's aim is to reconcile what he considers to be the two sides of criticism and formulation, to rescue "theoretically informed practice" from its reduction to technical implementation.[19] This instrumentalism has exigency in contemporary neo-liberal global culture, where culture is so diffused, expanded, and mutated that it now requires new forms of political legitimacy. George Yudice's "expedient" culture illuminates this rationale, where culture is reformulated as a "resource" for a new epistemology to understand how ideologies and institutions are absorbed into economic rationality.[20]

Yudice's "culture-as-resource" thesis has been influential in putting the discourse of pragmatism into debates in Cultural Studies. Peter Osborne claims it has become a "new form of metaculture" that has succeeded in mainstreaming policy analysis in Cultural Studies to the extent that it has now become the "new cultural positivism" of the discipline.[21] Although Osborne is critical of the danger that it may displace politics with "a new cultural-economic form," he nevertheless points to how pragmatism can be seen as "*the revenge* (of cultural policy studies) ... *on cultural studies for the untheorized presumption of its immediate practicality*."[22] While Osborne's criticism can be levelled at poor impact studies that can exaggerate the claims for arts and culture, Lisanne Gibson, like Bennett, argues that instrumentalism has always been integral to cultural policy, and that "instrumental cultural policies are in fact *policies of production*."[23] This lineage has resonance in the history of cultural policy development in Singapore.

History of Cultural Policy Development

Cultural policy initiatives began in the 1960s and developed to become "cultural economic policy" in the 1980s.[24] Evaluating ministerial statements and press releases, Lily Kong shows how the arts were recognised very early on as playing a vital role in nation-building.[25] Local music, dance, choirs, and orchestra, as part of traditional, classical and folk culture, were nurtured for patriotism and identity. As the arts emerged as a cultural institution with the aims of gatekeeping and cultural maintenance, culture (that is, tradition) was harnessed as a practice of social management for the service of economic development. In the late 1960s and 1970s, this conception of culture was mobilized to boost tourism. Under the campaign of "Instant Asia," multi-racialism was exploited to promote the country as the ultimate tourist destination in Asia.

In the 1980s, with accelerated rising standards of living, arts and cultural pursuits were used to promote "the quality of life."[26] This agenda was developed under the auspices of the Economic Committee, which saw the potential of the arts as a "service sector."[27] In its report, the arts were defined as "cultural and entertainment services"[28] that would improve the quality of life, and make Singapore more exciting for tourism and appealing to skilled migrants. It expanded from the traditional realms of high classics (literature, music, dance, orchestra) to the cultural industries of performing arts, film production, museums and art galleries, entertainment centres, and theme parks. The conception of culture as an economic driver was consolidated with the shift from culture (tradition) as a tourism resource to culture as a service industry.

The 1989 Report of the Advisory Council on Culture and the Arts was considered the first cultural policy statement for Singapore. It established the National Arts Council and the National Heritage Board. Like organizations elsewhere, these cultural agencies promoted the arts by nurturing local talent, and explored and maintained culture for the promotion of national identity. Although the government "did not champion either an economic or socio-political agenda,"[29] other government announcements and strategies in the following years continued to use the arts for national economic competitiveness. The 1991 statement from the then Minister for Information and the Arts, George Yeo, is instructive:

> We should not see the arts as luxury or mere consumption but as investment in people and the environment. We need a strong development of the arts to help make Singapore one of the major hub cities of the world

> … We also need the arts to help us produce goods and services which are competitive in the world market. We need an artistic culture … we also need taste. With taste, we will be able to produce goods and services of far greater value.[30]

Since 1991, the promotion of the arts as an exportable industry has been pursued aggressively through an industrial cultural policy that has seen statutory agencies such as the Economic Development Board and Trade Development Board promote "the local production of cultural goods to be consumed nationally or exported."[31] These include the manufacture of electronic goods, mass media, artistic productions, and fashion. Tax incentives, subsidies and the waiving of censorship laws were strategies put into place to entice foreign domestic investment. Alongside tourism, these cultural policy developments set the stage for Singapore's next stage of creative economy developments.

In 2002, Singapore released its *Creative Industries Development Strategy* (CIDS).[32] This is the country's current national plan for transforming its manufacturing and information industries into a creative economy. It was developed from its early genesis when the Economic Development Board set up a Creative Services Strategic Unit in the late 1980s and put forth its Creative Services Development Plan in 1991. Creative industries merge arts, technology, and business as a way of ensuring a nation's competitiveness within an integrated global economy, and can be found in the areas of arts and culture (Renaissance City 2.0), media (Media 21) and design (Design Singapore).[33] CIDS focuses on building creative capabilities through education, niche branding through product differentiation and place competitiveness (for example, the "New Asia" genre), and harnessing creative industries development through value-adding, content creation, interactivity, convergence, and new ways of storage and distribution. In June 2009, as part of its second-phase development, Media 21 was upgraded to a national media blueprint, the Singapore Media Fusion Plan (SMFP), which aims to transform Singapore into "a trusted global capital for New Asia Media."[34] It builds on its internationally recognized intellectual protection regime, leverages its global connectivity and identity, and promotes media from and for the newly industralized countries of Asia, and Asia's new media.

From post-colonial independence to its latest economic stimulus reform, Singapore's cultural policy developments have leveraged culture as an economic resource. Whether it was the cultivation of tradition for national identity, the pursuit of artistic and cultural activities to improve the quality of life, or the global integration of media capitals to leapfrog into the knowledge economy, these developments are enshrined in the logic of pragmatism. From the history of such a development, it can be argued that the conception of culture emerged in Singapore, as Bennett has cogently postulated, not as a way of life but through governance as a field of social management for the purpose of the economy. Similarly, as Gibson has also argued, the instrumentalism of Singapore's policies is indeed its policies for cultural production. As its 2006 GDP attests, the media sector currently employs 54,000 workers, contributes S\$19.5 billion revenue and value-adds S\$5 billion to the economy.

Catch-up

The implementation of the CIDS is not unlike similar strategies in the region.[35] The key feature of this strategy is the problematic discourse of "catch-up." For Singapore, this discourse stems from four decades of developmental capitalism that have seen a newly independent nation devoid of natural resources trying to "catch up" with the rest of the world, to becoming a manufacturing outpost, the world's busiest port city, a regional centre for multinational corporations, and now a media city for global capital. Well-rehearsed in studies of political economy and economics, this teleology of progress is increasingly cited in studies of creative economies of Asia. Questions such as "Can developing countries compete with the sophisticated products from the developed centres of production?", and terms like "transitional economies" are ubiquitous among planners, NGOs, practitioners and scholars both within and outside of Asia.[36] In these studies, the "catch-up" discourse is evident in its sectoral approach.

The sectoral approach consists of mapping specific types of production that should be included in the cultural economy. Cultural mapping "involves a comprehensive effort to identify all relevant cultural economic activities, organizations, employment in a given area such as a town or region."[37] Its purpose is to evaluate indicators to assess the economic impact of creativity. There is currently no standardized mapping and no regional framework for statistical indicators. The British government's Department of Culture, Media and Sport (DCMS) 1998 and 2001 cultural industries mapping documents have been widely influential,[38] and have been copied in many parts of the world, including Australia, Hong Kong, and Singapore.

Following Hong Kong's study of its creativity index, Singapore has also produced a study on the economic contributions of its creative industries.[39] While the report validates the economic growth of the creative economy — in 2001, for instance, creative industries contributed 3.2 per cent of Singapore's GDP, while the earnings from intellectual property generated S$43.2 billion in output and value added S$12.3 billion to the economy — its methodologies are not unproblematic. Normative and reductive tendencies are evident in benchmarking practices. For example, in the comparison of the national creative capability of Singapore, the proxy indicators of "manpower," "markets," and "infrastructure" are derived from influential studies on the creative economy, commissioned studies by governments in Australia, the United Kingdom, and the United States, and global reports and industry statistics on world competitiveness.[40] The British model, together with the theses of Richard Florida and John Howkins, is adopted as a norm.[41]

Measuring "manpower" through social diversity, the size of the creative workforce, and their innovative capability misses the complexity of cultural activity and reduces contradictions to a numerical scale. Measuring "infrastructure" through the size of the copyright industries, and public expenditure on arts, culture and media, as well as through the institutional framework of how an industry is able to protect and distribute creative property, misses the relationship of cultural infrastructure to the public good and is unable to account for cultural participation and access. Measuring "markets" through copyright export, GDP per capita, and the value-adding capacity of knowledge industries flattens the different logics of development in each country. The clustering of countries such as the United Kingdom, United States, Australia, Hong Kong, and Singapore, based on the World Bank's classification of high-income group, does not take into account the disparity in the hierarchy of cultural trade among these countries.[42]

The sectoral model focuses on production and uses copyright and intellectual property as its organizing principles. The value of creative industry is measured in purely economic terms. These types of cultural indicators singularize the cultural economy as one economy, and homogenize how different cultural economies have emerged in different geographies under different material conditions.[43] This model has implications for the way it accounts for the cultural economy and its geographical distribution of cultural capital — the cultural is not only economic, it is also social. The processes and experiences of consumption — factors such as quality of life and the aspirations of cultural citizenship — cannot be measured completely in economic terms.

UNESCO has since extended cultural mapping with a cultural indigenization approach to developing creative communities in the Asia-Pacific region.
The 2005 report, *Asia Pacific Creative Communities: Promoting the Cultural
Industries for Local Socio-economic Development*, introduces elements of a
regional policy framework.[44] It highlights how the new networks of cultural
industries can be incorporated into the national development plans to achieve
a more "sustainable development."[45] In this new framework, culture is defined
more through its anthropological origins, and sustainable development is
promoted as a new interdisciplinary and inter-sectoral approach that brings
together diverse stakeholders, from urban planners, educators, cultural pro-
grammers, and copyright offices to the population. Here, cultural policy is
integrated into national social development, cultural industries are central
to sustainable community development, and cultural content is valued as a
strategy for localisation and indigenization. This is a two-pronged approach:
culture can be an economic potential, and creative industries can also enable
countries to retain their national specificities in striving to compete in the
global cultural economy.[46] It is a relevant framework to evaluate the development of Singapore's creative industries.

Assessing the state of the cultural industries since the 1990s, Chua Beng
Huat shows how arts is used to add value to tourism by bringing in "big"
Broadway musicals such as *Les Misérables*, *Phantom of the Opera* and *Cats*.
These events, he argues, have created culture with "no consideration given to
the development of local cultural content."[47] The lack of cultural content is also
evident in how education has nurtured a talent base which offshore production
companies such as the recently established S$450 million animation produc-
tion factory Lucas Laboratory can use as a "high technology 'sweat-shop.'"[48]
Similar examples include co-funded and transnationally produced films
such as *Infernal Affairs 2* (Andrew Lau and Alan Mak, 2003) and *The Eye 1
and 2* (Danny and Oxide Pang, 2002, 2004), which — although Singapore co-
funded — used few or no leading Singapore artists and allowed for little or no
development of the local film industry. He also shows how locally produced
television serials, following the successful formats of Hong Kong, Japan and
Korea — are not exportable because of their low budgets and weak scripts,
and how the S$90 million dollar franchise partnership with the National
Geographic and Discovery Channels in 2003 to produce documentaries has
been financially and even critically successful because the factual documentaries contain no cultural content. Although Chua does not delve further into

his examples, four models of media globalization are evident from his analysis: (1) direct cultural export (Broadway musicals); (2) deterritorialization (Lucas Animation); (3) cloning (isomorphic pan-Asian television serial format); and (4) cultural technology transfer (Hong Kong film co-productions and global television documentary).[49] While these theoretical models champion both the wholesale borrowing and partial localizing of content, Chua's assertion that Singapore's cultural industries create "technolog[ies] with no content" suggests that in the case of Singapore, these models evince the thesis of cultural imperialism rather than indigenization, and clearly contradict and undermine UNESCO's logic of harnessing local cultural content as a mode of sustainable development.[50]

Similar to the cultural mapping approach, cultural indigenization, by focusing on cultural content and its Asian cultural specificity, is still locked in the one-way flow of Western cultural imperialism. Underpinning this approach is the assumed role of cultural and media institutions as traditional gatekeepers for maintaining, fostering, and differentiating national cultural identity within and outside the nation-state. In the new creative economy, cultural institutions are better conceptualized as gateway institutions for leveraging regional capacity. In Singapore, this is evident in the new aims of its diverse cultural institutions, from the campaigns of cultural tourism and the design of urban renewal to the broadcasting logics of its media institutions. For example, "New Asia" and "Uniquely Singapore," two recent tourism campaigns, continue to market Singapore as a stopover destination to Asia. Here, its geographical hub is literally capitalized upon to enhance the status of its symbolic interface in the region. In television institutions such as Channel News Asia, the gateway discourse is evident in its narrowcasting technology that transmits to niche, middle-class and English-speaking "new Asian" audiences rather than mainstream markets. In urban renewal creative city projects around the Singapore River, the metaphor of the gateway is also evident through the liminality of place — the cultural history of the port city and the new creative city as a flexible place in which to live, play, and work.[51] In these cultural institutions of tourism, television and heritage, Singapore's intersectional location as a regional and symbolic hub is exploited for the economy.[52]

The concept of the cluster critically illustrates the new gateway role of the cultural institution. In neo-liberal discourse, the term is usually used to refer to how industries and nations gain a competitive economic edge over others. Michael Porter defines the cluster as "a geographically proximate group of interconnected companies and associated institutions in a particular field, linked by commonalities and complementarities."[53] This concept has been appropriated to frame the economic innovation of creative industries and encourage the rise of creative cities. In Singapore, geographical clusters are evident in newly established science and technology parks (such as the complexes of Biopolis and Fusionpolis) and artist enclaves (for example, Esplanade Theatres on the Bay, Wessex Estate, and gentrified shop-houses in Chinatown, Little India, and Kampong Glam).[54] While the creative cluster tends to refer to how the agglomeration of similar industries can create innovative entrepreneurialism, my usage of the cluster concept as a gateway metaphor extends this emphasis on spatial concentration to refer to its potential as a concept of spatial flows characterized by "[i]nteractivity, convergence, customisation, collaboration and networks."[55] This mode produces a distinct way of organising data and the economy, and hence a new way of thinking about culture. The "Made-by-Singapore" film is an example of such a cluster.

"Made-by-Singapore" Film: A Media Capital Cluster

The "Made-by-Singapore" genre comes out of the 2002 CIDS to refer to films that have developed content for export through collaborations with foreign talent and partners.[56] Local media companies are assisted with venture capital to go abroad to find foreign partnerships. It does not mean "made in Singapore" or "made by Singapore;" the purpose is to internationalize local media companies, nurture local talent, and export the content that is generally less national, and more global and regional.[57] Two key film examples are useful to demonstrate the workings of the film cluster as a gateway institution.

Rice Rhapsody is Singapore Film Commission's first creative economy film released in 2004 under the Media 21 blueprint.[58] The story revolves around a single mother (played by Sylvia Chang) who owns a chicken rice stall coming to terms with the gay sexuality of her three sons. The film is a joint collaboration between a local content development company, Ground Glass Images, and the Hong Kong industry, including producer Jackie Chan's JCE Movies, director Kenneth Bi's Kenbiroli Films, and a cast including Sylvia Chang, Ivy Ling Po, Maggie Q, and Martin Yan, all of whom are either central to or associated with the Hong Kong film industry.[59] Apart from the supporting roles of the three sons, Tan Lepham, Alvin Chiang, and Craig Toh, who are Singapore actors, there are no visibly recognizable local cultural specificities such as the slang and resistance of Singlish or Hokkien.[60] Mandarin and English, the two nominated languages of official bureaucracy and nationalism, dominate the stilted script. Film-induced tourism is evident in the on-location realism of Chinatown's architectural heritage of Peranakan shop houses, and the country's culinary showcase of famous hawker cuisine.

Similarly, *Krrish* is the first film to be made under Media 21's Film-in-Singapore subsidy scheme, launched in 2006.[61] Directed by Rakesh Roshan, the doyen of contemporary Bollywood cinema, *Krrish* is India's fourth-highest-grossing film this decade, and the third-highest-grossing film of 2006. The story revolves around an Indian superhero, Krishna (played by Hrithik Roshan), who is born with magical powers, and traces his life as he meets Priya (played by Prinyanka Chopra), a Singapore-based non-resident Indian, and follows her to Singapore. More than 60 per cent of the film was shot in Singapore over sixty days. Written by an Indian team, and action choreographed by Hong Kong's Ching Siu-tung, Singapore's below-the-line input, from extras and through ancillary services such as set management and catering, evince the new international division of cultural labour.[62] The film exploits the city's futurist skyline, showcases the gleaming interiors of shopping malls, and features segments in the zoo, at theme parks, and by the riverside. As in *Rice Rhapsody*, where food and heritage are used to add value to tourism, *Krrish* uses these iconic locations and its high profile on-location shooting as a hallmark event, to make explicit its institutional association with tourism. When the film was released, promotional events such as the *Krrish* tour and the box office success of the film indeed increased Indian visitation and domestic tourism.[63]

The "Made-by-Singapore" genre follows the clustering mandate of the CIDS that positions the media as a hub in the region. The gateway of the hub has historical precedence in Singapore: as a developmental port colony, it distributed Western imports to the region and was also the region's export gateway for primary commodities. The media hub builds on this established regional capacity by insinuating itself at the intersection of two of the world's biggest media capitals — India and Hong Kong–China. These are the two largest Asian film industries and two of the world's emerging global economies. Singapore is not only sandwiched between China and India, it also has a diasporic population, which originated from these places and has already created the disjunctive mediascapes for these industries. This way of thinking about capital is not about capital as concentration (Singapore is not a film center in Asia), but rather as an intersection for economic, social, and cultural flows, "a nexus or switching point rather than a container."[64] Capital is used "not to perform conventional city functions but to leverage their relationships for innovative collaborations with global companies."[65] Regional media capacity internationalizes local industries and possesses the potential to generate cultural exports through the intellectual property from content origination and value-add from its multipliers.

At this stage, it is difficult to assess whether these films fulfil their economic aims. *Rice Rhapsody* generated only S$15,000 in local box office despite receiving critical acclaim for Best Director and Best Actress at the 25th Hong Kong Film Awards and being included in the Top Ten Best Chinese Films of 2005 by the Chinese Film Critics Association.[66] Although *Krrish* grossed S$21.3 million in 2006,[67] it is debatable how much returned to Singapore. However, what is significant here is the system of the gateway cluster and its capacity for new forms of social inclusion.

In the "Made-by-Singapore" film hub, culture is no longer content or context, but a network. A network is more than simply an interconnected system of resources, capital and people; it is also embedded in social ties and cultural relations. Justin O'Connor suggests that "social network markets" provide a new direction for theorising the creative industry because they emphasize "markets and consumption," and depart from the production-centered approach promoted in normative sectoral studies.[68] This model draws on theories of cultural democratization to include non-commercial activities that also create cultural value. It removes the false dichotomy between activities that are either intrinsic or instrumental so that creative economic activities are also vital to cultural life, and that underpinning cultural consumption is also the economic foundation of cultural production.[69] This model is relevant to the development of new regional co-production cultures in Asia. Social ties are used in the Hong Kong film industry to open up new cross-border markets into China.[70] Social capital is also central to successful venture capital fundraising in Beijing.[71] In *Rice Rhapsody*, Hong Kong's film network attracted the Singapore Film Commission, which saw the film as an opportunity to internationalize its nascent industry and nurture its local talent. For the Singapore gay community, it was a landmark film that put the issue of gay acceptance into the mainstream. In *Krrish*, the commercial benefit of the geographical network is also a way to promote economic and cultural proximity. For Singapore's Bollywood fans and local residents, it engendered creative nationalism as new forms of cultural pride and new practices of everyday leisure. Although the self-promotional discourse of the creative industry has led critics to highlight its complicity with neo-liberalism,[72] in Asian nation-states such as Singapore, neo-liberal creative industrial policy, with its innovative systems of the social network cluster, holds the potential to create new forms of inclusion.[73] From new resident-tourists and subcultural fans to the activist gay community, these forms of inclusion attest to the capacity of the new creative film institution as a gateway cluster to account for shifting cultural values, tastes, and lifestyles.

The following discusses cultural citizenship as another example to illustrate the gateway function of the cultural institution. It is a gateway metaphor because it is a bridging concept between individuals and community, individual rights and common good, individualism and communalism. It is also a site of cultural consumption because it addresses the right of citizens to participate in cultural life. I return to the Aware saga introduced at the beginning of this chapter, and use the third perspective on pragmatism as a political resource to evaluate how the "doing" of sexuality has emerged as a result of the "doing" of cultural citizenship.

Pragmatism as Political Resource: Cultural Citizens, Doing Sexuality, and Critical Action

Illiberal pragmatism has also shaped the social habitus and crafted new subjectivities. Aaron Koh links this mode of subjectivation to the metapragmatics of governing globalization.[74] Following Foucault, he shows how metapragmatism is tied to state discourses and practices on neo-liberal economic and public policies, language campaigns, and civic nationalism, and how these policies are intended for "managing people's conduct because once people are moulded into a way of behaving and thinking it would be easy to marshal resources for the ideological purposes of the state;" "[i]ts *telos*, is to regulate the Singapore habitus, and create new subjectivities suitable for the new economy."[75] This recourse to Foucault is also evident in Yudice's thesis, where the term "performativity," rather than pragmatism, is used to refer to how norms are legitimated as part of the political resource for social groups to make claims to access and representation.[76]

In Singapore, gays and lesbians have appropriated these new subjectivities in their performance of cultural democracy. The last decade has seen the proliferation of gay and lesbian-owned bars, karaoke pubs, dance clubs, and saunas, as part of the night-time economy encouraged by government rent subsidies in the creative enclave of Chinatown and its neighboring precincts. At its height in the mid-2000s, Singapore boasted more queer venues than Australia's gay capital, Sydney; hosted the region's biggest annual queer circuit party; and promoted provocative new butch-femme identities in its yearly lesbian beauty quests. Each year, at least two to three thousand people faithfully attend these parties; they generate, through pink tourism, at least S$6 million for the economy.[77] Elsewhere, I have discussed these consumption practices as part of the performance of "doing gay" and "doing butch."[78] Rather than celebrating identity (that is, "being gay"),[79] the practices of "doing" celebrate the shame associated with gay and lesbian sex; for gay men, it is associated with the post-AIDS era that stigmatizes gay sex with disease and promiscuity; for butch lesbians, it is associated with the feminine body that betrays the failure to pass. At these events and in these places, gay men, with their buffed and semi-naked bodies, expropriate the decadence and hedonism of the pre-AIDS era to celebrate that which has been side-lined in the conservative march for homonormalization and progressive sexual reforms; butch lesbians, competitors, and patrons alike appropriate and celebrate the breast-binder as the technology *par excellence* for their new female masculinities. In a country that criminalizes homosexuality, these performances of "doing" sexuality, themselves beneficiaries of disjunctive global flows, are part of the practices of "doing" cultural citizenship rather than embodying sexual citizenship.

Cultural citizenship refers to the right to make claims to and access culture. It is a concept that explains and justifies why culture is of central significance to an individual's capacity to participate in politics and society more broadly. It also explores how the failure to tolerate, recognize, and respect the significance and variability of culture can function to exclude and marginalize groups and individuals.[80] These concerns highlight difference by emphasizing the "redistribution of resources" and a politics of "recognition and responsiveness."[81] They also stress how multiculturalism and cosmopolitanism can shape common culture and provide the capacity for autonomy.[82] In Singapore, these discussions assume the narrow form of political culturalism, a governmental process of steering participation through ethnic channels to promote multiracial harmony as a public good.[83] In a state governed by illiberal pragmatism, political culturalism opens up pathways for participation in different spheres of everyday life, except in political contestation, and allows individuals to become cultural rather than liberal citizens. For minority groups such as gays and lesbians, cultural and creative industrial policy developments have extended the scope of political culturalism, and facilitated the potential to make claims to cultural citizenship.

While cultural rights provide recognition through reallocation, they also construct identities and lifestyles that question hegemonic norms. As Ong attests, cultural citizenship is a dual process "of self-making and being made in relation to nation-states and transnational processes," shaped by "negotiating the often ambivalent and contested relations with the state and its hegemonic forms that establish the criteria of belonging within a national population and territory."[84] At the level of cultural and arts policies, it relates to the role of citizens as producers and consumers in shaping material culture, and stresses "the capacity to participate effectively, creatively and successfully within a national culture."[85] A recent study on the quality of life of Singapore lesbians reveals that cultural citizenship is performed with resistant and complicit practices enacted through cultural and media consumption.[86] By actively participating in capital accumulation afforded to the new neo-liberal consumption cultures of the creative economy, lesbians are also able to create strong social networks, cultivate social capital, and be active in civic engagement.

Similarly, the new media consumption cultures of the creative economy have also facilitated the "doing" of feminism in the recent Aware saga. Notwithstanding the peaking of the Twitter trend on the night of May 2, 2009, or the proven capacity of social media networks to mobilize support and encourage online citizenry in the preceding three months, "doing" feminism has emerged as a practice of cultural citizenship that engages the political resource of pragmatism. Formed in 1985 against the backdrop of the Great Marriage Debate, Aware began as a state-sanctioned NGO, as an example of the loosening up of state control and an instance of an emerging civil society.[87] Although it is commonly known as a feminist organization, the terms "feminist" or "feminism" do not appear in its constitution. It promotes itself as a "women's organization" fighting for women's rights, and explicitly does not address issues of race, class, and sexuality. These conservative decisions, shaped by a model of consensus, moderation and reform, are steeped in the political astuteness of illiberal pragmatism, one that appeases the dominant status quo, which negatively associates feminism with the Western model of radical activism. It has led to criticisms that Aware is a state-defined feminist organization unable to address issues of structural inequality and difference, thus confirming the general theoretical perception that feminism in Asia is characterized by state intervention and the discourse of nationalism.[88] Lenore

Lyons, however, argues that by presenting "a publicly mediated and, hence, palatable definition of feminism based on indigenous tradition, tolerance and strategic conservatism [Aware] has successfully negotiated the possible pathways between suppression and co-option."[89] Rather than the transformative potential of feminist goals, Aware has "[subverted] two of the state's key principles of governance — multiracialism and meritocracy" by "keeping one eye on [the state], but actively asserting all women's right to define their own lives."[90] This state of ambivalence, between the illiberal pragmatics of complicity and resistance, has framed Aware's operational logic, functioned as political resource, and sustained its longevity.

The last twenty-five years since the inception of Aware have seen a new generation of women come to the fore as a result of the social changes brought about by the success of economic development. The thousand-fold increase in Aware's 2009 membership reflects a new polity consistent with a more educated population that values the civic pluralism of diversity and difference. That three thousand members joined and turned up in their rally of support attests not only to the political resource of pragmatism but its capacity for engaging critical action.

Cornel West's method of philosophical pragmatism provides a vantage point for situating this form of creative and participatory democracy. As a method for doing philosophy, philosophical pragmatism extends the commonsense view of pragmatism as an approach towards that which serves expediency. Its anti-foundationalism draws on the connection between theory, practice, and action. As a theory of truth and a criterion for meaning, it suggests that meaning is the outcome of its practical consequences. West's branch of pragmatism extends the engaged instrumentalism of John Dewey and revisions its "future-oriented instrumentalism" as a form of critical action: "Its basic impulse is a plebian radicalism that fuels an antipatrician rebelliousness for the moral aim of enriching individuals and expanding democracy."[91] Westian pragmatism — what he calls prophetic pragmatism — departs from the philosophical tradition of matching solutions to actions; rather, it is a sort of cultural commentary that promotes a "culture of creative democracy by means of critical intelligence and social action."[92] It is prophetic because it is sustained by a love ethic that compels one "to speak the truth in love with courage" and "relate ideas to collective praxis."[93] He locates it in the "everyday experiences of ordinary people," and considers it "a material force for individuality and democracy."[94]

The activism of the Aware saga demonstrates the political dimension of prophetic pragmatism. Collective social motion is evident in the masses of women who have turned up to vote, as well as in the thousands of comments and posts on social media networks and online print journalism in the months before and after the event.[95] Online and offline grassroots citizenry is not only a form of collective intelligence;[96] it is also a form of critical intelligence, with debates ranging from feminism, civil society, religion, secularism, and education to parenting and identity. Anti-patrician rebelliousness is evident in the crux of the struggle, which is the moral standpoint that a successful, long-standing, non-partisan, government-sanctioned women's organization can be hijacked by a small group of right-wing corporate Christian fundamentalists. The issue of lesbianism and the praxis of "doing" sexuality have emerged as the driving forces behind this democratic operation. As one trainer of the Comprehensive Sexuality Education Program stated: "The three words ... anal sex, homosexuality, and lesbianism are only mentioned in one and a half minute out of three hours of the program, of which half is spent on promoting abstinence ... how to refuse sex."[97] These are the three words that have irked the ire of the new guard and sparked the fight for control of the organization. Significant here is that in the debates that have ensued, the topic of lesbianism, whenever it is mentioned, is instantly displaced by a return to the universal rubric of women's rights. The following provides a sample log of this displacement during the night when the women from the floor took to the microphone:

> *7:55 p.m.:* we are not here because we are gay or lesbians ... We are here because we are deeply troubled how this exco came into power and the lack of respect for the values of pluralism, democracy that this new exco has demonstrated. We are here because we believe women are intelligent and rational enough to make our own choices on how a good life is. We are here to protect the rights and integrity of women everywhere.

> *7:15 p.m.:* ... I am a Muslim with three daughters ... We need to have ... the spirit of inquiry to enable our ladies to make informed choices and because of that, I would be very proud [for] my daughter to go through the CSE program.

> *6:32 p.m.:* I am a Christian and I have sex education in secondary school. I am for a system which enabled people to make informed choices and not to make judgment on others.

> *6:26 p.m.:* As a parent myself, I would like my child to go through this program. Just discussing a wide range of sexual behavior does not make one a homosexual. Your child won't come back and say, "Hey, I want to marry a person of same sex!"[98]

These responses share common values about the engaged instrumental-ism of education to engender better choices about moral and sexual conduct. Key here is women's right to choose. Rather than viewing the displacement of lesbian rights as a homophobic erasure, the recourse to women's rights can be seen as reflecting Aware's ambivalent logic of illiberal pragmatism. More specifically, however, this praxis of "doing" sexuality has enabled Aware's estab-lished discourse of feminism — through the palatable and feminine signifiers of autonomy and independence — to materialize as a collective force for social action. This material force is prophetic, participatory, and democratic: the col-lective chanting and coming together of the crowd is reminiscent of a spiritual awakening;[99] it is driven by the activisms of faith — religious and secular, the intensity of loyalty and belief not unlike any other social movement; it is also enshrined with "an ethics of respect" that allows the moral courage to speak, love, and accept the choices individuals make.[100]

The Aware saga has done more to raise the profile of Singapore lesbians than any other previous social movement. It has also heightened the reputation of Aware and made its status as an organization relevant and accessible to con-temporary young Singapore women more credible. It is the illiberal pragmatics of "doing" sexuality that has, perhaps not ironically, produced this renewed discourse of local feminism. This event also joins other practices of gendered consumption in the creative economy. Alongside "doing" gay and "doing" butch, "doing" feminism points to the materialization of a praxis as a form of collective and critical action negotiated through the technology of sexuality. The pragmatic outcomes of cultural and creative development policies, such as a highly educated, media-literate, multi-racial, and cosmopolitan population, has indeed turned itself around in this instance, and seized the force of its own complicity to resist the undercurrents of neo-conservatism and neo-liberalism. Similar to the direct claims of the right to culture exhibited in the literal con-sumption practices of the creative economy, here too is a praxis of cultural citizenship that promotes the rights to recognition and self-determination. The technology of sexuality has also reinvigorated the normative cultural institu-tions of education and religion. Their dogmas are not only extensively dis-sected in public discourse; they have allowed Aware to remake its own popular feminism while also inevitably lifting the status of minor lesbianism. As a re(new)ed cultural institution, Aware has shown how the gateway of cultural citizenship is a pragmatic force as potent as the thrust of the creative economy.

Conclusion

In August 2009, a few months after the Aware saga, I was invited to talk at the IndigNation festival, a month-long event celebrating queer pride in Singapore. As this was the first time I would speak about my queer Singapore research to a non-academic Singapore audience, I was quietly excited but also silently apprehensive — excited because I was finally returning my research to the place to which it belonged, the country of my birth and citizenship, and the locale of my own queer activist struggle; apprehensive because I was unsure how my work would be received despite having already been awarded IndigNation's inaugural Rascals Prize.[101]

I turned up at the address, a shop house in a lane off Serangoon Road, lost in the heritage cluster of Little India. In an area renowned for restaurants, wet-market shopping and wholesale import warehousing, refurbished shop houses have turned into newly converted cafes, museums, and art galleries. The speaking venue, a place called "Post-Museum" on Rowell Road, is one of these creative gems. This place, an empty shop with whitewashed walls and wooden bench-seats, is owned by a couple who run the organic vegetarian restaurant next door. Upstairs is a communal office with desks for rent. I was later told this was an activist hub; the office is populated by writers, artists, event organizers, and project workers of all sorts, who make a living working for NGOs, freelancing, or trying to plan for the next "big" thing. Downstairs is where the occasional art exhibition, weekly flea market or community gathering is held.

As I was packing up after my talk, I was discreetly led to a corner at the back of the room. There I was instructed to provide my identification details to two plainclothes policemen whom I immediately recognised as intimate members of the small audience. I was aghast. I knew foreigners could not speak publicly about local queer matters, which was why my colleague from Thailand was prevented from obtaining a visa in 2007 for the same festival, and also why my fellow panellist, a lawyer from Hong Kong who also co-won the Rascals Prize with me, could not present his paper despite being present at the event. Rather than shielding me from the harsh censorship and surveillance meted out to activist foreigners, my citizenship became the pragmatic tool to log my presence and record my crime. Like the three thousand or so women who turned up to vote at the Aware EGM, the state now has a dossier on me.

This chapter encapsulates the heart of the anecdote above, of how a new creative economy has pragmatically emerged with soft and hard cultural institutions that have provided the capacity for new ways of administering and doing culture. As a technology of cultural policy, sexuality has been inscribed in and transformed by these new forces of pragmatic production, consumption, and sociality.

It began with two critical discourses of pragmatism that have produced culture as an instrumental economic resource. One has its lineage in the ideology of post-colonial survival; the other is rooted in the history of cultural policy developments. In these lineages, cultural institutions assume the traditional gatekeeping role of maintaining cultural identity and national difference within and without the nation-state. These two discourses have also shaped the recent development of creative industries, and Singapore's bid to "catch up" in the new economy. In the haste to "catch up," however, the government has not only inadvertently expropriated the technology of sexuality, but its creative industry implementations have also problematically imported the norms of cultural mapping and cultural indigenization.

This chapter has suggested that cultural institutions are better situated through the gateway metaphor, evident in the branding of the city-state as a media hub and the generic formation of its "Made-by-Singapore" film cluster. As the new genre attests, the gateway cluster has redefined the role of the cultural institution as a site for leveraging capacity and acquiring capital. This shift in the function of the cultural institution is significant, as it provides a new direction in which to situate the role of the creative industries through the concomitant logics of production and consumption. The gateway cluster is not only the nexus for building new capital capacity, it is also an interface for the contestation of people, resources, and capital.

This chapter has also demonstrated cultural citizenship as a gateway, mediating individuals and communities, individual rights and common good, individualism, and communalism, and as an arena for the cultural politics of recognition and distribution. Using the Aware case study of "doing" sexuality, this chapter has shown how cultural citizenship is claimed by gays, lesbians, and feminists in a country steeped in the logic of illiberal pragmatics and the repression of homosexuality. Where pragmatism has shaped culture as an economic resource for ideological and neo-liberal legitimacy, the pragmatic "doing" of cultural policy has also enabled the "doing" of sexuality.

12

Culture, Institution, Conduct

The Perspective of Metaculture

Tony Bennett

What does it mean to be concerned with the institutional conditions and affiliations of Cultural Studies? What form do these take? What implications do — or should — they have for the ways in which Cultural Studies is conducted? In taking these to be the guiding questions for this collection, I shall approach them as part of a larger set of issues concerning the relations between culture, institution, and conduct. For this purpose, I interpret culture as a historically specific set of relations in which particular forms of expertise are entangled with institutional practices in forming and re-forming social conduct in varied and contested ways. I shall approach these forms of expertise — the disciplines of Heritage Studies, Art History, Literary Studies, Anthropology, Archaeology, and Public History, for example — as instances of "metaculture." And I shall argue that Cultural Studies is itself a form of metaculture, one that has been shaped by the longer history of the culture/institution/conduct plexus that, in turn, it has sought to reshape.[1]

What do I mean by metaculture? There are two senses of the term I want to put into play. The first I draw from Barbara Kirshenblatt-Gimblett's contention that heritage is created through "metacultural operations that extend museological values and methods (collection, documentation, preservation, presentation, evaluation, and interpretation) to living persons, their knowledge, practices, artifacts, social worlds, and life spaces."[2] It is not the specific focus on museological methods that I want to draw from this definition but the transformative effect Kirshenblatt-Gimblett attributes to the processes of collection, documentation, and so on in producing "a metacultural relationship to what was once just habitus."[3] For these have a more general provenance across the full range of cultural disciplines. It is, then, the general role of such disciplines in ordering, classifying, valuing, and presenting texts, artefacts, visual presentations, sounds, material environments, and so on in order to induce new relationships to such phenomena on the part of varied groups and agents that I take from this definition of metaculture. The further aspect I want to add to Kirshenblatt-Gimblett's formulations is that such metacultural practices are best interpreted institutionally as components of a historically distinctive set of cultural assemblages that bring together texts, objects, humans, techniques, and distinctive forms of expertise to produce varied ways of acting on the conduct of groups and individuals in programs of social governance.

The second definition of metaculture is a more particular one. I refer to Francis Mulhern's account of the forms of cultural commentary developed in the wake of post-Kantian aesthetic conceptions of *Kulturkritik*, and their tendency, in Mulhern's estimation, to substitute culture for politics as the preferred form of intervention into social life.[4] A similar conception — although one given a longer historical perspective and a sharper institutional dimension — informs William Ray's account of what he calls "the logic of culture" and the role it plays in relation to practices of self-formation, mechanisms of social differentiation, and an open-ended dialectic of historical becoming.[5] For both Mulhern and Ray, this longer history of *Kulturkritik* also comprises a continuing aspect of the contemporary practices of Cultural Studies, particularly in its British versions in the history that runs from Raymond Williams through to Stuart Hall.

There is, as I have argued elsewhere,[6] a good deal to be said in favor of Mulhern's account — although I do not share the Marxist conception of a pre-given form of class politics that shapes his assessments of Cultural Studies. My main purpose is to explore what follows from placing this account of metaculture, with its particular focus on the enduring influence of a particular form of aesthetic knowledge and expertise, in the context of the broader definition of metaculture reviewed above. There will be two main aspects to my argument in this regard. The first will draw on Foucauldian governmentality theory and assemblage theory to suggest how Cultural Studies might most productively take account of its own activities as a form of metaculture that operates alongside, and in the same way as, other metacultural practices in the sense proposed by Kirshenblatt-Gimblett. The second will be to argue the need to cut the ties that still bind many formulations within Cultural Studies to the more particular form of metaculture that Mulhern discusses, inasmuch as they pin their colors to a conception of cultural politics as speaking over and above the particular institutional entanglements in which it is — or so I will argue — inevitably tied up. I shall develop this aspect of my concerns by reviewing Jacques

Rancière's conception of metapolitics, in which formulations very similar to those informing the relationships between aesthetics and Cultural Studies have been offered a renewed lease of life.[7]

The Institutional Space of Culture

Perhaps the best way into the first set of questions is to ask how we can now best conceive the space within which Cultural Studies is conducted. This is a topographical question concerning the organization of the relations between the practices of Cultural Studies, its objects of analysis, and the nature of the political concern it has in these. Little progress can be made with these matters unless it is recognized how radically the coordinates of the intellectual land-scape have shifted from those in which the founding rhetorics and pragmatics of Cultural Studies were shaped. The blithe confidence of the moment of theory sustaining the aspiration to a heroic penetration of the illusions of ideology to arrive at a knowledge of the objective structures that shape the practices of social agents behind their backs has now surely passed.[8] So has the notion that the critical intellectual might serve as the locus of a truth that can be opposed to power. Our awareness, post-Foucault, of the complex entanglements of the relations between knowledge and power has long since emptied any simple truth/power opposition of any logic or purpose. Equally importantly, as the work of Luc Boltanski and Eve Chiapello suggests,[9] the overlapping of the per-spectives of the social and artistic (or, in the British context, cultural) critiques that proved so important to the critical intellectual perspectives of the 1960s and 1970s has since come undone. These two forms of critique are now largely disentangled from one another and have yet — either singly or in combina-tion — to articulate clear or persuasive reconceptualizations of their roles.

More challenging, perhaps, are those aspects of the contemporary theoreti-cal landscape that make it increasingly difficult to identify whether and, if so, how culture might be constituted as a reasonably coherent object of analysis. To define culture as the realm of the symbolic — of meaning-making practices — is clearly no longer adequate since this produces only an infinite and unstop-pable expansion of its domain. Since the symbolic is everywhere, implicated in all practices, it can be nowhere in particular. Moreover, the very enterprise of seeking to differentiate culture in these terms so that it might be constituted as a reality of a particular type (made up of the symbolic, meanings, representa-tions) that is distinct in its composition from other realities (for example, those of the social) has been called into question by the post-representational turn across the humanities and social sciences. The notion that it might be intelligible to distinguish a realm of representations or of the symbolic in such a way as to then define a set of problems concerning the nature of its relations to non-representational realities (Is it determined by these, if only in the last instance? Does it construct them?) has been challenged by actor-network and assemblage theory. Following in the wake of Foucault's work, particularly his concept of the *dispositif*, and seeking a counter-heritage in the work of Gabriel Tarde, this loosely but strategically connected set of traditions deploys what David Toews usefully has called a "compositional perspective." In place of the great founding separations of the nineteenth-century social sciences between culture, society, and economy, this perspective focuses on the more historically specific "gatherings" of varied elements (textual, technological, human, non-human) into provisional associations with one another, which traverse such great divides.[10]

It is from this perspective that we usefully might return to the first of the two senses of metaculture discussed earlier. For it suggests a light in which such metacultural practices might be reconsidered as both effecting, and being entangled within, gatherings of particular kinds — gatherings consisting in the roles performed by particular forms of expertise in bringing together (not from above, as in the logic of a master discourse, but in lateral processes of assembling) heterogeneous elements and organizing them into distinctive compositional configurations. It also suggests a basis on which a use might again be found for the concept of culture, provided that it is understood as the historically mutable and contingent product of such processes of gathering. The culturalness of culture, on this conception, does not precede the practices of metaculture — it is not something that is pre-given to such practices — but is rather their effect. It is not a matter of the properties of the symbolic or the logic of representation, but of the nature of the gathering that is produced by the ordering of the relations between the elements that constitute it.

This is the view I have proposed in suggesting that a distinctive object might be retrieved for cultural analysis in the form of what I have called the "culture complex."[11] This comprises a connected set of such gatherings or assemblages that are distinct from the social or the economy not because of the "stuff" of which they are made up, but because of the public ordering of their relations to one another. The historical and geographical distinctiveness of this complex consists in the way it produces and organizes forms of power that are connected to those ways of intervening in the conduct of conduct that Foucault calls governmental. Foucault, it will be recalled, characterizes governmental power as the result of a process that, in the West, "has led to the development of a series of specific governmental apparatuses (*appareils*) on the one hand, [and, on the other] to the development of a series of knowledges (*savoirs*)."[12] The value of characterizing a specific ensemble of knowledges and apparatuses as cultural depends on being able to show that it brings together persons, things, and techniques — ways of doing and making — in compositional configurations that give rise to, exercise, and perform historically specific forms of power by producing distinctive techniques of intervention into the conduct of conduct. The analytical wager of the concept of the culture complex is that a distinctive field of cultural government has been shaped into being as a specific public ordering of things and people via the deployment of the modern cultural disciplines (literature, aesthetics, art history, folk studies, drama, heritage studies, cultural and media studies) in the apparatuses of the culture complex (museums, libraries, cinema, broadcasting, universities, heritage sites, and so on). To reiterate, these metacultural practices do not operate as master discourses that subordinate the texts, technologies, artefacts, and persons they assemble to their control. They are rather contingent forms of expertise that emerge from and are constituted within the assemblages in which they are active constituents. The logic of connection between such assemblages and the social is that of connecting particular ways of doing and making — particular regimes of cultural practice — to regularized ways of acting on the social to bring about calculated changes in conduct related to particular rationalities of government.

The historical and geographical specificity of this complex cannot be stressed too strongly. There is no question here of an account of culture as a trans-historical constant, a component in the makeup of all societies. Of course, it makes no sense to say of some societies that they lack culture where this is understood as the realm of the symbolic. And to suggest that some societies lack culture understood, in its restrictive definition, as a set of higher intellectual and cultural forms has itself been a means of exercising colonial power. There are, however, many societies in which the distinctive ways of assembling materials and practices, and bringing these to bear on the organization of conduct, associated with the culture complex, have not been present. It is really only in its post-Enlightenment conception, for example, that the library in England emerges as a site for practices of classification and arrangement that detached books and writing practices from earlier religious assemblages, or their functioning as quasi-military aspects of state power against the threat of popular insurgency, to emerge instead as a key site for shaping the conduct of the population as a whole.[13] Similarly, owing to the lack of anything approaching a civic cultural infrastructure in colonial French West Africa, the strategies of governance in the "Greater France" of the 1920s and 1930s operated in accordance with different logics in metropolitan and colonial contexts: through the shaping of beliefs and opinions via civic cultural assemblages in the former, and via direct intervention into the milieu to shape conditions of life in the latter.[14] And while the history of the relations between aesthetic practices, the tea ceremony, and practices of civility played an important role in the exercise of distinctive forms of state power during the Tokugawa period in Japan,[15] the subsequent failure during the Meiji period to graft the practices of Western art museums on to the space that these practices produced testified to the operation of quite distinctive cultural assemblages.[16]

We are not dealing with universals here, but rather with the specific spaces and settings for action that are produced by specific gatherings of historically particular forms of expertise, texts, instruments, techniques, objects, and so on, which connect with the forms of conduct of the population — or differentiated sections of it — in distinctive ways. It is in terms of its relations to these spaces, and the positions it takes up within or *vis-à-vis* them through the metacultural framings of cultural practice that it has proposed, that the history of Cultural Studies should be written. This is partly a matter, to take the British case again, of understanding how its early trajectories were shaped by its relations to the workers' and adult education movements, and its role in channeling these through a range of leftist and social democratic "takes" on the concept of a common culture derived from the tradition of *Kulturkritik*.[17] Or, to take the Australian case, it involves considering how, *inter alia*, the concerns of Australian Cultural Studies have been shaped by the positions it has taken up in the range of "problem spaces" that define the relations between Indigenous Australians and mainstream collecting institutions, broadcasting, film, heritage sites, tourism, and so on.[18] In both cases, we have to deal with intellectual and practical interventions that aim to transform metacultural practices in ways that will affect how cultural institutions are implicated in the conduct of conduct. A good deal, however, hinges on the ways in which these aspects of metacultural practices are understood for assessments of the kinds of politics in which Cultural Studies is engaged and the means by which these should be conducted. It is to these matters that I now turn.

From Ideological Articulation to Ontological Politics

One of the most influential accounts of the procedures through which Cultural Studies operates politically is Stuart Hall's account of the mechanisms of articulation — or, more accurately, of disarticulation and rearticulation — through which particular ideological elements are detached from their association with dominant ideological formations and attached to counter-hegemonic ones.[19] The most positive aspect of this legacy is its anti-essentialism — that is, its insistence that the particular elements of an ideological formation derive their force and class belongingness from the combinatorial mix in which they are provisionally brought together with other ideological elements rather than from an essential relationship to a particular class. Yet, as Hall presents it, the politics of articulation is, at its root, a politics of consciousness, a struggle for the frames of reference that will organize the terms in which different social groups are brought together and forged into opposing political forces. There is no room in this account for the more pluri-dimensional anti-essentialisms of actor-network and assemblage theory, in which it is always the more complex combinatorial relations between signs, things, and persons that have to be netted analytically and in which the affordances of things — their give and take — are granted a force that has to be taken into account alongside the agency of persons.[20] I want, then, to illustrate briefly the light that these perspectives throw on the processes through which the relations between culture, institution, and conduct are subjected to different metacultural orderings and combinatorial framings before returning to discuss the limitations of aesthetic conceptions of metapolitics and their influence on Cultural Studies.

I shall do so by means of a particular example focused on the role played by the Musée de l'Homme as a key site for the coordination of a complex set of processes which, in the 1920s and 1930s, led to significantly new metacultural framings of the cultures of the populations of France's colonial territories.[21] These were expressed in two aspects of the Museum's practices. First, they were evident in what Christine Laurière calls the environmentalist concept of the object informing its displays, which were arranged to show how all humans transform their cultures in given environments through creative capacities common to all peoples.[22] This involved exhibitions of arts and crafts practices complemented by photographic and documentary evidence, and by maps — the intention being to convey an impression of a culture as a distinctive totality bound and shaped by a distinctive regional milieu. This anthropological humanism, affirming the equality of all peoples as testified to by their shared capacity for creativity in everyday cultural practices, was echoed in the laboratory of the Institut d'ethnologie housed in the Museum and the *salles de travail* of its different departments. Separated from the Museum's exhibition galleries, these spaces made available a selection of the objects, films, photographs, sound recordings, and field notes collected through its various scientific expeditions as a resource for study that would, first, make possible a detailed knowledge of the specifically distinguishing qualities of the different territorially defined cultures that fell under French colonial administration and, second, make that knowledge available (in varied ways) to colonial administrators.

What is perhaps most noteworthy about both these aspects of the Musée de l'Homme's practices, however, is the shift of balance away from the collection, exhibition, and examination of racialized human anatomies that they effected. This was a not a total shift: the Musée de l'Homme's Galerie anthropologique continued to be informed by evolutionary conceptions of such matters, and its racially and territorially defined galleries also displayed racially defined skulls and skeletons. Their role here, however, was clearly subordinate to and, in some respects, at odds with that played by photographs, maps, and textual descriptions in evoking the specificity of different cultures. This constituted a significant break with the earlier traditions of French anthropology — particularly those represented by Paul Broca, which undertook a seemingly limitless stockpiling of the anatomical remains of conquered and colonized peoples as a resource for an evolutionary version of racial science. Broca's role in relation to the Society for Mutual Autopsy, established in 1876 as a part of the Société d'Anthropologie de Paris, is telling in this regard. So called because its members dedicated their bodies to science by agreeing to have an autopsy performed on their remains by one of their fellow members, the Society's museum and laboratory played an important role in this respect.[23] The walls of the laboratory were lined with thousands of human and anthropoid skulls, and there were boxes of skulls and skeletons, and of miscellaneous bones, donated by anthropologists from their overseas excursions. The adjacent museum had over four thousand skulls of different races, forty human skeletons, and the skeletons and skulls of anthropoids and other large animals. And among these, but in a differentiated area, were the skulls, brains, and other body parts of the members of the Society, whose conceit was that, as representatives of the most intellectually advanced branches of the species, bequeathing their remains to science would assist in identifying the anatomical traits that needed to be cultivated in the interests of continuing species and social advancement.

The processes through which these metacultural framings of the colonized were transformed to those effected by the Musée de l'Homme in the 1930s are intricate and complex, involving multiple agents whose actions comingled with one another across a range of institutional contexts. These included the role of a range of new societies and institutes, particularly the Institut d'ethnologie, through which the Durkheimian and Maussian projects of ethnography challenged and eventually supplanted the bias toward physical anthropology favored by Broca; the emergence of the Musée de l'Homme, during its period of incubation within Le Musée d'Ethnographie du Trocadéro, as a key coordinating site for the activities of such institutes and societies, and a point of connection with the University of Paris; the role of Paul Rivet, initially a disciple of Broca and later the founding director of the Musée de l'Homme, and a crucial junction point for a range of scientific and administrative networks; the disentangling of the Musée de l'Homme's anthropological humanism from the exotic evocations of the "other" arising from its early associations with surrealism; and the organization of new actor networks arising from the Musée de l'Homme's role in arranging fieldwork expeditions, mainly to different parts of French West Africa. More important for my purposes here, however, are the consequences of these processes in producing a new metacultural framing of the cultures of the colonized, framings that made possible new forms of action on the colonial social as parts of new governmental rationalities.

Let's go back to Broca's laboratory and museum. For it was into this environment that France's leading *fin-de siècle* anthropologists went to do their work. By using anthropometric techniques of measurement to identify a range of cephalic types, Paul Broca, Jacques Bertillon, and their contemporaries sought to lay out the social in radically new, resolutely materialist terms as a series of body types existing in a secular developmental time and, as such, subject to management and rearrangement through scientific, proto-eugenic forms of intervention aimed at modifying the relationships between them. The ways of assembling, exhibiting, and working on colonized cultures at the Musée de l'Homme, by contrast, formed parts of two intersecting governmental rationalities that nonetheless operated differently depending on whether their point of application was the French public or the colonized themselves. As far as the former was concerned, the Musée de l'Homme, largely through its exhibition galleries, operated in connection with the institutions of the public sphere in aiming to effect a transformation of conduct by inducting the French population into a new pluralistic view of diversity in which a humanistic understanding of the colonized was connected to the anti-fascist politics of the Popular Front. As far as the latter was concerned, however, the Musée de l'Homme formed part of a new scientific-administrative complex in which a detailed and accumulating knowledge of the colonized was to be applied to the management of their milieux in ways calculated to manage their conduct via the manipulation of the material conditions of their existence rather than through public educational or civilizing programs.

This is an example of Anthropology as a metacultural practice reordering the relations between cultures and, in so doing, producing new surfaces for intervention into the conduct of conduct. It is not, however, a matter of Anthropology functioning as a purely intellectual form of knowledge practice. Rather, it concerns its operations as intimately tangled up in a complex set of relations between an array of knowledge institutions considered as parts of hybrid assemblages or actor networks involving both human and non-human actors. The stress here, as a number of commentators have pointed out, falls on the role played by knowledge practices — themselves conceived as always institutionally embedded — in making up and enacting new realities, thus producing and performing the social worlds on which they act.[24] This is not to be understood, however, in accordance with the logic of the "cultural turn" as a matter of representations shaping the real after their own fashion. It is rather a matter of knowledge practices operating through intellectual and institutional processes that are socially-materially constituted so as to fashion similarly constituted new realities.

The Interestedness of Aesthetics as Metapolitics

The example I have chosen — the deployment of Anthropology across a set of relations between the Musée de l'Homme, anthropological societies and institutes, the public sphere, and the scientific-administrative apparatuses of colonial rule — may seem a long way from the kinds of debates and issues that have informed the development of post-war Cultural Studies. Yet the connections become a little clearer if some of the intermediate steps are filled in. If we broaden the scale of the analysis, the activities of the Musée de l'Homme come into view as parts of a broader institutional ensemble inasmuch as the new political rationalities of colonial rule in which it was enmeshed were connected to the post-World War I establishment of the League of Nations and the international governmental organizations it sponsored in order to promote a new form of colonial rule that would work through, and profess respect for, the different values of different cultures. These institutions included the Office International des Musées (OIM) that was established in Paris in 1926 as a part of the Commission Internationale de Coopération Intellectuelle that had been founded in Geneva in 1922 under the auspices of the Society of Nations. The OIM's mission was to coordinate a set of relations between various knowledge practices — Anthropology, Art History, Archaeology, and so on — so as to transform museums into instruments of democratic popular education. As such, it was both a harbinger and incubator of the organizations for international cultural governance that were developed after the 1939–45 war. And the set of practices developed around the orbit of the Musée de l'Homme was a key point of connection between the two periods: Rivet was involved in the work of the OIM; Georges Henri Rivière, Rivet's deputy at the Musée de l'Homme, and later, the Director of the Musée des Arts et Traditions Populaires, became the first Director of its successor, the International Council of Museums (ICOM), which was established under the auspices of UNESCO in 1946.

It is not difficult to see connections between the operations of Cultural Studies in this second phase in the development of institutions of global cultural governance and the role of anthropology in the first phase. There are institutional and personal connections — Richard Hoggart's move from Birmingham to UNESCO, for example. There are clear lines of connection between the intellectual agendas of Cultural Studies and the cultural governmental agendas of UNESCO generally, and of ICOM specifically. Hall's work contributed to the influence of anti-essentialist conceptions of race in the development of UNESCO's cultural diversity agendas.[25] The 1996 UNESCO publication *Our Creative Diversity*, a report of the World Commission for Culture and Development, drew on Cultural Studies perspectives on the creativity of everyday cultural practices to reformat the governance/diversity interface so as to take it away from a concern with the administration of territorially marked ethnic cultures toward processes of trans-ethnic cultural intermingling as a source of "creative diversity."[26] The feedback loops from this through ICOMOS to national arts councils in turn provided an institutional/discursive assemblage in which Hall and others — myself included — have brought the perspectives of Cultural Studies to bear as a metacultural intervention into the processes through which cultural resources are mobilized as means for acting on the conduct of conduct in the context of cultural diversity policies.[27]

This, then, is to speak of Cultural Studies as a knowledge practice that operates alongside other knowledge practices in ways that are informed by the social, material, discursive, and institutional unfoldings of earlier knowledge practices. It is to speak of it as being involved in an ontological politics that, through its metacultural framing of the relations between social and cultural practices, is in play in the larger processes and relationships through which different forms of cultural expertise with a stake in the social business of shaping conduct interact, compete with, and contest one another.

The conception of aesthetics as a form of metapolitics pulls in the opposite direction by trying to lift aesthetics — interpreted as a transcendent, self-authorizing form of critique — out of and above the materially and institutionally entangled forms of contested political and civic calculations that such processes involve. We can see something of this in Michael Bérubé's assessment of Ian Hunter's account of the relations between aesthetics and literary education[28] as one that makes the whole enterprise of aesthetics look like "a swindle in which educational authorities get to mess with your mind."[29] In advocating instead an interpretation of the aesthetic that calls attention to the formal properties of literary works, Bérubé fails to register that it is precisely via the stress that aesthetics places on such properties that it was able to enter the machinery of popular schooling as a technique for "messing with minds" (what else could it be?) that worked through the newly instituted formal properties of literary texts.

A similar case for treating aesthetics as an exemption from the involvement of knowledge practices in processes of social governance is provided by Jacques Rancière's account of aesthetics and its discontents.[30] This constitutes a site of a tension within Rancière's work between, on the one hand, the ways in which his comments on the aesthetic regime of art open up the history of varied social inscriptions of art (or, in Rancière's terms, emplotments of the relations between art and life) to empirical inquiry,[31] and on the other, the ways in which his conception of aesthetics as a form of metapolitics seeks to privilege one such inscription above others. This tension is evident in the terms Rancière uses to distinguish aesthetics as metapolitics from any putative positive or negative ethical inscription of the aesthetic — as in public or community art projects, for example, or the line of critique (Adorno, Lyotard, Agamben) that links the aesthetic to the Holocaust. In place of these, Rancière proposes a conception of aesthetics as a form of metapolitics representing a standpoint of critique that is constitutively outside of, and occupying a position of transcendence in relation to, the mundane politics of the state, institutions, parties, bureaucracies, and so on. Rancière traces the source of this conception of the aesthetic to Kant's account of art's autonomy as a form of sensory experience that serves as the harbinger of a *sensus communis* that will provide the locus for a new humanity that is to come, a humanity no longer fractured by the sensory divisions that hitherto have marked the relations between art and the social division of occupations. Readers versed in the history of Cultural Studies will recognize a familiar structure here. For what Rancière proposes as an innovation is in fact a duplication of the place occupied by the idea of a common culture in the work of Raymond Williams and Terry Eagleton,[32] which — as Mulhern and Hunter have shown in different ways — is a legacy of the post-Kantian tradition of *Kulturkritik* as represented by the tradition of English criticism that leads from Matthew Arnold to Williams.

Yet if Rancière's formulations largely restate these earlier positions in Cultural Studies, they have also been marshalled in advocacy of a return to those positions as an alternative to various "pragmatic" or "instrumental" turns that have marked its subsequent development — the cultural policy moment, for example.[33] Yet it is surely evident that what is at stake in such endorsements of the anti-instrumental critiques of aesthetics is an attempt to constitute a particular form of expertise (the philosophical specification of art's autonomy) that seeks to clear a space for its exercise *vis-à-vis* that of other cultural knowledges (history and art history, for example) by mobilizing that particular architecture of personhood bequeathed by Kant in the form of a division between an ideal humanity yet to come and its currently self-divided and debased forms. It is within the historically instituted space produced by this division that the philosopher aesthetician operates as an interested party in seeking to organize a putatively transcendent space from which to intervene in the conduct of conduct in ways contrary to the directions proposed by other authorities and agents. Yet it is only from the point of view of a foreshortened view of the history of aesthetics — one that interprets the Kantian transcendental project as effecting the historical suppression of its antecedents — that such a view is tenable. Viewed in the light of its longer history, the Kantian architecture of a divided humanity is only too clearly a reworking of Christian metaphysics, just as the philosopher aesthetician who seeks to act on conduct from within such a space aspires to a new form of priestly authority via a commentary on a new set of canonized texts in the form of works of art.[34]

Some Conclusions

Where does all of this leave us? I have, in the foregoing, sketched a view of Cultural Studies as a set of metacultural practices through which specific forms of cultural expertise are deployed in various ways with a view to changing the conduct of, and/or the relations between, social agents. It is not, of course, unified in its methods, purposes, or modes of engagement with the social processes through which the "conduct of conduct" is enacted. Nor is it the only form of metaculture engaged in such processes. To the contrary, its operations in these regards have to be considered alongside those of a wide range of cultural disciplines. Its relations to these have been, and remain, mobile and fluid ones of mutual interaction rather than relations of a potential interdisciplinary transcendence. The somewhat heroic aspirations towards a totalizing form of interdisciplinary synthesis that characterized Cultural Studies in the 1970s and 1980s no longer have much credence. Indeed, in this chapter I have looked largely outside Cultural Studies to other intellectual traditions for productive ways of rethinking its nature as an intellectual practice and the issues that are at stake in its pursuit.

There have been three aspects to my arguments in these regards. The first has been to suggest that Cultural Studies should view itself as acting on a par with, and alongside, other forms of cultural expertise in relation to the organization of conduct. This is to deny it the possibility — to which some tendencies within it have often been prone — of staking its claims to a ground that is outside those processes through which the mechanisms of liberal government and the cultural disciplines are complexly entangled with one another. The second has been to suggest new ways in which those entanglements should be viewed by stressing their inherently socio-material nature. This is not an appeal to a materialism of a Marxist kind. On the contrary, the conception of *materiality* that is invoked here rebuts the concern of *materialisms* to explain one set of practices (cultural) as being grounded in and determined by another (economic). In place of such analytical enterprises, it substitutes a concern with the relational organization of the reciprocal agency of things and persons in and through the networks and assemblages in which they are gathered together. The constitution of these — whether they are social, economic, or cultural — includes technical instruments and devices as material operators in and of the relations between persons, equipping them with the capacities for specific kinds of agency and interrelation.[35]

Third and finally, the perspective I have proposed suggests that the political vocation of Cultural Studies can no longer be thought of as an endeavour to construct, by discursive means, where the lines of effective political division within a social formation will be drawn. Quite apart from the fact that it has never been the kind of political movement that might play such a role, such a conception abstracts political consciousness from the more complex forms of the organization and distribution of agency across intersecting networks and assemblages with which cultural analysis and politics have now to engage.

Notes

Introduction: Instituting Cultural Studies

1. Cornelius Castoriadis, *The Imaginary Institution of Society*, translated by Kathleen Blamey (Cambridge, MA: MIT Press, 1987), 133.
2. John R. Searle, "Social Ontology and the Philosophy of Society." In *On the Nature of Social and Institutional Reality*, edited by Eerik Lagerspetz, Heikki Ikäheimo and Jussi Kotkavirta (Jyväskylä: SoPhi, 2001), 37.
3. For an elaborated account of this methodological priority, see Lawrence Grossberg, *Cultural Studies in the Future Tense* (Durham, NC: Duke University Press, 2010).
4. Ted Striphas, "The Long March: Cultural Studies and Its Institutionalization." *Cultural Studies* 12(4) (1998): 454. Striphas's essay introduced his guest-edited special issue on "The Institutionalization of Cultural Studies."
5. Some examples of such accounts are in Brett de Bary, ed., *Universities in Translation: The Mental Labor of Globalization* (Hong Kong: Hong Kong University Press, 2010); Kuan-Hsing Chen and Chua Beng Huat, eds., *The Inter-Asia Cultural Studies Reader* (London: Routledge, 2007); Barak Kalir and Pál Nyíri, eds., "Evaluating Academia: Between Old Hierarchy and New Orthodoxy." *EspacesTemps.net,* July 12, 2010. http://www.espacestemps.net/document8318.html; Mikko Lehtonen, "Spaces and Places of Cultural Studies," *Culture Unbound* 1 (2009): 67–81. http://www.culture-unbound.ep.liu.se/v1/a06; Meaghan Morris, "Teaching versus Research? Cultural Studies and the New Class Politics in Knowledge." *Inter-Asia Cultural Studies* 9(3) (2008): 433–50; Ronald Schliefer, "The Institutions of Cultural Studies." *Surfaces* 2 (1992). http://www.pum.umontreal.ca/revues/surfaces/vol2/schleife.html; Graeme Turner, *What's Become of Cultural Studies?* (Thousand Oaks, CA: Sage, 2011); Handel K. Wright and Meaghan Morris, eds., *Cultural Studies of Transnationalism* (London: Routledge, 2012).
6. Cris Shore, "Audit Culture and Illiberal Governance." *Anthropological Theory* 8(3) (2008): 282. On the "New Public Management" (NPM) principles driving a wave of public sector reforms worldwide since the 1980s, see Sowaribi Tolofari, "New Public Management and Education." *Policy Futures in Education* 3(1) (2005): 75–89. For a broader argument that within these reforms the humanities in

Australia have nonetheless "won significant ground in influencing how government and the university sector have conceptualised research," see Graeme Turner, "Informing the Public: Is There a Place for a Critical Humanities?" in *Proceedings* (Canberra: Australian Academy of the Humanities, 2005), 136.

7. For an account of this, see Cris Shore and Susan Wright, "Coercive Accountability: The Rise of Audit Culture in Higher Education." In *Audit Cultures: Anthropological Studies in Accountability, Ethics and the Academy*, edited by Marilyn Strathern (London: Routledge, 2000), 67.

8. Simon Marginson and Mark Considine, *The Enterprise University: Power, Governance and Reinvention in Australia* (Cambridge: Cambridge University Press, 2000), 21.

9. On some of the educational complexities, see Meaghan Morris, "Humanities for Taxpayers: Some Problems." *New Literary History* 36(1) (2005): 111–29.

10. Our special thanks for their participation go to Lawrence Grossberg, Kim Soyoung, and Earl Jackson.

11. We are grateful to Lingnan University for a Direct Grant to fund the project titled "University Culture, Markets, Globalization and Norms"; Mette Hjort, PI, and Meaghan Morris. LU: DA06A7, 2005–06.

12. "Liveable Institutions: What Does It Take These Days?" was the title of Mette Hjort's paper for the Cultural Studies and Institution conference, and is the basis of part of her chapter here.

13. Our thanks to Ien Ang, Tony Bennett, Ib Bondebjerg, Pam Cooke, Kuan-Hsing Chen, John Frow, Josephine Ho, Dina Iordanova, Koichi Iwabuchi, Tejaswini Niranjana, Kevin Pask, Duncan Petrie, Kim Soyoung, and William Straw.

14. The classic analysis of how invocations of "excellence" function in neo-liberal university rhetoric is Bill Readings, *The University in Ruins* (Cambridge, MA: Harvard University Press, 1996). We borrow the notion of stories "to live by" from Charles Taylor: personal conversation with Mette Hjort.

15. Mary Douglas, *How Institutions Think* (Syracuse, NY: Syracuse University Press, 1986), 46.

16. The qualification "with Chinese characteristics" is widely used to signify the need to alter or adjust borrowed — usually Western — policies to allow for the cultural and historical difference of Chinese societies, and in Hong Kong it is just as widely used humorously to affirm the local subversion or *détournement* of that policy's intent.

17. Bill Readings, *The University in Ruins* (Cambridge, MA: Harvard University Press, 1996). On audit culture, see Marilyn Strathern, ed., *Audit Cultures: Anthropological Studies in Accountability, Ethics and the Academy* (London: Routledge, 2000). On the physical and psychic costs of those cultures, see Jody Berland, "Bodies of Theory, Bodies of Pain: Some Silences." In *Feminism–Art–Theory: An Anthology 1968–2000*, edited by Hilary Robinson (Oxford: Blackwell, 2001), 75–84; and Bronwyn Davies and Peter Bansel, "Governmentality and Academic Work: Shaping the Hearts and Minds of Academic Workers." *Journal of Curriculum Theorizing* 26(3) (2010): 5–20.

18. Introduction to Barak Kalir and Pál Nyíri, "Evaluating Academia." *EspacesTemps. net*, July 12, 2010. http://espacestemps.net/document8318.html.

19. On the relationality of place and locality, see Doreen Massey, *Space, Place and Gender* (Minneapolis, MN: University of Minnesota Press, 1994).

20. See http://www.inter-asia.org/ for an overview of the movement's activities.

21. See Kuan-Hsing Chen, ed., *Trajectories: Inter-Asia Cultural Studies* (London: Routledge, 1998) for publications based on this conference and a subsequent meeting in 1995. Authors coming to the project from "outside" Asian locations at the time were Ien Ang, Leo Ching, Kenneth Dean, Stuart Hall, Meaghan Morris, Stephen Muecke, Cindy Patton, Mark A. Reid, and Naoki Sakai. Among the contributors to this present volume, Tony Bennett, Stephen Ching-kiu Chan, Kuan-Hsing Chen, and Meaghan Morris attended the 1992 Trajectories conference.

22. Jacques Derrida, *The Other Heading: Reflection on Today's Europe*, translated by Pascale-Anne Brault and Michael B. Naas (Bloomington, IN: Indiana University Press, 1992).

23. Marginson and Considine, *The Enterprise University*, 19. On Chinese participation, see Lin Ye, "Audit Culture with Chinese Characteristics?" *EspacesTemps.net*, Textuel, July 12, 2010. http://espacestemps.net/document8298.html.

24. On the complex work of deciding the "point" of a story told in a given context, see Ross Chambers, *Story and Situation: Narrative Seduction and the Power of Fiction* (Minneapolis, MN: University of Minnesota Press, 1984).

25. Theodor Adorno, *The Culture Industry* (London: Routledge, 1991), 121.

26. Jennifer Lindsay, "A Drama of Change: Cultural Policy and the Performing Arts in Southeast Asia." In *Global Culture: Media, Arts, Policy, and Globalization*, edited by Diana Crane, Nobuko Kawahima and Ken'ichi Kawasaki (New York: Routledge, 2002), 63–4.

27. Rita Felski, "The Doxa of Difference." *Signs* 23(1) (1997): 1–21.

28. Thanks for this nice phrase to an anonymous reviewer for Hong Kong University Press.

29. The phrase "critical potential" here is from Douglas Crimp: personal correspondence. For the double movement initiating a turn to Cultural Studies in Crimp's own work at this time, see Douglas Crimp, *AIDS: Cultural Analysis/Cultural Activism* (Cambridge MA: MIT Press, 1988); and Douglas Crimp, *On the Museum's Ruins* (Cambridge MA: MIT Press, 1993).

30. Tony Bennett, *Culture: A Reformer's Science* (London: Sage, 1998), 2–3.

31. On the relationship of the academy to public and professional spheres, see Michael Denning, *Culture in the Age of Three Worlds* (London: Verso, 2004), 121–46; and Iain McCalman and Meaghan Morris, "'Public Culture' and Humanities Research in Australia: A Report," *Public Culture* 11(2) (1999): 319–45. The theme of collusion is discussed in Striphas, "The Long March: Cultural Studies and Its Institutionalization."

32. Adorno, *The Culture Industry*, 107.

33. Zygmunt Bauman, "Culture and Management." *Parallax* 10(2) (2004): 71.

34. Peter Osborne, "'Whoever Speaks of Culture Speaks of Administration as Well': Disputing Pragmatism in Cultural Studies." *Cultural Studies* 20(1) (2006): 34.
35. Osborne, "Whoever Speaks," 46. The notion of culture as resource is developed by George Yúdice, *The Expediency of Culture: Uses of Culture in the Global Era* (Durham, NC: Duke University Press, 2003).
36. For a case study of the impact of managerial choices on Aston University in the United Kingdom in 1981–94, see Henry D.R. Miller, *The Management of Change in Universities: Universities, State and the Economy in Australia, Canada and the United Kingdom* (Milton Keynes: Society for Research into Higher Education and Open University Press, 1995), 125–49. A classic account in economic history that understands institutions through the interplay of constraints and choice is Douglass C. North, *Institutions, Institutional Change and Economic Performance* (Cambridge: Cambridge University Press, 1990).
37. See, respectively, Michel Foucault, *The History of Sexuality: An Introduction*, translated by Robert Hurley (Harmondsworth: Penguin, 1984); and Louis Althusser, "Ideology and Ideological State Apparatuses (Notes towards an Investigation)." In Louis Althusser, *Lenin and Philosophy and Other Essays*, translated by Ben Brewster (New York: Monthly Review Press, 1971), 127–86.
38. On the conflation of accountability with accountancy, see Shore, "Audit Culture and Illiberal Governance."
39. Simon Marginson, "Making Space in Higher Education." In *Global Creation: Space, Mobility and Synchrony in the Age of the Knowledge Economy*, edited by Simon Marginson, Peter Murphy and Michael A. Peters (New York: Peter Lang, 2010), 154.
40. Marginson, "Making Space in Higher Education," 155.
41. Michel Foucault, "Governmentality." In *The Foucault Effect: Studies in Governmentality*, edited by Graham Burchell, Colin Gordon and Peter Miller (London: Harvester/Wheatsheaf, 1978), 87–104. For an influential example of this kind of institutional study, see Tony Bennett, *The Birth of the Museum: History, Theory, Politics* (London: Routledge, 1995).
42. Editors' Introduction to *On the Nature of Social and Institutional Reality*, edited by Eerik Lagerspetz, Heikki Ikäheimo and Jussi Kotkavirta (Jyväskylä: SoPhi, 2001), 4.
43. Stanley Taylor, cited in Elwin H. Powell, "On Choosing Institutions: Ideas from Stanley Taylor," in Stanley Taylor, *Conceptions of Institutions and the Theory of Knowledge*, 2nd ed. (New Brunswick, NH: Transaction, 1989), 5.
44. Michel Foucault, in Rux Martin, "Truth, Power, Self: An Interview with Michel Foucault." In *Technologies of the Self: A Seminar with Michel Foucault*, edited by Luther H. Martin, Huck Gutman and Patrick H. Hutton (London: Tavistock, 1982), 10.
45. Adorno, *The Culture Industry*, 122.
46. Althusser, "Ideology and Ideological State Apparatuses," 174.
47. Althusser, "Ideology and Ideological State Apparatuses," 185.

48. Cited in Powell, "On Choosing Institutions: Ideas from Stanley Taylor," 6.
49. Douglas, *How Institutions Think*, 92.
50. Douglas, *How Institutions Think*, 92.
51. Douglas, *How Institutions Think*, 92.
52. Douglas, *How Institutions Think*, 126.

Chapter 1: The Desire for Cultural Studies

1. For early attempts to articulate this continuity, see the *Journal of Arts and Ideas* in the 1980s. Overlaps of concerns and authors are to be found in Tejaswini Niranjana, P. Sudhir, and Vivek Dhareshwar, eds., *Interrogating Modernity: Culture and Colonialism in India* (Kolkata: Seagull Books, 1993), now seen as the first Cultural Studies reader to be published in India.
2. While the Subaltern Studies historians, among others, have written about the crisis in nationalist discourse, the parallel crises in disciplines and institutions have not yet received the same kind of attention.
3. This formulation, which emerged in CSCS (Centre for the Study of Culture and Society) discussions in the late 1990s, owes much to the work of Partha Chatterjee.
4. See, for example, C. L. R. James, *The Black Jacobins* (New York: Vintage, 1989 [1938]); Aimé Césaire, *Cahier d'un retour au pays natal* (*Return to my Native Land*) (Paris: Volontés, 1939); Jawaharlal Nehru, *Discovery of India* (Oxford: Oxford University Press, 1946); Jomo Kenyatta, *Facing Mount Kenya* (London: Martin, Secker and Warburg, 1938).
5. Satish Deshpande, *Contemporary India: A Sociological Introduction* (Delhi: Penguin, 2003).
6. A key figure here is Sir William Jones, an early Indologist who founded the Asiatic Society in 1784 and whose work is still reprinted, and revered, in India. For a critical account of Jones' work, see Tejaswini Niranjana, *Siting Translation: History, Post-structuralism and the Colonial Context* (Berkeley, CA: University of California Press, 1992).
7. For a lucid account of the development of this critique, see Susie Tharu's Introduction to Vol. II of *Women Writing in India* (Delhi: Oxford University Press, 1993).
8. C. T. Kurien, *Rethinking Economics* (Delhi: Sage, 1996).
9. Deshpande, *Contemporary India*.
10. Inspired in large measure by Edward Said's *Orientalism* (New York: Vintage, 1979), the critique of English Studies found articulation in Gauri Viswanathan, *Masks of Conquest* (London: Faber, 1990); Rajeswari Sunder Rajan, ed., *The Lie of the Land* (Delhi: Oxford University Press, 1992); Svati Joshi, ed., *Rethinking English* (Delhi: Trianka, 1991); and Susie Tharu, ed., *Subject to Change* (Hyderabad: Orient Longman, 1998).
11. "Higher Education in India," Country Paper for UNESCO, World Conference on Higher Education in the Twenty-first Century, 2000.

12   For the discussion in this section, I am indebted to the inputs of CSCS colleagues and the many proposals and reports we have assembled over the last ten years.

13.   The Master's program in Cultural Studies was introduced at the behest of Kuvempu University, a local state university that has had a long-standing engagement with CSCS. After one successful year of the program, the Kuvempu University administrators ran afoul of the Open University system in Karnataka, which claimed that no other institution could offer distance learning courses. The MA in Cultural Studies has since been suspended.

Chapter 2: Social Movements, Cultural Studies, and Institutions

1.   Inter-Asia Cultural Studies, also known as the Movements project, is a trans-border collective undertaking to confront Inter-Asia cultural politics. Among other networking activities it publishes a refereed journal, *Inter-Asia Cultural Studies*, links research centers and organizes a biennial conference. See http://www.inter-asia.org.

2.   See Kuan-Hsing Chen, ed., *Trajectories: Inter-Asia Cultural Studies* (London: Routledge, 1998).

3.   In January 2006, a five-day Teaching Cultural Studies Workshop was held at National Central University, Chung-li, Taiwan. Without prior preparation, a Memorandum of Understanding was signed by friends who represented eleven different institutions in the region. For details, see Josephine Ho, "Forging the Trail: Teaching Cultural Studies Workshop, Taiwan, 2006." *Inter-Asia Cultural Studies* 9(3) (2008): 429–32.

4.   Hanasaki Kohei, "Decolonialization and Assumption of War Responsibility." *Inter-Asia Cultural Studies* 1(1) (2000): 71–84.

5.   *Inter-Asia Cultural Studies* 6(2) (2005).

6.   These journals include Seoul-based *Creation and Criticism* (*Changbi*), Tokyo-based *Contemporary Thought* (*Gendai Shiso*) and IMPACTION, Beijing-based *Dushu*, Taipei-based *Taiwan: A Radical Quarterly in Social Studies*, and *Inter-Asia Cultural Studies*. A conference on Historical Culture of the Cold War took place in Kinmen in November 2010.

7.   See "Editorial Statement," *Inter-Asia Cultural Studies* 1(1) (2000): 5.

8.   See Kuan-Hsing Chen and Chua Beng Huat, "Introduction: The *Inter-Asia Cultural Studies: Movements* Project." In *The Inter-Asia Cultural Studies Reader*, edited by Kuan-Hsing Chen and Chua Beng Huat (London: Routledge, 2007), 1–6.

9.   Carolyn Cooper, "'Pedestrian Crosses': Sites of Dislocation in 'Post-colonial' Jamaica." *Inter-Asia Cultural Studies* 10(1) (2009): 3–11.

Chapter 3: Life of a Parasite

1.   The term "gadfly" was used by Plato in the *Apology* to describe Socrates' role of dissent in stinging the complacent establishment into action. Cultural Studies, as a

gadfly, could be said to direct its sting at the power bloc, the status quo or popular beliefs.

2. These pockets, all active in the field of Cultural Studies, include the Graduate Institute of Building and Planning at National Taiwan University (est. 1988), the Center for Asia-Pacific/Cultural Studies at Tsing-Hua University (est. 1992), the Center for the Study of Sexualities at National Central University (est. 1995), the Graduate School for Social Transformation Studies at Shih-Hsin University (est. 1997), and a vibrant group in the Department of Psychology at Fu-Jen Catholic University (est. 2000). Established or operated by left-wing scholars who had returned to Taiwan after the lifting of martial laws in 1987, but who refused to dance to the tunes of nationalist politics, such critical gatherings, scattered in many different fields, have maintained active involvement in Taiwan's various social movements not only by sharing their own social respectability — and thus legitimacy — with marginal groups, but also by producing critical discourses and research results, as well as non-conforming students, to challenge mainstream academic mechanisms of knowledge production.

3. "Democratization" has been considered a liberalizing, liberating restructuring of society, but I am putting the word in quotation marks exactly to point to the inimical dimensions of such a seemingly benevolent process.

4. My own clandestine slogan of "We want orgasms, not sexual harassment," uttered in the 1994 anti-sexual harassment march in Taipei, followed by my controversial book *The Gallant Woman: Feminism and Sexual Emancipation* (1994), not only opened up discursive space for female sexuality but also resulted in a silent purge of my membership from feminist scholarly organizations henceforth. As one weathered feminist put it in a private conversation: "It took us so many years of effort to reach this level of social acceptance, we cannot afford to have it tarnished by any controversy."

5. Other members came from the Graduate Institute of Philosophy at National Central University and the Chinese Department of National Tsinghua University, but most of us were concentrated in the English Department of National Central University. The title of the Center was chosen to demonstrate our resolve to discuss gender issues without losing sight of sexuality as well as other social differences, such as class, race, age, and so on. We chose to put a slash in between *xing-bie* (性別, which means "gender" in Chinese, but taken apart, the two characters signify sex and difference) to mark our position. The Center's English title was later changed to the "Center for the Study of Sexualities," not only for the sake of brevity but also to mark the stalemate in gender studies as mainstream women began sharing state power in 2000, and as the rapid development in sexuality studies as activism in the area of marginal sexualities took off.

6. Since the establishment of our center in 1995, I have often been asked by the curious but friendly: "Has the university given you any trouble? Is there any opposition to your Center at your university?" The frequency of such questions is a constant reminder that although gender has marched on to the university map and national

policy, we are still faced with the difficulty of dealing with a subject — sexuality — that easily evokes shame, guilt, fear, ignorance, and consequently anger and bigotry. And our difficulties are doubled because of the against-the-grain approach we are determined to embrace.

7.   To intervene in the rapid development of mainstream gender education, the Center organized a series of gender equity education workshops in 1998 and 1999 that not only provided platforms for progressive middle school teachers to address and influence their peers but also, because the workshops were funded and certified by the County Bureau of Education, helped boost respectability and credibility for the Center. We also published various kinds of teacher training materials, as well as gender education material for middle school students in the form of a popular *manga*. All materials, in Chinese, are now available online (http://sex.ncu.edu.tw/course/young/young.html).

8.   In 1997, at the urging of mainstream women's groups, Taipei mayor Chen Shui-Bian revoked the licenses of the last remaining 128 prostitutes in order to demonstrate his resolve to purify the city of vice. Unexpectedly, the middle-aged, illiterate prostitutes rose in protest, and labor groups as well as sex-positive feminists came to their support, thus igniting a wave of fierce debates among feminists over the issue of sex work. The debates had other practical and tangible consequences. Staff members at the Awakening Foundation, the most prominent feminist group at the time, who worked tirelessly to support the sex workers as well as advocating for lesbian issues, were collectively fired later that year for "ignoring their work assignment and disobeying the orders of the Board of Directors." The discharged activists formed Gender/Sexuality Rights Association of Taiwan (GSRAT) two years later to continue their fight for marginal genders and sexualities (http://gsrat.net/en/aboutus.php). In contrast, mainstream women's groups that stood with the city government in 1997 have since been rewarded generously with both funding and political power of influence as mayor Chen became the president of the country in 2000. As their assistance in consolidating governance is both effective and necessary, President Ma's regime since has also maintained good relations with these women's groups.

9.   The Chinese term "state-feminism" was first used by feminist scholar Yu-Xiou Liu in a 1996 interview. Liu believes that feminist ideals are to be carried out by none other than housewives becoming political agents through entering the public realm of the state apparatus *en masse*. The sheer presence and number of women would then swallow up the public realm with the private realm, thus feminizing the state and forcing it to take up the job of caring, while the self-professed "philosophy queen" dethrones the "philosophy king." See Yu-Xiou Liu, "From Women Ruling the State to Gender Liberation: Subverting Familial Patriarchy with State-Feminism." *Stir Quarterly* 2 (1996): 23–4 (in Chinese). It is with this vision in mind that mainstream feminists developed an unusually high interest and investment in the project of state-building.

10. Lin Fang-mei, "Identity Politics in Contemporary Women's Movement in Taiwan: The Case of Licensed Prostitution." *Chung-Wai Literary Monthly* 313 (1998): 58 (in Chinese). Author's emphasis. Lin herself became a Cabinet member after the opposition DPP party assumed state power in 2000.

11. This leftist bent was later noted as our work was seen as continuously producing "a body of indigenous Marxist writings that mobilizes different senses of 'queerness' to demonstrate that the official celebration of diversity and human rights [in Taiwan] has actually further alienated and disempowered sex workers, promiscuous homosexuals, gay drug-users, and other social subjects that are considered to be a threat to the liberal-democratic order." See Petrus Liu, "Queer Marxism in Taiwan." *Inter-Asia Cultural Studies*, 8(4) (2007): 517–39.

12. The influx of such writings totally transformed the *Fu-kan* (literary supplement) of major newspapers, turning the space for creative literary writing to that of critical expository writing. This was the key site for Cultural Studies during that period of time, and helped popularize the approach and analytical style of Cultural Studies. Cf. Yin-Bin Ning, "Cultural Politics as 'Real Politics' and Cultural Studies as Applied Philosophy: Cultural Criticism in Taiwan." Paper presented at the International Conference on Cultural Criticism, Chinese University of Hong Kong, January 2, 1993.

13. One review committee member insisted that our conference theme and content "looked very much like a conference for social movements," which I would not have disputed at all. I am sure that at one time or another some may have even considered us "parasitic" on the English Department.

14. Ironically, the English Department of National Central University has since become well known for its strengths in gender/sexuality studies and film studies. However, being recognized as a Cultural Studies stronghold, the department has suffered repeated defeats in its efforts to launch a PhD program, as reviewers were assigned by the Ministry of Education along traditional disciplinary lines and reviewers in English studies do not look upon Cultural Studies kindly. A fourth attempt to launch a PhD program is now under discussion within the department.

15. The third proposal, drafted by someone who was more closely related to the actual organization of the sex workers in their struggles, still could not pass the appeals review despite a strong rebuttal.

16. In that sense, the lifting of martial law in Taiwan in 1987 was likewise necessitated by the crisis that followed upon its booming economy. In other words, political liberalization was necessitated by a desperate need to liberalize the market as well as the capital so as to attract international investment while shifting the manufacturing industries to regions with lower wages.

17. Research teams making their collective presence felt at international conferences is highly encouraged; conventions or congresses of international academic organizations are solicited to hold their conferences in Taiwan; executive positions in such organizations are deemed equal to academic merit.

18. The number of visits by international scholars now constitutes one important figure on the quantified assessment table required of all research-oriented universities in their annual evaluation.

19. Kuan-Hsing Chen and Chien Yong-Hsiang, "Academic Production under Globalized New Liberalism." In *Globalization and Knowledge Production: Critical Reflections on the Practices of Academic Evaluation*, Tai-She Forum Series 4 (Taipei: Tangshan, 2005), 6.

20. Our speakers included such illustrious names as Cindy Patton, Fran Martin, Eve Kosofsky Sedgwick, Judith Halberstam, Jose Neil Cabanero Garcia, Leslie Feinberg, Minnie Bruce Pratt, Jamison Green, Ann Bolin, Laura Kipnis, and Katrien Jacobs.

21. The tendency of quantification in neo-liberal, market-oriented professionalism may be faulted on many fronts, but it has helped the Center survive on its own impressive quantity of academic output. The university is then left with a sense of strong ambivalence toward us: we could be problematic in our public statements and involvements, yet we are too valuable an asset to do without. Our choice to remain administratively under the jurisdiction of the English Department, where members of the Center make up the most senior faculty, also ensures the complete autonomy of the Center's functioning. It is this delicate status, and our self-determined accountability, that have ensured the Center enjoys a rare combination of academic professionalism and social activism.

22. In the meantime, publishing sites and spaces are rapidly dwindling due to commercialization. This crisis has prompted the editors of newspaper literary supplements to define their pages in a purely literary fashion that would stave off cultural commentaries. All these developments have worked to a certain extent to discourage the crossing over of the academics and their progressive ideas into other social realms.

23. In the more practice-oriented disciplines, such as social work or urban planning, such packaging is widely practiced by the expatriated left-wing scholars. Among all the pockets of Cultural Studies, the Department of Psychology at Fu-Jen Catholic University has been the most effective in opening up the department to marginal students. Its graduate student pool includes members from the sado-masochism, sex work, and transgender groups, and the program has been training them to become professionals who serve marginal populations.

24. The project is headed by Kuan-Hsing Chen, the tireless champion of inter-Asia Cultural Studies.

25. We succeeded in gathering delegates from twelve Cultural Studies programs across Asia to sign a Memorandum of Understanding of cooperation in the 2006 Teaching Cultural Studies Workshop held at National Central University, Taiwan. As the universities seemed to be slow in responding, another Memorandum of Understanding of cooperation — this time involving eighteen institutions spread across Asia — was signed at Tokyo University in the summer of 2009. The banding together of otherwise isolated pockets of Cultural Studies proves to be quite inspiring. Delegates from these participating institutions gathered in Seoul to launch

the Inter-Asia Cultural Studies Consortium on July 2, 2010. This was viewed as a monumental step toward regional collaboration and was carried further in ensuing Cultural Studies conferences and colloquiums in the region.
26. Michel Serres, *The Parasite*, translated by Lawrence R. Schehr (Baltimore, MD: Johns Hopkins University Press, 1982), 35.

Chapter 4: The Assessment Game

1. See http://chroniclegreatcolleges.com.
2. Robin Wilson, "Globe Trotting Academics Find New Career Paths." *The Chronicle of Higher Education*, December 6, 2009. http://chronicle.com/article/Globe-Trotting-American/49349/.
3. Simon Marginson, "Rankings Ripe for Misleading." *The Australian*, December 6, 2006. http://www.theaustralian.news.com.au/story/0,20867,20877456–12332,00.html.
4. Marginson, "Rankings Ripe for Misleading."
5. See http://www.ln.edu.hk/research.
6. All citations are from *120ᵗʰ Anniversary of the Founding of Lingnan University & 40ᵗʰ Anniversary of the Re-establishment of Lingnan University in Hong Kong* (Hong Kong: Public Affairs Office, Lingnan University, 2007). See also Huang Ju-yan, ed., *Modern Education in Guangdong and Lingnan University* (Hong Kong: Commercial Press, 1995).
7. Mette Hjort, "Affinitive and Milieu-Building Transnationalism: The 'Advance Party' Initiative." In *Cinema at the Periphery*, edited by Dina Iordanova, David Martin-Jones and Belén Vidal (Detroit, MI: Wayne State University Press, 2010); Mette Hjort, "Dogma 95: A Small Nation's Response to Globalisation." In *Purity and Provocation: Dogma 95*, edited by Mette Hjort and Scott MacKenzie (London: BFI, 2003).
8. Mette Hjort, "Style and Creativity in *The Five Obstructions*." In *Dekalog 01: On "The Five Obstructions,"* edited by Mette Hjort (London: Wallflower); Mette Hjort, "Denmark." In *The Cinema of Small Nations*, edited by Mette Hjort and Duncan Petrie (Edinburgh: Edinburgh University Press, 2007).
9. http://www.oma.eu/index.php?option=com_projects&view=project&id=1187&Itemid=10.
10. Björn G. Olafsson, *Small States in the Global System: Analysis and Illustrations from the Case of Iceland* (Aldershot: Ashgate), 14.
11. See, for example, Tony Coady, ed., *Why Universities Matter* (Sydney: Allen & Unwin, 2000); and Cary Nelson and Stephen Watt, *Academic Keywords: A Devil's Dictionary for Higher Education* (London: Routledge, 1999).
12. Mok Ka-ho, *Education and the Market Place in Hong Kong and Mainland China* (Hong Kong: Department of Public and Social Administration, City University of Hong Kong, 1998), 5.
13. James L. Fisher and James V. Koch, *Presidential Leadership: Making a Difference* (Phoenix, AZ: Oryx Press, 1996), ix–x.

14. Howard Gardner, *Intelligence Reframed: Multiple Intelligences for the 21st Century* (New York: Basic Books, 1999), 41–3, 47–8.
15. Gardner, *Intelligence Reframed*, 128.
16. Gardner, *Intelligence Reframed*, 126.
17. Gardner, *Intelligence Reframed*, 126.
18. Association of Commonwealth Universities, "Engagement as a Core Value for the University: A Consultation Document," 6; www.viu.ca/integratedplanning/.../AcademicPlanAppendixAugust162010.pdf.
19. Office of Service-Learning, *Annual Report 2008/09: Uniting Social Capitals for the Global Society* (Hong Kong: Lingnan University, Office of Service-Learning, 2010), 10.
20. For a discussion of moral sources, see Charles Taylor, *Sources of the Self: The Making of the Modern Identity* (Cambridge, MA: Harvard University Press, 1992).

Chapter 5: Three Tough Questions of Cultural Studies

1. I develop this argument further in Wang Xiaoming, "China on the Brink of a 'Momentous Era,'" *positions: east asia cultures critique* 11(3) (2003).
2. These courses are taught by Cultural Studies scholars from the five universities/institutes mentioned above. Proposed new courses are "Selected Readings in Modern Chinese Thought," "Analysis of the Modern Dominant Culture," and "Methodology of Cultural Studies."
3. An anthology of the seminar's reports is published as a teaching resource: Wang Xiaoming, ed., *Cultural Studies in the Chinese World* (Shanghai: Shanghai Bookstore, 2010).
4. To this day, the Ministry of Education in China does not include Cultural Studies in its "first class subjects" list.
5. There are three elective courses in this category: "Introduction to Cultural Studies," "Introduction to Selected Cultural Studies Theories," and "Theory and Practice of Cultural Studies." These courses target third- and fourth-year undergraduate students. From 2009, another undergraduate version of "Introduction to Cultural Studies" became one of the four core courses for all Arts Faculty undergraduate students of Shanghai University. The "elective" nature of the course remains, as students are only required to choose two from the four core courses.
6. The Master's degree programs offered by the Program in Cultural Studies are subordinated to five majors: "Chinese Modern and Contemporary Literature," "Literature Studies," "Anthropology," "Film and Television Studies," and "Media Studies"; the PhD programs are subordinated to "Sociology" and "Chinese Modern and Contemporary Literature."
7. The number of forums varies according to real teaching schedules. Usually, lecturers post the lecture outlines and reading list on the corresponding forum; some would post the lecture notes too. Students' posts are mainly reflections on the lectures (including questions) and electronic files of some readings.

8. Apart from research objects and methodology, you must have an outline of the analytical theory in order to establish Cultural Studies as an independent "subject." Our preliminary efforts in this regard are outlined below.

9. For example, from the late 1990s to the mid-2000s, Wen Tiejun and others set up a "Village Construction College" in Ding County of Hebei Province.

10. Modern society is highly permeated by ideology. A young person from a village in Eastern China might not know a term like "modernization," but nonetheless acts and treats his or her daily experience according to a vulgar version of modernization theory acquired from television and secondary school textbooks: the city equals progress, the village equals backwardness, the meaning of life is to escape from the village and enjoy the life of a city dweller.

11. "The three-dimensional rural issues" include agriculture, rural villages, and farmers. From 2003 to 2006, discussion of these issues overwhelmed the whole country and finally led to the abolition of the agriculture tax. *Zhi Jiao* is short for "village education support," and this program is mainly about organizing university students, including postgraduates, to teach in village schools for short terms and to help establish schools and libraries.

12. The establishment of the People's Republic of China in 1949 was the first epoch-making triumph of the "Chinese revolution." During the 1950s, the many radical policies implemented by the Chinese Communist Party (CCP) to remake society continued this revolution. However, from the mid-1950s the "socialist" project led by the CCP gradually turned sour. Conflicts within society became serious and led to the beginning of the Cultural Revolution; the failure of the Cultural Revolution triggered the "Reform" in the 1980s, and this resulted in the "Fourth of June" tragedy in 1989. By this point, all energy for the intellectual and social movements of the "Chinese revolution" was used up and society as a whole turned to the right. China entered into the first "anti-revolution" or "post-revolution" phase, dominated by the right wing in its modern history. From this perspective, the 1950s to the 1970s was the period when the Chinese revolution started to decline. Therefore, this article fixes the end of the high tide of the Chinese revolution in the mid-twentieth century.

13. Lu Xun, *Wild Grass* [1927], translated by Yang Xianyi and Gladys Yang (Hong Kong: Chinese University of Hong Kong, 2003), 2.

14. Wang Xiaoming and Zhou Zhan-an, eds. *Anthology of Modern Chinese Thought* (Shanghai: Shanghai Bookstore, 2011).

Chapter 6: Doing Cultural Studies

1. As David Harvey explains, the latest trend in "the neo-liberal turn" has also resulted in developments that affect the Asia-Pacific region to a great extent. See Harvey, *A Brief History of Neoliberalism* (Oxford: Oxford University Press, 2005); especially Chapter 5, "Neoliberalism with Chinese Characteristics," 120–51.

2. Stephen Chan, "Mapping the Global Popular in Hong Kong: Re-Articulations of the Local, National and Transnational in Contemporary Cultural Flows." In *Re-Inventing Hong Kong in the Age of Globalization*, edited by Yee Leung et al. (Hong Kong: Chung Chi College and Faculty of Social Sciences, Chinese University of Hong Kong, 2002).

3. John Erni, "Like a Post-Colonial Culture: Hong Kong Re-Imagined," *Cultural Studies* 15(3–4) (2001): 400.

4. Chan, "Mapping the Global Popular in Hong Kong."

5. Erni, "Like a Post-Colonial Culture."

6. Stephen Chan, ed., *Cultural Imaginary and Ideology: Critical Essays in Contemporary Hong Kong Cultural Politics* (Hong Kong: Oxford University Press, 1997); Wing-Sang Law, ed., *Whose City?* (Hong Kong: Oxford University Press, 1997).

7. Ngai Pun, book review of *Cultural Imaginary and Ideology* by Stephen Chan and *Whose City?* by Wing-Sang Law, *Hong Kong Journal of Social Sciences*, 11 (1998).

8. See Inaugural Editorial, *The Hong Kong Cultural Studies Bulletin* 1 (1994).

9. Stephen Chan, ed., *The Practice of Affect: Studies in Hong Kong Popular Song Lyrics* (Hong Kong: Oxford University Press, 1997).

10. See Stephen Chan, "On the Postmodern Condition of Hong Kong: At the Limits of Status Quo and Anomaly in 1997." In *Hong Kong Literature as/and Cultural Studies*, edited by Mee-kwan Cheung and Yiu-wai Chu (Hong Kong: Oxford University Press, 2002); Ching-kiu Chan, "On Urban Cultural Imagination in Xi Xi's Narratives of Hong Kong." In *Hong Kong Literature as/and Cultural Studies*, edited by Mee-kwan Cheung and Yiu-wai Chu (Hong Kong: Oxford University Press, 2002).

11. Eric Ma, "Peripheral Vision: Chinese Cultural Studies in Hong Kong." In *A Companion to Cultural Studies*, edited by Toby Miller (Oxford: Blackwell, 2001), 262.

12. Stephen Chan, "Figures of Hope and the Filmic Imaginary of *Jianghu* in Contemporary Hong Kong Cinema." *Cultural Studies* 15(3–4) (2001).

13. Erni, "Like a Post-Colonial Culture," 405, 407.

14. Stephen Chan, "Building Cultural Studies for Postcolonial Hong Kong: Aspects of the Postmodern Ruins in Between Disciplines." In *Cultural Studies: Interdisciplinarity and Translation*, edited by Stefan Herbrechter (Amsterdam: Rodopi, 2002).

15. Wing-Sang Law, *Collaborative Colonial Power: The Making of the Hong Kong Chinese* (Hong Kong: Hong Kong University Press, 2009).

16. See Arjun Appadurai, "Disjuncture and Difference in the Global Cultural Economy." In *Modernity at Large* (Minneapolis, MN: University of Minnesota Press, 1996).

17. Stephen Chan as interviewed by Wendy Kan, in "Identity Crisis," *South China Morning Post*, July 5, 1997.

18. Po-Keung Hui, "Introduction," in *Integrated Humanities and Liberal Studies: A Research Assessment*, edited by Choi Po-King, Hui Po-Keung et al. (Hong Kong: Kwan Fong Cultural Research and Development Programme, Lingnan University, 2009).

19. See the analysis by Iam-Chong Ip, "When Cultural Studies Meets Cultural Preservation." In *Cultural Studies and Cultural Education*, edited by Wing-Sang Law (Hong Kong: Department of Cultural Studies, Lingnan University, 2010).

20. See《告別殖民、土地歸人民》（一‧二一人民登陸皇后聲明）("Farewell to the Colonial Mindset: Reclaiming Our Own City: People Landing on the Queen's Pier, January 21, 2007 Declaration"); commentaries by King-fai Chan "From Star Ferry Preservation Movement to Local Cultural Politics"《從天星保衞運動到本土文化政治》, *Ming Pao Daily*, January 4, 2007; "Victoria Harbour, Lee Tung Street, Star Ferry: The First Urban Space Movement since the Handover"《維港‧利東街‧天星：回歸後的首場空間運動》, *Ming Pao Daily*, February 6, 2007.

21. See Wing-Suen Kwong, ed., *Standing on the Side of the Eggs: The Hong Kong Post-80s* (Hong Kong: UP Publications, 2010).

22. Ma, "Peripheral Vision," 265. My emphasis.

23. Erni, "Like a Post-Colonial Culture," 406.

24. Tony Bennett, *Culture: A Reformer's Science* (London: Sage, 1998), 217, 224.

25. Bennett, *Culture: A Reformer's Science*, 231.

26. According to the Four-Year BACS Programme Review (2003), the aims of the BA (Hons) Cultural Studies program at Lingnan University are:

    (i) to engage actively in the contemporary analysis of culture; to become sensitive to, and critical of, the issues of identity, value and affection about which the various forms of culture they study are concerned; (ii) to be aware of the complex interplay between the modern self, society and history through intensive work in an inter-disciplinary curriculum; to learn how the multiple perspectives with which people see the world today are crucial to our understanding of contemporary cultural realities; and (iii) to open themselves intellectually to the wide-ranging texts and contexts that have been transforming the contemporary age, so as to develop independent judgement on the cultural practices and social institutions they must deal with now and in the future.

27. See, for example, "The Legacy and Rupture in Social Movement: Interview with Lau Sai-Leung." In Kwong, *Standing on the Side of the Eggs*, 47.

28. Interview with Stephen Chan, in Erni, "Like a Post-Colonial Culture," 401.

29. Stephen Chan and Po-Keung Hui, "Cultural Studies through Education: Moments of Pedagogy and Pragmatics." *Inter-Asia Cultural Studies* 9(3) (2008): 484–95.

30. Bennett, *Culture: A Reformer's Science*, 224.

31. See Stephen Chan and Muriel Law, "Taking Education Seriously as Reform: School Curriculum Policy Research and Its Implications for Cultural Studies" and Po-Keung Hui and Chak-Sang Pang, "Doing Cultural Studies in the Hong Kong

Educational Context: A Tale of Two Action Research Experiments." *Cultural Studies* 24(1) (2011), 25–41, 109–22.

32. See Law, "The Challenge Posed to Cultural Studies by Cultural Education." In Law, *Cultural Studies and Cultural Education*, 76.

33. Bennett, *Culture: A Reformer's Science*, 17.

34. Bennett, *Culture: A Reformer's Science*, 51.

35. See Stephen Chan: "Under the current system, 'excellence' cannot serve as a carrier of content, for it seems capable of drawing one single boundary, that of 'the unrestricted power of the bureaucracy' (Bill Readings). Worse, it permits exhaustive accounting, often taken to mean the same as accountability. In short, it would appear that the quest for 'excellence' works only to tie the university into an 'excellent' net of bureaucratic institutions." In "Building Cultural Studies for Postcolonial Hong Kong: Aspects of the Postmodern Ruins in Between Disciplines." In *Cultural Studies: Interdisciplinarity and Translation*, edited by Stefan Herbrechter (Amsterdam: Rodopi, 2002), 224–5.

36. Chan and Hui, "Cultural Studies through Education."

Chapter 7: Coordinates, Confusions, and Cultural Studies

1. In January 1993, the Department of English at the Chinese University of Hong Kong organized the first international Cultural Studies conference in the Chinese-speaking territories. During the same period, some universities in Hong Kong and Taiwan introduced courses on Cultural Studies. In 1995, the Comparative Literature and Culture Research Centre of Beijing University set up the Cultural Studies Working Group and introduced Cultural Studies courses. In 1999, the Cultural Studies Association was established in Taiwan; Lingnan University of Hong Kong established the Department of Cultural Studies; while many comprehensive universities in mainland China started to organize Cultural Studies programs, publications and websites. In July 2004, Shanghai University established the Program in Cultural Studies.

2. Jim McGuigan, *Cultural Populism* (London: Routledge, 1992).

3. Alan Swingewood, *The Myth of Mass Culture* (London: Macmillan, 1977).

4. This was a cultural debate on vernacular Chinese, colloquial Chinese, and literary Chinese in Shanghai in 1934.

5. Ji Dong, "Inside Story of China's Biggest Fan Club." *Southern Metropolis Weekly*, May 9, 2007.

6. *Time Asia Magazine*, Asian Heroes special issue, October 3, 2005.

7. In 2005, the lifestyle magazine *New Weekly* dedicated an issue to the discussion of the phenomenon of the "drifting generation."

8. Zhang Xi, "Han Shao Gong: The Director of *Shi Bing Tu Ji* has a Spine, a Fine Brain and a Conscience." *Southern Weekly*, February 15, 2008.

9. Zhao Yu, "*Shi Bing Tu Ji*: The Yelling Inside Behind the Vanity." *Guangming Daily*, March 6, 2008.

Chapter 8: Uses of Media Culture, Usefulness of Media Culture Studies

1. George Yúdice, *The Expediency of Culture: Uses of Culture in the Global Era* (Durham, NC: Duke University Press, 2003).

2. Adorno's original words in his seminal essay titled "Culture and Administration" are as follows: "Whoever speaks of culture speaks of administration as well, whether this is his intention or not." Theodor W. Adorno, *The Culture Industry: Selected Essays on Mass Culture*, edited with an introduction by Jay M. Bernstein (London: Routledge, 1991), 107.

3. As was the case with the Western Orientalist gaze on Japan in the construction of national identity, the above-mentioned American observations are still crucial for the confirmation of the "cool Japan" phenomenon within Japan. And as with traditional culture such as Ukiyoe, Western appreciation has a determining power on the international quality of Japanese culture. The fact that Japanese popular culture has been much more actively and massively received in East Asia has never spurred the same extent of euphoria. In this sense, the "Cool Japan" discourse still testifies to Japan's appreciation of the Western Orientalist gaze and complicit uses of it to enhance the sense of national pride both domestically and internationally. In this sense, "Cool Japan" is basically a Western phenomenon. See Koichi Iwabuchi, "Complicit Exoticism: Japan and Its Other." *Continuum* 8(2) (1994): 49–82.

4. Cited by the Director of Japan Information Center, Kazuhiro Koshikawa's speech at the City University of New York Graduate Center, December 12, 2003. http://www.ny.us.emb-japan.go.jp/en/c/vol_11–5/title_01.html.

5. Christopher Palmeri and Nanette Byrnes, "Is Japanese Style Taking Over the World?" *Business Week*, July 26, 2004.

6. Anthony Faiola, "Japan's Empire of Cool; Country's Culture Becomes Its Biggest Export." *Washington Post*, December 27, 2003.

7. Douglas McGray, "Japan's Gross National Cool." *Foreign Policy*, May–June 2002.

8. Joseph Nye, *Bound to Lead: The Changing Nature of American Power* (New York: Basic Books, 1990), 32.

9. Nye, *Bound to Lead*, 32.

10. http://www.glocom.org/opinions/essays/20051205_nye_allure/index.html.

11. http://www.bunka.go.jp/1kokusai/kokusaikondankaihoukoku.html

12. Chua Beng Huat and Koichi Iwabuchi, eds. *East Asian Pop Culture: Approaching the Korean Wave* (Hong Kong: Hong Kong University Press, 2008).

13. Joseph Nye, *Soft Power: The Means to Success in World Politics* (New York: Public Affairs, 2004).

14. Peter van Ham, "The Rise of the Brand State: The Postmodern Politics of Image and Reputation." *Foreign Affairs*, September/October 2001.

15. van Ham, "The Rise of the Brand State," 3–4.

16. As for "cultural odor," see Koichi Iwabuchi, *Recentering Globalization: Popular Culture and Japanese Transnationalism* (Durham, NC: Duke University Press, 2002).

17. Aso Taro, "A New Look at Cultural Diplomacy: A Call to Japan's Cultural Practitioners." Speech made at Digital Hollywood University, Tokyo, April 28, 2006.

18. Joseph Nye, "Soft Power Matters in Asia." *Japan Times*, December 5, 2005. http://search.japantimes.co.jp/cgi-bin/eo20051205a1.html.

19. Joseph Nye. Interview about Koizumi's visit to Yasukuni Shrine. *Tokyo Newspaper*, October 22, 2005.

20. Koichi Iwabuchi, "Uses of Japanese Popular Culture: Media Globalization and Postcolonial Desire for 'Asia.'" *Emergences: Journal of Media and Composite Cultures* 11(2) (2001).

21. See Koichi Iwabuchi, *Bunka no taiwaryoku* (Culture's Dialogic Capacity) (Tokyo: Nihonkeizaishinbun Shuppansha, 2007), Chapter 3.

22. Tessa Morris-Suzuki, *The Past within Us: Media, Memory, History* (London: Verso, 2005).

23. *Bunka gaiko no suishin ni kasuru kondankai houkokusho* (A Report by the Discussion Group on the Promotion of Cultural Diplomacy), July 2005.

24. Ulf Hannerz, *Transnational Connections: Culture, People, Places* (London: Routledge, 1996).

25. Stuart Hall, "The Local and the Global: Globalization and Ethnicity." In *Culture, Globalization, and the World-System*, edited by A. King (London: Macmillan, 1991).

26. John Urry, *Global Complexity* (London: Polity, 2003), 87.

27. David Hesmondhalgh, "Neoliberalism, Imperialism, and the Media." In *The Media and Social Theory*, edited by David Hesmondhalgh and Jason Toynbee (London: Routledge, 2008).

28. For the critique of creative industries, see Toby Miller, "A View from a Fossil: The New Economy, Creativity and Consumption — Two or Three Things I Don't Believe In." *International Journal of Cultural Studies* 7(1) (2004).

29. Toby Miller, Nitin Govil, John McMurria, Richard Maxwell, and Ting Wang, eds. *Global Hollywood 2* (London: British Film Institute, 2005).

30. Naomi Klein, *No Logo: Taking Action at the Brand Bullies* (London: HarperCollins, 2000).

31. See, for example, Ae-ri Yoon, "In Between the Values of the Global and the National: The Korean Animation Industry." In *Cultural Studies and Cultural Industries in Northeast Asia: What a Difference a Region Makes*, edited by Chris Berry, Jonathan D. Mackintosh and Nicola Liscutin (Hong Kong: Hong Kong University Press, 2009).

32. Nobuyuki Takahashi, "Kitty-chan wo tsukutteitanowa dare?" (Who produced Kitty?). *Shukan Kinyoubi* 357 (2001): 56–7.

33. Jim McGuigan, *Rethinking Cultural Policy* (London: Open University Press, 2004).

34. Otsuka Eiji and Nobuaki Osawa, *"Japanimation" wa naze yabureruka* (Why Japanimation should be defeated) (Tokyo: Kadokawa Shoten, 2005).

35. David Hesmondhalgh. "Neoliberalism, Imperialism and the Media." In *The Media and Social Theory*, edited by David Hesmondhalgh and Jason Toynbee (London: Routledge, 2008).
36. Michael Billig, *Banal Nationalism* (London: Sage, 1995).
37. Urry, *Global Complexity*, 107.
38. Urry, *Global Complexity*, 107.
39. See Andreas Wimmer and Nina Glick Shiller, "Methodological Nationalism and Beyond: Nation-State Building, Migration and Social Sciences." *Global Networks* 2(4) (2002).
40. See Iwabuchi, *Bunka no taiwaryoku*.
41. See Iwabuchi, *Recentering Globalization*.
42. See Koichi Iwabuchi, "When Korean Wave Meets Resident Koreans in Japan." In *East Asian Pop Culture: Approaching the Korean Wave*, edited by Chua Beng Huat and Koichi Iwabuchi (Hong Kong: Hong Kong University Press, 2007).
43. Raymond Williams, "State Culture and Beyond." In *Culture and the State*, edited by L. Apignanesi (London: Institute of Contemporary Arts, 1984), 3–5.
44. McGuigan, *Rethinking Cultural Policy*.
45. Williams, "State Culture and Beyond," 3.
46. McGuigan, *Rethinking Cultural Policy*, 5.
47. Adorno, *The Culture Industry*, 113.

Chapter 9: Way Out on a Nut

1. "Daniel Buren: In Conversation." Guggenheim Museum, March 29, 2005. *The Eye of the Storm: Works in Situ by Daniel Buren*, Solomon R. Guggenheim Museum, New York, March 25–June 8, 2005.
2. "Daniel Buren: In Context." Guggenheim Museum, April 12, 2005; participants included Roselee Goldberg, John Knight, James Meyer, and Anne Rorimer. *Couleurs Superposées*, Solomon R. Guggenheim Museum, New York, March 26, 2005.
3. I paraphrase Buren here from my notes.
4. Michael Kimmelman, "Tall French Visitor Takes Up Residence in the Guggenheim." *New York Times*, March 25, 2005: E27.
5. *The New York Times Style Magazine*, April 3, 2005. The ad is on p. 105.
6. A photograph by Horst P. Horst of this cape is the frontispiece for Elizabeth Ann Coleman, *The Genius of Charles James* (New York: The Brooklyn Museum and Holt, Rinehart and Winston, 1982). The cape is catalogue number 374, p. 149.
7. Daniel Buren, "Beware." In *Five Texts* (New York: John Webber Gallery and Jack Wendler Gallery, 1973), 13, 15.
8. Quoted in Alison M. Gingeras, "The Decorative Strategy: Daniel Buren's 'The Museum Which Did Not Exist.'" *Parkett* 66 (2002): 89.
9. Dan Flavin, "The Guggenheim Affair: Letters to *Studio International*." *Studio International* 182(935) (1971): 6.

10. Daniel Buren, "Round and About a Detour." *Studio International* 181(934) (1971): 246–7.

11. Alison M. Gingeras, "Who is Daniel Buren?" *The Buren Times* (New York: The Solomon R. Guggenheim Museum, 2005), Section 3A, 1. Buchloh's review appears in *Artforum* 35(1) (1997): 116.

12. Buchloh continues to apply this early=pure/late=decadent view to Buren. In a roundtable discussion for the catalogue of the exhibition *Flashback*, an exhibition looking at the art of the 1980s, the following exchange takes place:

    > *John M Armleder:* ... In the seventies, [Buren] is not the same as in the eighties or nineties. If you follow a linear construction, then you have to ask how his work changed.
    >
    > *Benjamin H. D. Buchloh:* Buren in 1970 is like Picasso in 1912, and in 1980 how Picasso was in 1930. In the 1990s Buren is like Picasso was in the 1950s and 1960s. Do I think Buren is the best artist? Yes, sure. Absolutely, until 1975.

    "The Eighties Are in Our Midst: Roundtable Discussion, Basel, June 18, 2005." In Philipp Kaiser, *Flashback: Revisiting the Art of the 80s* (Basel: Kunstmuseum Basel, Museum für Gegenwartskunst, 2005).

13. Kimmelman, "Tall French Visitor," E27.

14. Kimmelman, "Tall French Visitor," E27.

15. This essay initially was occasioned by an invitation to participate in the educational programming in conjunction with *In the Eye of the Storm: Works in Situ by Daniel Buren*, March 25–June 8, 2005, and was further developed for the conference Cultural Studies and Institution, co-organized by the Department of Cultural Studies and the Kwan Fong Cultural Research and Development Program, Lingnan University, Tuen Mun, N.T., Hong Kong, May 26–28, 2006.

16. Rosalyn Deutsche, "Inadequacy." In *Silvia Kolbowski: Inadequate ... Like ... Power* (Vienna and Cologne: Secession and Verlag der Buchhandlung Walther König, 2004), 69.

17. Alan Reed Sawyer, *Mastercraftsmen of Ancient Peru* (New York: Solomon R. Guggenheim Museum, 1968).

18. See Kynaston McShine, *The Museum as Muse: Artists Reflect* (New York: Museum of Modern Art, 1999), 186.

19. According to Elizabeth Ann Coleman, James had begun discussions with Harper & Row for an autobiography as early as 1956, and he received a Guggenheim Fellowship in 1975 to write a book on his techniques. None of his book projects came to fruition. See Coleman, *The Genius of Charles James*, 98–9.

20. *Decade of Design* (New York: Brooklyn Museum, 1948).

21. See Coleman, *The Genius of Charles James*, 79.

22. Richard Martin, *Charles James* (London: Thames and Hudson, 1997), 18.

23. Martin, *Charles James*, 12.

24. Mary St. John Hitchinson, quoted in Coleman, *The Genius of Charles James*, 9.

25. Quoted in Coleman, *The Genius of Charles James*, 111.

26 *Form Follows Fashion* (New York: The Museum at FIT, October 6–December 31, 2004).

27. *Guggenheim International Exhibition 1971* (New York: The Solomon R. Guggenheim Museum, 1971).

28. See "Statement by Dianne Waldman." *Studio International* 181(933) (1971): 248.

29. Daniel Buren, "Round and About a Detour." *Studio International* 181(933) (1971): 246.

30. I wrote about Buren's work for his exhibition at the Van Abbemuseum in Eindhoven in 1976 ("Daniel Buren's New York Work." In R. H. Fuchs, *Discordance/Cohérence* [Eindhoven: Stedelijk Vanabbemuseum, 1976], 75–8) and again in "The End of Painting." *October* 16 (1981): 69–86.

31. Alex Alberro, "The Turn of the Screw: Daniel Buren, Dan Flavin, and the Sixth Guggenheim International Exhibition." *October* 80 (1997): 81.

32. Roberta Smith, "On Daniel Buren." *Artforum* 12(1) (1973): 67.

33. Daniel Buren, "Preface: Why Write Texts or the Place from Where I Act," translated by Patricia Railing. In *Five Texts*, 6–7.

34. Alberro, "The Turn of the Screw," 71–2.

35. Frank O'Hara, *Art Chronicles 1954–1966* (New York: George Braziller, 1975), 1–2.

36. Mark Wigley, *White Walls, Designer Dresses: The Fashioning of Modern Architecture* (Cambridge, MA: MIT Press, 1995).

37. William Middleton, "A House that Rattled Texas Windows." *New York Times*, June 3, 2004, F1, 10.

38. I refer here to Hal Foster's *Design and Crime (and Other Diatribes)* (London: Verso, 2002), in which the author asks more than once, and with an answer already firmly in mind: "To what extent has the 'constructed subject' of postmodernism become the 'designed subject' of consumerism?" (xiv), hoping to finally be rid of contemporary theory's interest in both subjectivity and design by linking them to the evils of global capitalism.

39. During the restoration of the building that was completed in 2008, "conservators stripped away 11 layers of paint from the landmark building's exterior and found that it was originally coated with a light brownish-yellow shade." The New York City Landmarks Preservation Commission decided nevertheless to "maintain the same light-gray paint shade it has had since 1992, when a major expansion of the museum by Gwathmey Siegel & Associates Architects was completed." One dissenter on the Commission, Pablo E. Vengoechea, was quoted as saying, "'I've heard arguments that the lighter color is less jarring, less controversial and so forth, but I think that that really doesn't persuade … This building was designed to stand out.'" (Sewell Chan, "Pale Gray or Light Yellow? A Ruling on Guggenheim." *New York Times*, November 21, 2007.

40. "'Which is in fact what happened,' Thomas Messer in an interview with Barbara Reise 25 April, 1971." *Studio International* 182(935) (1971): 37.

Chapter 10: Who Needs Human Rights?

1. David Luban, "The War on Terrorism and the End of Human Rights." In *War After September 11*, edited by Verna V. Gehring (New York: Rowman & Littlefield, 2003).
2. Jean L. Cohen, "Whose Sovereignty?: Empire Versus International Law." In *Global Institutions and Responsibilities: Achieving Global Justice*, edited by Christian Barry and Thomas W. Pogge (Malden, MA: Blackwell, 2005), 159–89.
3. Some notable works that attempt to think cultural analysis, critical theory, and law together include: Wendy Brown and Janet Halley, eds., *Left Legalism/Left Critique* (Durham, NC: Duke University Press, 2002); Austin Sarat and Jonathan Simon, eds., *Cultural Analysis, Cultural Studies, and the Law: Moving Beyond Legal Realism* (Durham, NC: Duke University Press, 2003); Kate Nash, *The Cultural Politics of Human Rights: Comparing the US and UK* (Cambridge: Cambridge University Press, 2009); Rosemary Coombe, *The Cultural Life of Intellectual Properties: Authorship, Appropriation, and the Law* (Durham, NC: Duke University Press, 1998); Costas Douzinas, *Human Rights and Empire: The Political Philosophy of Cosmopolitanism* (London: Routledge-Cavendish, 2007); John Nguyet Erni, "New Sovereignties and Neoliberal Ethics: Remapping the Human Rights Imaginary." *Cultural Studies* 23(3) (2009).
4. Nancy Fraser's discussion of redistribution and recognition politics appeared as early as 1997, and continued until more recent times. See Nancy Fraser, "From Redistribution and Recognition? Dilemmas of Justice in a 'Postsocialist' Age." In *Justice Interruptus: Critical Reflections on the "Postsocialist" Condition* (New York: Routledge, 1997); Nancy Fraser, "Reframing Justice in a Globalizing World." *New Left Review* 36 (2005): 1–19; Nancy Fraser, "Abnormal Justice." *Critical Inquiry* 34(3) (2008): 393–422.
5. Rosemary J. Coombe, "Is There a Cultural Studies of Law?" In *A Companion to Cultural Studies*, edited by Toby Miller (Malden, MA: Blackwell, 2001), 36.
6. Lawrence Grossberg, *We Gotta Get Out of This Place: Popular Conservatism and Postmodern Culture* (New York: Routledge, 1992).
7. Grossberg, *We Gotta Get Out of This Place*, 385.
8. Grossberg, *We Gotta Get Out of This Place*, 391.
9. Grossberg, *We Gotta Get Out of This Place*, 391.
10. Examples of the more recent critique of Cultural Studies' political relevance include: Jan Baetens, "Cultural Studies after the Cultural Studies Paradigm." *Cultural Studies* 19(1) (2005); Marcus Breen, "US Cultural Studies: Oxymoron?" *Cultural Studies Review* 11(1) (2005): 11–26. On the other hand, some have challenged the (unreflective) practicality of Cultural Studies. See Peter Osborne, "'Whoever Speaks of Culture Speaks of Administration as Well': Disputing Pragmatism in Cultural Studies." *Cultural Studies* 20(1) (2006).
11. Joanna Zylinska, "'Arous[ing] the Intensity of Existence': The Ethics of Seizure and Interruption." Paper presented at the international conference Ethics and Politics: The Work of Alain Badiou, Centre for Critical and Cultural Theory, Cardiff

University, May 25–26, 2002. See also Joanna Zylinski, *The Ethics of Cultural Studies* (London: Continuum, 2005).

12. Stuart Hall, "Cultural Studies and Its Theoretical Legacies." In *Cultural Studies*, edited by Lawrence Grossberg, Cary Nelson, and Paula Treichler (New York: Routledge, 1992), 284.

13. Hall, "Cultural Studies and Its Theoretical Legacies."

14. See, for example, Pepi Leistyna, "Revitalizing the Dialogue: Theory, Coalition-Building, and Social Change." In *Cultural Studies: From Theory to Action*, edited by Pepi Leistyna (Malden, MA: Blackwell, 2005), 1–16.

15. See http://www.cumc.columbia.edu/dept/gender.

16. In 2005, the author completed a Master of Laws specializing in human rights at the University of Hong Kong.

17. Lawrence Grossberg, "Does Cultural Studies Have Futures? Should It? (Or What's the Matter with New York?)." *Cultural Studies* 20(1) (2006): 8.

18. See Micheline R. Ishay, "Human Rights: Historical and Contemporary Controversies." In *The Human Rights Reader*, edited by Micheline R. Ishay, 2nd ed. (New York: Routledge, 2007), xxi–xxviii; Mark Goodale, "Human Rights and Anthropology." In *Human Rights: An Anthropological Reader*, edited by Mark Goodale (Malden, MA: Wiley-Blackwell, 2009).

19. See Andrea Durbach, Catherine Renshwa and Andrew Byrnes, "'A Tongue but No Teeth?': The Emergence of a Regional Human Rights Mechanism in the Asia Pacific Region." *The Sydney Law Review* 31 (2009). I also thank Meaghan Morris for her help with this idea.

20. Pheng Cheah, *Inhuman Conditions: On Cosmopolitanism and Human Rights* (Cambridge, MA: Harvard University Press, 2006), 148, original emphasis.

21. Peter Korner, Gero Maass, Thomas Siebold, and Rainer Tetzlaff, *The IMF and the Debt Crisis: A Guide to the Third World's Dilemma*, translated by Paul Knight (London: Zed Books, 1986), 5–73, 128–61.

22. Shelley Wright, *International Human Rights, Decolonisation and Globalisation: Becoming Human* (London: Routledge, 2001).

23. Christopher G. Weeramantry, *Universalising International Law* (Leiden: Martinus Nijhoff, 2004).

24. Sundhya Pahuja, "Comparative Visions of Global Public Order (Part I): The Postcoloniality of International Law." *Harvard International Law Journal* 46 (2005): 467.

25. Julie Mertus, "From Legal Transplants to Transformative Justice: Human Rights and the Promise of Transnational Civil Society." *American University International Law Review* 14 (1999): 1335.

26. Boaventura de Sousa Santos, "Human Rights as an Emancipatory Script? Cultural and Political Conditions." In *Another Knowledge Is Possible: Beyond Northern Epistemologies*, edited by Boaventura de Sousa Santos (London: Verso, 2007), 3–37.

27. See, for example, Emily Grabham, Davina Cooper, Jane Krishnadas, and Didi Herman, eds., *Intersectionality and Beyond: Law, Power and the Politics of Location* (New York: Routledge-Cavendish, 2009).

28. Balakrishnan Rajagopal, "International Law and Social Movements: Challenges of Theorizing Resistance." *Columbia Journal of Transnational Law* 41 (2003): 397.

29. Rajagopal, "International Law and Social Movements," 402.

30. Andrew Ross, "Components of Cultural Justice." In *Cultural Pluralism, Identity Politics, and the Law*, edited by Austin Sarat and Thomas R. Kearns (Ann Arbor, MI: University of Michigan Press, 1998), 203–28.

31. David Kennedy, "The International Human Rights Movement: Part of the Problem?" *The Harvard Human Rights Journal* 15 (2002): 99, 189.

32. Kennedy, "The International Human Rights Movement," 180.

33. Rosemary J. Coombe, "Contingent Articulations: A Critical Cultural Studies of Law." In *Cultural Pluralism, Identity Politics, and the Law*, edited by Austin Sarat and Thomas R. Kearns (Ann Arbor, MI: University of Michigan Press, 1998), 35.

34. Grossberg, "Does Cultural Studies Have Futures?", 5.

35. For example, a critique of the United Nations appears in Frédéric Mégret and Florian Hoffmann, "The UN as a Human Rights Violator? Some Reflections on the United Nations' Changing Human Rights Responsibilities." *Human Rights Quarterly* 25(2) (2003).

Chapter 11: From Gatekeepers to Gateways

1. Kum Hong Siew, "What I Took Away from 2 May." May 6, 2009. http://siewkumhong.blogspot.com/2009/05/what-i-took-away-from-2-may.html.

2. Chua Beng Huat, "Defining Moment for Liberalism." *The Straits Times*, May 6, 2009. http://www.straitstimes.com/Review/Others/STIStory_372878.html.

3. Loh Chee Kong, "A Coming of Age for Civil Society: Could Aware Saga Be Watershed for Public Discourse on Taboo Topics?" *TODAY*, May 5, 2009; see also Simon Tay, "A Tale of Two Communities." *TODAY*, May 5, 2009.

4. Terence Chong, "Affirmation of Diversity." *The Straits Times*, May 6, 2009. http://www.straitstimes.com/Review/Others/STIStory_372877.html.

5. The ministry's letter to *The Straits Times*, cited in Diana Othman, "Aware Sex Guide Suspended." *The Straits Times*, May 6, 2009. http://www.straitstimes.com/print/Breaking%2BNews/Singapore/Story/STIStory_373200.htm.

6. Robbie Goh, "Christian Identities in Singapore: Religion, Race and Culture between State Controls and Transnational Flows." *Journal of Cultural Geography* 26(1) (2009): 1–23.

7. Nirmala Purushotam, "'Woman' as Boundary: Raising the Communitarian Against Critical Imaginings." *Inter-Asia Cultural Studies* 3(3) (2002): 349.

8. On the intersection between the development of education and cultural policy in Singapore, see Lai Ah Eng, ed., *Beyond Rituals and Riots: Ethnic Pluralism and Social Cohesion in Singapore* (Singapore: Eastern Universities Press, 2004). On the positive benefits of the arts, see Eleonora Belfiore and Oliver Bennett, "Rethinking the Social Impact of the Arts." *International Journal of Cultural Policy* 13(2) (2007): 135–41.

9. Andrew Ross, *Nice Work If You Can Get It: Life and Labor in Precarious Times* (New York: New York University Press, 2009), 39.

10. See Audrey Yue, "Creative Queer Singapore: The Illiberal Pragmatics of Cultural Production." *Gay and Lesbian Issues and Psychology Review* 3(3) (2007): 149–60; Audrey Yue, "Hawking in the Creative City: *Rice Rhapsody*, Sexuality and the Cultural Politics of New Asia in Singapore." *Feminist Media Studies* 7(4) (2007): 365–80.

11. Chua Beng Huat, *Communitarian Ideology and Democracy in Singapore* (New York: Routledge, 1995), 59.

12. Chua Beng Huat, *Political Legitimacy and Housing: Stakeholding in Singapore* (New York: Routledge, 1997), 131.

13. Chua, *Communitarian Ideology*, 73; Chua Beng Huat, *Life is Not Complete without Shopping: Consumption Culture in Singapore* (Singapore University Press, 2003), 3.

14. Chua, *Communitarian Ideology*, 69.

15. On Singapore as an illiberal democracy, see Gary Rodan, "Preserving the One-party State in Contemporary Singapore." In *Southeast Asia in the 1990s: Authoritarianism, Democracy, and Capitalism*, edited by Kevin Hewison, Richard Robison, and Gary Rodan (Sydney: Allen & Unwin, 1993).

16. Tony Bennett, "Putting Policy into Cultural Studies." In *Cultural Studies*, edited by Lawrence Grossberg, Cary Nelson, and Paula Treichler (London: Routledge, 1992), 23.

17. Bennett, "Putting Policy into Cultural Studies," 26.

18. Jim McGuigan, *Culture and the Public Sphere* (London: Routledge, 1996), 5.

19. McGuigan, *Culture and the Public Sphere*, 187.

20. George Yúdice, *The Expediency of Culture: Uses of Culture in the Global Era* (Durham, NC: Duke University Press, 2003), 1.

21. Peter Osbourne, "'Whoever Speaks of Culture Speaks of Administration as Well': Disputing Pragmatism in Cultural Studies." *Cultural Studies* 20(1) (2006): 35, 43.

22. Osbourne, "'Whoever Speaks of Culture," 38, 43. Italics in original.

23. Lisanne Gibson, "In Defence of Instrumentality." *Cultural Trends* 17(4) (2008): 248. Italics in original.

24. Lily Kong, "Cultural Policy in Singapore: Negotiating Economic and Socio-Cultural Agendas." *Geoforum* 31(4) (2000): 410.

25. See also Terence Chong, "The State and the New Society: The Role of the Arts in Singapore Nation Building." *Asian Studies Review* 34(2) (2010): 131–49.

26. Kong, "Cultural Policy in Sinapore," 413.

27. Kong, "Cultural Policy in Sinapore," 413.

28. Kong, "Cultural Policy in Sinapore," 413.

29. Kong, "Cultural Policy in Sinapore," 414.

30. George Yeo, "Building in a Market for the Arts." *Speeches: A Bi-monthly Selection of Ministerial Speeches* 18:4 (1991): 54, cited in Kong, "Cultural Policy in Sinapore," 415.

31. Yeo, cited in Kong, "Cultural Policy in Sinapore," 415.

32. Media Development Authority, *Creative Industries Development Strategy: Propelling Singapore's Creative Economy* (Singapore: Ministry of Information, Communication and the Arts, 2002).
33. Media Development Authority, *Creative Industries Development Strategy*, 4.
34. Media Development Authority, *Singapore Media Fusion Plan*. May 4, 2009. http://www.smf.sg/smfp/index.html, 14–15.
35. In the region, Australia, New Zealand, Japan, Hong Kong, Korea, and China have also embarked on this developmental path. For a list of the current thirty-five countries in 2009 with such cultural planning policies, see Graeme Evans, "Creative Cities, Creative Spaces and Urban Policy." *Urban Studies* 46(5/6) (2009): 1003–40.
36. For studies on Singapore using this discourse, see Linda Low, "The Singapore development state in the new economy and polity." *The Pacific Review* 14:3 (2001): 411–41; Tan Kim-Song, "From Efficiency-Driven to Innovation-Driven Economic Growth: Perspectives from Singapore." *World Bank Policy Research Working Paper* (April 1, 2005), http://econ.worldbank.org/external/default/main?pagePK=64165259&theSitePK=469382&piPK=64165421&menuPK=6416609393&entityID=000012009_20050425133228; Wong Poh Kam, Ho Yuen Ping, and Annette Singh, "Singapore as an Innovative City in East Asia: An Explorative Study of the Perspectives of Innovative Industries." *World Bank Policy Research Working Paper* (April 1, 2005), http://econ.worldbank.org/external/default/main?pagePK=64165259&theSitePK=469382&piPK=64165421&menuPK=64166093&entityID=000012009_20050425130701; Clive Edwards, "Singapore: Reflections and Implications of Another Smart State." *Queensland Review* 10(1) (2003): 53–69. In the fields of creative industry studies in Asia using this discourse, see, for example, Diana Barrowclough and Zeljka Kozul-Wright, eds., *Creative Industries and Developing Countries: Voice, Choice and Economic Growth* (London: Routledge, 2008).
37. UNESCO/Global Alliance for Cultural Diversity, "Understanding Creative Industries: Cultural Statistics for Public Policy-Making." March 6, 2006. Paris: UNESCO/Global Alliance for Cultural Diversity, 2006, 6. http://portal.unesco.org/culture/en/files/30297/...stat_EN.../cultural_stat_EN.pdf.
38. Department for Culture, Media and Sport, *Creative Industries Mapping Documents* (London: DCMS, 1998); Department for Culture, Media and Sport, *Mapping Creative Industries Technical Document* (London: DCMS, 2001).
39. Toh Mun Heng, Adrian Choo and Terence Ho, "Economic Contributions of Singapore's Creative Industries." *Economic Survey of Singapore First Quarter* (Singapore: Ministry of Trade and Industry, 2003): 51–75.
40. Heng, Choo and Ho, "Economic Contributions of Singapore's Creative Industries," 63.
41. Florida's work focuses on the creative capability of talent by showing how industries are attracted to places that nurture creative people. See Richard Florida, *The Rise of the Creative Class* (Melbourne: Basic Books, 2002). Howkins emphasizes

how creativity can flourish when intellectual property is recognized. He argues that marked economic growth is generated not from the actual products, but from the exploitation of products through distribution and trade. See John Howkins, *The Creative Economy* (Harmondsworth: Penguin, 2001).

42. For an account of the disparity in cultural trade between these countries, see UNESCO, *International Flows of Selected Cultural Goods and Services 1994–2003: Defining and Capturing the Flows of Global Cultural Trade* (Montreal: UNESCO Institute for Statistics, 2005).

43. Chris Gibson and Lily Kong, "Cultural Economy: A Critical Review." *Progress in Human Geography* 29(5) (2005): 549. For a critique of how the British model has been exported to Asia, see Lily Kong and Justin O'Connor, eds., *Creative Cities: Asian-European Perspectives* (Springer: New York, 2009). For a critique on how cultural indicators can be valued for the social impact of the arts, see Christopher Madden, "Indicators for Arts and Cultural Policy: A Global Perspective." *Cultural Trends* 14(3) (2005): 217–47.

44. UNESCO, *Asia-Pacific Creative Communities: Promoting the Cultural Industries for Local Socio-economic Development: A Strategy for the 21st Century* (Bangkok: UNESCO, 2005).

45. UNESCO, *Asia-Pacific Creative Communities*, 1.

46. This perspective is also promoted by leading scholars such as Stuart Cunningham. See, for example, Stuart Cunningham, Michael Keane and Mark David Ryan, "Finance and Investment in Creative Industries in Developing Countries." Paper presented at the Asia-Pacific Creative Communities: A Strategy for the 21st Century Senior Expert Symposium, Jodhpur, India, February 22–26, 2005.

47. Chua Beng Huat, "Cultural Industry and the Next Phase of Economic Development of Singapore." Paper presented at the Workshop on Port Cities and City-States in Asia, Europe, Asia-Africa Institute, University of Hamburg, Germany, November 4–7, 2004, 6.

48. Chua, "Cultural Industry and the Next Phase," 9.

49. These frameworks are borrowed from Michael Keane, "Once Were Peripheral: Creating Media Capacity in East Asia." *Media, Culture and Society* 28(6) (2006): 835–55.

50. Chua, "Cultural Industry and the Next Phase," 8.

51. For these examples, see Audrey Yue, "The Regional Culture of New Asia: Cultural Governance and Creative Industries in Singapore." *International Journal of Cultural Policy* 12(1) (2006): 17–33.

52. On the features and problems of the media hub, see Audrey Yue, "Doing Cultural Citizenship in the Global Media Hub: Illiberal Pragmatics and Lesbian Consumption Practices in Singapore." In *Circuits of Visibility: Gender and Transnational Media Cultures*, edited by Radha Hegde (New York: New York University Press, 2011), 250–67.

53. Michael Porter, *On Competition* (Boston, MA: Harvard Business School Publishing, 1998), 199.

54. For a critique of some of these clusters, see Aihwa Ong, *Neoliberalism as Exception: Mutations in Citizenship and Sovereignty* (Durham, NC: Duke University Press, 2006), 177–94; Lily Kong, "Making Sustainable Creative/Cultural Space in Shanghai and Singapore." *Geographical Review* 99(1) (2009): 1–22; K. C. Ho, "The Neighbourhood in the Creative Economy: Policy, Practice and Place in Singapore." *Urban Studies* 46(5/6) (2009): 1188–201.

55. Stuart Cunningham, "From Cultural to Creative Industries: Theory, Industry and Policy Implications." *Media International Australia* 102 (2002): 59.

56. Media Development Authority, *Creative Industries Development Strategy,* 44–5.

57. Television serials in this genre include *Rouge* (2004), a fourteen-episode female action comedy drama produced by Mega Media in partnership with MTV Asia, and starring five actresses from the Philippines, Singapore, the United States, and Vietnam; *Tao Shu: The Warrior Boy* (2004), a fifty-two-episode animation series from Peach Blossom Media, a company renowned for creating the world's first Asian originated cartoon series *Tomato Twins* for the Nickelodeon channel; and *House of Harmony* (2005), a S$10 million dollar German–Singapore telemovie, with a cast from China and Hong Kong, that was screened on free-to-air German television to an audience of about fifteen million viewers.

58. For a further study of this film, see Yue, "Hawking in the Creative City."

59. Ling is a Shaw Brothers veteran; Chang's early career as a Taiwanese teen star of Mandarin romance melodramas in the 1970s received an unprecedented boost after she appeared in New Wave and comedy classics such as *The Secret* (Ann Hui, 1979) and *Aces Go Places 1 and 2* (Eric Tsang, 1982); Q is an Hawaiian-born American-Vietnamese model whose film career was launched with *Gen-Y Cops* (Benny Chan, 2000) and *Naked Weapon* (Ching Siu-tung, 2002); Yan is a diasporic Canadian Chinese food celebrity who is famous for his cooking shows on Hong Kong cuisine.

60. On the resistance to Hokkien in film and everyday life, see Chua Beng Huat, *Life is Not Complete without Shopping,* 164; on the cultural specificity of Singlish as slang, see Olivia Khoo, "*Slang* Images: On the Foreignness of Contemporary Singaporean Films." *Inter-Asia Cultural Studies* 7(1) (2006): 81–98.

61. For a further study of this film, see Audrey Yue, "Film-Induced Domestic Tourism in Singapore: The Case of *Krrish.*" In *Domestic Tourism in Asia: Diversity and Divergence*, edited by Shalini Singh (London: Earthscan, 2009).

62. For a discussion of the framework of the new international division of cultural labour, see Toby Miller, *Global Hollywood* (London: British Film Institute, 2001).

63. For statistics on these visitations, see Yue, "Film-Induced Tourism in Singapore," 276–7.

64. Michael Curtin, "Media Capital: Towards the Study of Spatial Flows." *International Journal of Cultural Studies* 6(2) (2003): 204.

65. Ong, *Neoliberalism as Exception*, 8.

66. See Singapore Film Commission, "List of Singapore Movies (1991–2008)." *Film Industry: Fact and Figures*, http://www.sfc.org.sg/main.html; see also Internet

Movie Database, *Hainan Jifan: Awards (2004)*, http://www.imdb.com/title/tt0383388/awards.

67. See Box Office India, *Box Office 2006*, http://www.boxofficeindia.com/showProd.php?itemCat=212&catName=MjAwNg==.

68. Justin O'Connor, "Creative Industries: A New Direction?" *International Journal of Cultural Policy* 15(4) (2009): 387–402.

69. See also Paul du Gay and Michael Pryke, *Cultural Economy: Cultural Analysis and Commercial Life* (London: Sage, 2002).

70. Lily Kong, "The Sociality of Cultural Industries: Hong Kong's Cultural Policy and Film Industry." *International Journal of Cultural Policy* 11(1) (2005): 61–76.

71. Jing Zhang and Poh-Kam Wong, "Networks vs Market Methods in High-Tech Venture Fundraising: The Impact of Institutional Environment." *Entrepreneurship and Regional Development* 20 (2008): 409–30.

72. For a summary of such criticisms, see David Hesmondhalgh, "Cultural and Creative Industries." In *The Sage Handbook of Cultural Analysis*, edited by Tony Bennett and John Frow (London: Sage, 2008).

73. Ong, *Neoliberalism as Exception*, 3.

74. Aaron Koh, "Living with Globalization Tactically: The Metapragmatics of Globalization in Singapore." *Sojourn: Journal of Social Issues in Southeast Asia* 72(2) (2007): 179–201.

75. Koh, "Living with Globalization Tactically," 181, 183.

76. Yúdice, *The Expediency of Culture*, 31.

77. Anonymous, "Singapore Public Gay Parties." *Wikipedia.* http://en.wikipedia.org/wiki/Singapore_public_gay_parties.

78. Yue, "Creative Queer Singapore," 156–8.

79. On the difference between "being" gay and "doing" gay, see Gary Dowsett, "'I'll Show You Mine, if You Show Me Yours': Gay Men, Masculinity Research, Men's Studies, and Sex." *Theory and Society* 22 (1993): 697–709.

80. Nick Stevenson, *Cultural Citizenship: Cosmopolitan Questions* (Maidenhead: Open University Press, 2003).

81. Renato Rosaldo, "Cultural citizenship, inequality, and multiculturalism." In *Race, Identity, and Citizenship*, edited by Rofoldo Torres, Louis Miron, and Jonathan Inda (Boston: Beacon Press, 1999), 255.

82. Will Kymlicka, *Multicultural Citizenship: A Liberal Theory of Minority Rights* (Oxford: Oxford University Press, 1995).

83. Chua Beng Huat, "Political Culturalism, Representations and the People's Action Party of Singapore." *Democratization* 14(5) (2007): 911–27.

84. Aihwa Ong, "Cultural Citizenship as Subject Making: Immigrants Negotiate Racial and Cultural Boundaries in the United States." In *Race, Identity, and Citizenship*, edited by Rodolfo Torres, Louis Miron, and Jonathan Inda (Boston: Beacon Press, 1999), 262–4.

85. Brian Turner, "Outline of a General Theory of Cultural Citizenship." In *Culture and Citizenship*, edited by Nick Stevenson (London: Sage, 2002), 12; David Chaney,

"Cosmopolitan Art and Cultural Citizenship." *Theory, Culture and Society* 19(2) (2002): 151–74.

86. Yue, "Doing Cultural Citizenship in the Global Media Hub."

87. For a history of Aware, see Lenore Lyons, *A State of Ambivalence: The Feminist Movement in Singapore* (London: Brill, 2004).

88. Geraldine Heng, "'A Great Way to Fly': Nationalism, the State, and the Varieties of Third-World Feminism." In *Feminist Genealogies, Colonial Legacies, Democratic Futures*, edited by M. Jacqui Alexander and Chandra T. Mohanty (New York: Routledge, 1997).

89. Lyons, *A State of Ambivalence*, 171.

90. Lenore Lyons, "The Limits of Feminist Political Intervention in Singapore." *Journal of Contemporary Asia* 30(1) (2000): 67.

91. Cornel West, *The American Evasion of Philosophy: A Genealogy of Pragmatism* (Madison, WI: University of Wisconsin Press, 1989), 5.

92. West, *The American Evasion of Philosophy*, 212.

93. West, *The American Evasion of Philosophy*, 233–4.

94. West, *The American Evasion of Philosophy*, 213, 232.

95. For a coverage of the debates and networks online, see "Daily SG: 3 May 2009 AWARE Weekend Special." *Singapore Daily*, May 3, 2009. http://singaporedaily.net/2009/05/03/daily-sg-3-may-2009-aware-weekend-special; "Aware Saga," *We are Aware*. http://www.we-are-aware.sg/sections/saga.

96. On collective intelligence, see Pierre Levy, *Cyberculture* (Minneapolis, MN: University of Minnesota Press, 2001), 10.

97. Field Reporter, "LIVE from Suntec: AWARE EGM." *The Temasek Review*, May 2, 2009. http://74.125.153.132/search?q=cache:RXFKo0WkAAgJ:temasekreview.com/%3Fp%3D8732+live+report+Aware+saga+log+2+May+2009&cd=1&hl=en& ct=clnk&gl=au&client=firefox-a.

98. Field Reporter, "LIVE from Suntec."

99. For video and photo coverage of the event, see "More Than a Thousand Turn Up for Aware EOGM." *The Online Citizen*, May 2, 2009. http://the-onlinecitizen.com/2009/05/more-than-a-thousand-turn-up-for-aware-eogm/; Boris Chan, "Exclusive Video Coverage of Aware EOGM — Part One." *The Online Citizen*, May 3, 2009. http://theonlinecitizen.com/2009/05/toc-exclusive-video-coverage-of-aware-eogm-part-one.

100. Lyons, *A State of Ambivalence*, 21.

101. The Rascals Prize is a biennial award for the best research work related to the subject of gays, lesbians, bisexuals, and trans-genders, and Singapore. It commemorates a seminal event in local gay history when police raided and detained all the patrons at gay nightclub Rascals on May 30, 1993. The indignation over the raid galvanized the gay community into action and the country's leading activist group, People Like Us, was born. See People Like Us, "People Like Us Launches the Rascals Prize." August 2, 2008. http://www.plu.sg/society/?p=121.

Chapter 12: Culture, Institution, Conduct

1. I borrow the term "plexus" from Patrick Carroll, who prefers it to the more familiar "nexus" in suggesting a more plural and multiform set of connections. See Patrick Carroll, *Science, Culture, and Modern State Formation* (Berkeley, CA: University of California Press, 2006).
2. Barbara Kirshenblatt-Gimblett, "World Heritage in Cultural Economics." In *Museum Frictions: Public Cultures/Global Transformations*, edited by Ivan Karp, Corinne A. Kratz, Lynn Szwaja, and Tomás Ybarra-Frausto (Durham, NC: Duke University Press, 2006), 161.
3. Kirshenblatt-Gimblett, "World Heritage," 161.
4. Francis Mulhern, *Culture/Metaculture* (London: Routledge, 2000).
5. William Ray, *The Logic of Culture: Authority and Identity in the Modern Era* (Oxford: Blackwell, 2001).
6. Tony Bennett, "Making Culture, Changing Society: The Perspective of Culture Studies." *Cultural Studies* 21(4–5) (2007): 610–29.
7. As elaborated in Jacques Rancière, *Aesthetics and Its Discontents* (Cambridge: Polity Press, 2009).
8. Latour's work has been perhaps the most influential in this regard. See particularly Bruno Latour, "Why Has Critique Run Out of Steam: From Matters of Fact to Matters of Concern." In *Things*, edited by Bill Brown (Chicago: University of Chicago Press).
9. Luc Boltanski and Eve Chiapello, *The New Spirit of Capitalism* (London: Verso, 2005).
10. David Toews, "The New Tarde: Sociology after the End of the Social." *Theory, Culture & Society* 20(5) (2009): 90.
11. See Tony Bennett, "'Culture Studies' and the Culture Complex." In *Culture: A Sociological Handbook*, edited by John R. Hall, Laura Grindstaff and Ming-cheng Lo (London: Routledge, 2010). I draw here on my formulations in this and two earlier papers: "Making Culture, Changing Society" and "The Work of Culture." *Journal of Cultural Sociology* 1(1) (2007): 31–48.
12. Michel Foucault, *Security, Territory, Population: Lectures at the Collège de France, 1977–1978* (London: Palgrave Macmillan, 2007), 108.
13. See the wonderful discussion in Jennifer Summit, *Memory's Library: Medieval Books in Early Modern England* (Chicago: University of Chicago Press, 2008).
14. See Gary Wilder, *The French Imperial Nation-State: Negritude and Colonial Humanism between the Two World Wars* (Chicago: University of Chicago Press, 2005), and my discussion of the Musée de l'Homme in "Museum, Field, Colony: Colonial Governmentality and the Circulation of Reference." *Journal of Cultural Economy* 2(1/2) (2009): 99–116.
15. See Eiko Ikegami, *Bonds of Civility: Aesthetic Networks and the Political Origins of Japanese Culture* (Cambridge: Cambridge University Press, 2005).

16. See Masaaki Morishita, "Empty Museums: Transculturation and the Development of Public Museums in Japan." PhD dissertation. Open University, 2003. Morishita demonstrates an enduring lack of fit between the ordering of the relations between artistic forms of expertise, artworks, and publics in the two cases of the Japanese emperor *iomoto* system and the Western art system.

17. See Richard E. Lee, *Life and Times of Cultural Studies: The Politics and Transformation of the Structures of Knowledge* (London: Lawrence and Wishart, 2004).

18. See, for an exceptionally alert navigation of this difficult territory, Chris Healy, *Forgetting Aborigines* (Sydney: UNSW Press, 2008).

19. Stuart Hall, "On Postmodernism and Articulation: An Interview with Stuart Hall," edited by Lawrence Grossberg. *Journal of Communication Inquiry* 10(2) (1986): 45–60.

20. There is an extensive literature here, but for an authoritative distillation of its implications, see Bruno Latour, *Reassembling the Social: An Introduction to Actor-Network Theory* (Oxford: Oxford University Press, 2005).

21. I draw here on my discussion of the Musée de l'Homme in "Museum, Field, Colony" and, *inter alia*, on the following: Alice C. Conklin, "Skulls on Display: The Science of Race in Paris's Musée de l'Homme, 1928–1950." In *Museums and Difference*, edited by Daniel Sherman (Bloomington, IN: Indiana University Press, 2008); Nélia Dias, *Le musée d'ethnographie du Trocadéro (1878–1908): anthropologie et muséologie en France* (Paris: Éditions du Centre National de la Recherche Scientifique, 1991); Nina Gorgus, *Le magicien des vitrines: le muséologue Georges Henri Rivière* (Paris: Éditions de la Maison des Sciences de l'Homme, 2003); Benoît de L'Estoile, *Le goût des autres: de l'exposition coloniale aux arts premiers* (Paris: Flammarion, 2007); Daniel Sherman, "'Peoples Ethnographic': Objects, Museums, and the Colonial Inheritance of French Ethnology." *French Historical Studies* 27(3) (2004): 669–703; Emmanuelle Sibeud, "The Metamorphosis of Ethnology in France, 1839–1930." In *A New History of Anthropology*, edited by Henrika Kuklik (Malden, MA: Blackwell, 2007).

22. See Christine Laurière, *Paul Rivet: le savant et le politique* (Paris: Musée National d'Histoire Naturelle, 2008), 410–26.

23. See Jennifer Michael Hecht, *The End of the Soul: Scientific Modernity, Atheism, and Anthropology in France* (New York: Columbia University Press, 2003).

24. See, for example, John Law and John Urry, "Enacting the Social." *Economy and Society* 33(3) (2004).

25. Stuart Hall, "Race, Articulation and Societies Structured in Dominance." In UNESCO, *Sociological Theories: Race and Colonialism* (Paris: UNESCO, 1980).

26. World Commission for Culture and Development, *Our Creative Diversity* (Paris: UNESCO).

27. See Stuart Hall, "Unsettling 'The Heritage': Re-Imagining the Post-Nation." In *Whose Heritage? The Impact of Cultural Diversity on Britain's Living Heritage* (London: Arts Council of England, 1999); and Tony Bennett, "Culture and

Differences: The Challenges of Multiculturalism." In *When Culture Makes the Difference: Heritage, Arts and Media in Multicultural Society*, edited by S. Boda and Maria Rita Cifarelli (Rome: Meltemi Editore, 2006).

28. Ian Hunter, *Culture and Government: The Emergence of Literary Education* (London: Macmillan, 1988).

29. Michael Bérubé, "Introduction: Engaging the Aesthetic." In *The Aesthetics of Cultural Studies*, edited by Michael Bérubé (Oxford: Blackwell, 2005), 15.

30. Jacques Rancière, *Aesthetics and Its Discontents*.

31. For a more detailed discussion of the suggestiveness of Rancière's work in this regard, see my "Habitus Clivé: Aesthetics and Politics in the Work of Pierre Bourdieu." *New Literary History* 38(1) (2005): 201–28.

32. Notwithstanding his criticisms of Cultural Studies, Eagleton has never unsubscribed from this aspect of its formation. See, for example, his discussion of the common culture in his *The Idea of Culture* (Oxford: Blackwell, 2000).

33. See, for example, Peter Osborne, "Whoever Speaks of Culture Speaks of Administration as Well: Disputing Pragmatism in Cultural Studies." *Cultural Studies* 20(1) (2006): 33–47.

34. I offer a more extended discussion of these questions in "Sociology, Aesthetics, Expertise," *New Literary History* 41(2) (2010): 253–76, which draws on the discussion of Kant's relations to Christian metaphysics in Ian Hunter, *Rival Enlightenments: Civil and Metaphysical Philosophy in Early Modern Germany* (Cambridge: Cambridge University Press, 2001).

35. For a fuller elaboration of this position, see the introduction to *Material Powers: Cultural Studies, History and the Material Turn*, edited by Tony Bennett and Patrick Joyce (London: Routledge, 2010).

Bibliography

Introduction: Instituting Cultural Studies

Adorno, Theodor W. "Culture and Administration." In Theodor Adorno, *The Culture Industry: Selected Essays on Mass Culture*, edited by J. M. Bernstein. London: Routledge, 1991.

Althusser, Louis. "Ideology and Ideological State Apparatuses (Notes towards an Investigation)." In Louis Althusser, *Lenin and Philosophy and Other Essays*, translated by Ben Brewster. New York: Monthly Review Press, 1971.

Bauman, Zygmunt. "Culture and Management." *Parallax* 10(2) (2004): 63–72.

Bennett, Tony. *Culture: A Reformer's Science*. London: Sage, 1998.

——. *The Birth of the Museum: History, Theory, Politics*. London: Routledge, 1995.

Berland, Jody. "Bodies of Theory, Bodies of Pain: Some Silences." In *Feminism-Art-Theory: An Anthology 1968–2000*, edited by Hilary Robinson. Oxford: Blackwell, 2001.

Castoriadis, Cornelius. *The Imaginary Institution of Society*, translated by Kathleen Blamey. Cambridge, MA: MIT Press, 1987.

Chambers, Ross. *Story and Situation: Narrative Seduction and the Power of Fiction*. Minneapolis, MN: University of Minnesota Press, 1984.

Chen, Kuan-Hsing, ed. *Trajectories: Inter-Asia Cultural Studies*. London: Routledge, 1998.

Chen, Kuan-Hsing and Chua Beng Huat, eds. *The Inter-Asia Cultural Studies Reader*. London: Routledge, 2007.

Crimp, Douglas. *AIDS: Cultural Analysis/Cultural Activism*. Cambridge, MA: MIT Press, 1988.

——. *On the Museum's Ruins*. Cambridge MA: MIT Press, 1993.

Davies, Bronwyn and Peter Bansel. "Governmentality and Academic Work: Shaping the Hearts and Minds of Academic Workers." *Journal of Curriculum Theorizing* 26(3) (2010): 5–20.

de Bary, Brett, ed. *Universities in Translation: The Mental Labor of Globalization*. Hong Kong: Hong Kong University Press, 2010.

Denning, Michael. *Culture in the Age of Three Worlds*. London: Verso, 2004.

Derrida, Jacques. *The Other Heading: Reflection on Today's Europe*, translated by Pascale-Anne Brault and Michael B. Naas. Bloomington, IN: Indiana University Press, 1992.

Douglas, Mary. *How Institutions Think*. Syracuse: Syracuse University Press, 1986.

Felski, Rita. "The Doxa of Difference." *Signs* 23(1) (1997): 1–21.

Foucault, Michel. "Governmentality." In *The Foucault Effect: Studies in Governmentality*, edited by Graham Burchell, Colin Gordon and Peter Miller. London: Harvester/ Wheatsheaf, 1978.

—— *The History of Sexuality: An Introduction*, translated by Robert Hurley. Harmondsworth: Penguin, 1984.

Grossberg, Lawrence. *Cultural Studies in the Future Tense*. Durham, NC: Duke University Press, 2010.

Kalir, Barak and Pál Nyíri. "Evaluating Academia." *EspacesTemps.net*, July 12, 2010. http://espacestemps.net/document8318.html.

Lagerspetz, Eerik, Heikki Ikäheimo and Jussi Kotkavirta, eds. *On the Nature of Social and Institutional Reality*. Jyväskylä: SoPhi, 2001.

Lehtonen, Mikko. "Spaces and Places of Cultural Studies." *Culture Unbound* 1 (2009): 67–81. http://www.cultureunbound.ep.liu.se/v1/a06.

Lindsay, Jennifer. "A Drama of Change: Cultural Policy and the Performing Arts in Southeast Asia." In *Global Culture: Media, Arts, Policy, and Globalization*, edited by Diana Crane, Nobuko Kawahima, and Ken'ichi Kawasaki. New York: Routledge, 2002.

McCalman, Iain and Meaghan Morris. "'Public Culture' and Humanities Research in Australia: A Report." *Public Culture* 11(2) (1999): 319–45.

Marginson, Simon. "Making Space in Higher Education." In *Global Creation: Space, Mobility and Synchrony in the Age of the Knowledge Economy*, edited by Simon Marginson, Peter Murphy and Michael A. Peters. New York: Peter Lang, 2010.

Marginson, Simon and Mark Considine. *The Enterprise University: Power, Governance and Reinvention in Australia*. Cambridge: Cambridge University Press, 2000.

Martin, Rux. "Truth, Power, Self: An Interview with Michel Foucault." In *Technologies of the Self: A Seminar with Michel Foucault*, edited by Luther H. Martin, Huck Gutman and Patrick H. Hutton. London: Tavistock, 1982.

Massey, Doreen. *Space, Place and Gender*. Minneapolis, MN: University of Minnesota Press, 1994.

Miller, Henry D.R. *The Management of Change in Universities: Universities, State and the Economy in Australia, Canada and the United Kingdom*. Milton Keynes: Society for Research into Higher Education and Open University Press, 1995.

Morris, Meaghan. "Humanities for Taxpayers: Some Problems." *New Literary History* 36(1) (2005): 111–29.

———. "Teaching versus Research? Cultural Studies and the New Class Politics in Knowledge." *Inter-Asia Cultural Studies* 9(3) (2008): 433–50.

North, Douglass C. *Institutions, Institutional Change and Economic Performance*. Cambridge: Cambridge University Press, 1990.

Osborne, Peter. "'Whoever Speaks of Culture Speaks of Administration as Well': Disputing Pragmatism in Cultural Studies." *Cultural Studies* 20(1) (2006): 33–47.

Powell, Elwin H. "On Choosing Institutions: Ideas from Stanley Taylor." Introduction to *Conceptions of Institutions and the Theory of Knowledge* by Stanley Taylor, 2nd ed. New Brunswick, NH: Transaction, 1989.

Readings, Bill. *The University in Ruins*. Cambridge, MA: Harvard University Press, 1996.

Schliefer, Ronald. "The Institutions of Cultural Studies." *Surfaces* 2 (1992). http://www.pum.umontreal.ca/revues/surfaces/vol2/schleife.html.

Searle, John R. "Social Ontology and the Philosophy of Society." In *On the Nature of Social and Institutional Reality*, edited by Eerik Lagerspetz, Heikki Ikäheimo, and Jussi Kotkavirta. Jyväskylä: SoPhi, 2001.

Shore, Cris. "Audit Culture and Illiberal Governance." *Anthropological Theory* 8(3) (2008): 278–98.

Shore, Cris and Susan Wright. "Coercive Accountability: The Rise of Audit Culture in Higher Education." In *Audit Cultures: Anthropological Studies in Accountability, Ethics and the Academy*, edited by Marilyn Strathern. London: Routledge, 2000.

Strathern, Marilyn, ed. *Audit Cultures: Anthropological Studies in Accountability, Ethics and the Academy*. London: Routledge, 2000.

Striphas, Ted. "The Long March: Cultural Studies and Its Institutionalization." *Cultural Studies* 12(4) (1998). Special issue: "The Institutionalization of Cultural Studies": 453–75.

Tolofari, Sowaribi. "New Public Management and Education." *Policy Futures in Education* 3(1) (2005): 75–89.

Turner, Graeme. "Informing the Public: Is There a Place for a Critical Humanities?" *Proceedings*. Canberra: Australian Academy of the Humanities, 2005.

——. *What's Become of Cultural Studies?* London: Sage, 2011.

Wright, Handel K. and Meaghan Morris, eds. *Cultural Studies of Transnationalism*. London: Routledge, 2012.

Yi, Lin. "Audit Culture with Chinese Characteristics?" *EspacesTemps.net*, Textuel, July 12, 2010. http://espacestemps.net/document8298.html.

Yúdice, George. *The Expediency of Culture: Uses of Culture in the Global Era*. Durham, NC: Duke University Press, 2003.

Chapter 1: The Desire for Cultural Studies

Césaire, Aimé. *Cahier d'un retour au pays natal (Return to My Native Land)*. Paris: Volontés, 1939.

Deshpande, Satish. *Contemporary India: A Sociological Introduction*. Delhi: Penguin, 2003.

James, C. L. R. *The Black Jacobins*. Vintage: New York, 1989 [1938].

Joshi, Svati, ed. *Rethinking English*. Delhi: Trianka, 1991.

Kenyatta, Jomo. *Facing Mount Kenya*. London: Martin, Secker and Warburg, 1938.

Kurien, C.T. *Rethinking Economics*. Delhi: Sage, 1996.

Nehru, Jawaharlal. *Discovery of India*. Oxford: Oxford University Press, 1946.

Niranjana, Tejaswini. *Siting Translation: History, Post-structuralism and the Colonial Context*. Berkeley, CA: University of California Press, 1992.

Niranjana, Tejaswini, P. Sudhir, and Vivek Dhareshwar, eds. *Interrogating Modernity: Culture and Colonialism in India*. Kolkata: Seagull Books, 1993.

Rajan, Rajeswari Sunder, ed. *The Lie of the Land*. Delhi: Oxford University Press, 1992.

Said, Edward. *Orientalism*. New York: Vintage, 1979.

Tharu, Susie, ed. *Subject to Change*. Hyderabad: Orient Longman, 1998.

———. "Preface" to *Women Writing in India*, Vol. II. Delhi: Oxford University Press, 1993.

Viswanathan, Gauri. *Masks of Conquest*. London: Faber, 1990.

Chapter 2: Social Movements, Cultural Studies, and Institutions

Chen, Kuan-Hsing, ed. *Trajectories: Inter-Asia Cultural Studies*. London: Routledge, 1998.

Chen, Kuan-Hsing and Chua Beng Huat, eds. *The Inter-Asia Cultural Studies Reader*. London: Routledge, 2007.

Cooper, Carolyn. "'Pedestrian Crosses': Sites of Dislocation in 'Post-colonial' Jamaica." *Inter-Asia Cultural Studies* 10(1) (2009): 3–11.

Editorial Collective. "Editorial Statement." *Inter-Asia Cultural Studies* 1(1) (2000): 5–6.

Hanasaki, Kohei. "Decolonialization and Assumption of War Responsibility." *Inter-Asia Cultural Studies* 1(1) (2000): 71–84.

Ho, Josephine. "Forging the Trail: Teaching Cultural Studies Workshop, Taiwan, 2006." *Inter-Asia Cultural Studies* 9(3) (2008): 429–32.

Rajadhyaksha, Ashish, ed. *Inter-Asia Cultural Studies*, South Asia Special Issue 6(2) (2005).

Chapter 3: Life of a Parasite

Chen, Kuan-Hsing and Sechin Y.-S Chien. "Academic Production under Globalized New Liberalism." In *Globalization and Knowledge Production: Critical Reflections on the Practices of Academic Evaluation*, edited by conference organizing committee. Tai-She Forum Series 4. Taipei: Tangshan, 2005 (in Chinese).

Ho, Josephine. *The Gallant Woman: Feminism and Sexual Emancipation*. Taiwan: Crown, 1994 (in Chinese).

Lin, Fang-mei. "Identity Politics in Contemporary Women's Movement in Taiwan: The Case of Licensed Prostitution." *Chung-Wai Literary Monthly* 313 (1998): 56–87 (in Chinese).

Liu, Petrus. "Queer Marxism in Taiwan." *Inter-Asia Cultural Studies* 8(4) (2007): 517–39.

Liu, Yu-Xiou. "From Women Ruling the State to Gender Liberation: Subverting Familial Patriarchy with State-Feminism." *Stir Quarterly* 2 (1996): 20–26 (in Chinese).

Ning, Yin-Bin. "Cultural Politics as 'Real Politics' and Cultural Studies as Applied Philosophy: Cultural Criticism in Taiwan." Paper presented at the International Conference on Cultural Criticism, Chinese University of Hong Kong, January 2, 1993 (in Chinese).

Serres, Michel. *The Parasite,* translated by Lawrence R. Schehr. Baltimore, MD: Johns Hopkins University Press, 1982.

Websites

Center for the Study of Sexualities at National Central University, gender equity education workshop materials: http://sex.ncu.edu.tw/course/young/young.html

Gender/Sexuality Rights Association Taiwan (GSRAT): http://gsrat.net/en/aboutus.php

Chapter 4: The Assessment Game

120th Anniversary of the Founding of Lingnan University & 40th Anniversary of the Re-establishment of Lingnan University in Hong Kong. Hong Kong: Public Affairs Office, Lingnan University, 2007.

Association of Commonwealth Universities. *Engagement as a Core Value for the University: A Consultation Document (April 2001).* www.viu.ca/integratedplanning/.../AcademicPlanAppendixAugust162010.pdf.

Coady, Tony, ed. *Why Universities Matter: A Conversation about Values, Means and Directions.* Sydney: Allen & Unwin, 2000.

Fisher, James L. and James V. Koch. *Presidential Leadership: Making a Difference.* Phoenix, AZ: Oryx Press, 1996.

Gardner, Howard. *Intelligence Reframed: Multiple Intelligences for the 21st Century.* New York: Basic Books, 1999.

"Great Colleges to Work For." http://chroniclegreatcolleges.com.

Hjort, Mette. "Affinitive and Milieu-Building Transnationalism: The *Advance Party* Initiative." In *Cinema at the Periphery*, edited by Dina Iordanova, David Martin-Jones, and Belén Vidal. Detroit, MI: Wayne State University Press, 2010.

——. "Denmark." In *The Cinema of Small Nations*, edited by Mette Hjort and Duncan Petrie. Edinburgh: Edinburgh University Press, 2007.

——. "Dogma 95: A Small Nation's Response to Globalisation." In *Purity and Provocation: Dogma 95*, edited by Mette Hjort and Scott MacKenzie. London: BFI, 2003.

——. "Style and Creativity in *The Five Obstructions*." In *Dekalog 01: On "The Five Obstructions,"* edited by Mette Hjort. London: Wallflower, 2008.

Huang Ju-yan, ed. *Modern Education in Guangdong and Lingnan University.* Hong Kong: Commercial Press, 1995.

Marginson, Simon. "Rankings Ripe for Misleading." *The Australian*, December 6, 2006. http://www.theaustralian.news.com.au/story/0,20867,20877456–12332,00.html.

Mok Ka-ho. *Education and the Market Place in Hong Kong and Mainland China.* Hong Kong: Department of Public and Social Administration, City University of Hong Kong, 1998: 1–35.

Nelson, Cary and Stephen Watt. *Academic Keywords: A Devil's Dictionary for Higher Education*. London: Routledge, 1999.

Office of Metropolitan Architecture (OMA). "West Kowloon Cultural District, Hong Kong, 2009." http://www.oma.eu/index.php?option=com_projects&view=project&id=1187&Itemid=10.

Office of Service-Learning. *Annual Report 2008/09: Uniting Social Capitals for the Global Society*. Hong Kong: Lingnan University, Office of Service-Learning, 2010.

Olafsson, Björn G. *Small States in the Global System: Analysis and Illustrations from the Case of Iceland*. Aldershot: Ashgate.

"Research." http://www.ln.edu.hk/research.

Wilson, Robin. "Globe Trotting Academics Find New Career Paths." *The Chronicle of Higher Education*, December 6, 2009. http://chronicle.com/article/Globe-Trotting-American/49349.

Chapter 5: Three Tough Questions of Cultural Studies

Lu Xun. *Wild Grass,* translated by Yang Xianyi and Gladys Yang. Hong Kong: Chinese University of Hong Kong, 2003 [1927].

Wang Xiaoming. "China on the Brink of a 'Momentous Era.'" *positions: east asia cultures critique* 11(3) (2003): 585–611.

——. ed. *Cultural Studies in the Chinese World*. Shanghai: Shanghai Bookstore, 2010.

Wang Xiaoming and Zhou Zhan-an, eds. *Anthology of Modern Chinese Thought*. Shanghai: Shanghai Bookstore, 2011.

Chapter 6: Doing Cultural Studies

Appadurai, Arjun. "Disjuncture and Difference in the Global Cultural Economy." In *Modernity at Large*. Minneapolis, MN: University of Minnesota Press, 1996.

Bennett, Tony. *Culture: A Reformer's Science*. London: Sage, 1998.

Chan, Stephen Ching-Kiu, ed. *Cultural Imaginary and Ideology: Critical Essays in Contemporary Hong Kong Cultural Politics* 《文化想像與意識形態：當代香港文化政治論評》. Hong Kong: Oxford University Press, 1997.

——. ed. *The Practice of Affect: Studies in Hong Kong Popular Song Lyrics* 《情感的實踐：香港流行歌詞研究》. Hong Kong: Oxford University Press, 1997.

——. "Building Cultural Studies for Postcolonial Hong Kong: Aspects of the Postmodern Ruins in Between Disciplines." In *Cultural Studies: Interdisciplinarity and Translation*, edited by Stefan Herbrechter. Amsterdam: Rodopi, 2002. A slightly different version, in Chinese, is published as 《從文學到文化研究：香港的視角》 ("From Literary to Cultural Studies: A Hong Kong Perspective"). In *Methodologies: Routes of Research on Literature*, edited by Han-Liang Chang, 283–315. Taipei: National Taiwan University Press, 2002. An expanded version also appears as 《在廢墟中築造文化研究：並論當代大學教育的頹敗形式與意義》 in the special issue on University, *E+E* 6 (2003), 10–22.

——. "Figures of Hope and the Filmic Imaginary of *Jianghu* in Contemporary Hong Kong Cinema." *Cultural Studies* 15(3–4) (2001): 486–514.

——. "Mapping the Global Popular in Hong Kong: Re-Articulations of the Local, National and Transnational in Contemporary Cultural Flows." In *Re-Inventing Hong Kong in the Age of Globalization*, edited by Yee Leung et al. Hong Kong: Chung Chi College and Faculty of Social Sciences, The Chinese University of Hong Kong, 2002.

——. "On the Postmodern Condition of Hong Kong: At the Limits of Status Quo and Anomaly in 1997"《後現代的常態與異狀：窮想九七香港如常》. In *Hong Kong Literature as/and Cultural Studies*《香港文學@文化研究》, edited by Mee-kwan Cheung and Yiu-wai Chu. Hong Kong: Oxford University Press, 2002.

—— "On Urban Cultural Imagination in Xi Xi's Narratives of Hong Kong"《論都市的文化想像：並讀西西說香港》. In *Hong Kong Literature as/and Cultural Studies*, edited by E. M. K. Cheung and S. Y. W. Chu. Hong Kong: Oxford University Press, 2002. Originally published in *Transit: A Journal of Hong Kong Arts & Culture*《過渡》, 1 (1995): 6–14. Also collected in *Forty Years of Chinese Literatures*《四十年來中國文學》, edited by Yu-min Shao et al. Taipei: Unitas, 1995.

Chan, Stephen Ching-Kiu, Choi Po-King, Hui Po-Keung et al. *Integrated Humanities and Liberal Studies: A Research Assessment*《盤點 IH，認真通識》. Hong Kong: Kwan Fong Cultural Research and Development Programme, Lingnan University, 2009.

Chan, Stephen Ching-Kiu and Hui, Po-Keung. "Cultural Studies through Education: Moments of Pedagogy & Pragmatics." *Inter-Asia Cultural Studies* 9(3) (2008): 484–95.

——. "Redesigning Critical Pedagogy in the Era of Knowledge-based Economy: The Case of Hong Kong." Paper presented at the international conference on "Redesigning Pedagogy: Research, Policy, Practice" organized by the National Institute of Education, Nanyang Technological University, Singapore, May 31–June 2, 2005.

Erni, John. "Like a Post-Colonial Culture: Hong Kong Re-Imagined." Introduction to the special issue on "Becoming (Postcolonial) Hong Kong." *Cultural Studies* 15(3–4) (2001): 389–418.

Harvey, David. *A Brief History of Neoliberalism.* Oxford: Oxford University Press, 2005.

Hong Kong Cultural Studies Bulletin《香港文化研究》(1994–98), nos. 1–9, edited by Program for Hong Kong Cultural Studies. Hong Kong: Chinese University of Hong Kong.

Hui, Po-Keung. "Introduction." In *Integrated Humanities and Liberal Studies: A Research Assessment*, edited by Choi Po-King, Hui Po-Keung et al. Hong Kong: Kwan Fong Cultural Research and Development Programme, Lingnan University, 2009.

Hui, Po-Keung and Stephen Ching-Kiu Chan. "Contextual Utility and Practicality: Cultural Research for the School Community in Hong Kong." *Cultural Studies Review* 12(2) (2006): 165–82.

Ip, Iam-Chong. "When Cultural Studies Meets Cultural Preservation" 《當文化研究遇上文化保育》. In *Cultural Studies and Cultural Education*, edited by Wing-Sang Law.

Kwong, Wing-Suen, ed. *Standing on the Side of the Eggs: The Hong Kong Post-80's* 《站在蛋的一邊：香港八十後》. Hong Kong: UP Publications, 2010.

Law, Wing-Sang. "The Challenge Posed to Cultural Studies by Cultural Education" 《文化教育對文化研究的挑戰》. In *Cultural Studies and Cultural Education*. Hong Kong: Step Forward Multimedia, 64–78.

——. *Collaborative Colonial Power: The Making of the Hong Kong Chinese*. Hong Kong: Hong Kong University Press, 2009.

——. ed. *Cultural Studies and Cultural Education*.《文化研究與文化教育》. Hong Kong: Department of Cultural Studies, Lingnan University, 2010.

Law, Wing-Sang, ed. *Whose City?: Civic Culture and Political Discourse in Post-War Hong Kong*《誰的城市？：戰後香港的公民文化與政治論述》. Hong Kong: Oxford University Press, 1997.

Ma, Eric Kit-wai. "Peripheral Vision: Chinese Cultural Studies in Hong Kong." In *A Companion to Cultural Studies*, edited by Toby Miller. Oxford: Blackwell, 2001.

Pun, Ngai. Book review of *Cultural Imaginary and Ideology* by Stephen Ching-Kiu Chan and *Whose City?* by Wing-Sang Law, *Hong Kong Journal of Social Sciences* 11 (1998): 184–6.

Chapter 7: Coordinates, Confusions, and Cultural Studies

Ji Dong. "Inside Story of China's Biggest Fan Club." *Southern Metropolis Weekly*, May 9, 2007.

McGuigan, Jim. *Cultural Populism*. London: Routledge, 1992.

Swingewood, Alan. *The Myth of Mass Culture*. London: Macmillan, 1977.

Time Asia Magazine, Asian Heroes special issue, October 3, 2005.

Zhang Xi, "Han Shao Gong: The Director of *Shi Bing Tu Ji* has a Spine, a Fine Brain and a Conscience." *Southern Weekly*, February 15, 2008.

Zhao Yu, "*Shi Bing Tu Ji*: The Yelling Inside Behind the Vanity." *Guangming Daily*, March 6, 2008.

Chapter 8: Uses of Media Culture, Usefulness of Media Culture Studies

Adorno, Theodor W. *The Culture Industry: Selected Essays on Mass Culture,* edited with an introduction by J.M. Bernstein. London: Routledge, 1991.

Billig, Michael. *Banal Nationalism*. London: Sage, 1995.

Bunka gaiko no suishin ni kasuru kondankai houkokusho (A Report by the Discussion Group on the Promotion of Cultural Diplomacy), July 2005.

Chua, Beng Huat and Koichi Iwabuchi, eds. *East Asian Pop Culture: Approaching the Korean Wave*. Hong Kong: Hong Kong University Press, 2008.

Eiji, Otsuka and Nobuaki Osawa. *"Japanimation" wa naze yabureruka* (Why Japanimation should be defeated). Tokyo: Kadokawa Shoten, 2005.

Faiola, Anthony. "Japan's Empire of Cool: Country's Culture Becomes Its Biggest Export." *Washington Post*, December 27, 2003.

Hall, Stuart. "The Local and the Global: Globalization and Ethnicity." In *Culture, Globalization, and the World-System*, edited by A. King. London: Macmillan, 1991.

Hannerz, Ulf. *Transnational Connections: Culture, People, Places*. London: Routledge, 1996.

Hesmondhalgh, David. "Neoliberalism, Imperialism, and the Media." In *The Media and Social Theory*, edited by David Hesmondhalgh and Jason Toynbee. London: Routledge, 2008.

Iwabuchi, Koichi. *Bunka no taiwaryoku* (Culture's Dialogic Capacity) (Tokyo: Nihonkeizaishinbun Shuppansha, 2007).

——. "Complicit Exoticism: Japan and Its Other." *Continuum* 8(2) (1994): 49–82.

——. *Recentering Globalization: Popular Culture and Japanese Transnationalism*. Durham, NC: Duke University Press, 2002.

——. "Uses of Japanese Popular Culture: Media Globalization and Postcolonial Desire for 'Asia.'" *Emergences: Journal of Media and Composite Cultures* 11(2) (2001): 197–220.

——. "When Korean Wave Meets Resident Koreans in Japan." In *East Asian Pop Culture: Approaching the Korean Wave*, edited by Chua Beng Huat and Koichi Iwabuchi. Hong Kong: Hong Kong University Press, 2007.

Klein, Naomi. *No Logo: Taking Action at the Brand Bullies*. London: HarperCollins, 2000.

Kongo no kokusai bunka kouryu no suishin ni tsuite (A Report by the Discussion Group on the International Cultural Exchange), 2003. http://www.bunka.go.jp/1kokusai/kokusaikondankaihoukoku.html.

McGray, Douglas. "Japan's Gross National Cool." *Foreign Policy*, May–June 2002.

McGuigan, Jim. *Rethinking Cultural Policy*. London: Open University Press, 2004.

Miller, Toby. "A View from a Fossil: The New Economy, Creativity and Consumption — Two or Three Things I Don't Believe In." *International Journal of Cultural Studies* 7(1) (2004): 55–65.

Morris-Suzuki, Tessa. *The Past within Us: Media, Memory, History*. London: Verso, 2005.

Nye, Joseph. *Bound to Lead: The Changing Nature of American Power*. New York: Basic Books, 1990.

——. "The Allure of Asia and America's Role." Paper presented to Global Communication Platform, December 5, 2005. http://www.glocom.org/opinions/essays/20051205_nye_allure/index.html.

——. Interview about Koizumi's visit to Yasukuni Shrine. *Tokyo Newspaper*, October 22, 2005.

——. "Soft Power Matters in Asia." *Japan Times*, December 5, 2005. http://search.japan-times.co.jp/cgi-bin/eo20051205a1.html.

——. *Soft Power: The Means to Success in World Politics*. New York: Public Affairs, 2004.

Palmeri, Christopher and Nanette Byrnes. "Is Japanese Style Taking Over the World?" *Business Week*, July 26, 2004.

Takahashi, Nobuyuki. "Kitty-chan wo tsukutteitanowa dare?" (Who produced Kitty?). *Shukan Kinyoubi* 357 (2001): 56–7.

Taro, Aso. "A New Look at Cultural Diplomacy: A Call to Japan's Cultural Practitioners." Speech made at Digital Hollywood University, Tokyo, April 28, 2006.

Toby Miller, Nitin Govil, John McMurria, Richard Maxwell, and Ting Wang, eds. *Global Hollywood 2*. London: British Film Institute, 2005.

Urry, John. *Global Complexity*. London: Polity, 2003.

van Ham, Peter. "The Rise of the Brand State: The Postmodern Politics of Image and Reputation." *Foreign Affairs*, September/October 2001: 1–6.

Williams, Raymond. "State Culture and Beyond." In *Culture and the State*, edited by L. Apignanesi. London: Institute of Contemporary Arts, 1984.

Wimmer, Andreas and Nina Glick Shiller. "Methodological Nationalism and Beyond: Nation-State Building, Migration and Social Sciences." *Global Networks* 2(4) (2002): 301–34.

Yoon, Ae-ri. "In Between the Values of the Global and the National: The Korean Animation Industry." In *Cultural Studies and Cultural Industries in Northeast Asia: What a Difference a Region Makes*, edited by Chris Berry, J.D. Mackintosh and N. Liscutin. Hong Kong: Hong Kong University Press, 2009.

Yúdice, George. *The Expediency of Culture: Uses of Culture in the Global Era*. Durham, NC: Duke University Press, 2003.

Chapter 9: Way Out on a Nut

Alberro, Alex. "The Turn of the Screw: Daniel Buren, Dan Flavin, and the Sixth Guggenheim International Exhibition." *October* 80 (1997): 57–84.

Buchloh, Benjamin H. D. "Sculpture Projects in Münster." *Artforum* 35(1) (1997): 115–7.

Buren, Daniel. *Five Texts*. New York and London: John Webber Gallery and Jack Wendler Gallery, 1973.

—— "Round and About a Detour." *Studio International* 181(934) (1971): 246–7.

The Buren Times. New York: The Solomon R. Guggenheim Museum, 2005.

Chan, Sewell. "Pale Gray or Light Yellow? A Ruling on Guggenheim." *New York Times*, November 21, 2007.

Coleman, Elizabeth Ann. *The Genius of Charles James*. New York: The Brooklyn Museum and Holt, Rinehart and Winston, 1982.

Crimp, Douglas. "Daniel Buren's New York Work." In R. H. Fuchs, *Discordance/ Cohérence* 8. Eindhoven: Stedelijk van Abbemuseum, 1976.

——. "The End of Painting." *October* 16 (1981): 69–86.

Deutsche, Rosalyn. "Inadequacy." In *Silvia Kolbowski: Inadequate … Like … Power*. Vienna: Secession, 2004.

Flavin, Dan. "The Guggenheim Affair: Letters to *Studio International*." *Studio International* 182(935) (1971): 6.

Foster, Hal. *Design and Crime (and Other Diatribes)*. London: Verso, 2002.

Gingeras, Alison M. "The Decorative Strategy: Daniel Buren's 'The Museum which Did Not Exist.'" *Parkett* 66 (2002): 84–92.

Guggenheim International Exhibition 1971. New York: The Solomon R. Guggenheim Museum, 1971.

Kaiser, Philipp. *Flashback: Revisiting the Art of the 80s.* Basel: Kunstmuseum Basel, Museum für Gegenwartskunst, 2005.

Kimmelman, Michael. "Tall French Visitor Takes Up Residence in the Guggenheim." *New York Times*, March 25, 2005, Arts Section.

Martin, Richard. *Charles James.* London: Thames and Hudson, 1997.

McShine, Kynaston. *The Museum as Muse: Artists Reflect.* New York: Museum of Modern Art, 1999.

Middleton, William. "A House that Rattled Texas Windows." *New York Times*, June 3, 2004.

O'Hara, Frank. *Art Chronicles 1954–1966.* New York: George Braziller, 1975.

Sawyer, Alan Reed. *Mastercraftsmen of Ancient Peru.* New York: Solomon R. Guggenheim Museum, 1968.

Smith, Roberta. "On Daniel Buren." *Artforum* 12(1) (1973): 66–7.

"Statement by Dianne Waldman." *Studio International* 181(933) (1971): 247–8.

"'Which is in fact what happened,' Thomas Messer in an interview with Barbara Reise 25 April, 1971." *Studio International* 182(935) (1971): 37.

Chapter 10: Who Needs Human Rights?

Baetens, Jan. "Cultural Studies after the Cultural Studies Paradigm." *Cultural Studies* 19(1) (2005): 1–13.

Breen, Marcus. "US Cultural Studies: Oxymoron?" *Cultural Studies Review* 11(1) (2005): 11–26.

Brown, Wendy and Janet Halley, eds. *Left Legalism/Left Critique.* Durham, NC: Duke University Press, 2002.

Cheah, Pheng. *Inhuman Conditions: On Cosmopolitanism and Human Rights.* Cambridge, MA: Harvard University Press, 2006.

Cohen, Jean L. "Whose Sovereignty?: Empire Versus International Law." In *Global Institutions and Responsibilities: Achieving Global Justice*, edited by Christian Barry and Thomas W. Pogge. Malden, MA: Blackwell, 2005.

Coombe, Rosemary. "Contingent Articulations: A Critical Cultural Studies of Law." In *Cultural Pluralism, Identity Politics, and the Law*, edited by Austin Sarat and Thomas R. Kearns. Ann Arbor, MI: University of Michigan Press, 1998.

——. *The Cultural Life of Intellectual Properties: Authorship, Appropriation, and the Law.* Durham, NC: Duke University Press, 1998.

——. "Is There a Cultural Studies of Law?" In *A Companion to Cultural Studies*, edited by Toby Miller. Malden, MA: Blackwell, 2001.

de Sousa Santos, Boaventura. "Human Rights as an Emancipatory Script? Cultural and Political Conditions." In *Another Knowledge Is Possible: Beyond Northern Epistemologies*, edited by Boaventura de Sousa Santos. London: Verso, 2007.

Douzinas, Costas. *Human Rights and Empire: The Political Philosophy of Cosmopolitanism*. London: Routledge-Cavendish, 2007.

Durbach, Andrea, Catherine Renshwa, and Andrew Byrnes. "'A Tongue but No Teeth?': The Emergence of a Regional Human Rights Mechanism in the Asia Pacific Region." *The Sydney Law Review* 31 (2009): 211–38.

Erni, John Nguyet. "New Sovereignties and Neoliberal Ethics: Remapping the Human Rights Imaginary." *Cultural Studies* 23(3) (2009): 417–36.

Fraser, Nancy. "Abnormal Justice." *Critical Inquiry* 34(3) (2008): 393–422.

——. "From Redistribution and Recognition? Dilemmas of Justice in a 'Postsocialist' Age." In *Justice Interruptus: Critical Reflections on the "Postsocialist" Condition*, edited by Nancy Fraser. New York: Routledge, 1997.

——. "Reframing Justice in a Globalizing World." *New Left Review* 36 (2005): 1–19.

Goodale, Mark. "Human Rights and Anthropology." In *Human Rights: An Anthropological Reader*, edited by Mark Goodale. Malden, MA: Wiley-Blackwell, 2009.

Grabham, Emily, Davina Cooper, Jane Krishnadas, and Didi Herman, eds. *Intersectionality and Beyond: Law, Power and the Politics of Location*. New York: Routledge-Cavendish, 2009.

Grossberg, Lawrence. "Does Cultural Studies Have Futures? Should it? (Or What's the Matter with New York?)." *Cultural Studies* 20(1) (2006): 1–32.

——. *We Gotta Get Out of This Place: Popular Conservatism and Postmodern Culture*. New York: Routledge, 1992.

Hall, Stuart. "Cultural Studies and Its Theoretical Legacies." In *Cultural Studies*, edited by Lawrence Grossberg, Cary Nelson, and Paula Treichler. New York: Routledge, 1992.

Ishay, Micheline R. "Human Rights: Historical and Contemporary Controversies." In *The Human Rights Reader*, 2nd ed., edited by Micheline R. Ishay. New York: Routledge, 2007.

Kennedy, David. "The International Human Rights Movement: Part of the Problem?" *The Harvard Human Rights Journal* 15 (2002): 99–125.

Korner, Peter, Gero Maass, Thomas Siebold, and Rainer Tetzlaff, *The IMF and the Debt Crisis: A Guide to the Third World's Dilemma*, translated by Paul Knight. London: Zed Books, 1986.

Leistyna, Pepi. "Revitalizing the Dialogue: Theory, Coalition-Building, and Social Change." In *Cultural Studies: From Theory to Action*, edited by Pepi Leistyna. Malden, MA: Blackwell, 2005.

Luban, David. "The War on Terrorism and the End of Human Rights." In *War After September 11*, edited by Verna V. Gehring. New York: Rowman & Littlefield, 2003.

Mégret, Frédéric and Hoffmann, Florian. "The UN as a Human Rights Violator? Some Reflections on the United Nations' Changing Human Rights Responsibilities." *Human Rights Quarterly* 25(2) (2003): 314–42.

Mertus, Julie. "From Legal Transplants to Transformative Justice: Human Rights and the Promise of Transnational Civil Society." *American University International Law Review* 14 (1999): 1335–89.

Nash, Kate. *The Cultural Politics of Human Rights: Comparing the US and UK.* Cambridge: Cambridge University Press, 2009.

Osborne, Peter. "'Whoever Speaks of Culture Speaks of Administration as Well': Disputing Pragmatism in Cultural Studies." *Cultural Studies* 20(1) (2006): 33–47.

Pahuja, Sundhya. "Comparative Visions of Global Public Order (Part I): The Postcoloniality of International Law." *Harvard International Law Journal* 46 (2005): 459–69.

Program for the Study of Sexuality, Gender, Health, and Human Rights at Columbia University in New York City. http://www.cumc.columbia.edu/dept/gender.

Rajagopal, Balakrishnan. "International Law and Social Movements: Challenges of Theorizing Resistance." *Columbia Journal of Transnational Law* 41 (2003): 397–433.

Ross, Andrew. "Components of Cultural Justice." In *Cultural Pluralism, Identity Politics, and the Law,* edited by Austin Sarat and Thomas R. Kearns. Ann Arbor, MI: University of Michigan Press, 1998.

Sarat, Austin and Jonathan Simon, eds. *Cultural Analysis, Cultural Studies, and the Law: Moving Beyond Legal Realism.* Durham, NC: Duke University Press, 2003.

Weeramantry, Christopher G. *Universalising International Law.* Leiden: Martinus Nijhoff, 2004.

Wright, Shelley. *International Human Rights, Decolonisation and Globalisation: Becoming Human.* London: Routledge, 2001.

Zylinska, Joanna. "'Arous[ing] the Intensity of Existence': The Ethics of Seizure and Interruption." Paper presented at the Ethics and Politics: The Work of Alain Badiou conference, Centre for Critical and Cultural Theory, Cardiff University, May 25–26, 2002.

——. *The Ethics of Cultural Studies.* London: Continuum, 2005.

Chapter 11: From Gatekeepers to Gateways

"Aware Saga." *We are Aware.* http://www.we-are-aware.sg/sections/saga.

Barrowclough, Diana and Zeljka Kozul-Wright, eds. *Creative Industries and Developing Countries: Voice, Choice and Economic Growth.* London: Routledge, 2008.

Belfiore, Eleonora and Oliver Bennett. "Rethinking the Social Impact of the Arts." *International Journal of Cultural Policy* 13(2) (2007): 135–41.

Bennett, Tony. "Putting Policy into Cultural Studies." In *Cultural Studies,* edited by Lawrence Grossberg, Cary Nelson, and Paula Treichler. London: Routledge, 1992.

Box Office India. *Box Office 2006*. http://www.boxofficeindia.com/showProd.php?item
Cat=212&catName=MjAwNg==.

Chan, Boris. "Exclusive Video Coverage of Aware EOGM — Part One."
The Online Citizen, May 3, 2009. http://theonlinecitizen.com/2009/05/
toc-exclusive-video-coverage-of-aware-eogm-part-one.

Chong, Terence. "Affirmation of Diversity." *The Straits Times*, May 6, 2009. http://www.
straitstimes.com/Review/Others/STIStory_372877.html

——. "The State and the New Society: The Role of the Arts in Singapore Nation
Building." *Asian Studies Review* 34(2) (2010): 131–49.

Chua, Beng Huat. *Communitarian Ideology and Democracy in Singapore*. New York:
Routledge, 1995.

——. *Political Legitimacy and Housing: Stakeholding in Singapore*. New York: Routledge,
1997.

——. *Life is Not Complete without Shopping: Consumption Culture in Singapore*.
Singapore: Singapore University Press, 2003.

——. "Cultural Industry and the Next Phase of Economic Development of Singapore."
Paper presented at the Workshop on Port Cities and City-States in Asia, Europe,
Asia-Africa Institute, University of Hamburg, Germany, November 4–7, 2004.

——. "Political Culturalism, Representations and the People's Action Party of Singapore."
Democratization 14(5) (2007): 911–27.

——. "Defining Moment for Liberalism." *The Straits Times*, May 6, 2009. http://www.
straitstimes.com/Review/Others/STIStory_372878.html

Cunningham, Stuart. "From Cultural to Creative Industries: Theory, Industry and
Policy Implications." *Media International Australia* 102 (2002): 54–65.

Cunningham, Stuart, Michael Keane and Mark David Ryan. "Finance and Investment
in Creative Industries in Developing Countries." Paper presented at Asia-Pacific
Creative Communities: A Strategy for the 21st Century Senior Expert Symposium.
Jodhpur, India, February 22–26, 2005.

Curtin, Michael. "Media Capital: Towards the Study of Spatial Flows." *International
Journal of Cultural Studies* 6(2) (2003): 202–28.

Department for Culture, Media and Sport. *Creative Industries Mapping Documents*.
London: DCMS, 1998.

——. *Mapping Creative Industries Technical Document*. London: DCMS, 2001.

Dowsett, Gary. "'I'll Show You Mine, if You Show Me Yours': Gay Men, Masculinity
Research, Men's Studies, and Sex." *Theory and Society* 22 (1993): 697–709.

du Gay, Paul and Michael Pryke. *Cultural Economy: Cultural Analysis and Commercial
Life*. London: Sage, 2002.

Edwards, Clive. "Singapore: Reflections and Implications of Another Smart State."
Queensland Review 10(1) (2003): 55–69.

Evans, Graeme. "Creative Cities, Creative Spaces and Urban Policy." *Urban Studies*
46(5/6) (2009): 1003–40.

Field Reporter. "LIVE from Suntec: AWARE EGM." *The Temasek Review*, May 2, 2009.
http://74.125.153.132/search?q=cache:RXFKo0WkAAgJ:temasekreview.com/%3F

p%3D8732+live+report+Aware+saga+log+2+May+2009&cd=1&hl=en&ct=clnk &gl=au&client=firefox-a

Florida, Richard. *The Rise of the Creative Class*. Melbourne: Basic Books, 2002.

Gibson, Chris and Lily Kong. "Cultural Economy: A Critical Review." *Progress in Human Geography* 29(5) (2005): 541–61.

Gibson, Lisanne. "In Defence of Instrumentality." *Cultural Trends* 17(4) (2008), 247–57.

Goh, Robbie. "Christian Identities in Singapore: Religion, Race and Culture between State Controls and Transnational Flows." *Journal of Cultural Geography* 26(1) (2009): 1–23.

Heng, Geraldine. "'A Great Way to Fly': Nationalism, the State, and the Varieties of Third-World Feminism." In *Feminist Genealogies, Colonial Legacies, Democratic Futures*, edited by M. Jacqui Alexander and Chandra T. Mohanty. New York: Routledge, 1997.

Hesmondhalgh, David. "Cultural and Creative Industries." In *The Sage Handbook of Cultural Analysis*, edited by Tony Bennett and John Frow. London: Sage, 2008.

Ho, K. C. "The Neighbourhood in the Creative Economy: Policy, Practice and Place in Singapore." *Urban Studies* 46(5/6) (2009): 1188–201.

Howkins, John. *The Creative Economy*. Harmondsworth: Penguin, 2001.

Internet Movie Database. *Hainan Jifan: Awards (2004)*. http://www.imdb.com/title/ tt0383388/awards.

Keane, Michael. "Once Were Peripheral: Creating Media Capacity in East Asia." *Media, Culture and Society* 28(6) (2006): 835–55.

Khoo, Olivia. "*Slang* Images: On the Foreignness of Contemporary Singaporean Films." *Inter-Asia Cultural Studies* 7(1) (2006): 81–98.

Koh, Aaron. "Living with Globalization Tactically: The Metapragmatics of Globalization in Singapore." *Sojourn: Journal of Social Issues in Southeast Asia* 72(2) (2007): 179–201.

Kong, Lily. "Cultural Policy in Singapore: Negotiating Economic and Socio-Cultural Agendas." *Geoforum* 31(4) (2000): 409–24.

——. "The Sociality of Cultural Industries: Hong Kong's Cultural Policy and Film Industry." *International Journal of Cultural Policy* 11(1) (2005): 61–76.

——. "Making Sustainable Creative/Cultural Space in Shanghai and Singapore." *Geographical Review* 99(1) (2009): 1–22.

Kong, Lily and Justin O'Connor, eds. *Creative Cities: Asian-European Perspectives*. New York: Springer, 2009.

Kum, Hong Siew. "What I Took Away from 2 May." May 6, 2009. http://siewkumhong. blogspot.com/2009/05/what-i-took-away-from-2-may.html.

Kymlicka, Will. *Multicultural Citizenship: A Liberal Theory of Minority Rights*. Oxford: Oxford University Press, 1995.

Lai, Ah Eng, ed. *Beyond Rituals and Riots: Ethnic Pluralism and Social Cohesion in Singapore* (Singapore: Eastern Universities Press, 2004).

Levy, Pierre. *Cyberculture*. Minneapolis: University of Minnesota Press, 2001.

Loh, Chee Kong. "A Coming of Age for Civil Society: Could Aware Saga Be Watershed for Public Discourse on Taboo Topics?" *TODAY*, May 5, 2009.

Low, Linda. "The Singapore Development State in the New Economy and Polity." *The Pacific Review* 14(3) (2001): 411–41.

Lyons, Lenore. "The Limits of Feminist Political Intervention in Singapore." *Journal of Contemporary Asia* 30(1) (2000): 67–83.

——. *A State of Ambivalence: The Feminist Movement in Singapore*. London: Brill, 2004.

Madden, Christopher. "Indicators for Arts and Cultural Policy: A Global Perspective." *Cultural Trends* 14(3) (2005): 217–47.

Media Development Authority. *Creative Industries Development Strategy: Propelling Singapore's Creative Economy*. Singapore: Ministry of Information, Communication and the Arts, 2002.

——. *Singapore Media Fusion Plan*. May 4, 2009. http://www.smf.sg/smfp/index. html14–15.

McGuigan, Jim. *Culture and the Public Sphere*. London: Routledge, 1996.

Miller, Toby. *Global Hollywood*. London: British Film Institute, 2001.

"More than a Thousand Turn Up for Aware EOGM." *The Online Citizen*, May 2, 2009. http://theonlinecitizen.com/2009/05/more-than-a-thousand-turn-up-for-aware-eogm.

O'Connor, Justin. "Creative Industries: A New Direction?" *International Journal of Cultural Policy* 15(4) (2009): 387–402.

Ong, Aihwa. "Cultural Citizenship as Subject Making: Immigrants Negotiate Racial and Cultural Boundaries in the United States." In *Race, Identity, and Citizenship*, edited by Rofoldo Torrres, Louis Miron and Jonathan Inda. Boston: Beacon Press, 1999.

——. *Neoliberalism as Exception: Mutations in Citizenship and Sovereignty*. Durham, NC: Duke University Press, 2006.

Osbourne, Peter. "'Whoever Speaks of Culture Speaks of Administration as Well': Disputing Pragmatism in Cultural Studies." *Cultural Studies* 20(1) (2006): 33–47.

Othman, Diana. "Aware Sex Guide Suspended." *The Straits Times*, May 6, 2009. http://www.straitstimes.com/print/Breaking%2BNews/Singapore/Story/STIStory_373200.htm.

People Like Us. "People Like Us Launches the Rascals Prize." August 2, 2008. http://www.plu.sg/society/?p=121.

Porter, Michael. *On Competition*. Boston, MA: Harvard Business School Publishing, 1998.

Purushotam, Nirmala. "'Woman' as Boundary: Raising the Communitarian Against Critical Imaginings." *Inter-Asia Cultural Studies* 3(3) (2002): 337–70.

Rodan, Gary. "Preserving the One-party State in Contemporary Singapore." In *Southeast Asia in the 1990s: Authoritarianism, Democracy, and Capitalism*, edited by Kevin Hewison, Richard Robison, and Gary Rodan. Sydney: Allen & Unwin, 1993.

Rosaldo, Renato. "Cultural Citizenship, Inequality, and Multiculturalism." In *Race, Identity, and Citizenship*, edited by Rodolfo Torres, Louis Miron, and Jonathan Inda. Boston: Beacon Press, 1999.

Ross, Andrew. *Nice Work If You Can Get It: Life and Labor in Precarious Times*. New York: New York University Press, 2009.

Singapore Daily. "Daily SG: 3 May 2009 AWARE Weekend Special." *The Singapore Daily*. May 3, 2009. http://singaporedaily.net/2009/05/03 daily-sg-3-may-2009-aware-weekend-special.

Singapore Film Commission. "List of Singapore Movies (1991–2008)." *Film Industry: Facts and Figures*. http://www.sfc.org.sg/main.html.

"Singapore Public Gay Parties." *Wikipedia*. http://en.wikipedia.org/wiki/Singapore_public_gay_parties.

Stevenson, Nick. *Cultural Citizenship: Cosmopolitan Questions*. Maidenhead: Open University Press, 2003.

Tan, Kim-Song. "From Efficiency-Driven to Innovation-Driven Economic Growth: Perspectives from Singapore." *World Bank Policy Research Working Paper*. April 1, 2005. http://econ.worldbank.org/external/default/main?pagePK=64165259&theSitePK=469382&piPK=64165421&menuPK=64166093&entityID=000012009_20050425133228.

Tay, Simon. "A Tale of Two Communities." *TODAY*, May 5, 2009.

Toh, Mun Heng, Adrian Choo, and Terence Ho. "Economic Contributions of Singapore's Creative Industries." *Economic Survey of Singapore First Quarter*. Singapore: Ministry of Trade and Industry, 2003.

Turner, Brian. "Outline of a General Theory of Cultural Citizenship." In *Culture and Citizenship*, edited by Nick Stevenson. London: Sage, 2002.

UNESCO. *Asia-Pacific Creative Communities: Promoting the Cultural Industries for Local Socio-economic Development: A Strategy for the 21st Century*. Bangkok: UNESCO, 2005.

——. *International Flows of Selected Cultural Goods and Services 1994–2003: Defining and Capturing the Flows of Global Cultural Trade*. Montreal: UNESCO Institute for Statistics, 2005.

UNESCO/Global Alliance for Cultural Diversity. "Understanding Creative Industries: Cultural Statistics for Public Policy-Making." March 6, 2006. Paris: UNESCO/Global Alliance for Cultural Diversity, 2006. http://portal.unesco.org/culture/en/files/30297/...stat_EN.../cultural_stat_EN.pdf.

West, Cornel. *The American Evasion of Philosophy: A Genealogy of Pragmatism*. Madison, WI: University of Wisconsin Press, 1989.

Wong, Poh Kam, Yuen Ping Ho, and Annette Singh. "Singapore as an Innovative City in East Asia: An Explorative Study of the Perspectives of Innovative Industries." *World Bank Policy Research Working Paper*. April 1, 2005. http://econ.worldbank.org/external/default/main?pagePK=64165259&theSitePK=469382&piPK=64165421&menuPK=64166093&entityID=000012009_20050425130701.

Yúdice, George. *The Expediency of Culture: Uses of Culture in the Global Era*. Durham, NC: Duke University Press, 2003.

Yue, Audrey. "The Regional Culture of New Asia: Cultural Governance and Creative Industries in Singapore." *International Journal of Cultural Policy* 12(1) (2006): 17–33.

——. "Creative Queer Singapore: The Illiberal Pragmatics of Cultural Production." *Gay and Lesbian Issues and Psychology Review* 3(3) (2007): 149–60.

——. "Hawking in the Creative City: *Rice Rhapsody*, Sexuality and the Cultural Politics of New Asia in Singapore." *Feminist Media Studies* 7(4) (2007): 365–80.

——. "Film-Induced Domestic Tourism in Singapore: The Case of *Krrish*." In *Domestic Tourism in Asia: Diversity and Divergence*, edited by Shalini Singh. London: Earthscan, 2009.

——. "Doing Cultural Citizenship in the Global Media Hub: Illiberal Pragmatics and Lesbian Consumption Practices in Singapore." In *Circuits of Visibility: Gender and Transnational Media Cultures*, edited by Radha Hegde. New York: New York University Press, 2011.

Zhang, Jing and Poh-Kam Wong. "Networks vs Market Methods in High-Tech Venture Fundraising: The Impact of Institutional Environment." *Entrepreneurship and Regional Development* 20 (2008): 409–30.

Chapter 12: Culture, Institution, Conduct

Carroll, Patrick. *Science, Culture, and Modern State Formation*. Berkeley, CA: University of California Press, 2006.

Conklin, Alice C. "Skulls on Display: The Science of Race in Paris's Musée de l'Homme, 1928–1950." In *Museums and Difference*, edited by Daniel Sherman. Bloomington, IN: Indiana University Press, 2008.

Bennett, Tony. "'Culture Studies' and the Culture Complex." In *Culture: A Sociological Handbook*, edited by John R. Hall, Laura Grindstaff, and Ming-cheng Lo. London: Routledge, 2010.

——. "Culture and Differences: The Challenges of Multiculturalism." In *When Culture Makes the Difference: Heritage, Arts and Media in Multicultural Society*, edited by S. Boda and Maria Rita Cifarelli. Rome: Meltemi Editore, 2006.

——. "Habitus Clivé: Aesthetics and Politics in the Work of Pierre Bourdieu." *New Literary History* 38(1) (2005): 201–28.

——. "Making Culture, Changing Society: The Perspective of Culture Studies." *Cultural Studies* 21(4–5) (2007): 610–29.

——. "Museum, Field, Colony: Colonial Governmentality and the Circulation of Reference." *Journal of Cultural Economy* 2(1/2) (2009): 99–116.

——. "Sociology, Aesthetics, Expertise." *New Literary History* 41(2) (2010): 253–76.

——. "The Work of Culture." *Journal of Cultural Sociology* 1(1) (2007): 31–48.

Bennett, Tony and Patrick Joyce, eds. "Introduction." In *Material Powers: Cultural Studies, History and the Material Turn*. London: Routledge, 2010.

Bérubé, Michael. "Introduction: Engaging the Aesthetic." In *The Aesthetics of Cultural Studies*, edited by Michael Bérubé. Oxford: Blackwell, 2005.

Boltanski, Luc and Eve Chiapello. *The New Spirit of Capitalism*. London: Verso, 2005.

Dias, Nélia. *Le musée d'ethnographie du Trocadéro (1878–1908): anthropologie et muséologie en France*. Paris: Éditions du Centre National de la Recherche Scientifique, 1991.

Eagleton, Terry. *The Idea of Culture*. Oxford: Blackwell, 2000.

Foucault, Michel. *Security, Territory, Population: Lectures at the Collège de France, 1977–1978*. London: Palgrave Macmillan, 2007.

Gorgus, Nina. *Le magicien des vitrines: le muséologue Georges Henri Rivière*. Paris: Éditions de la Maison des Sciences de l'Homme, 2003.

Hall, Stuart. "On Postmodernism and Articulation: An Interview with Stuart Hall," edited by Lawrence Grossberg. *Journal of Communication Inquiry* 10(2) (1986): 45–60.

——. "Race, Articulation and Societies Structured in Dominance." In UNESCO, *Sociological Theories: Race and Colonialism*. Paris: UNESCO, 1980.

——. "Unsettling 'The Heritage': Re-Imagining the Post-Nation." In *Whose Heritage: The Impact of Cultural Diversity on Britain's Living Heritage*. London: Arts Council of England, 1999.

Healy, Chris. *Forgetting Aborigines*. Sydney: UNSW Press, 2008.

Hecht, Jennifer Michael. *The End of the Soul: Scientific Modernity, Atheism, and Anthropology in France*. New York: Columbia University Press, 2003.

Hunter, Ian. *Culture and Government: The Emergence of Literary Education*. London: Macmillan, 1988.

——. *Rival Enlightenments: Civil and Metaphysical Philosophy in Early Modern Germany*. Cambridge: Cambridge University Press, 2001.

Ikegami, Eiko. *Bonds of Civility: Aesthetic Networks and the Political Origins of Japanese Culture*. Cambridge: Cambridge University Press, 2005.

Kirshenblatt-Gimblett, Barbara. "World Heritage in Cultural Economics." In *Museum Frictions: Public Cultures/Global Transformations*, edited by Ivan Karp, Corinne A. Kratz, Lynn Szwaja, and Tomás Ybarra-Frausto. Durham, NC: Duke University Press, 2006.

Latour, Bruno. *Reassembling the Social: An Introduction to Actor-Network Theory*. Oxford: Oxford University Press, 2005.

——. "Why Has Critique Run Out of Steam: From Matters of Fact to Matters of Concern." In *Things*, edited by Bill Brown. Chicago: University of Chicago Press, 2004.

Laurière, Christine. *Paul Rivet: le savant et le politique*. Paris: Musée National d'Histoire Naturelle, 2008.

Law, John and John Urry. "Enacting the Social." *Economy and Society* 33(3) (2004): 390–410.

Lee, Richard E. *Life and Times of Cultural Studies: The Politics and Transformation of the Structures of Knowledge*. London: Lawrence and Wishart, 2004.

L'Estoile, Benoît de. *Le goût des autres: de l'exposition coloniale aux arts premiers*. Paris: Flammarion, 2007.

Morishita, Masaaki. "Empty Museums: Transculturation and the Development of Public Museums in Japan." PhD dissertation. Open University, 2003.

Mulhern, Francis. *Culture/Metaculture*. London: Routledge, 2000.

Osborne, Peter. "Whoever Speaks of Culture Speaks of Administration as Well: Disputing Pragmatism in Cultural Studies." *Cultural Studies* 20(1) (2006): 33–47.

Rancière, Jacques. *Aesthetics and Its Discontents*. Cambridge: Polity Press, 2009.

Ray, William. *The Logic of Culture: Authority and Identity in the Modern Era*. Oxford: Blackwell, 2001.

Sherman, Daniel. "'Peoples Ethnographic': Objects, Museums, and the Colonial Inheritance of French Ethnology." *French Historical Studies* 27(3) (2004): 669–703.

Sibeud, Emmanuelle. "The Metamorphosis of Ethnology in France, 1839–1930." In *A New History of Anthropology*, edited by Henrika Kuklik. Malden, MA: Blackwell, 2007.

Summit, Jennifer. *Memory's Library: Medieval Books in Early Modern England*. Chicago: University of Chicago Press, 2008.

Toews, David. "The New Tarde: Sociology after the End of the Social." *Theory, Culture & Society* 20(5) (2003): 81–98.

Wilder, Gary. *The French Imperial Nation-State: Negritude and Colonial Humanism between the Two World Wars*. Chicago: University of Chicago Press, 2005.

World Commission for Culture and Development. *Our Creative Diversity*. Paris: UNESCO.

Index